CHANGING CORPORATE AMERICA
FROM INSIDE OUT

Social Movements, Protest, and Contention

Series Editor: Bert Klandermans, Free University, Amsterdam

Associate Editors: Ron R. Aminzade, University of Minnesota
David S. Meyer, University of California, Irvine
Verta A. Taylor, University of California, Santa Barbara

For more books in the series, see page 336.

CHANGING CORPORATE AMERICA FROM INSIDE OUT

Lesbian and Gay Workplace Rights

Nicole C. Raeburn

Social Movements, Protest, and Contention
Volume 20

University of Minnesota Press
Minneapolis • London

Published by the University of Minnesota Press
111 Third Avenue South, Suite 290
Minneapolis, MN 55401-2520
http://www.upress.umn.edu

Library of Congress Cataloging-in-Publication Data

Raeburn, Nicole C.
    Changing corporate America from inside out : lesbian and gay workplace
rights / Nicole C. Raeburn.
        p.   cm. — (Social movements, protest, and contention ; v. 20)
    Data gathered from Fortune 1000 companies.
    Includes bibliographical references and index.
    ISBN 0-8166-3998-1 (hc : alk. paper) — ISBN 0-8166-3999-X (pb : alk.
paper)
    1. Gays—Employment—United States.   2. Gay rights—United States.
    3. Corporations—United States.   4. Organizational change—United
States.   5. Domestic partner benefits—United States.   6. Gay liberation
movement—United States.   7. Industrial management—Social aspects—
United States.   I. Title: Lesbian and gay workplace rights.   II. Title.
III. Series.
    HD6285.5.U6R34 2004
    331.5'3'0973—dc22

                                                                2004008523

12 11 10 09 08 07 06   10 9 8 7 6 5 4 3 2

To my mom, my first and best teacher,
and to my dad, my first and best study partner

and to Li'l Bee and Li'l Frog Man,
for the blue lights and the joy

Contents

Acknowledgments

Many people deserve continued thanks for all of the support, assistance, and feedback they provided to me while I was conceptualizing this project, gathering the data, analyzing, and writing. Since this book is based on my doctoral dissertation, I first thank my dissertation committee. Verta Taylor, Craig Jenkins, and Randy Hodson were incredibly supportive. They offered guidance through their insightful questions and comments and through their own research, which inspired me to combine social movement theory and organizational analysis. As my adviser, Verta Taylor emboldened me to think broadly and deeply and to not scale back the project despite her and others' warnings that it was big enough for two or three dissertations (she also didn't tell me, more than once a week, that I was crazy for trying to finish while teaching a full load). I will always treasure her mentoring and her friendship.

I also thank the numerous people who helped me through the course of the dissertation and this book by offering kind and crucial gestures: giving feedback on my proposal and on the papers I presented at sociological conferences, helping me find contacts in corporations, encouraging me in my efforts toward theoretical synthesis, providing methodological advice, solving computer problems, sending me clippings on workplace issues, showing a genuine interest in my work, engaging in intellectually stimulating dialogue, and reminding me that research and writing can be tools for social change. For all of this and more, I thank Barry Adam, Joan Arnfield, Mary Bernstein, Kathy Blee, Egan and Jerry Bradnan, Elizabeth Cooksey, John D'Emilio, Kim Dill, Kim Dugan, Rachel Einwohner, Mary Margaret

Fonow, Bill Form, the late Clyde Franklin, Steph Gabis, Pat Gagné, Josh Gamson, Christine Hahn, Gia Hinkle, Joan Huber, Bert Klandermans, the late Marty Levine, Pat Yancey Martin, Doug McAdam, Betty Menaghan, David Meyer, Debra Minkoff, Aldon Morris, Andrew Newman, Jodi O'Brien, Cynthia Pelak, Liz Pesch, the late Marie Pesch, Townsand Price-Spratlen, Jo Reger, Barbara Reskin, John Reynolds, Leila Rupp, Michael Schwartz, the late Linda Singer, Larry Spencer, Sid Tarrow, Verta Taylor, Marieke Van Willigen, and the late Jim Woods.

For their long-distance help and friendship, having done so many things in Columbus for me after I moved to San Francisco, I thank Betsy Kaminski and Beckett Broh. For assistance with library research and checking bibliographic sources, I thank Nicole LaFlamme, Keely McCave, Jen Moreno, and Molly Wallace. For providing contact lists or other important information on lesbian, gay, and bisexual issues in the workplace, I thank Christian Arthur Bain, editor of the *Gay/Lesbian/Bisexual Corporate Letter;* Demian, of the Partners Task Force for Gay and Lesbian Couples; Daryl Herrschaft, deputy director of the WorkNet workplace project of the Human Rights Campaign (HRC); Gerald Hunt, of the Academy of Management; Sally Kohn, formerly of the National Gay and Lesbian Task Force (NGLTF); Kelly Lobel, former executive director of NGLTF; Kim Mills, education director of HRC; and diversity consultants Mark Kaplan, Jay Lucas, Brian McNaught, and Liz Winfeld.

I also express my appreciation to the individuals who agreed to be surveyed and interviewed for this project. Confidentiality prevents me from acknowledging them by name, but I send my sincere thanks to each one of them. I especially recognize all of the activists and their allies, whose dedication to creating change in the workplace and larger society was constantly inspiring and whose stories provide the heart and soul of this book.

I am grateful for the following sources of financial support, which helped make this project possible: National Science Foundation Doctoral Dissertation Research Grant SBR-9700763; an American Sociological Association/ National Science Foundation Fund for the Advancement of the Discipline Award; a Martin P. Levine Memorial Dissertation Fellowship Honorable Mention from the Sex and Gender section of the American Sociological Association; and various scholarly and financial awards from Ohio State University, including a Presidential Fellowship, a Graduate Student Alumni Research Award from the Graduate School, the Elizabeth D. Gee Research Award from the Center for Women's Studies, a Research-Intense Summer Fellowship from the Department of Sociology, two Sociology Graduate Student Research Support Awards from the Rabbi Morris Silverman Fund for Research in Human Rights, and an Outstanding Graduate Student Award from the Office of Gay, Lesbian, and Bisexual Student Services.

I thank the terrific team of people at the University of Minnesota Press for providing such thoughtful attention to editing, production, and publicity. I especially thank Carrie Mullen, executive editor, for her support, enthusiasm, and expertise; and Bert Klandermans, editor of the Social Movements, Protest, and Contention series, for supporting this project even before I began gathering data. My sincere thanks as well to Doug Armato, director of the Press; Alison Aten, for her dedicated work on publicity and marketing; Adam Grafa, for his creativity in the design and printing of the book; Jason Weidemann, for his good-humored editorial assistance; Laura Westlund, managing editor, for expertly overseeing production; and Tammy Zambo, for her careful copyediting of the manuscript.

On a personal note, I send my deep thanks to the Pesch, Michalak, Albano, and Raeburn families for all of their love and support. I am grateful for my colleagues and students at the University of San Francisco, where I found my dream job. My colleagues in the Department of Sociology (Bill Edwards, Josh Gamson, Becky Chiyoko King-O'Riain, the late Esther Madriz, who was both mentor and sister to me, Kim Richman, Cecilia Santos, Stephanie Sears, Mike Webber, and Steve Zavestoski) are generous with their gifts of friendship, laughter, insight, and shared commitment to social justice.

Most of all, I thank my parents, Duane and Mary Raeburn; my brother Chris, his wife, Dani, and their son, Christopher; and my partner and wife, Liz Pesch, and our son, Joshua Ian Pesch Raeburn. Their constant love, support, guidance, and faith in me serve as my rock, my joy, my inspiration. Liz, I could never thank you enough for the countless things you did to help me finish—from doing all the housework, cooking gourmet meals, and being so patient about having to put off our vacations and evenings and weekends, to preparing the charts for the book, reading my work, listening to my ideas, and encouraging me and believing in me. And Joshua, our precious son, thank you for reminding me of the sweet, profound, flesh-and-blood rewards of working for social change.

Introduction

Corporations as the New Frontier for Lesbian, Gay, and Bisexual Rights

Given the often contentious intersection between advocates for change and profit-oriented companies, a central question is how the rights of various groups are negotiated and secured in the workplace. Despite the backlash against gay and lesbian rights occurring in cities and states across the country, a rapidly expanding number of corporations are including sexual orientation in nondiscrimination policies, providing gay-inclusive diversity training, and extending health insurance and other benefits to domestic partners of lesbian and gay employees. Focusing on the Fortune 1000, or *Fortune* magazine's list of the top 1,000 revenue-generating companies in the United States, my study reveals that the majority of equitable-benefits adopters instituted this policy change only after facing internal pressure from mobilized groups of lesbian, gay, and bisexual employees (see also D. Baker, Strub, and Henning 1995). Serving as powerful reminders that the state is not the sole contested terrain, these "institutional activists" (Santoro and McGuire 1997) demonstrate that committed individuals "do" politics not simply on the streets or in voting booths but also in the cubicles, offices, and boardrooms of companies across the country.

Yet not all gay employee groups have succeeded in their fight for inclusive policies, and some corporations have instituted these changes in the absence of employee activism. How, then, do we account for variation in companies' willingness to adopt such policies? That question provides the grounding point for this book. My analysis focuses on the emergence and outcomes of the workplace movement, as it is typically called by challengers, a form of institutional activism that is long overdue for study. I concentrate particularly

I

on the mobilization of gay, lesbian, and bisexual employee networks over the past fifteen years to win equitable benefits, often called domestic partner benefits, in Fortune 1000 companies. My multimethod approach utilizes surveys of 94 corporations with and without gay networks, intensive interviews with vice presidents of human resources and gay employee activists, and a small number of case studies.

Research shows that in 1990 just 3 corporations provided family and bereavement leave for lesbian and gay employees (Mickens 1994a), and none provided health-insurance coverage for domestic partners (D. Baker, Strub, and Henning 1995; Navarro 1995). But, by the middle of the 1990s, domestic partner benefits had practically become a household word, given their adoption by numerous big-name companies. By fall 1999, the rate of adoption among major employers had climbed to approximately 2 per week, up from an average of 1 per week in the first half of the decade (Herrschaft 1999; HRCF 1999a, 4). In just the first quarter of 2001, over 20 Fortune 500 companies instituted the benefits or announced that they would do so by midyear (Data Lounge 2001b). According to data gathered by the WorkNet workplace project of the Human Rights Campaign, as of February 14, 2004, 211 Fortune 500 companies (42 percent) had adopted equitable benefits. Joining these corporations were 6,863 other companies, nonprofit organizations, and unions, along with 198 colleges and universities, 10 states, the District of Columbia, and 130 local governments. In all, then, by mid-February 2004, at least 7,412 employers had instituted domestic partner benefits (HRCF 2004).

Looked at from the perspective of the U.S. workforce as a whole, by the year 2000, 15 percent of workers were employed in organizations that provide equitable benefits, up from 11 percent in 1999, according to a study done by the Kaiser Family Foundation (Elswick 2001). Focusing solely on corporate America, organizational research shows that nearly 1 in 4 companies now provides health insurance to the partners of gay and lesbian employees (Simanoff 2002). According to a survey of 570 large U.S. employers conducted by Hewitt Associates, a global management-consulting firm specializing in employee benefits, 22 percent of corporations offered equitable benefits as of spring 2000. Of the yet-to-adopt companies, over a third (35 percent) said they were considering the extension of such benefits in the next three years (Hewitt Associates 2000, 11). Likewise, a 2002 study done by the Society for Human Resource Management found that 23 percent of U.S. firms provide same-sex domestic partner benefits, up from 7 percent only five years earlier (Simanoff 2002).

My study reveals the crucial role of the workplace movement in bringing about this sea change. Of the 20 companies that first adopted equitable benefits, at least 16 did so in response to internal mobilization (D. Baker, Strub, and Henning 1995). Nevertheless, while employee activists clearly spearheaded this major corporate transformation, institutional processes have since come into greater play such that the presence of an employee network is now less necessary for policy change. This progression is detailed in Table 1, which focuses on equitable-benefits adoption among the Fortune 1000 by year and by presence of a gay employee group.

As shown in the table, between 1991 and 1993, all 11 of the Fortune 1000 adopters changed their policies in response to pressure from gay employee networks. Between 1994 and 1997, 72 percent of new adopters (21 out of 29) had faced internal mobilization. In contrast, between 1998 and 1999, only 56 percent of new adopters (24 out of 43) had been pressured by organized groups of gay and lesbian workers. Although corporations with activist networks still constituted two-thirds of Fortune adopters as of 1999 (56 out of 83, or 67 percent), over time the presence of a gay employee group has become less necessary for gay-inclusive policy change. Institutional

Table 1. Adoption of Domestic Partner Benefits among the Fortune 1000 by Year and by Presence of a Gay Employee Network

Year	Number of Fortune 1000 Adopters	Number (and Percentage) of Adopters with Gay Employee Networks
1991	1	1 (100%)
1992	1	1 (100%)
1993	9	9 (100%)
Subtotal, 1991–93	11	11 (100%)
1994	6	3 (50%)
1995	5	4 (80%)
1996	5	4 (80%)
1997	13	10 (77%)
Subtotal, 1994–97	29	21 (72%)
1998	28	15 (54%)
1999	15	9 (60%)
Subtotal, 1998–99	43	24 (56%)
Total, 1991–99	83	56 (67%)

Source: Adapted with permission from data provided by the WorkNet workplace project of the Human Rights Campaign and the Human Rights Campaign Foundation, supplemented with data gathered by the author.

theorists would attribute this shift to what they call mimetic isomorphism (DiMaggio and Powell 1991a, 1991b): as leading organizations adopted equitable benefits, others began to follow suit in order to remain competitive.

Of course, it is also possible, and perhaps even likely, that some of the corporations that appear to have adopted benefits in the absence of internal pressure were in fact responding to requests from individual employees or informal groups that would remain invisible to outside observers. Likewise, some adopters may have faced pressure from gay employee networks that later disbanded after their victory and would thus no longer appear on the mobilization radar screen. Moreover, local or state organizations in the wider gay rights movement sometimes pressure particular companies, but, unless these groups receive press coverage, their role is often obscured from public sight. In addition, leaders from national gay rights organizations occasionally work quietly with certain companies to persuade elites to adopt equitable benefits. Such efforts would likewise remain unseen by outside observers. If anything, then, the figures in Table 1 underestimate the importance of workplace activism. Nonetheless, my research also shows that institutional processes have recently begun to figure more prominently such that mobilization is not as necessary as it was in previous waves of adoption.

Among institutional scholars, a key theoretical and empirical question centers on institutionalization, or how particular policies or practices diffuse within and across organizational fields and become invested with legitimacy and are eventually taken for granted (J. Meyer and Rowan 1977; Zucker 1977, 1983; Abell 1995; Scott 1995b; Scott and Christensen 1995a; Tolbert and Zucker 1996; Fligstein 1997; Scully and Creed 1998). Clearly, the adoption of equitable benefits has not yet reached a taken-for-granted status. On the contrary, it is still a highly contentious issue. It is this very point that makes the topic interesting and important in both a theoretical and a practical sense.

How is it possible that, amid widespread backlash against gay and lesbian rights in the United States, a rapidly increasing number of corporations are instituting gay-inclusive policies and practices? Indeed, companies far outpace educational, nonprofit, and government employers in offering equitable benefits to the partners of lesbian and gay employees. How has this remarkable change come about? To answer these questions, in this book I first situate the workplace movement in a wider historical context, documenting the quiet and cautious beginnings of workplace mobilization by activists who organized *outside* the walls of the corporation. In later chapters, I turn to the institutional and social movement literatures for theoretical guidance in understanding the emergence and outcomes of *internal* mobilization. In the remainder of this introducton, after tracing the early struggles of external activists, I close with a brief discussion of my data and methods, followed by an outline of the book.

Early Battles against Antigay Employment Discrimination

Quiet and Cautious Beginnings

The struggle for gay rights in the United States began with the emergence of the "homophile" movement in the early 1950s and was transformed by the Stonewall Riots of 1969, which scholars typically use to mark the start of the gay liberation movement (D'Emilio 1983; Adam 1995). To varying degrees, activists in both of these periods targeted antigay employment policies. Given the McCarthy era's witch hunts against homosexuals in government and other employment sectors, few would question the quiet, accommodationist stance of the early homophile movement (D'Emilio 1983). Functioning largely as self-help groups to counter the prevailing images of homosexuality as sick or immoral, homophile organizations in the 1950s attempted to provide members with support and affirmation by inviting sympathetic professionals as speakers (Valocchi 1999).

Just as the early homophiles relied on outside "experts" to educate the rest of society, groups would also urge unsympathetic professionals to attend their meetings so that they could open a dialogue with authorities, whom they hoped would change their opinions of homosexuality when faced with the "reasonableness" of members (D'Emilio, 1983, 109). Public events, if held at all, were designed mostly to convince others that homosexuals were "just like any other good citizens" (Faderman 1991, 190). To demonstrate civic-mindedness, for example, homophile groups would hold charity events or sponsor blood drives (D'Emilio 1983; Valocchi 1999). Desperately seeking respectability for "sexual variants," many leaders of the two earliest homophile organizations in the United States, the Mattachine Society and Daughters of Bilitis, criticized gay bars and other aspects of gay subculture and encouraged members to adopt conservative styles of dress and comportment (D'Emilio 1983; Faderman 1991). In the early 1960s, however, deeply affected by civil rights demonstrations, some segments of the homophile movement began to adopt a more militant stance.

A Brave New Approach

After losing an extended court battle against wrongful discharge from his civil service job, Frank Kameny decided to join the movement and became one of its most visible leaders. He urged homophiles to abandon accommodationist strategies, fight for equal rights, and take up direct-action tactics (D'Emilio 1983). Influenced by Kameny and other activists who favored a confrontational approach, in the early 1960s the Homophile League of New York staged the first gay rights protest in the country by picketing outside an induction center, carrying signs that read, "If you don't want us don't take us, but don't ruin our lives" (Faderman 1991, 191).

While some in the homophile movement avoided protests out of fear or distaste for contentious politics, others borrowed from the strategies and master frame of the civil rights movement (Snow and Benford 1992) and began to target the antigay employment policies of the federal government and civil service sector. By 1964, lesbians in dresses and gay men in suits were picketing outside the White House, the Pentagon, and other governmental buildings with signs bearing messages such as "End employment policies against homosexuals," "Homosexual Americans demand their civil rights," and "Discrimination against homosexuals is immoral" (Faderman 1991, 87, 191; *Out of the Past* 1997). Despite the bravery of these homophiles, however, very few tangible gains were made in the fight for equal rights (D'Emilio 1983).

Then, suddenly, beginning on June 27, 1969, gay rights were catapulted to a far more prominent position in the country's consciousness. That night at the Stonewall Inn, a gay bar in Greenwich Village, several lesbian, gay, and drag-queen patrons fought back against what was supposed to have been a routine police raid. Their resistance drew a crowd of more than two thousand sympathetic protesters who confronted over four hundred police officers with chants of "Gay power!" (D'Emilio 1983, 232). Thus began the gay liberation movement. Diffusing rapidly through networks of activists who were already radicalized by their participation in the New Left, "gay liberation fronts" soon appeared on college campuses and in cities across the country (D'Emilio 1983; Adam 1995). Drawing on the energy, strategies, and ideologies of other radical movements of the day, particularly black power, women's liberation, and the New Left generally, gay liberationists adopted direct-action tactics and proffered collective action frames that called for gay power and sexual liberation while simultaneously criticizing heterosexism and the interrelated nature of multiple oppressions (Valocchi 1999).

Zapping the Corporate Pigs

Although their approach was a bold break from the accommodationist tactics of the homophiles, in many ways early gay liberationists faced a cultural context that varied little from that of their predecessors. Placed in a familiar but unenviable position, activists in the late 1960s and early 1970s were attempting to win gay-inclusive change in a society that viewed homosexuality as pathological. But while early homophiles largely sought the acceptance of society through contact with individual professionals in the psychiatric and psychological communities, gay liberationists took a sharply different tack.

As movement scholar Steve Valocchi (1999, 69) puts it, the "post-Stonewall assault . . . called into question the values and principles of the broader society and connected the psychiatrists' oppressiveness to that of other powerful institutions." Quoting the San Francisco Gay Liberation Front during one of its "zap actions" at the national meetings of the American Psychiatric Association, Valocchi describes how liberationists drew from the revolutionary narratives of the New Left to attack the interlocking and institutional nature of oppression: "You [psychiatrists] are the pigs who make it possible for the cops to beat homosexuals; they call us queer; you—so politely—call us sick. But it's the same thing. You make possible the beatings and rapes in prisons. You are implicated in the torturous cures perpetuated on desperate homosexuals" (69, originally quoted in Teal 1971, 274–75).

In addition to targeting the mental health establishment and the state, gay liberationists set their sights on the antigay policies of corporate America. In what appears to be the earliest protest ever staged against a major corporation, gay liberationists in San Francisco, Los Angeles, and New York picketed ABC in the spring of 1970 after a San Francisco station fired an employee who had joined the "gay militant movement" (*Advocate* 1970a).

Other gay liberation fronts began to survey companies about their policies toward gays and lesbians. In 1970, FREE (Fight Repression of Erotic Expression), a liberationist group at the University of Minnesota, combined its survey approach with a warning. In its letters to the twelve largest companies in the Twin Cities area, the group promised to "act against" those employers who discriminated (*Advocate* 1970b). Leaving no room for companies that wished to avoid protest by lying or simply not participating in the survey, the letter informed recipients that FREE was planning test cases to see whether openly gay applicants would be turned down and that members would interpret a nonresponse to the survey as discrimination.

In a striking reminder of the cultural constraints under which gay liberationists operated, FREE made sure to discuss in its letter a report submitted to the National Institute of Mental Health by Evelyn Hooker, whose research showed that homosexuality was not a "mental health problem" (see also Fetner 2001). The tone then quickly shifted as the letter writers moved from a psychiatric frame to a co-optation of corporate discourse. In perhaps the earliest documented example of what I call an "ideology of profits," FREE argued that motivation and productivity suffer if employees have to keep their sexual orientation a secret. Citing both positive and negative incentives, the letter touched on the recruitment advantages of gay-inclusive policies and the costs of antigay practices. Members informed companies that survey results would be given to graduating seniors and that FREE would urge the university to break off all ties with discriminatory employers, whose names would be forwarded to the Minnesota Human Rights Commission.

When a vice president at Honeywell responded to the survey by writing, "We would not employ a known homosexual," a graduate student member of FREE filed a bias charge against the company, citing the University of Minnesota's policy against discrimination by recruiters (*Advocate* 1973c). Unfazed, Honeywell maintained its antigay stance until almost one year later when, upon the retirement of the aforementioned vice president, his replacement adopted a policy of nondiscrimination (Bjornson 1974). Activist success thus depended on an opening of what I call "institutional opportunities." Similar to Sidney Tarrow's discussion of political realignments as a key component of political opportunity structure (1989, 1998), organizational realignments that derive from elite turnover can help turn the tables for challengers.

Rather than surveying corporations, other gay liberation fronts took a decidedly more aggressive approach. In the fall of 1971, when a spokesperson for Pacific Telephone and Telegraph (PT&T) said that the company would "not knowingly hire a homosexual," the Gay Activists Alliance picketed both PT&T and its parent company, American Telephone and Telegraph (AT&T) (*Advocate* 1971). Although headquartered in San Francisco, which instituted a nondiscrimination ordinance against antigay bias among city contractors in 1972, PT&T still refused to sign a hiring pledge against discrimination based on sexual orientation (*Advocate* 1972a, 1972b).

After gay activists in the Pride Foundation filed a complaint the following year, the city attorney ruled that the company was not mandated to comply, since it operated in an industry that was regulated by the Public Utilities Commission. In the face of continued intransigence, gay liberationists staged a highly dramatic Good Friday zap action that featured a young gay man dragging a heavy "cross" made from a telephone pole, which he carried through the downtown area to the PT&T premises (*Advocate* 1973d). A couple of weeks later, protesters held another rally, but to no avail.

During that same summer of 1973, gay liberationists picketed and leafleted for six days outside Northwestern Bell in Minnesota after the AT&T subsidiary announced on the front page of the newspaper that it would not hire "admitted homosexuals" (*Advocate* 1973b). Although the Minnesota

American Civil Liberties Union (ACLU) filed suit against parent company AT&T in 1973, it was not until May 1974, with the lawsuit still pending, that Northwestern Bell rescinded its antigay policy (*Advocate* 1973a, 1974b). The change was preceded by the passage of a gay rights ordinance in Minneapolis three days earlier. While similar laws elsewhere had not persuaded other affiliates to add sexual orientation to their nondiscrimination policies, it seems likely that the gay rights ordinance, paired with the ACLU lawsuit, worked to tip the scales at Northwestern Bell.

This seems an especially plausible interpretation given the fact that AT&T had just recently settled a highly publicized class-action suit for discrimination against women. In January of 1973, the company had agreed to pay the women plaintiffs $38 million in back pay and increased wages. This decision came after a damning investigation by the Equal Employment Opportunity Commission, which had concluded that "the Bell monolith is, without doubt, the largest oppressor of women workers in the United States" (quoted in Freeman 1975, 189).

Thus, it is not surprising that in May 1974 Northwestern Bell, faced with both a lawsuit and a newly passed nondiscrimination ordinance, officially ended its antigay policy, thereby demonstrating the power of what institutional theorists have called coercive isomorphism (DiMaggio and Powell 1991b). Approximately three months later, parent company AT&T announced in an issue of *AT&T News,* framed in response to a reader's question, that the corporation would not discriminate against gays and lesbians (*Advocate* 1974a). The CEO also sent a letter to the National Gay Task Force, which had contacted the company, to verify the inclusion of sexual orientation in the corporate nondiscrimination policy.

These early examples of gay-inclusive policy change illustrate the importance of movement processes, organizational realignments inside corporations, and coercive institutional pressures in the wider legal environment. The cases also demonstrate the significance of "early risers," who open up opportunities for later challengers (Tarrow 1998). For example, gay liberationists were able to win an inclusive hiring policy at AT&T only after the women's movement had convinced the corporate giant that employment discrimination, when legally prohibited, could be costly. Despite these early victories, however, lesbians and gay men were reluctant to mobilize *within* the workplace.

Holding Off on Mobilization inside Corporations

By the mid-1970s, gay and lesbian caucuses had sprung up in a handful of professional associations (S. Lewis 1979; see also Taylor and Raeburn 1995), but these submerged networks did not form within—nor did they target the antigay policies of—particular workplaces. This is hardly surprising given the fact that antigay employment discrimination was perfectly legal outside of a handful of cities. Many employers in both the public and private sectors expressed open hostility toward gays and lesbians. In fact, the federal government prohibited lesbians and gay men from civil service employment until 1975, with the ban on openly gay military personnel still in full effect (G. Lewis [1997] 2003). Early issues of the *Advocate* (1967 to 1982), the national newsmagazine of the gay and lesbian movement, are replete with stories about blatant discrimination by major corporations (for an index, see Ridinger 1987).

In 1976 the co–executive director of the National Gay Task Force commented on the fears that prevented lesbians and gay men from joining a national gay rights organization (S. Lewis 1979, 7): "About 75 percent of the problem is that a lot of people are afraid to make out checks to gay organizations or to have their names on gay mailing lists." How much stronger those fears must have been when it came to organizing in one's own place of work. While some ad hoc alliances of lesbian and gay union members had begun to emerge in the 1970s and early 1980s (Krupat [1999] 2001)—such as the gay union caucus that formed at the *Village Voice* in 1982, one of the first such caucuses in the state of New York—for the vast majority of gays and lesbians mobilization inside corporations was considered too high-risk.

It is also possible that lesbians and gay men were avoiding workplace activism because they were hopeful about the prospects of federal legislation that had been introduced by Bella Abzug and Edward Koch in 1974 (Thompson 1994, 97). As the first gay rights bill ever considered by Congress, the measure would have outlawed employment discrimination on the basis of sexual orientation. While in retrospect this optimism seems incredibly naive (the Employment Non-discrimination Act has yet to pass), at that time gays and lesbians had reason to believe that change was on its way. By the mid-1970s a number of cities had already passed gay rights ordinances, and by early 1975 eight states were considering similar bills (*Advocate* 1975a, 1975b, 1975c). The hopes of gay and lesbian people were buoyed as well in 1973 by the American Psychiatric Association's removal of homosexuality from its official list of mental disorders (Adam 1995).

Fearful of job loss and pinning their hopes on continued progress in the formal political domain, lesbians and gay men thus avoided mobilization in their own places of work. Indeed, it wasn't until 1978 that the first known gay employee network formed inside the walls of a Fortune 1000 corporation. And, given the powerful right-wing backlash that arose against gay rights in the late 1970s, it would take another decade before the number of corporate networks could be counted on two hands. This slow and cautious start of the workplace movement makes its successes in the 1990s and beyond all the more surprising. How, despite these hesitant beginnings, did the workplace movement achieve such startling victories, winning not only nondiscrimination protections in over half of the Fortune 500 but also equitable benefits in almost 20 percent of these 500 giants by the end of the 1990s (HRCF 2000b). Indeed, by mid-February 2004, nearly three-fourths of the Fortune 500 had adopted inclusive nondiscrimination policies, and over 40 percent had granted equitable benefits (HRCF 2004).

As discussed earlier, while some employers now play "follow the leader" and adopt domestic partner benefits in the absence of internal pressure, it is gay employee activists who deserve credit for the entire first wave of corporate adoptions and for a significant proportion of policy extensions even still. Having finally found the courage to come out and organize inside the walls of their own workplaces, lesbian and gay employees achieved groundbreaking changes that eventually began to ripple through the wider business world. The early and continued success of these inside agitators demonstrates the power of social movements, particularly those that mobilize within institutions beyond the formal political arena.

Data and Methods

In order to address the theoretical and empirical questions that drive this book, namely, those centered on the emergence and outcomes of the workplace movement, I relied on five main sources of data. First were telephone surveys of lesbian, gay, and bisexual employee networks in the Fortune 1000, along with the vice presidents or directors of human resources at companies with and without gay networks. Second, I conducted intensive interviews with all of the gay employee groups for which I had contact information, as well as a subsample of corporate elites and key informants from the workplace projects of the country's largest gay rights organizations, namely, the National Gay and Lesbian Task Force (NGLTF) and the Human Rights Campaign (HRC). All interviews were tape-recorded and transcribed. The third type of data came from print and virtual sources on gay-related workplace topics, including mainstream and gay press accounts, popular books, professional literature geared toward human resource managers and other business executives, and Web sites directed to the lesbian and gay community and to human resource professionals. To locate these varied sources, I conducted electronic searches using the Internet, LexisNexis, and the ABI/Inform business-news database, as well as archival searches of various lesbian and gay newspapers and magazines that had not been indexed electronically. My fourth source of data consisted of organizational documents from three case studies, as well as press releases and other documents published by HRC and NGLTF. Finally, I gathered extensive field data by attending several workplace conferences at both the regional and national levels, participating in the social activities of a local umbrella organization, and observing the weekly meetings of one of the oldest and most respected employee networks in the movement.

Prior to selecting my sample, I attempted to compile a list of gay employee networks that was as complete as possible. I retrieved contact lists from the workplace projects of NGLTF and HRC. These lists were current as of April 1998. To seek additional contacts, I also conducted an exhaustive search of the Internet; read all of the books and articles I could locate on sexual orientation issues in the workplace (see chapters 3 and 4); contacted diversity consultants who were well known for their knowledge of lesbian and gay issues; and attended movement conferences, both general and workplace-focused.

Combining all of these sources, there appeared to be 97 Fortune 1000 companies with gay employee groups. However, some of these sources were either inaccurate or could not be verified. As of April 1998, I was able to verify 85 networks that existed at one time or another, representing approximately 9 percent of the Fortune 1000. I attempted to contact all of them, but a couple had disbanded and I was unable to locate any former members. In other cases I lacked contact information and so sent my survey request in care of the vice president of human resources. In one such case I was told that my request would not be forwarded to the gay network, since the company did not allow employee groups to participate in external surveys. In other cases I never heard back from executives even after repeated attempts on my part; I thus never knew whether my request had been forwarded to the gay network.

In all, 71 gay employee groups responded to my survey request, all of whom agreed to participate. Of the 83 documented networks still in existence, this represents a response rate of 86 percent. Of those 71 activist networks, I was able to conduct telephone surveys and in-depth interviews with 70 of them, 69 of which provided complete data. These interviews were conducted mainly in a five-month period, from mid-May to the end of October 1998. While the surveys were semistructured questionnaires intended to be completed in approximately twenty minutes, all of the network informants also provided in-depth interviews that ranged from forty-five minutes to over three hours.

Summary Characteristics of Lesbian, Gay, and Bisexual Employee Networks

Of the 69 networks for which I have complete data, the average size was 142 members, with totals ranging from a low of 10 to a high of 2,000 members. In terms of gender composition, the workplace movement consists of more men than women. On average, women constitute only 38 percent of gay employee activists in the Fortune 1000. Gender representation is evenly balanced in only 26 percent of networks, while in 61 percent of networks men outnumber women. The workplace movement is also disproportionately white. In only 9 percent of networks do people of color constitute 15 percent or more of members. An equal percentage of networks is entirely white. On average, people of color make up only 7 percent of workplace activists in the Fortune 1000. While the movement is primarily fueled by lesbian, gay, and bisexual employees, heterosexuals constitute 8 percent of all workplace activists.

Nonmanagement employees make up a greater proportion of the movement (71 percent) than do management-level employees. The vast majority of gay employee groups have no union members. In many cases this is because companies themselves lack unions, as was true for 42 percent of all networks. When unions do exist, gay employees often find it difficult to win union participation because of three main obstacles that many union members face: inflexible work schedules, which make attendance at daytime meetings difficult; a hostile factory environment, which creates fear of harassment or violence; and lack of access to e-mail, which is the primary form of communication among network members. While some networks attempt to overcome these obstacles, they have largely met with limited success. Nonetheless, union members constitute, on average, 17 percent of the workplace movement's membership base.

Regardless of variation in the composition of the movement, gay employee groups typically share four main goals: to provide support, socializing, and networking opportunities for members; to gain official corporate recognition; to educate employees on sexual orientation issues; and to bring about gay-inclusive policies and practices, including nondiscrimination policies, diversity training, and domestic partner benefits. Some networks also encourage their employers to donate to lesbian and gay organizations or events in the wider community and/or to expand their marketing efforts to specifically target the gay community. A growing number of networks, especially those that have achieved all of their internal goals, are engaging in community outreach or other service projects, including scholarships for lesbian, gay, bisexual, and transgender students. Some have even established foundations to support such endeavors.

Selecting the Wider Sample

Using purposive sampling and drawing from the Fortune 1000 list published in *Fortune* magazine on April 29, 1996, I selected a total of 230 companies that reflected variation in industry type, degree of competition, location, size, and presence of a gay activist network. I also relied on numerous workplace-related Web sites, the WorkNet workplace project database of HRC, LexisNexis searches, and the ABI/Inform business-news database to determine whether corporate headquarters were located in areas that had adopted gay rights laws and whether companies had been the target of lawsuits, boycotts, or shareholder activism.

Since the response rate for mail questionnaires is typically far below adequate (Neuman 2002), the letters I sent to executives and activists requested that individuals participate in a telephone survey. Of the 230 corporations I contacted, I was able to find willing participants in 94 companies (76 with a gay network and 18 without), for an overall response rate of 41 percent. I attempted to survey comparable numbers of executives from corporations with and without gay activist groups in order to gauge the relative importance of environmental and internal pressures. However, corporate elites largely proved unwilling to participate in the study. Among the 230 Fortune 1000 companies I contacted, only 51 human resource executives agreed to be surveyed, resulting in a response rate of 22 percent. Not surprisingly, the response rate was higher among executives from companies that had a gay employee group. While 43 percent of these elites participated in the study (33 out of 76), only 12 percent of those from companies without a gay network agreed to be surveyed (18 out of 154). Of those human resource executives who responded to my request for participation, 10 also agreed to intensive interviews. Ranging from one to two hours, the interviews took place in the summer and fall of 1998.

Of the Fortune 1000 industries that are represented in my sample, those most likely to have gay employee groups were in entertainment (75 percent), high-tech/computer as well as scientific and photographic industry (both 35 percent), and telecommunications (30 percent), followed by soaps and cosmetics (22 percent), pharmaceuticals (21 percent), and airlines (20 percent). Not surprisingly, these industries are also far more likely to have instituted equitable benefits. In contrast, of the 56 industries represented on the Fortune 1000 list, half had no gay networks whatsoever as of mid-1998, when data collection on network formations ended. These included healthcare firms, grocery and drugstore chains, retailers, wholesalers, and most of the "old economy" or heavy-industry sectors, such as building materials, construction and engineering, industrial and farm equipment, metals, mining, oil, textiles, transportation, and trucking. Aside from these sectors, the industries least likely to have gay employee groups were in chemicals (2 percent), forest and paper products (3 percent), utilities (4 percent), electronics and electrical equipment (5 percent), and food manufacturers (6 percent).

Tellingly, businesses in those sectors with no or very few gay employee groups have also been laggards with regard to equitable-benefits adoption. (For a complete list of industries with gay employee networks, see Table A.1 in the appendix, and for a comparison of benefits adoption by industry, see Table A.3 in the appendix.)

Who Counts as an Equitable-Benefits Adopter?

Although true equality for lesbian and gay employees would mean complete access to all of the benefits already provided to heterosexual employees and their spouses, for the purposes of this study my operationalization of equitable-benefits adoption required, at a minimum, health-care coverage for same-sex partners, the same criterion used by HRC in compiling its WorkNet database. In addition to granting "hard" benefits (medical, dental, and vision coverage) to domestic partners, many companies provided "soft" benefits as well, which often came before the extension of health insurance itself (Mickens 1994a; D. Baker, Strub, and Henning 1995; Winfeld and Spielman 1995).

As mentioned earlier, according to a survey of 570 large U.S. employers, 22 percent of companies offered domestic partner benefits as of March 2000 (Hewitt Associates 2000, 1). Of the corporations that grant benefits to same-sex partners, nearly all (98 percent) provide medical coverage, while 95 percent offer dental and 77 percent vision coverage (13). Among the soft benefits that some companies extend to gay and lesbian employees are family leave (56 percent), bereavement leave (61 percent), life insurance (51 percent), and COBRA or similar benefits that provide health-insurance coverage for a departing worker's partner for up to eighteen months after the worker leaves a job (71 percent) (14). Less common but still sought by lesbian and gay employees are the soft benefits designated in the Hewitt study as "other," which only 21 percent of adopters provide (13). They include, but are not limited to, the following: partners' access to employee assistance programs, partners as beneficiaries for pension or 401(k) plans, relocation expenses, adoption assistance, long-term-care insurance, tuition assistance, dependents' scholarships, child-care services, and discounts on company products or services (14; see also Adams and Solomon 2000).

Other simple but meaningful steps on the path toward equality include inviting domestic partners as well as spouses to company events and including the name of an employee's partner on holiday cards or other correspondence. As explained in an equitable-benefits guide for employers written by two attorneys specializing in compensation and benefits (Adams and Solomon 2000, 11), "At a minimum, such gestures foster a culture of acceptance, which is often what gay and lesbian employees want nearly as much as they want health coverage for their partners."

A Note on Confidentiality

Given the fear that elites often expressed over the possibility of backlash, and to protect the identities of activists who often revealed highly sensitive information about particular executives, I promised all survey and interview respondents complete confidentiality. In many cases I had to assure executives multiple times that I would not be identifying their companies and that I would disguise any revealing characteristics. I struggled with this decision, as did many of the activists themselves, since my personal commitment to workplace change includes my preference that the policies and practices of all employers be brought out into the open. On scholarly grounds as well, I wish that this project could be a typical movement study, where the names of activist organizations are published and more detailed information is provided. But given the choice between confidentiality (which hopefully elicited honest and forthcoming responses) and identification of participants in the name of movement goals (which would have drastically reduced my response rate), I chose the former. It is my hope that this study, regardless of its limitations, will contribute to the ongoing struggle for equality in the workplace.

In those instances where I discuss companies by name, it is because the information already has been made public through, for example, press releases or newspaper articles. Since corporate names often change as a result of mergers and acquisitions, it is also important to note that the companies identified in the text bear the names they used at the times indicated.

Data Analysis

This research uses a comparative design that allowed me to explore different patterns of policy change across the cases in my sample (Ragin 1994). I used the survey data mainly as background information in discussing the significance of the social and political environment, industry and corporate characteristics, and internal social movement factors on the adoption of inclusive policies. For a rich understanding of the institutional and movement processes that underlie corporate policy decisions, I relied primarily on qualitative analysis. In addition to integrating data from seventy-nine in-depth interviews (sixty-nine with gay employee networks and ten with human resource executives), I selected three cases that illuminate the central theoretical processes posited by the study. These intensive case studies embody key differences found among the corporations in my sample.

The case studies represent a transportation company where equitable policies were adopted in the absence of a lesbian and gay employee group; a financial services corporation whose gay employee network, which I call LGB (Lesbians, Gays, and Bisexuals), succeeded early in its existence; and a telecommunications company whose employee group, which I call GLUE (Gay and Lesbian United Employees), fought unsuccessfully for years, winning equitable benefits only relatively recently. A comparative design allowed me to gather in-depth information about a diversity of cases in order to understand the relative effects of institutional factors and activist challenges on policy change. Aside from the practical benefits that this study can provide for institutional activists, my goal is to advance theories of social change by highlighting the institutional and movement processes that underlie the transformation of complex organizations.

Outline of the Book

While this study addresses a number of intriguing issues, my overarching question revolves around a central paradox: with lesbian, gay, and bisexual rights still so hotly contested in the sociopolitical arena, how is it possible that gay-inclusive policies have become standard practice in so many companies across the country? The answers to that question will provide guidance not only to the numerous groups still fighting for equal rights in the workplace but also to scholars who are interested in explaining the outcomes of social movements, particularly those aimed at institutions other than the state. In this way I contribute to two relatively neglected areas of study: movement outcomes in general and institutional activism in particular.

In chapter 1, which traces the rise and trajectory of the corporate workplace movement, I examine the formation and spread of gay and lesbian employee networks among the Fortune 1000. After a decade of slow and halting growth following its emergence in the late 1970s, the workplace movement took off at the start of the 1990s, mushroomed at a rapid pace, but then just as suddenly experienced a slowdown in new corporate organizing beginning in 1995. Using a wide-angle lens to help make sense of these findings, I analyze the distinctive patterning of network formations in relation to four key shifts in the broader institutional environment: changes in the sociopolitical climate, the actions of the larger gay and lesbian rights movement, the expanded attention of the media, and institutional openings in the workplace. Aside from variations in the political environment, I am especially interested in the relationship between direct-action groups such as Queer Nation, with their purposefully outrageous media-grabbing tactics, and the mobilization of corporate challengers, whose unobtrusive style could not contrast more sharply with that of their raucous sisters and brothers in the streets. I also consider the impact of discordant events in the corporate arena itself, including the announcement of an explicitly antigay hiring policy by one particularly audacious employer and, in comparison, the extension of domestic partner benefits by the first few big-name companies, a move that was complemented by the growing number of corporations that had begun "talking the talk" of diversity.

Chapter 2 addresses the puzzling drop-off in corporate mobilization beginning in 1995. By the middle of the 1990s, lesbian and gay employees had won equitable benefits in a sizable number of major companies, and sexual orientation issues in the workplace had received widespread coverage in both gay and mainstream media and in the business and professional literature. Why, then, amid growing policy victories and heightened publicity, did new corporate organizing drop precipitously? I analyze this paradoxical decline by treating both political and institutional opportunities as socially constructed. I argue that the decisions of potential challengers were shaped at that time by three primary factors in the sociopolitical and institutional environments: contrasting interpretations and political battles over the presumed imminence of gay marriage following Hawaii's move toward legalization; media representations of equitable-benefits adoption in the corporate arena; and movement-issued accounts of inclusive policy change. Focusing on what I call the irony of partial success and the dangers of complacency, I also address the perplexing quiescence of gay and lesbian workers in yet-to-adopt companies after two surprising announcements of equitable-benefits adoption—one by an employer long known for its antigay politics and the other by a company widely seen as a "family values" giant.

In chapter 3, I show how workplace challengers built and continue to benefit from an extensive infrastructure that helps connect gay employee activists from a wide variety of institutional settings and provides the movement with staying power despite the decline in new corporate organizing. My discussion has a dual purpose: to explain the institutional and movement processes by which previously isolated networks became linked to one another; and to highlight the resources, structures, and strategies that arose from these interorganizational ties. First I consider the importance of what I call "virtual opportunities," namely, expanded access to e-mail and the Internet, and the ways that activists have used these communication technologies to provide both long-distance emotional support and technical assistance. Next I discuss the rise of workplace conferences, which I consider to be the movement's greatest mobilizers, and the establishment of workplace projects by national organizations in the larger gay rights movement, which provide the workplace wing with some of its most critical resources. I then address the formation of local, regional, and national umbrella organizations that bring gay employee networks into coalition with one another and help sustain the commitment of challengers amid harsh conditions in the corporate or wider sociopolitical environment.

In the next two chapters I present the key dimensions of what I call an "institutional opportunity framework," which synthesizes a political opportunity approach to social movements and a neoinstitutional perspective on organizational change. My theoretical model offers a systematic framework for understanding how the "nested" and often contradictory environments of challengers—the targeted corporation, the surrounding field of competitors or other relevant players, and the wider sociopolitical context—can aid and/or constrain the fight for institutional transformation. Focusing on the winds of change outside the corporation, chapter 4 details macro-level opportunities in the sociopolitical and field environments, while chapter 5 concentrates on meso-level opportunities present in the corporation itself. In both chapters I lay out the key processes and structures that facilitate gay-inclusive policy change, particularly the adoption of domestic partner benefits among Fortune 1000 companies. Rather than delineating those dimensions of opportunity here, I simply touch on a few of the interesting questions that are addressed by my institutional opportunity framework.

In chapter 4, for example: What impact does the legal environment have on companies, particularly since no more than a handful of cities require corporate contractors to provide equitable benefits to their employees? How have corporations responded to coercive pressures such as boycotts and shareholder activism—tactics that are now used by gay rights supporters and opponents alike? What effects do competitive pressures have on companies' willingness to adopt gay-inclusive policies, and how have Web-based benchmarking tools, which rate corporations on such policies, expanded the competitive referent groups that corporate elites use when making policy decisions? How did activist-generated frames, particularly those which rationalize gay-inclusive policies as profitable, become so widely reflected in the pages of the business press and in personnel and other professional journals, and to what effect?

And here, a glimpse of some of the key questions addressed in chapter 5, where I shift down a level to examine opportunities in the corporation itself: How are lesbian and gay activists aided by the prior successes of employee networks for women and people of color and by diversity offices, councils, or task forces? What are the policy impacts of turnovers in top management, shifts in the corporate boards of directors, or mergers and acquisitions? How important are allies within and outside of management, and what are the various roles played by unions, other employee networks, and "executive sponsors"? Besides a diversity-embracing corporate culture, what other cultural supports facilitate policy success for workplace challengers? How does the personal background of elites affect corporate decision making with regard to gay-inclusive policies?

Chapter 6 highlights the role that activists themselves play in bringing about inclusive policy change. I focus particularly on the impact of two movement processes: the use of "identity-oriented strategies" that emphasize the visibility of gay, lesbian, and bisexual employees and their allies; and the mobilization of "profits- versus ethics-oriented collective action frames" that rationalize inclusive policies as "good for the bottom line" rather than simply "the right thing to do." First I discuss the impact of various identity tactics and the different settings in which they are deployed. Focusing especially on the ways that lesbian and gay challengers utilize coming-out stories and other personal narratives, I emphasize the transformative power of emotions in winning allies and persuading elites to embrace equality. Next I examine the innovative programs that employee activists have developed to heighten the visibility of their allies. Closing the chapter with an analysis of framing strategies, I then consider the particular ways that workplace challengers blend ideologies of profits and ethics in their call for gay-inclusive policy change, and I delineate the various components that constitute those frames.

In the conclusion, which weaves together theoretical and practical considerations, I first summarize the key components of my institutional opportunity framework, tracing both its derivation from and its contributions to social movement and new institutional perspectives. As a theory of movement success, this approach can be used to understand the outcomes of not simply gay employee mobilization but a wide variety of institutional challenges. Aside from widening the focus of dominant social movement perspectives, which so often treat the state as the sole site of contention, my approach also expands the purview of neoinstitutional theory by highlighting the role of mobilized constituencies as agents of organizational change. In the second half of the chapter, I consider the practical implications of my findings for the workplace movement as a whole and draw out the important lessons that institutional activists can take with them in the ongoing fight for equal rights. I review how my research confirms the crucial role of employee activists in securing a wide range of gay-inclusive policies and practices in the corporate world. Turning next to a cross-sector comparison, I consider various explanations as to why corporate America is so far ahead of other types of employers in embracing equality for lesbian and gay workers, particularly in providing equitable benefits. Finally, I discuss what my study reveals about the relative effects of external institutional processes and internal activist challenges on policy change over time. With an eye on continued and more expansive success, I offer some concluding thoughts on the future course of the workplace movement and its relationship with the larger gay, lesbian, bisexual, and transgender rights movement.

1

The Rise of the Corporate Workplace Movement

Although the gay, lesbian, and bisexual movement is one of the most highly mobilized campaigns on the current political landscape (Adam 1995; J. Gamson 1995; Jenness 1999; Taylor and Raeburn 1995; Adam, Duyvendak, and Krouwel 1999), scholars have yet to direct their attention to a significant development in the struggle for equal rights: the rise of a lesbian, gay, and bisexual workplace movement. With a fledgling start in the late 1970s and early 1980s, when only two major corporations witnessed the birth of gay employee networks, by the late 1980s small numbers of lesbians and gay men began to mobilize for inclusive policies and practices in their places of work. Still, by the end of that decade, only ten gay employee groups had sprung up among the Fortune 1000. By the late 1990s, however, the numbers had swelled to over 80 documented networks, which together constitute a pioneering force for social change.

Amid the long-standing backlash against gay rights in the United States (Adam 1995; Vaid 1995; S. Epstein 1999), how did the workplace movement take off and gain enough visibility and success such that the *New York Times* referred to gay and lesbian concerns in the corporate arena as "the workplace issue of the '90s" (D. Baker, Strub, and Henning 1995)? To answer this question, in this chapter I first discuss the patterned emergence and diffusion of lesbian and gay employee networks among the Fortune 1000 in relation to four key areas of the institutional environment: the wider sociopolitical context, the larger gay and lesbian rights movement, mainstream media and the gay press, and institutional openings in the workplace. I then briefly discuss the development of interorganizational linkages among gay employee networks beginning in the early 1990s. In the next chapter I address the surprisingly sluggish pace of new corporate organizing beginning in 1995 and consider alternative explanations for the slowdown.

The Emergence and Diffusion of the Corporate Workplace Movement

Examining the number of lesbian, gay, and bisexual employee groups that have emerged each year among Fortune 1000 companies reveals a distinctive patterning of network formations across time. As shown in Figure 1, organizational births are clustered within three main periods such that the trajectory of corporate organizing can be described as follows: (1) a slow rise between 1978 and 1989; (2) rapid growth from 1990 to 1994; and (3) a decline in new organizing from 1995 to mid-1998 (when data collection on network formations ended).

Table 2 details the number and percentage of gay employee networks that emerged each year and, in aggregate, the organizational birthrate for each of the three periods. (Table A.2 in the appendix sketches the growth and diversification of the workplace movement by focusing on this periodized clustering of network formations by industry and region of the country. For a complete list of organizational births by year, industry, and geographic region, see Table A.1 in the appendix.)

As shown in Table 2, during the first period of the workplace movement, between 1978 and 1989, only 10 gay networks appeared among the Fortune 1000. The slow rate of mobilization over that twelve-year stretch

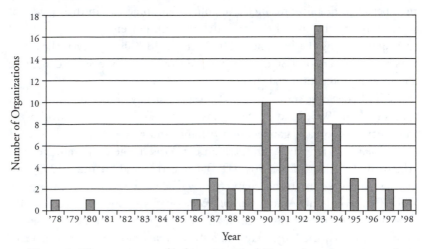

Figure 1. The emergence of lesbian, gay, and bisexual employee networks among the Fortune 1000: organizational births by year.

Table 2. Emergence and Diffusion of the Corporate Workplace Movement: The Clustering of Organizational Births across Time

Year	n	Percentage of Organizational Population (N = 69)
1978–89: Slow rise		
1978	1	1.4%
1979	0	
1980	1	1.4%
1981	0	
1982	0	
1983	0	
1984	0	
1985	0	
1986	1	1.4%
1987	3	4.3%
1988	2	2.9%
1989	2	2.9%
Subtotal	10	14%
Birthrate: Less than 1 (0.83) new organization per year		
1990–94: Rapid growth		
1990	10	14.5%
1991	6	8.7%
1992	9	13.0%
1993	17	24.6%
1994	8	11.6%
Subtotal	50	72%
Birthrate: 10 new organizations per year		
1995–mid-1998: Decline in new organizing		
1995	3	4.3%
1996	3	4.3%
1997	2	2.9%
Through mid-1998	1	1.4%
Subtotal	9	13%
Birthrate: Fewer than 3 (2.57) new organizations per year		
Total	69	
Birthrate: More than 3 (3.37) new organizations per year		

Note: Data are from surveys and interviews with 69 gay, lesbian, and bisexual employee networks in the Fortune 1000, conducted primarily between May and October 1998. Subtotal percentages are rounded to the nearest whole percentage.

contrasts sharply with the next five years, which witnessed the birth of 50 new groups. Put differently, while during the first wave of mobilization the organizational founding rate was less than 1 new group per year, that figure climbed to 10 per year between 1990 and 1994. Examining the distribution trends from the perspective of the entire organizational sample (N = 69), only 14 percent of corporate networks were born during the first wave, compared to 72 percent in the second.

The third period of the workplace movement is marked by a significant decline in the pace of new organizing. Only 9 employee groups emerged between 1995 and mid-1998, which represents only 13 percent of the total sample. At first glance the decrease may appear to be an artifact of unequal time comparisons (5 years in period 2 versus 3.5 years in period 3). But this does not explain the fact that the organizational birthrate dropped from 10 new networks per year in the second wave to fewer than 3 per year in the third.

All of these contrasting patterns will begin to make sense when viewed through the trifocal lens of the shifting political climate, the actions of the broader gay and lesbian movement, and the variable conditions present in other institutional spheres, namely, the media and the workplace. For now it bears mentioning that by the end of the third period, after over twenty years of workplace mobilization, lesbian and gay employee groups had emerged in 85 documented Fortune 1000 companies, 69 of which are included in my sample here (see the methods section of the introduction for an explanation of the discrepancy).

The Sociopolitical Context of Corporate Organizing

As political process theorists suggest, shifts in the wider political environment help to explain the rise and trajectory of social movements (Tilly 1978; McAdam 1982; Katzenstein and Mueller 1987; Tarrow 1989, 1998; Jenkins and Klandermans 1995b; McAdam, McCarthy, and Zald 1996a; W. Gamson and Meyer 1996). For example, Doug McAdam (1982) contends that the civil rights movement emerged in response to new political opportunities that were made possible by the collapse of the cotton-based economy in the South and the mass migration of African Americans to industrial regions of the North. Similarly, Craig Jenkins and Charles Perrow (1977) argue that the success of the farm workers' movement in the late 1960s grew out of political realignments, policy reform, and broad economic trends that created a more supportive set of conditions for insurgent activity. The rise of the gay and lesbian workplace movement and the distinctive patterns of network formation over the past twenty years likewise reflect changes in the broader sociopolitical context.

The New Right and the First Wave of Employee Activism

The tentative pace of early corporate organizing is understandable, given the rise of the New Right in the late 1970s and its consolidation of power in the

1980s. Mobilized around fiscally and socially conservative goals, including the defense of traditional gender and sexual norms, and drawing from a broad network of well-organized single-issue groups, evangelical Christians, and various members of the corporate elite, the New Right took aim at the gains that had been made by the gay liberation movement in the 1970s (Adam 1995; S. Epstein 1999). Beginning with Anita Bryant's highly publicized so-called Save Our Children campaign in 1977, which resulted in the repeal of a gay rights ordinance in Dade County, Florida, a wave of similar repeals spread across the United States (Adam 1995; Fetner 2001; Werum and Winders 2001). The day after the Dade County repeal, California state senator John Briggs introduced the infamous Briggs Initiative, which aimed to purge the school system of gay men and lesbians as well as anyone who presented homosexuality in a positive light (D'Emilio 1992).

In response to the growing antigay backlash, three hundred thousand people turned out for San Francisco's Gay Pride Day in 1978 (D'Emilio 1992, 89), and over thirty organizations sprang up across the state to fight the initiative (S. Epstein 1999, 47), a groundswell of mobilization that historian John D'Emilio (1992, 89) describes as "the most far-reaching and sustained gay organizing campaign" the movement had ever seen. Later that same year, Dan White, a disgruntled former member of the San Francisco Board of Supervisors and former police officer, assassinated mayor George Moscone and city supervisor Harvey Milk, one of the first openly gay officeholders in the country. When White received a manslaughter rather than murder conviction, from five thousand to ten thousand people marched on city hall (D'Emilio 1992, 92), where some smashed windows and others torched police cars to express their rage at the injustice (Adam 1995).

It was during that turbulent year of 1978 that the earliest known gay employee group formed in corporate America. Not surprisingly, its location was California, as was the case for four of the ten employee networks that emerged during the first wave of the workplace movement. During the same year, the organization then known as the National Gay Task Force released the first movement study of antigay workplace discrimination in the private sector. Nonetheless, aside from the second corporate network, which formed in 1980, no other gay employee groups were formed until 1986. The emergence of the New Right in the late 1970s and the increasingly hostile political climate had halted new corporate organizing among lesbian and gay employees and radically altered the terrain of struggle for the gay rights movement in general (Adam 1995; S. Epstein 1999).

The stunted growth of the workplace movement also may have stemmed from the recessions of the late 1970s and early 1980s, since, as many scholars have pointed out, economic downturns make it more difficult for progressive social movements to advance their causes (Ryan 1992; Taylor and Rupp 1993; Adam 1995; Whittier 1995). Lesbians and gay men were already concerned for their economic situation, given their vulnerability to job loss and other forms of antigay employment discrimination (Weinberg and Williams 1974; Levine 1979, 1992; S. Lewis 1979; Blumstein and Schwartz 1983; Levine and Leonard 1984; Schneider 1984, 1986, 1988; Woods 1993; Badgett 1995; Taylor and Raeburn 1995; G. Lewis [1997] 2003). How much stronger the fear of coming out and mobilizing at work must have been when compounded by the rising rate of unemployment generally.

Commenting on the social and political impact of economic decline during the period in question, Barry Adam (1995, 122) explains, "The economic recession of the late 1970s and the retrenchment of major industries increased unemployment, creating greater defensiveness in a population anxious for its livelihood. . . . American workers, women, and minorities were forced toward 'concessions' and 'conservation' of their positions and away from the struggle for greater equality." In contrast, during periods of economic growth, when demand for labor rises, companies feel pressure to woo workers and to distinguish themselves from competitors by offering better compensation and benefits packages (Bond 1997; Darcé 1997; Ginsberg 1997; Kelly and Dobbin 1999; Frase-Blunt 2002). During such times, workplace activists emphasize how low unemployment and tight labor markets make equitable benefits all the more necessary for employers hoping to attract and retain top talent (HRC 1999c). But, from the perspective of lesbian and gay workers at the end of the 1970s and start of the 1980s, rosier economic conditions were still a long way off. With the early 1980s bringing massive layoffs, or the more euphemistic "corporate downsizing," and the worst economic recession the country had seen in over thirty-five years (*Dun's Business Month* 1983; Knoke 2001), mobilization in the corporate workplace had come to a complete standstill.

But an even more direct explanation for the five-year hiatus in corporate organizing can be found in the New Right's consolidation of power in the early 1980s, which "stalemated the gay and lesbian movement" as a whole, "forcing it into a defensive mode" (Adam 1995, 122). The presidential election of Ronald Reagan in 1980 and the announcement of a renewed antigay campaign by Jerry Falwell's Moral Majority served to entrench the New Right (D'Emilio 1992), thereby compelling the gay rights movement to redirect energy and crucial resources away from the proactive efforts of the 1970s—such as pressing for state and corporate nondiscrimination policies, overturning sodomy laws, and winning elected office (S. Epstein 1999)—and toward defensive measures and simple community preservation (Adam 1995).

Struggling against the powerful conservative momentum of the Reagan era and the rise of the AIDS epidemic, gay and lesbian activists did not concentrate on gaining advances in the workplace or any other arena; instead they focused by necessity on preventing further assaults on gay rights, battling the deadening silence of the media and political establishment over AIDS from 1981 to 1983, caring for those who were sick and dying, and then, once word of the epidemic hit the news, defending against widespread panic and virulently antigay attacks such as street and police violence as well as discrimination against, including calls to quarantine, people living with HIV and AIDS (Adam 1995; S. Epstein 1999; Werum and Winders 2001). Early news reports of the deadly virus, both reflecting and reinforcing the dominant cultural mythology, strengthened the supposed link between gay men and pathology and fed the right wing's continuing attempts to equate homosexuality with inherent deviance and public threat (Schmidt 1994). "In this environment," explains Steven Epstein (1999, 52), "gay communities faced a nearly overwhelming set of political challenges."

Thus, it comes as no great shock that the first two gay employee networks, both in the high-tech industry, remained the solitary representatives of the corporate workplace movement from 1980 until well into the second term of Ronald Reagan, when they were finally joined by a slow trickle of other gay networks beginning in 1986. By 1989, lesbian, gay, and bisexual employees had mobilized in 10 Fortune 1000 companies. The workplace movement was thus slowly moving into gear after the doldrum years of the early to mid-1980s, a period of "abeyance," to borrow Verta Taylor's term (1989), during which activists had been forced into a holding pattern amid a harsh political climate (see also Rupp and Taylor [1987] 1990).

The revival of corporate activism by the end of the 1980s came on the heels of what Barry Adam has called the "faltered" momentum of the New Right in the middle of the decade. These changes, compounded by sex scandals among the Christian-fundamentalist leadership of the Right beginning in 1987 and Pat Robertson's failure to obtain the Republican presidential nomination in 1988, portended a shifting political environment. Lesbians and gay men then increasingly mobilized "in all spheres of civil society . . . at work, in communities, in churches, in health and social services, in sport, and in the media, education, and the arts" (Adam 1995, 130).

Clinton's Rise to Office and the Second Wave of Employee Activism

The second wave of the workplace movement is marked by a significant jump in corporate organizing beginning in 1990, which ushered in a five-year period of rapid growth and diversification. While during the first wave of the movement it took twelve years to produce 10 gay networks, the year 1990 alone brought 10 more groups, starting a growth trend that would continue throughout the second wave of mobilization such that by the end of 1994, 60 networks had formed among the Fortune 1000. The relative explosion of corporate organizing during the second wave corresponds to the changing political climate that eventually brought Bill Clinton to the presidency.

Beginning in the early 1990s, the larger gay and lesbian movement encountered a more favorable set of environmental conditions, including the aggressive courting of the gay vote by Clinton (Vaid 1995). Openly gay people were prominent on Clinton's campaign team and his list of presidential appointments (S. Epstein 1999). Discussing other significant openings in the structure of political opportunity for the gay rights movement, Sidney Tarrow (1994) notes the split among the political elite over the definition of "family values," the electoral realignment of 1992 that brought a Democrat into the White House after twelve years of Republican occupancy, Clinton's attempt to end the long-standing military ban on gay and lesbian service members (see also Korb 1996), and the increasing presence of gay-friendly allies among the women's movement, civil rights groups, and various members of Congress.

Just days after the election, President Clinton sent a letter to the National Gay and Lesbian Task Force in which he thanked members for their advocacy work and campaign support, asked for help in implementing positive change, and extended a warm welcome to those who were attending NGLTF's annual Creating Change conference. Describing both the immediate impact and wider significance of Clinton's gesture, one audience member later reflected, "When Urvashi Vaid [then NGLTF director] read Bill Clinton's letter . . . the crowd went wild. The President Elect's letter to *us,* lesbian, bisexual, and gay activists from all over the U.S., was at once a recognition of the role of our community in his victory and a positive sign for the future" (quoted in Bain 1992d, 7; emphasis in the original).

Issues of fairness and equal treatment in the workplace also gained considerable attention as politicians began to furiously debate Clinton's 1991 campaign pledge to rescind the military's antigay policies (Vaid 1995). Fifty years earlier the military had taken a strikingly similar stance against racial integration of the armed forces. Faced with Clinton's promise, the military dusted off its racist arguments and sent them into battle over gays in uniform, warning again of breakdowns in unit cohesion and threats to combat-readiness (Raeburn 1998; Herek, Jobe, and Carney 1996). The controversy culminated in 1993 with the so-called compromise policy known as "Don't ask, don't tell, don't pursue," which even conservatives describe as varying little from the former ban (Korb 1996, 295). Nevertheless, the furor brought to the public eye not only the exclusionary policies of the armed forces but also the holes that could be shot through the military's defense of the ban. These weaknesses in military rhetoric revealed deeper questions about the rationale for—and rationality of—antigay attitudes in the workplace generally.

New Strategies of the Right

In 1992 the workplace movement experienced a different kind of jolt following passage of Colorado's Amendment Two. A statewide ballot initiative that legally banned civil rights protection for lesbians, gay men, and bisexuals, the measure overturned gay rights laws that had been passed in Aspen, Boulder, and Denver (Adam 1995, 133; Dugan 1999). While the lesbian and gay movement was accustomed to battling the repeal of gay rights ordinances, this measure and others like it in Oregon and later in Idaho and Cincinnati, Ohio, represented a new form of legislation "that sought to make it legally impossible for gay rights laws ever to be established" (S. Epstein 1999, 68; see also Blain 1997; Dugan 1999). Although in 1996 the United States Supreme Court ruled the Colorado amendment unconstitutional, its passage in 1992 by 53 percent of voters led outraged lesbian and gay activists to issue a national boycott of travel to the state (S. Epstein 1999, 68).

Media attention to this new and more virulent strain of antigay legislation, a "suddenly imposed grievance" in movement terms (Walsh 1981), also precipitated an increase in corporate mobilization. As shown earlier, in Table 2, nine new employee groups (13 percent of the current sample) emerged in 1992, making it the third most "fertile" year of the workplace movement's twenty-year history. Commenting on the mobilizing impact of the legislation, one Colorado-based activist explained in our interview, "After voters in my district supported Amendment Two, I decided it was time for a gay employee resource group at my company." While none of the other employee networks that formed in that year were located in Colorado, the New Right's success in passing a more insidious form of antigay legislation created a wave of gay and lesbian mobilization that reverberated across state lines and into corporations around the country. As Traci Sawyers and David Meyer (1999) argue, unfavorable legislation or hostile judicial rulings can be seen as opportunities, since challengers can use them to generate publicity, to raise consciousness and money, and to gain new recruits or even increased leverage in other policy domains (see also Burstein 1991; D. Meyer and Staggenborg 1996).

The Impact of the Wider Gay, Lesbian, and Bisexual Movement

Taking It to the Streets . . . and into the Workplace

Situated within nested political environments, the workplace movement faces windows of opportunities and walls of constraint that stem not simply from actions of the state and of countermovements but also from the efforts of the broader lesbian, gay, and bisexual movement. Just as suddenly imposed grievances can incite activism, so too can movement protest itself lead to increased and more widespread mobilization (Sawyers and Meyer 1999). For example, the cluster of first-wave employee groups that sprang up during the late 1980s followed the record-breaking turnout for the second National March on Washington for Gay and Lesbian Rights, in 1987.

In response to the New Right's vitriolic attacks and the ever-expanding AIDS crisis, and in the aftermath of the *Bowers v. Hardwick* Supreme Court decision in 1986, which upheld sodomy statutes and denied lesbians and gays the right to privacy, anywhere from 500,000 to over 650,000 people descended on the Capitol in the 1987 march to demand justice, equality, and a cure (D'Emilio 1992, 267; Vaid 1995, 99; S. Epstein 1999). Accounting for the heightened and more militant wave of activism that began in 1986, Deborah Gould (2001, 149) emphasizes the "moral shock" (Jasper and Poulsen 1995; Jasper 1997) delivered by the high court's ruling: "Emanating from the highest echelons of the state and amidst increasingly repressive legislation, government negligence, and the ever-increasing AIDS deaths, the *Hardwick* ruling shocked lesbians and gay men into a greater recognition of the life-threatening nature of state-sponsored and socially sanctioned homophobia."

The radical presence at the 1987 march of the newly formed ACT UP (AIDS Coalition to Unleash Power), a direct-action, grassroots alliance, and the participation of five thousand activists at the national Civil Disobedience Action the following day at the Supreme Court (Vaid 1995, 99), attracted considerable media attention. ACT UP expanded the strategic repertoire of the movement by reincorporating tactics that had been abandoned after the heyday of gay liberation (D'Emilio 1992; Berzon 1994; S. Epstein 1999). As ACT UP's "SILENCE = DEATH" slogan diffused rapidly to the public spaces of mainstream America, its message struck a responsive chord among many (see also Gould 2001). While fear of discrimination and harassment had kept countless gay men and lesbians from coming out at work, the AIDS crisis and the life-saving necessity of speaking out pushed many out of the closet (Swan 1997c). In the words of journalist Thomas Stewart (1991, 44–45), who interviewed over one hundred lesbian and gay people

in corporate America, volunteering in AIDS organizations and mobilizing against the disease had "ended the isolation that confined many gay
professionals."

Once connected through AIDS organizing, and once empowered to be
visible, many gay men and lesbians decided to mobilize in their own places
of work. The first gay network to emerge in a utility company, for example,
grew out of the efforts of six employees who had persuaded their West Coast
employer to sponsor an internal AIDS hotline. Although one of the founders was a gay rights activist who had previously worked for a civil rights
organization, the gay employee network started out as a purely social group.
Shortly thereafter, however, members took on explicitly political aims both
within and outside of the company. Many other gay networks in the Fortune
1000 likewise began as informal "support groups," but members soon expanded their goals, renamed themselves "diversity networks" or "employee
resource groups" (terms commonly used by preexisting networks for women
and people of color), and sought meetings with corporate decision makers
about the need for gay-inclusive policies (see also Swan 1997c).

As alluded to earlier, however, the birth of several gay employee networks in the late 1980s after a five-year hiatus did not come simply from the
mobilizing carryovers of the AIDS epidemic; the 1987 March on Washington fanned the flames of that organizing impulse. As activist-writer Urvashi
Vaid (1995, 99) explains, the march and day-long demonstrations of civil
disobedience "ignited gay and lesbian activism" in local communities across
the country and in multiple institutional spheres, sparking a trend of movement growth and organizational diversification that continued well into the
next decade. Movement scholar John D'Emilio (1992, 267) comments elo-
quently on the impact of the 1987 march: "[T]he weekend in Washington
proved uncontainable. The display of the Names Project quilt, the massive
wedding ceremony at the National Cathedral, and the impressive parade
of contingents from every state in the nation, struck a chord of self-respect
so deep that it could not be ignored. People returned to their home communities transformed, ready to do what seemed unimaginable a few days
before."

D'Emilio's words ring true in the founding account of the largest lesbian and gay employee group in the country, a telecommunications case
study that I refer to as GLUE (Gay and Lesbian United Employees). Located in a company headquartered on the East Coast and formed in 1987 by
a small circle of friends who had attended the march, the network had over
two thousand members in thirty chapters across the United States by 1996.
Even though the group's membership was reduced after the corporation

split into three separate companies, two of which entered the high-tech industry, GLUE is still the largest network in the movement, with over 1,300 members and twenty-eight chapters nationwide. The 1987 March on Washington made such an impression on the founders that even their informational brochure mentions its significance. As explained in the pages of the flyer, GLUE's first chapter formed after some friends in the company who had been meeting informally "returned home from the March on Washington inspired, energized, and convinced that they could change their part of the world . . . that they could make [their company] a place that welcomed ALL of its employees!" (emphasis in the original).

We're Here, We're Queer, We're Fabulous, Get Used to Us . . .

Although GLUE witnessed the emergence of gay employee groups in six other companies between 1987 and 1989, it was not until the 1990s that gay networks began to appear in far greater numbers, in part because of an attention-grabbing development in the wider gay and lesbian movement. In 1990, word spread like wildfire about a new social movement organization called Queer Nation. Formed in New York City, where it mobilized large and visible demonstrations against gay bashings, the group distributed fifteen thousand flyers at the New York Lesbian and Gay Pride Parade (S. Epstein 1999, 60). News of Queer Nation's loud and raucous entry at the pride march traveled fast, and "within days it seemed that groups calling themselves Queer Nation were springing up around the country" (Gross 1993, 82, quoted in S. Epstein 1999, 60).

Adopting a grassroots, direct-action, in-your-face style of organizing and a binary-smashing position that rejected the notion of fixed sexual identities, Queer Nation was a purposeful reaction against the mainstream tactics and essentialist stance of the larger gay and lesbian rights movement (J. Gamson 1995). As a means of challenging what queer theorists have called heteronormativity (Ingraham 1994), Queer Nation claimed public—and implicitly heterosexualized—space by holding "kiss-ins" or "queer-ins" while leafleting at shopping malls and bars (S. Epstein 1999). Posting neon-colored stickers and wearing T-shirts with confrontational slogans such as "Queers bash back," members popularized the "We're here, we're queer" chant that now echoes through the crowds of pride marches across the country (Faderman 1991; Podolsky 1994; Vaid 1995).

The corporate activism that took off in the early 1990s and gathered momentum throughout the second wave was, to be sure, a far cry from the transgressive style of queer politics. Nevertheless, the rise of Queer Nation and its offshoots in 1990 and the heightened militancy of ACT UP injected a new energy into the lifeblood of the larger movement, garnering an increased visibility that facilitated multiple forms of organizing. As shown in Table 2, 10 gay employee groups (15 percent of the current total) formed among the Fortune 1000 in 1990, making it the second-most-prolific year of the workplace movement. Of course, this eruption of corporate organizing was not generated simply by a spillover of activist energy from the streets to the workplace; the second wave was fueled as well by the momentous turning of the media spotlight to lesbian and gay employment issues.

Although queer activists were not solely responsible for this pivotal shift in media attention, their success in generating mainstream visibility clearly benefited the campaign for equal rights in the workplace. At the start of the 1990s, queer activists succeeded in shifting the gaze of the media to lesbian and gay concerns (Rouilard 1994). Once journalists and news producers widened their focus of coverage to include queer politics, it was only a short matter of time before light was cast on the workplace movement itself. Since the media tends to give short shrift to social movement concerns generally (McCarthy, Smith, and Zald 1996) and gay and lesbian issues in particular (Adam 1995), this remarkable interest in gay topics merits further analysis.

Mainstream Media's "Year of the Queer"

In a published chronicle of the lesbian and gay movement, 1990 earned the title "Year of the Queer" given the unprecedented media coverage of gay activism (Rouilard 1994). While media attention to movement concerns is often a crucial component of successful mobilization, such visibility can be exceedingly difficult to come by (McCarthy and Zald 1977; McAdam 1996). Owing in part to what scholars have termed "corporate hegemony," the news media are not apt to grant much access to movement actors whose demands are seen as threatening to the interests of media elites or their corporate sponsors (McCarthy, Smith, and Zald 1996, 297). Why, then, in 1990, did the mainstream news establishment suddenly devote so much airtime to queer politics?

Perhaps the answer lies at least in part in the propensity for much of queer activism to be directed not simply or even predominantly at specific institutions but at more diffuse targets. Joshua Gamson's work (1995, [1989] 1998) has revealed, for example, that many of ACT UP's efforts are aimed at what he calls an "invisible enemy" and what Michel Foucault (1979) has termed the "normalization process," that is, the cultural delineation and exclusion of the "abnormal" from the "normal" (J. Gamson [1989] 1998, 335). But, as Gamson points out, queer activists do sometimes level their actions at specific institutional practices, such as when ACT UP challenges the budgetary priorities of the federal government or the testing protocols and pricing policies of pharmaceutical companies (see also S. Epstein 1996), or when groups such as the Lesbian Avengers protest exclusionary curricula by giving grade-schoolers lavender balloons (a color associated with gay pride) that read, "Ask about lesbian lives" (Taylor and Rupp 1993; James 1995).

In fact, in 1990 queer activists targeted the media establishment directly, issuing charges of bias against the *New York Times,* the *Washington Post,* and other major news carriers (Rouilard 1994, 358; Vaid 1995, 201). Well aware of the fact that media discourse can be harmful if coverage presents a "biased and ridiculed picture of the movement" (Klandermans and Goslinga 1996, 319; see also Gitlin 1980), gay and lesbian activists mobilized within and against the mainstream media. Queer Nation, ACT UP, NGLTF, *OutWeek* magazine, and organized groups of lesbian and gay journalists challenged the corporate media giants on inaccurate reporting, urged more extensive coverage of the gay community and movement, and pushed for nondiscrimination in employment (Rouilard 1994, 358; Vaid 1995, 201).

News executives had also been facing pressure from the Gay and Lesbian Alliance against Defamation (GLAAD), which formed in 1985 to push for fairness and accuracy in the media. In 1992 the *Los Angeles Times* described GLAAD as "possibly the most successful organization lobbying the media for inclusion" (quoted in GLAAD 1999a). It seems likely, therefore, that the increased and more accurate coverage of gay issues beginning in 1990 stemmed in part from the self-interest of major corporate players in the news industry, who were defending themselves against public attacks that threatened their reputation as upholders of the highest journalistic standards.

But expanded media access also came in response to another important force, namely, innovations in the strategic repertoire of the lesbian, gay, bisexual, and transgender movement. Because of the increasingly creative symbolic politics of "self-proclaimed queers" who were "seasoned media-savvy activists" (Rouilard 1994, 357), the movement finally met what Doug McAdam (1996, 346) would call "the first requirement of media coverage": it had achieved the description "newsworthy" in the eyes of media gatekeepers. Faced with tight resources and restricted access to advertising, movements typically have to "induce the media to give free attention" (McCarthy and Zald 1977, 1229), yet those in control of the media rarely find interesting a movement's "actual, thought-out reasons" for organizing (Molotch 1979, 80). Given this indifference to the ideologies or collective action frames that justify mobilization (Snow et al. 1986), not to mention the ratings-driven emphasis of news producers (McCarthy, Smith, and Zald

1996), movements must often resort to "extraordinary techniques to gain coverage" (Molotch 1979, 91; see also W. Gamson 1995a; J. Gamson 1998). In other words, and rather ironically, outsiders have to disrupt the public order in order to gain mainstream visibility.

By moving beyond those forms of protest that have become institutionalized and hence ordinary, tactical innovations can invite repression (McCarthy and McPhail 1998; McPhail, Schweingruber, and McCarthy 1998; Waddington 1998), but so too can they open up new possibilities for challengers (McAdam 1983; W. Gamson 1990; Tarrow 1996, 1998). Queer tactics, which harken back to the zap actions of the women's and gay liberation movements (Freeman 1975; Adam 1995), are a textbook example of what Sidney Tarrow has called "innovation at the margins." By "adding elements of play and carnival or ferocity and menace" to more conventional forms of collective action, tactical developments can expand a movement's opportunities (Tarrow 1998, 102). This is because novel tactics can throw targets and countermovements off guard, attract new adherents, and, equally important, catch the eye of the otherwise disinterested media.

As the flashy new tactics of queer activists grew ever more spectacular—figuratively and literally, in the sense of a "media spectacle" (see McCarthy, Smith, and Zald 1996, 309)—they brought much-needed visibility not only to the street fighters themselves but also to gay and lesbian issues in general. Given the dramatically disruptive nature of myriad queer actions in 1990, major television networks and newspapers suddenly began to focus on the concerns of lesbian and gay people, including their experiences with employment discrimination. In the words of activist and writer Richard Rouilard (1994, 357), "Week after week, we were six o'clock news." From AIDS activists interrupting the Rose Parade in Pasadena, California, challenging President Bush during his first speech on AIDS, and halting traffic on the Golden Gate Bridge during rush hour and deadlocking fourteen thousand cars, to street protesters issuing a national boycott of Miller beer and Marlboro cigarettes because of manufacturer Philip Morris's corporate donations to antigay senator Jesse Helms, the movement in 1990 at last grabbed the serious attention of the media (Rouilard 1994, 357–58; Thompson 1994, 359–60).

Understanding all too well that an action without media publicity amounts to a "nonevent" (W. Gamson 1995a, 94), Queer Nation and ACT UP planned numerous and dazzling demonstrations that made for good copy, thereby winning extraordinary coverage in mainstream news outlets (Rouilard 1994). Certainly the media framing was not always favorable, but, as William Gamson (1995a, 94) has so aptly put it, "No news is bad news." Whether positive or negative, media attention validates challengers as "important players" (94). When in 1990 queer activism hit the news as never before, employee mobilization spiked as well. Thus, the benefits of media validation are not necessarily limited to the media-featured activists themselves, nor even to their particular wing of the movement. Once the media casts its glance on one type of challenger, the focus is more easily widened to include others within the broader movement. Indeed, the splash of queer actions that generated widespread press coverage in 1990 created a ripple effect as major business publications then turned their attention to sexual orientation issues in the workplace. Later in this chapter I will examine how the workplace movement itself played a part in and benefited from this new media focus, but first I will delve more deeply into the relationship between queer politics and employee mobilization.

We're Here, We're Gay, and Professional We'll Stay . . .

Aside from winning expanded media access, queer activists provided additional aid to corporate challengers in the form of a "radical flank effect" (Haines 1988). Many employee activists reasoned that their "professional" requests for equality at work seemed far less threatening to corporate elites than did the militant stance of queer activists. Explicitly contrasting their tactics with those of ACT UP and Queer Nation, employee respondents repeatedly emphasized that network members always behaved "professionally" and never made "demands."

In at least one company, however, this more moderate approach became a point of contention. In the telecommunications case study, after years of patient and methodical work had failed to persuade the corporation to adopt equitable benefits, some members of GLUE began urging the group to take up more aggressive tactics. A few people talked about sit-ins, while others wanted to plant themselves along the highway exit near corporate headquarters with signs calling on management to end the discriminatory benefits policy. "Then when [the company's recent spinoff] got domestic partner benefits and we didn't, . . . there was uproar," explained GLUE's national copresident. "My members wanted to picket. It was all I could do to keep some of them from doing that. It would have blown everything, so we'd explain to members what was going on behind the scenes." The rest of the story unwinds in later chapters, but what warrants emphasis here is the fact that GLUE stayed the course of "professionalism," albeit with strong pleadings for moderation from leadership. While it is unclear how many other networks faced internal struggles over strategy, all of the other gay employee groups in my sample likewise chose the path of "unobtrusive mobilization" (Katzenstein 1990), whether at the urging of leadership or not, and thus avoided street tactics altogether, even in the face of repeated setbacks.

While respecting the boldness of radical groups such as ACT UP—at times even expressing a frustrated desire to adopt similar strategies—most employee activists defined their own collective identity through a distancing from queer politics. Students of various social movements have documented a similar process of identity construction, whereby activists develop a collective self-definition through emphasizing boundaries not just between themselves and outsiders (Taylor and Whittier 1992; Taylor and Raeburn 1995) but also between themselves and others *within* the larger movement (Mueller 1994; Whittier 1995; Einwohner 1999a, 1999b, 2002; Rupp and Taylor 1999; Reger 2002; Robnett 2002). In the case of the workplace movement, however, boundary demarcations between institutional activists and "queer nationalists" seem to stem less from ideological divisions than from strategic necessity. Situated within multiple institutional spheres, and with none of the protections typically afforded to workers who mobilize within unions, employee activists feel compelled to strike a more restrained course through the corporate terrain. But, regardless of the apparent inappropriateness of queer strategies at work, the burst of corporate activism beginning in 1990 clearly corresponded to the heightened media visibility of queer organizing during that same year. Workplace activists were thus drawing energy from, if at times envying, the activities of their queer peers on the streets.

In sum, queer radicals can simultaneously inspire workplace activism and temper its apparent threat to corporate elites who, when faced with both kinds of challengers, see extremism and bad press in one and moderation and professionalism in the other. Through this process of "indexicality," to borrow a term from phenomenological analysis (Pfohl 1994), the meaning of workplace activism is constituted as "reasonable" vis-à-vis queer politics. The "radical flank" thereby improves the bargaining position of institutionally based activists and their allies (Sawyers and Meyer 1999). "It is this unity of purpose, even in the face of ideological and strategic differences," argue Traci Sawyers and David Meyer (203), "that makes social movements challenging and potentially powerful."

And the Movement Marches On . . .

Much like the shot in the arm that the birth of Queer Nation delivered in 1990, the third National March on Washington for Lesbian, Gay, and Bisexual Rights and Liberation, in 1993, stimulated the largest growth spurt that the workplace movement has ever experienced. Depending on the estimates used, the march drew to the Capitol anywhere from 300,000 to 1,000,000 participants (S. Epstein 1999, 68). The enthusiasm generated by the march obviously carried over into the workplace wing of the movement. While in 1990 10 new gay networks had formed among the Fortune 1000, followed by 6 more in 1991 and 9 others in 1992, the number of organizational births in 1993 shot up to 17. Looked at from the perspective of the current organizational sample (N=69), one-quarter of all corporate networks were born in 1993 (see Table 2). With the help of the March on Washington, then, the workplace movement had grown to include 52 Fortune 1000 companies by the end of 1993.

As employee activists' numbers reached a critical mass, their grievances, goals, and successes became the subject of media attention, which in turn furthered the growth of the movement. In the next section, I examine expanded media access as both a process and an element of institutional opportunity. I touch briefly on the role of queer activism in triggering this new "issue attention cycle" (Downs 1972, quoted in McCarthy and Zald 1977, 1229; McCarthy, Smith, and Zald 1996). Drawing from gay publications, mainstream news outlets, and the business press, I then analyze media representations of employment discrimination and workplace activism in order to assess the mobilizing impact of media visibility.

Expanded Media Access as an Element of Institutional Opportunity: The Benefits of Mainstream Visibility for Workplace Activists

Given the variable openness of the media system to movement concerns, political process theorists have recently begun to consider the mass media as important components of political opportunity (W. Gamson and Meyer 1996; McAdam 1996). However, since the term "political opportunity structure" has been used almost exclusively in reference to the state, a focus that has been criticized as overly narrow and structurally biased (McAdam 1994; Goodwin and Jasper 1999), it seems more appropriate to view media access as an element of what I call *institutional opportunity*. Openings in institutional arenas such as the media and the corporate sector can facilitate collective action in much the same way as shifts in the traditional political domain. Activists, however, do not simply wait for opportunities such as expanded media attention. As discussed earlier, challengers can create openings for themselves and others by drawing on the power of disruptive tactics or by planning other media-focused events (W. Gamson and Wolfsfeld 1993; W. Gamson and Meyer 1996; McAdam 1996; Tarrow 1996, 1998; Koopmans [1993] 1997).

As queer activists in 1990 engaged in purposefully outrageous and imaginatively obtrusive acts of symbolic resistance, interrupting the flow of everyday life, the mass media finally took notice, sparking a novel period of mainstream visibility. Put differently, the "Year of the Queer" was the start of a new issue attention cycle. The new queer presence extended to the institutions of popular culture as well. While the news media began to cover gay issues and made much ado about the newly coined "outing" phenomenon, wherein some queer activists dragged various gay politicians and corporate power brokers, like Malcolm Forbes, out of the closet (Thompson 1994, 365), the movie industry released three films in 1990 that gave additional voice and visibility to the diversity of the gay, lesbian, bisexual, and transgender community. All three soon became queer classics: Marlon Riggs's *Tongues Untied*, on the lives of black gay men; Jennie Livingston's *Paris Is Burning*, on drag balls in New York's black and Puerto Rican gay communities; and the even more widely seen *Longtime Companion*, on the devastating impact of AIDS on a circle of affluent gay friends in New York, a film that won critical acclaim in the mainstream press (372).

Energized by the numerous queer images reflected on the big screen and in mainstream news venues, and cognizant of the opportunity afforded by this new visibility, lesbian and gay employees mobilized within their companies at a more rapid pace than ever before. With the increased media attention to queer lives in 1990, 10 new networks emerged among the Fortune 1000, thus creating in only twelve months what had taken the earlier workplace movement twelve years to achieve. The doubling of the organizational population from 10 to 20 networks meant that lesbian and gay employee groups would become far more visible not just within but also outside of the corporate arena where they arose.

"Corporate Bullies" and the Gay Press

The jump in workplace organizing in the early 1990s, however, was not simply a response to the new mainstream visibility of gay issues; the lesbian and gay movement's own media also contributed to the upswing in corporate activism (see Klandermans and Goslinga 1996 on the use of movement media). In 1990 the gay and lesbian movement's national newsmagazine, the *Advocate*, "changed dramatically" and adopted an "aggressive investigative reporting" style (Rouilard 1994, 358), including a cover story in one issue entitled "Corporate Gay Bashing" (Hollingsworth 1990). The article attacked several major "corporate bullies" for antigay employment discrimination, especially their refusal to adopt domestic partner benefits.

The sudden focus of the *Advocate* on the lack of equitable benefits came on the heels of the decision by Ben and Jerry's, the popular ice cream maker that prides itself on its socially responsible reputation, to adopt the benefits in late 1989. Besides the *Village Voice* newspaper, Ben and Jerry's, with six hundred employees, was the only company to have opened its health-care plan to domestic partners (D. Baker, Strub, and Henning 1995). The AIDS epidemic had also added tragic salience to the issue of equitable benefits. Without bereavement leave, for example, many gay men who had just lost their partners to the disease were forced to stay at work and "grieve in the bathroom." Reporting on a small number of lawsuits brought by individual employees seeking equitable benefits, the author of the *Advocate* cover story, Gaines Hollingsworth, commented, "Many believe it is time to stop grieving in the bathroom and say it is time to receive equal pay for equal work, and that includes benefits."

Expanding on the equal rights angle, Hollingsworth pointed out that, "although employee benefits are, under law, considered to be part of wages," even companies with gay-inclusive nondiscrimination statements did not view the policies as applicable to benefit plans. As will be discussed in later chapters, some lesbian and gay employee activists now frame their arguments for equitable benefits by highlighting this inconsistency, mainly by describing the lack of benefits as compensation discrimination. At the time the "corporate bullies" article was published, however, the push for domestic partner benefits by gay employee networks had barely begun. Noting the emergence of "gay and lesbian support groups" in the corporate workplace, Hollingsworth lamented their reluctance to fight for equitable benefits: "Gays and lesbians who are currently fighting employment and compensation discrimination publicly . . . can be counted on fewer than two hands." This story published by the movement's national news source thus sounded a call to arms.

While bemoaning the scarcity of gay-inclusive nondiscrimination policies, let alone equitable benefits, Hollingsworth nevertheless made clear that as of 1990 the struggle for gay rights in the workplace was being waged on multiple fronts: lawsuits in the court system by individuals and gay advocacy organizations, lobbying by activists for federal protection in the legislative arena, nascent attempts at shareholder activism, and mobilization efforts within corporations by "a younger generation without fear." The list of workplace endeavors also included a survey designed to document the hiring policies of over three hundred companies, an undertaking of the Gay and Lesbian Employment Rights Project at the Interfaith Center on Corporate Responsibility in New York. Discussing the preliminary results of the study, Hollingsworth noted whether various corporations included sexual orientation in their nondiscrimination statements. He emphasized, however, that without municipal or state legislation to back them up, such policies were not typically treated as legally binding.

While lesbian and gay employees are painfully aware of their lack of legal rights, the wider public remains largely ignorant of the situation, a state perpetuated, no doubt, by the New Right's extensive campaigns against gay rights as "special rights" (Blain 1997; Duggan [1994] 1998; Dugan 1999). Nevertheless, press coverage of particularly blatant cases of discrimination can chip away at misinformation and jar people from a state of passivity. The audacity of some employers to publicly announce their antigay policies—and of some localities to preemptively ban any legal protections against such discrimination (S. Epstein 1999)—can actually be a boon to advocates of equal rights in the workplace.

Cracker Barrel's Crusade and the Impact of "Suddenly Publicized Grievances"

In January 1991, the Cracker Barrel corporation, a chain of restaurants located in sixteen southern and midwestern states, issued a press release announcing an official policy against employment of "homosexuals." Signed by the vice president of human resources, the policy mandated the termination of individuals "whose sexual preferences fail to demonstrate normal heterosexual values, which have been the foundation of families in our society" (quoted in Bain 1992b, 1). The company then fired at least eleven gay and lesbian employees, all from jurisdictions that lacked gay rights ordinances. When word hit the national news networks, protesters quickly staged demonstrations and sit-ins at various restaurant locations, and activists from across the country issued calls for a boycott (Vaid 1995). NGLTF launched a nationwide campaign against the company, and, for the first time in the history of shareholder activism, a U.S. corporation was faced with a shareholder resolution that sought to institute explicit protections against antigay discrimination (Bain 1992b, 1).

Much like the lunch-counter sit-ins of the civil rights movement (McAdam 1983; Morris 1984), the Cracker Barrel sit-ins helped to elicit additional and "highly sympathetic" press coverage of lesbian and gay employees' grievances (Bain 1992b, 2). Stories appeared on programs such as *The Oprah Winfrey Show, Larry King Live,* and *20/20* (Equality Project 1999). Even months later the company's policy was receiving national media attention. On the one hand, during a November 1991 segment of *20/20,* which was said to have been rescheduled so that it would air prior to Cracker Barrel's annual shareholder meeting, Barbara Walters announced that she would not patronize the chain (Bain 1992b). Dan Quayle, on the other hand, showed public support for the corporation's intransigence by visiting one of the restaurants during his campaign for the presidency (Vaid 1995).

Nonetheless, the Cracker Barrel protesters had won support from several public officials and a broad range of organizations, including the NAACP, labor unions, pension funds that held stock in the company, and liberal religious institutions (Bain 1992b). The company's actions were later featured in a first-ever documentary on antigay workplace discrimination, entitled *Out at Work*. Premiering on PBS, the film subsequently aired on HBO in January 1999 as part of the cable channel's *America Undercover* documentary series (*Gay People's Chronicle* 1999). Long before then, however, in the words of corporate activist and writer C. Arthur Bain (1992b, 8), Cracker Barrel's decision to trumpet its policy far and wide had "brought the issue of homophobic discrimination into sharp focus in boardrooms and living rooms across the country."

Scholars and activists alike have long recognized the galvanizing impact of media attention to movement concerns (McCarthy and Zald 1977; Molotch 1979; Gitlin 1980; W. Gamson 1988; Gamson and Wolfsfeld 1993; McCarthy 1994; Tarrow 1994, 1998; W. Gamson 1995a; Gamson and Meyer 1996; Klandermans and Goslinga 1996; J. Gamson 1998; della Porta and Diani 1999). From the powerfully disturbing images of fire hoses, guns, and bombs aimed at African Americans in the South who were fighting for civil rights while practicing nonviolence, and reports of antiwar student protesters at Kent State University being gunned down by the National Guard, interspersed with shocking footage of the human carnage of the Vietnam War, to the depiction of the gruesome gay-bashing and crucifixion-style murder of Matthew Shepard, media coverage can strengthen the commitment of activists and invoke sympathy and support from nonactivists. Visibility of grievances and of committed collectivities seeking redress can alert people to both the urgency and possibility of change, leading "bystander publics" to question the inequity and inevitability of the status quo (Turner 1970, quoted in McCarthy and Zald 1977, 1221).

Realizing that the system can be transformed, or experiencing what Doug McAdam (1982) calls "cognitive liberation," is a necessary precondition of collective action. Lesbians or gay men who have not yet ventured out of the closet can be moved to join the ranks of the out and proud through the potentially transformative images broadcast over the media. Activists thus seek media publicity not just to educate the public and influence elites but also because images and sound bites, even if distorted through the filter of media producers' focus on ratings and profits (J. Gamson 1998), can convert those who are "tuned in" from passive audience members to firm believers, and from vocal sideliners to active participants.

Put differently, to borrow the language of movement scholars, media attention can help activists turn uninformed or nonsupportive individuals into "adherents," who believe in movement goals, and adherents into "constituents," who offer resources in support of the cause. As a recruiting mechanism, press coverage of movement concerns can also motivate "potential beneficiaries" to join the struggle (McCarthy and Zald 1977). Thus, mainstream media's Year of the Queer in 1990, followed by extensive coverage of the Cracker Barrel protests in 1991, sounded like beacons for the movement, calling, "Come out, come out, wherever you are."

In his delineation of key types of "expanding cultural opportunities" that can spur people to action, Doug McAdam (1994, 40) highlights the impact of "suddenly imposed grievances," such as the Three Mile Island nuclear reactor disaster, which incited numerous antinuclear protests at both the local and national levels (Walsh 1981; Walsh and Warland 1983). The aftermath of the Cracker Barrel disclosure suggests that suddenly *publicized* grievances can have the same mobilizing impact. While the firings were certainly nothing new to the gay community, the company's brazen announcement brought into the open what other equally discriminatory employers practiced but rarely codified: a ban on the hiring or promotion of "known or suspected" gay, lesbian, bisexual, and transgender people.

Functioning as a "moral shock" (Jasper and Poulson 1995; Jasper 1997), Cracker Barrel's policy evoked a sense of outrage that motivated people to act. As Traci Sawyers and David Meyer (1999, 202) argue, "[H]arsh rhetoric and unsympathetic policy . . . can strengthen a movement by creating a crisis which mobilizes its adherents." Thus, as the media publicized a particularly striking example of long-held grievances in the gay and lesbian community, 6 more employee networks formed among the Fortune 1000 in 1991, followed by 9 others the next year.

In 1990, the second wave of corporate activism had begun with the birth of 10 gay networks. Comparatively speaking, then, the workplace movement experienced a drop in new organizing after the Cracker Barrel story hit the news in 1991. Nonetheless, media coverage of the incident set in motion a new cluster of developments in corporate organizing that helped to mitigate the potentially chilling effect of the firings. Cracker Barrel's crusade against gays and lesbians persuaded many employee networks that had been mobilizing separately to join forces in order to share resources and hone strategies for making the workplace a safer space.

In the wake of the Cracker Barrel fury in 1991, activists from several different companies organized the first two conferences in the country to focus on lesbian, gay, and bisexual issues in the workplace. As will be discussed in a later section, both of these events, held in 1991, constituted a

critical turning point for the workplace movement. The East Coast conference, which focused on educating corporate elites, generated considerable
press coverage (Swan 1997c, 1997d). The West Coast effort, called "Out
and Equal in the Workplace," was organized primarily for gay and lesbian
employees and was so successful that it became an annual event.

The Business Press Takes Note

Even staid, buttoned-down business publications began to devote some of
their pages to gay issues generally and the workplace movement in particular. In a first in the world of business publishing, on December 16, 1991,
Fortune magazine ran a cover story called "Gay in Corporate America,"
with the subheading "What It's Like, and How Business Attitudes Are
Changing." Above the byline on the first page of the featured article was the
following statement, set off in bold print: "In the company closet is a big,
talented, and scared group of men and women. They want out—and are
making the workplace the next frontier for gay rights" (Stewart 1991, 42).

Reporting that lesbians and gay men in major corporations were "rapidly forming employee groups," journalist Thomas Stewart described the
agenda of this "new activism": gay-inclusive nondiscrimination policies, diversity training, and equitable benefits (43). The article also mentioned one
of the two conferences on gay and lesbian workplace issues that had taken
place earlier that year, to which CEOs and human resource directors from
companies across the country had been invited. Emphasizing the need for
such events, Stewart cited one of the replies that organizers received in response to their invitation: "To all the fags, gays, homos, and lezzies. Do not
mail me any of your fag shit lezzie homo paperwork to my business" (56).

Citing a few of the companies that had begun to require attendance at
antihomophobia workshops, Stewart's article indicated how far some segments of corporate America had come in their treatment of lesbian and
gay employees. But the author was careful not to overstate the extent of
progress. Stewart relayed the painful experiences of several gay professionals
who were struggling with what one executive described as "rampant homophobia" (43). Commenting on the results of a 1987 *Wall Street Journal*
survey, in which 66 percent of the CEOs of major corporations stated that
"they would be reluctant to put a homosexual on management committees,"
Stewart concluded, "[W]hile attitudes may have changed since, there's no
evidence of a revolution" (45).

Nonetheless, without realizing it, Stewart was reporting on the very
beginnings of a different kind of revolution in the workplace: the rise of domestic partner benefits. In a sidebar called "A Cutting-Edge Issue: Benefits,"

Stewart discussed the "historic" move by high-tech Lotus Corporation in September 1991 to extend to same-sex domestic partners all of the benefits already offered to the spouses of heterosexual employees (50). Referred to by the company as "spousal equivalent benefits," the policy was adopted in response to the organizing work of an informal group of lesbian and gay employees who had requested the benefits over two years earlier (Laabs 1991; D. Baker, Strub, and Henning 1995). The policy change made Lotus, with its workforce of 3,100, the first major corporate adopter of equitable benefits. "Will Lotus set a trend? Probably not," concluded Stewart (50). Little did he know. As I will discuss in the next section, Lotus's move reflected a significant institutional opening for the workplace movement. Inspired by the news and committed to winning equal rights in their own places of work, other gay activist networks would eventually push many other companies to follow in Lotus's footsteps.

In sum, the cover story appearing in the widely read pages of *Fortune* magazine brought much-needed visibility to the workplace movement and to the cutting-edge issue of equitable benefits. The author's focus on gay employment topics and his mentioning of several specific employee networks further expanded the ranks of the movement. That same year, articles on lesbian and gay issues in the workplace, including domestic partner benefits, began to appear in personnel journals as well. To this day, employee activists celebrate such articles, especially those published in outlets like *Fortune* that reach far wider audiences than do specialty journals. At one of the many employee network meetings I attended, members excitedly pored over the pages of a magazine article on gay workplace issues and then distributed copies to everyone on their mailing list, including those who worked for other companies. Thus, as greater numbers of lesbian and gay employees heard about the struggles and successes of some of the early networks, many decided to mobilize in their own places of work, creating a new wave of activism that would eventually usher in a sea change in corporate America.

Institutional Openings in the Workplace: Early Adopters of Equitable Benefits and "Walking the Walk" of Diversity

The Rise of Domestic Partner Benefits

The dawning of equitable benefits on the corporate horizon spurred many gay and lesbian employees into action. Several founders of second-wave networks said that hearing the good news about early adopters prompted them to form employee organizations in their own companies. Other gay networks decided to add the benefits to their list of goals or, if already present, to give them higher priority. Although the *Village Voice* newspaper in

New York City was actually the first employer in the country to adopt equitable benefits, back in 1982 (D. Baker, Strub, and Henning 1995), word of the policy change did not spread far. The successful efforts of the union's gay and lesbian caucus thus went unnoticed in the wider business world. In contrast, after Lotus's decision in 1991, national newspapers started to cover stories about domestic partner benefits, which had already begun to arise in a small number of cities.

Municipal employees had first won equitable benefits in Berkeley in 1984, West Hollywood in 1985, Santa Cruz in 1986, and then Los Angeles and Takoma Park, Maryland, in 1988. (All dates are from a list provided by the Human Rights Campaign.) After Santa Cruz County adopted the benefits in 1989, Seattle and Laguna Beach followed suit in 1990. When Ben and Jerry's announced its decision in 1989, and Lotus in 1991, the momentum spread from the arena of municipal government to the business sector. The scales then began to tip away from city politics such that, for every year since 1993, the majority of adopters have been companies, both large and small, followed by universities. Lists of adoption dates gathered by the WorkNet project of the Human Rights Campaign document the shift.

From 1982 through 1990, just 20 employers adopted domestic partner benefits, and only 4 of these were companies. The bulk of adopters during this period were cities or counties (9), national gay rights organizations (2), or other nonprofit organizations (5) such as the American Civil Liberties Union, the American Psychological Association, and Planned Parenthood. In 1991, however, with national newspaper coverage of equitable-benefits adoption by Lotus, and the similar move by Montefiore Medical Center in the Bronx after threat of a lawsuit, other companies started to come on board. Of the 7 adopters that year, 4 were either small or large companies.

In 1992 there was an acceleration of benefits adoption: 21 employers extended their plans to cover domestic partners, including major corporations such as West Coast–based Levi Strauss & Co., Silicon Valley's Borland International, MCA/Universal Studios, a few hospitals and legal firms, and five universities (Oberlin College in Ohio, the University of Rochester, American University in Washington, DC, Golden Gate University in San Francisco, and the University of Iowa). Of the 21 adopters, only three were cities. The following year, in 1993, 36 employers, 20 of which were companies, adopted equitable benefits. Corporate America had begun to outpace employers in other sectors and has been in the forefront of change ever since, a paradox that I address in the conclusion of the book. (For a breakdown of policy change by sector and by industry, see Table A.3 in the appendix.)

As previously discussed, the vast majority of early corporate adopters extended their policies only after being persuaded to do so by groups of lesbian and gay employees. Chapters 4 through 6, on institutional and movement processes, explain how these groundbreaking changes came about. For the purposes of the present discussion, however, the relevance of early benefits adoption by major corporations lies in the energizing impact that it had on the workplace movement. As Lotus's policy change in the fall of 1991 jump-started the corporate campaign for equitable benefits, leading to a dramatic increase in adopters between 1992 and 1993, the pace of new organizing quickened in response. While 6 gay employee networks formed among the Fortune 1000 in 1991, the next year brought 9 new groups, followed by 17 more in 1993.

"Walking the Walk" of Diversity

Given the buzz in the lesbian and gay community about the rise of equitable benefits and the new queer visibility in mainstream media, as well as the *Advocate*'s more aggressive coverage of employment issues and employee organizing, the workplace movement picked up considerable steam in the early 1990s. But the second-wave momentum that generated new gay employee networks across the country also drew fuel from another institutional opening in the corporate world. According to many network founders, the surge of corporate organizing in the early years of the decade stemmed in part from the glaring omission of gay men and lesbians from their companies' newfound interest in diversity issues.

While some executives began to see diversity training and the formation of diversity task forces, councils, and offices as examples of corporate "best practices," lesbian and gay employees largely found themselves excluded altogether from these initiatives. Nevertheless, as greater numbers of corporate elites came to view diversity as a business imperative, reflecting the diffusion of what institutional scholars Frank Dobbin and John Sutton (1998) describe as a new human resources paradigm, lesbian and gay employees saw in this expanded corporate mind-set an institutional opening that offered new hope for a place at the table.

In diversity-embracing companies, gay employees watched the doors begin to open wider for people of color and women in general. Responding to this "open moment" (Gourevitch 1986) that indicated "Big Opportunity" (W. Gamson and Meyer 1996, 280), and taking a collective deep breath, lesbians and gay men attempted to walk through those doors as well. Although they were sometimes met by corporate bouncers on the other side, gay employee activists remained steadfast in their determination to join the party. The swell of workplace organizing in the first half of the 1990s, hence, grew not simply out of a more favorable political climate or out of the expanded opportunities afforded by media visibility and early benefits adoption; the rush of corporate activism during this period was also a response to a new institutional opening available to those whose employers had begun "talking the talk" of diversity. Responding to their changing corporate culture, lesbian and gay employees stepped in—or, rather, "out"—to be sure that their companies would, as workplace activists like to say, "walk the walk" when it came to addressing gay concerns.

The emergence of the largest gay employee network in the country clearly demonstrates the importance of expanded institutional opportunities at the organizational or corporate level. As already discussed, "GLUE" was formed in a telecommunications company by a small group of friends who were inspired by the 1987 March on Washington. But even before the march, when meeting for lunch in restaurants or after work in their homes, the friends had talked about the need for an officially recognized lesbian and gay employee organization "like the other diversity groups" in their company, for women and people of color. The majority of gay networks that eventually emerged in the Fortune 1000 likewise cited the existence of preexisting diversity groups in their companies as indirect but important motivators behind their decision to organize. These preexisting networks, which Sidney Tarrow would call "early risers," had already successfully mobilized for official recognition and resources, alerting gays and lesbians to the potential fruitfulness of making claims on the corporate elite. As Tarrow (1998, 87) puts it, early risers "can pry open institutional barriers through which the demands of others can pour."

Thus, much like periods of change or instability in the political system that make the state "vulnerable to political challenges" (W. Gamson and Meyer 1996, 280), the changing corporate culture in some companies signaled possible openings for lesbian and gay employees, who quickly mobilized in response. With an eye trained only on the formal political arena, as is the habit of political process theorists (Goodwin and Jasper 1999), one would miss the presence of opportunities that materialized in other institutional spheres. Obscured from one's gaze would be the transformations that were taking place in more and more companies whose executives saw dollar signs in the face(s) of diversity. By widening the theoretical focus to include other institutional arenas, this research extends the applicability of the political process approach to uncover the impact of opportunities that arise beyond the state.

Summary

The markedly greater fertility of the workplace movement during the second wave was the fruitful result of multiple factors. The more receptive political climate and unprecedented media coverage of queer activism and employment discrimination, in combination with early institutional shifts toward corporate diversity and equitable benefits, made for relatively inviting waters during the early 1990s. Lesbian, gay, and bisexual employees hence took the plunge in greater numbers than ever before, creating visible workplace organizations aimed at effecting widespread institutional change. While most of the first-wave networks had labored in relative isolation, gay employee groups that mobilized during the second period could draw courage—and vastly improved networking opportunities—from the knowledge that they were not alone.

During the second wave of the movement, between 1990 and 1994, institutional activists worked hard to create and foster interorganizational linkages among gay employee networks. These connections ranged from informal social gatherings and e-mail exchanges to more fully institutionalized networking mechanisms such as annual workplace conferences, hyperlinked Web sites, and formal umbrella groups consisting of gay employee networks from a wide variety of institutional settings. In response to the burgeoning grassroots movement for workplace equality, the two most prominent national gay rights organizations in the country, NGLTF and HRC, instituted workplace projects to provide resources and additional networking opportunities for employee activists across the country.

As the linkages among employee activists grew increasingly dense and formalized during the second wave, the workplace movement experienced a certain coming of age. Much like other rites of passage, this period of development came with its own set of tensions and a heightened reflexivity as leaders struggled over the type and degree of formalization that would best suit networking at the regional and national levels. Some local umbrella groups folded, while other regional organizations attempted to broaden their geographic reach. Efforts to form umbrella networks at the national level underwent a series of bumps and starts. In all, however, these growing pains resulted in a bigger, stronger, more densely connected movement.

By the mid-1990s, after a slow and tentative start back in 1978, the workplace wing of the gay and lesbian movement had finally come into its own. Numerous umbrella groups, two national workplace projects, and an abundance of conferences and Web sites that focused on gay employment issues were all well established by the middle of the decade. Their continued presence signifies the successful institutionalization of the workplace movement. Given the beneficial mobilization and policy outcomes that were facilitated by these multinetwork structures, I offer a more extended analysis of movement infrastructure in chapter 3, where I trace the development and impact of interorganizational networks and consider the larger movement and institutional processes that facilitated their emergence.

In addition to sustaining the commitment of employee networks and increasing the visibility of the workplace campaign, interorganizational linkages educated corporate decision makers as well as individual activists, thereby improving what Paul Burstein, Rachel Einwohner, and Jocelyn Hollander (1995) would call the movement's "bargaining" position in the institutional policy domain. Indeed, the infrastructural efforts of activists during the second wave helped the workplace movement achieve relatively remarkable policy success. By the middle of the 1990s, domestic partner benefits had practically become a household word, given their adoption by numerous big-name companies across the country.

Despite the rapidly increasing number of policy victories, however, the third wave's organizational birthrate dropped significantly. Beginning in 1995, the momentum of new corporate organizing slowed to a snail's pace. As revealed in Table 2, while the second wave of the corporate workplace movement (1990–1994) averaged 10 new employee organizations per year, the third period (1995–mid-1998) produced fewer than 3 networks per year. What factors account for this paradoxical decline in corporate organizing? In the next chapter I turn to the surprisingly sluggish pace of mobilization in the second half of the decade and consider the likely causes of this apparent quiescence.

2

The Slowdown in New Corporate Organizing

Accounting for the puzzling drop-off in corporate mobilization beginning in 1995 requires the same wide-angle lens used to explain the slow rise and then rapid growth of the workplace movement during the first and second waves. In this chapter I therefore discuss the third-wave decline in new organizing in relation to the larger sociopolitical and institutional environments. I also address the role of movement-countermovement interactions (Meyer and Staggenborg 1996) and the impact of the media on the decisions of potential challengers. Drawing on social movement and new institutionalist perspectives, I treat political and institutional opportunities as socially constructed. I thus emphasize the interpretive processes that mediate the relationship between the environment and social actors, who must perceive both the possibility of change and the necessity of activism before they will engage in collective action (McAdam 1982; W. Gamson and Meyer 1996).

The Sociopolitical Context of Third-Wave Organizing

Advances of the New Right since the Mid-1990s

In many ways the third-wave decline in corporate mobilization is hardly surprising. In the November 1994 elections, conservatives secured a majority in both the United States Senate and House of Representatives. The New Right's increased strength was apparent not only in the unprecedented number of antigay measures considered by Congress but also in the actions taken by the Clinton administration. In an edited volume on gay, lesbian, bisexual, and transgender public policy issues, Kathleen DeBold (1997, xviii) describes the mid-1990s as a particularly "troubling period" for gay rights advocates:

> Whether it is a congressman "accidentally" calling an openly gay congressman "Barney Fag"; the decision of the U.S. Justice Department not to act as *amicus curiae* in the Supreme Court appeal of Colorado and Cincinnati antigay initiatives; the elimination of an outspoken surgeon general who supported gay rights; a proposal by Senator Jesse Helms to place unprecedented curbs upon federal gay/lesbian workplace groups; [or] the introduction and passage of the virulently antigay (and cynically misnamed) Defense of Marriage Act (DOMA)—to name just a few— there is a definite and deliberate trend toward reversing the gains only recently garnered by the gay and lesbian community.

Reacting to the gains of the workplace movement, in 1995 Senator Helms introduced a bill that would have restricted the right of lesbian and gay federal employees "to meet and organize, use office e-mail, and exert other rights that are given to numerous employee groups" (HRC 1995a). In addition the measure would have prohibited the federal government from instituting nondiscrimination protections for gay and lesbian federal employees.

Antigay state legislation also increased dramatically in the middle of the decade. Between 1990 and 1994, no more than five states per year faced antigay measures at either the local or state level (NGLTF 1996c). In 1995, however, twenty-nine states saw the introduction of 64 antigay measures (NGLTF 1996a, 1997). In 1996, thirty-nine states faced a total of 99 antigay pieces of legislation (NGLTF 1996b). The following year, those numbers increased to forty-four and 120, respectively (NGLTF 1997). In 1998, elected officials in thirty-six states considered 126 antigay measures (NGLTF 1999a, 1999b), with the numbers increasing the following year to forty-four states facing 205 unfavorable pieces of legislation (NGLTF 1999c, 1999d). Much of this conservative legislative activity has revolved around the presumed possibility of same-sex marriage.

The New Right's Newest Fear: The Prospect of Gay Marriage

Beginning in the mid-1990s many lesbian and gay activists were forced to redirect their energy and resources toward staving off antigay marriage bills that arose in response to a landmark ruling by the Hawaii Supreme Court. In the 1993 case *Baehr v. Lewin,* the state bench surprised observers on both ends of the political spectrum by ruling that if the government could not provide evidence of a "compelling state interest" for denying the right of marriage to gay and lesbian people, Hawaii must grant marriage licenses to same-sex couples (Swan 1997b, 118). The case was then sent back to trial court, where few expected that the state would be able to meet the strict scrutiny standard (Stacey 1996, 121). Confirming those suspicions, a lower court ruled in favor of gay marriage in 1997, but the decision was appealed to the Hawaii Supreme Court (LLDEF 1999). In late 1999 the issue was ruled moot. Taking the matter out of the hands of the high court, voters ratified an amendment to the state constitution that gave the legislature the power to restrict marriage to a man and a woman (LLDEF 2000; see also Hull 2001).

In response to the 1993 Hawaii decision, conservatives quickly developed legislation that would allow states to refuse recognition of gay marriages that might eventually be performed elsewhere in the country. Although some legal scholars have argued that these so-called defense of marriage acts violate the "full faith and credit" clause of the U.S. Constitution (Swan 1997b, 119), antigay marriage bills continue to appear in state legislatures across the country. By May 1995, twenty-two states had considered such measures, 8 of which eventually became law (Stacey 1996, 119). In 1996 conservative legislators proposed antigay marriage bills in thirty-seven states, sixteen of which adopted them as law (LLDEF 1999). In the fall of that same year, Congress passed the federal-level Defense of Marriage Act (DOMA), which reiterated the legal definition of marriage as an exclusively heterosexual institution (Stacey 1996, 120), thereby reinforcing the long-standing exclusion of same-sex couples from access to what the U.S. General Accounting Office has found to be over one thousand federal benefits that are granted upon marriage (HRCF 2002g; City and County of San Francisco Human Rights Commission 2003).

Bowing to conservatives in his bid for reelection, which was just forty-five days away, and cognizant that his support of DOMA would be seen as a betrayal by the gay and lesbian community, President Clinton signed the bill into law under cover of darkness on September 20, 1996, waiting until the middle of the night to affix his signature (P. Baker 1996). Although, as federal law, DOMA made state-level measures redundant, antigay marriage bills continued apace. Additional DOMAs were adopted by ten out of the thirty-three states that considered them in 1997, six out of sixteen states in 1998, and one out of sixteen states in 1999 (LLDEF 1999; NGLTF 1999c, 1999d). As of fall 2002, thirty-six states, had passed antigay marriage statutes (HRCF 2002i), and that number increased to thirty-eight by mid-February 2004, when Ohio not only banned gay marriage but also went further than any other state by prohibiting domestic partner benefits for state employees (Welsh-Huggins 2004).

Civil Unions, Civil Marriage, and the New Trend in Antigay Organizing

As lesbian and gay activists attempted to fight off the DOMA forces, Vermont made a historic move in the struggle over gay marriage. Responding to a ruling by the Vermont Supreme Court, on April 25, 2000, the state legislature approved same-sex "civil unions," thereby extending to gay and lesbian couples all the state-level rights, responsibilities, and benefits of marriage except the name itself (Lockhead 2000). The groundbreaking law ignited a fury of antigay organizing both in and outside of the state. Signifying what the Human Rights Campaign Foundation (HRCF), an affiliated organization of the Human Rights Campaign, called a "new trend" in antigay mobilization, right-wing legislators began to introduce bills that "were even more restrictive than most anti-gay marriage laws currently on the books," in that "instead of simply barring recognition of marriage, they also address civil unions, domestic partnerships, and/or 'other forms' of same-sex relationships" (HRC 2002g).

Riding this wave of legislative activity, in May 2002 a conservative group of legislators in the House of Representatives proposed an antigay amendment to the U.S. Constitution, stating that marriage "shall consist only of the union of a man and a woman" and that no state or federal law "shall be construed to require that marital status *or the legal incidents thereof* be conferred upon unmarried couples or groups" (HRC 2002i; emphasis added). Originally proposed in July 2001 by the Alliance for Marriage, a group whose self-described goal is to "strengthen American families and reintegrate the role of a strong father figure," the Federal Marriage Amendment was, beginning in the summer of 2002, "quietly being pushed through Congress" (*Humanist* 2002, 47; see also Coltrane 2001).

No longer so quiet about it, the Right has recently thrust the amendment to the top of its political agenda in light of two landmark legal decisions. On June 26, 2003, the U.S. Supreme Court struck down all sodomy laws and declared for the first time that lesbians and gay men have a constitutional right to privacy and to "retaining their dignity as free persons." Liberals and conservatives alike agree that the 6–3 *Lawrence v. Texas* decision has "laid the groundwork for legal challenges to all laws that discriminate against gays and lesbians" (Lockhead 2003). Just five months after the decision was handed down, the highest court in Massachusetts ruled, on November 18, that same-sex couples in the state are legally entitled to civil marriage. On February 4, 2004, confirming its initial ruling, the state court declared, "The history of our nation has demonstrated that separate is seldom, if ever, equal" (quoted in Lockhead 2004). The judges reiterated that the Massachusetts legislature had until May 2004 to bring existing statutes into line, and that "civil unions" and "domestic partnerships" would not be acceptable alternatives (Greenberger 2004). Then, on February 12, 2004, San Francisco made history when, on the mayor's initiative, city hall began issuing marriage licenses to, and performing wedding ceremonies for, same-sex couples, making the newlyweds the first legally married gay and lesbian couples in the country (Gordon 2004). As a result, right-wing calls for the passage of the Federal Marriage Amendment continue to grow louder and more urgent.

While aiming to ban the recognition of gay and lesbian marriage, "[r]ealistically, the amendment is [also] a thinly veiled attempt to overturn state statutes that currently provide domestic partner benefits" (*Humanist* 2002, 47). Indeed, a spokesperson for the American Civil Liberties Union described the proposed law as "the nuclear bomb of anti-gay attacks," since it would "wipe out forever the protections given to unmarried couples and gay and lesbian couples" (quoted in Data Lounge 2001c). According to legal experts, the amendment could "in one stroke render null and void domestic partnership arrangements, gay and lesbian adoptions, equal benefits policies, hospital visitation—virtually the entire spectrum of gay civil rights successes won over the last 25 years" (Data Lounge 2001c).

The chances of the measure's becoming law are unclear. Although constitutional amendments require approval from two-thirds of both the House and Senate and ratification by three-quarters of the states, the proposed ban may gain momentum given President Bush's endorsement. On February 24, 2004, standing in the White House with a small group of religious leaders, Bush called on Congress to "protect marriage in America" by promptly passing the amendment, which he described as a matter of "national importance" (quoted in Sandalow 2004). Whether or not it passes, as the farthest-reaching of the recent attacks on gay marriage and domestic partnerships, the proposed amendment could help antigay forces push through less drastic but still damaging measures, a prospect all the more likely if Bush is reelected and Republicans retain control of both houses of Congress.

Such measures add to the load of an already overburdened and vastly underfunded gay rights movement. As shown by Lisa Duggan ([1994] 1998, 564), who has compared the combined budgets of the country's six largest right-wing religious organizations with the six largest gay rights groups, the religious Right has funding over seventeen times greater than the lesbian and gay movement.

A Queer Fight over the Right to Marry: The Tangled Relationship between Gay Marriage and Domestic Partnerships

Although many activists have felt compelled to fight preemptive attacks on same-sex marriage, the lesbian and gay community has long been divided over the issue of marriage, given its historical grounding as a heterosexist and patriarchal institution (Ettelbrick [1989] 1993; Stoddard [1989] 1993; Stacey 1996; S. Epstein 1999). Commenting on the larger implications of the same-sex marriage debate, lesbian activist and legal scholar Nancy Polikoff draws on both lesbian-feminist and socialist critiques of marriage when she argues as follows: "Advocating lesbian and gay marriage will detract from, and even contradict, efforts to unhook economic benefits from marriage and make basic health care and other necessities available to all" (quoted in Stacey 1996, 122).

Indeed, the fight for domestic partner benefits rests on the horns of a dilemma. Some advocates of equitable benefits see them as a temporary fix that, in the absence of the right to legally marry, provides symbolic recognition and material support for gay and lesbian relationships. Others view the movement for domestic partner benefits as settling for second-class citizenship, since it leaves the institution of marriage as the sole preserve of heterosexuals, who remain firmly ensconced in what Gayle Rubin ([1984] 1998) has called the "charmed circle." Still others, mirroring Polikoff's arguments, praise the domestic partner movement for its radical potential. In this view the campaign for equitable benefits in the workplace challenges, or at least bypasses, the state's right to define family and to deny economic benefits to those who fall outside the bonds of marriage, whether by choice or by legal fiat (Ettelbrick [1989] 1993).

Regardless of internecine struggles over the meaning of gay marriage and domestic partner benefits, the New Right continues to wage fierce attacks against both. Whether pushing for legislation that would prevent same-sex marriage and/or the legal recognition of domestic partnerships and civil unions, waging court battles to overturn gay-inclusive employment legislation, or boycotting companies that offer equitable benefits, antigay conservatives are trying desperately to hold back the forces of change (D. Baker, Strub, and Henning 1995; Swan 1997a; Data Lounge 1999a, 1999b; HRC 2002i).

Mixed Signals: Acknowledging the Complexity of the Sociopolitical Environment

Given the numerous advances of the New Right since 1995, the political climate may have seemed overwhelmingly unfavorable for lesbian and gay challengers in the latter half of the 1990s. Looked at from this angle, the third-wave decline in new corporate organizing comes as no surprise. It would appear that gays and lesbians, faced with an increasingly hostile environment, were either afraid to organize in the workplace or consumed by battles in the formal political arena. Yet an alternative explanation for the drop-off in new organizing seems equally plausible.

One could interpret the slowdown in employee mobilization as stemming not from the right-wing backlash itself but rather from the very prospect that same-sex marriage could be legalized. With headlines such as *USA Today*'s "Legal Gay Marriage on the Nation's Horizon: Hawaii May Be First State to Take Step" (Weiser 1996), which appeared January 2, 1996, and similar stories being published through the end of the 1990s, such an interpretation would not seem out of place. As the original and subsequent Hawaii decisions on gay marriage "thrust [the] issue into escalating levels of front-page and prime-time prominence" (Stacey 1996, 119), it is possible that a growing number of gay men and lesbians began to view same-sex marriage as a development right around the corner. In the minds of all but the most progressive members of the lesbian and gay rights movement, such institutionalization would render obsolete the fight for domestic partner benefits.

In her criticism of the New Right's war against gay marriage, Judith Stacey (119) refers to the "rampant rumors" that began to circulate in the mid-1990s claiming that "thousands of mainland gay and lesbian couples were stocking their hope chests with Hawaiian excursion fares, poised to fly to tropical altars the instant the first gay matrimonial bans falter[ed]." Although Stacey casts this vision as a figment of the New Right's reactionary imagination, it is nonetheless true that in that period lesbian and gay travel agencies began to advertise Hawaiian marriage packages. In his analysis of gay and lesbian activism, Steven Epstein (1999, 70) notes how lesbians and gay men from across the country "began imagining wedding-and-honeymoon trips to Hawaii." Although conservatives dashed those dreams, soon thereafter Vermont's civil unions law entered the mix, followed by the Massachusetts high court ruling on civil marriage.

Since the middle of the 1990s, then, the sociopolitical environment has sent out a complex array of mixed signals to lesbians and gay men (see Werum and Winders 2001). Although the New Right gained a stronghold in the 1994 elections and proceeded to deliver a barrage of antigay measures, a 1994 *Newsweek* poll showed that 74 percent of Americans opposed workplace discrimination against gays and lesbians (cited in HRC 1994), a figure that has since climbed to 85 percent, according to a June 2001 Gallup poll (HRC 2002h). Indeed, the Employment Non-discrimination Act (ENDA), which proposed to ban discrimination on the basis of sexual orientation, was first introduced in Congress during the summer of 1994 with the backing of 185 religious, labor, and civil rights organizations. With high-profile support from Senator Edward Kennedy, a lead sponsor, and Coretta Scott King, 30 senators and over 120 members of the House quickly signed on as cosponsors (HRC 1994). In 1995 Clinton endorsed ENDA, making him the first U.S. president to support gay rights legislation, and corporate and civil rights groups' endorsements of the bill more than doubled (HRC 1995b). By the spring of 1996, over twenty-five major corporations had expressed public support for ENDA, and in the summer of that year several business leaders, including the CEO of Eastman Kodak, delivered congressional testimony in favor of the bill (HRC 1996a, 1996b).

In the fall of 1996, ENDA came within one vote of passing the Senate (*New York Times* 1996). Perhaps many nonactivist members of the gay and lesbian community interpreted both the introduction of ENDA and its near win in the Senate as evidence that mobilization in the workplace would soon be unnecessary, thereby justifying inaction on their part. Moreover, since press coverage of the legislation rarely mentioned that it would not apply to benefits packages, many people may have incorrectly assumed that its adoption would mandate equitable benefits. In any case, while ENDA has yet to pass either house of Congress, as of fall 2002 it had 45 cosponsors in the Senate (40 Democrats, 4 Republicans, 1 Independent); 194 in the House (172 Democrats, 21 Republicans, 1 Independent); and public endorsements from over eighty companies (HRC 2002b).

Besides ENDA's near passage in the Senate in 1996, which may have planted false hope among some gays and lesbians, other elements of the political and cultural environment signaled a rosier future as well. At a November 1997 HRC fund-raising dinner, Bill Clinton made history as the first president ever to speak at a gay and lesbian movement event (S. Epstein 1999, 71). As he succinctly put it, "Being gay, the last time I thought about it, seemed to have nothing to do with the ability to read a balance book, fix a broken bone or change a spark plug" (quoted in HRCF 2000a, 11).

Earlier that same year, Ellen DeGeneres made history of her own when she and her sitcom character came out on prime-time television. Whether heterosexual audiences viewed the coming-out episode of *Ellen* as overblown hype, mundane television, or glorification of deviance (J. Gamson 1998), countless lesbians and gay men were glued to their television screens on the night of April 30, 1997. At *Ellen* parties across the country, friends gathered to watch the latest advance on the path toward major cultural transformation: the mainstreaming of homosexuality. Ironically, this enormous breakthrough in media visibility may have further reinforced the notion that lesbian and gay activism was no longer needed. Such is the danger of "virtual equality" (Vaid 1995).

Trying to militate against the perception that gays and lesbians had already obtained equal rights, HRC designed a commercial that was supposed to air on ABC during *Ellen*'s coming-out episode. Made possible by a generous donation and centered around the little-known fact that antigay job discrimination remained legal in forty-one (now thirty-six) states, the ad portrayed a lesbian leaving the office after having been fired, with her shocked colleagues looking on in disbelief as they wondered aloud how her termination could be legal. Their astonishment reflected a widespread misperception: of those surveyed nationally, 42 percent incorrectly believed that there was already a federal law prohibiting antigay employment discrimination (HRCF 2001b). Originally set to broadcast nationally, the commercial was seen only in select cities, since ABC refused to allow HRC to purchase nationwide airtime (HRC 1997). Thus, as conservatives attacked both Ellen and *Ellen*, interpreting DeGeneres's media visibility as the "promotion of homosexuality" (J. Gamson 1998, 262), the New Right's rhetoric against gay rights as "special rights" retained its secure position in the cultural imagination.

Theoretical Interpretations of Environmental Complexity

Since its inception, the workplace movement, like other movements, has faced a complex mix of environmental conditions that, in many ways, cannot be defined a priori as either favorable or unfavorable. Although the more stable components of political and institutional opportunity seem readily susceptible to "objective" definition, some of the more volatile aspects are open to widely varying interpretations (W. Gamson and Meyer 1996). Hostile legislation, for example, can be seen as a setback for or barrier to a movement, but so too can it incite increased mobilization (D. Meyer and Staggenborg 1996; Sawyers and Meyer 1999).

Much as poststructuralists argue that multiple discursive meanings make a unitary reading of text virtually impossible (Weedon 1987), social movement scholars have begun to render problematic simplistic treatments of political opportunity. Not only are discourses or frames subject to multiple meanings— a condition that poststructuralists refer to as "polysemy" or "multivalence" (Blain 1997)—but the environmental conditions that challengers face are also open to different, and sometimes conflicting, interpretations. Recent advances in social movement theory help make sense of this complexity.

Attempting to correct the structural biases of early resource mobilization and political process approaches, which took grievances as a given, many social movement theorists began to incorporate social-psychological insights to better understand the role of interpretive processes in the emergence and development of collective action (Morris and Mueller 1992). Moving toward a synthesis of structural and cultural approaches, many scholars today attend not simply to the impact of political opportunities and mobilizing structures but also to the mediating influence of "framing processes," a term that has come to refer broadly to the construction of meaning, grievances, collective identities, and interpretive schemata that identify systemic problems and solutions (McAdam, McCarthy, and Zald 1996b).

Taking seriously the argument that opportunity, organization, and framing are interactive rather than independent components of collective action (McAdam, McCarthy, and Zald 1996b, 8), William Gamson and David Meyer (1996) highlight the "framing of political opportunity." They describe opportunity as relative, in that social movement actors must define a particular situation as favorable or unfavorable. Indeed, they argue that "the definition of opportunity is often at the center of what is most contentious." In other words, political opportunity, while predominantly viewed in structural terms, is also socially constructed, since the strategic actions of challengers depend on their perceptions of particular circumstances as either hopeful or hopeless. As Gamson and Meyer conclude, "An opportunity unrecognized is no opportunity at all" (283).

Traci Sawyers and David Meyer (1999) likewise refer to "missed opportunities," focusing on situations that appear unfavorable on the surface but that nevertheless contain seeds of possibility. For example, movement leaders can create opportunities out of hostile legislation or rancorous court rulings if they use them to increase publicity, raise consciousness, and woo additional adherents and resources (see also D. Meyer and Staggenborg 1996). While I agree that activists' interpretations of their environment as overly unfavorable can result in missed opportunities, this scholarly focus leaves unexplored another possible scenario in the complex framing of political and institutional opportunities. Namely, actors can define a situation as so hopeful or favorable that additional collective action is seen as unnecessary. In the next section I consider this interpretation as another possible explanation for the third-wave decline in new corporate organizing.

The Paradox of Success: The Ironic Impact of the Institutionalization Process and the Mythical Domino Effect

To fully understand the varying levels of corporate mobilization over time, the focus must be widened to include not simply the political environment but also the other institutional conditions that potential challengers face. In other words, when deciding whether to mobilize in their own places of work, lesbian and gay employees look not only at the sociopolitical climate but also at the state of affairs in corporate America generally. At the end of the first wave, in 1989, after twelve years of workplace mobilization, fewer than 20 employers had adopted domestic partner benefits. In contrast, by the end of the second wave, in 1994, the workplace movement was thriving and had won equitable benefits in a sizable number of organizations. According to data provided to me by HRC, by the close of 1994, the number of adopters had risen to almost 150, most of which were companies, including 17 Fortune 1000 corporations or their subsidiaries. Yet, beginning in 1995, the pace of new organizing among the Fortune 1000 slowed considerably.

Why, at a time when the workplace movement had much to celebrate and seemed on the brink of even greater success, did gay and lesbian employees not rush to the party in droves, hoping to win similar victories in their own places of work? Even as the pace of equitable-benefits adoption accelerated throughout the third period, very few gay and lesbian employees in the Fortune 1000 formed networks of their own. From 1995 to mid-1998, only 9 new corporate networks joined the movement. This relative inactivity seems especially puzzling when one considers the fact that, by the end of 1998, domestic partner benefits had been instituted in 427 workplaces (HRC data provided to author). Most of the adopters were corporations, 67 of them in the Fortune 1000. Why, in the face of greater publicity, resources, and favorable outcomes, did the number of gay network formations plummet rather than mushroom during the third wave?

Complacency: The Irony of Partial Success

Scholars have found that policy victories can energize a movement and inspire increased mobilization (McAdam 1982; Costain 1992; Sawyers and Meyer 1999). Less attention has been paid to the opposite possibility, namely, that success on the part of some challengers can lead to complacency among other potential beneficiaries. Scholars interested in the so-called postfeminist era have documented a similar process. Although the notion of postfeminism has been duly criticized by feminist scholars, the term nevertheless arose in response to the complacency of some young women who, while benefiting from the gains of feminism, no longer saw a need for it (Stacey [1987] 1997; Taylor and Rupp 1993; Whittier 1995; Taylor and Whittier 1997).

Ironically, then, the institutionalization of certain movement goals, although favorable in terms of policy outcomes, can result in unfavorable mobilization outcomes (for the distinction between types of outcomes, see Staggenborg 1995). Although the pace of new organizing in the Fortune 1000 began to slow considerably in 1995, by then the workplace movement had achieved a staying power capable of sustaining it through relatively infertile times. Indeed, I propose that it is the visible success of the workplace movement that helps to explain the third-wave decline in new corporate mobilization.

But it is not simply the quickened pace of equitable-benefits adoption, or the media's increased attention to it, that accounts for inaction on the part of other gay and lesbian employees. The meaning of corporate policy change—that is, how it will be interpreted by potential challengers as well as potential adopters—varies, depending in part on *who* is doing the adopting. I argue, in other words, that it is not simply the number of adopters that matters. The wider impact of a particular employer's policy change depends on the significance that is attributed to it by the actors in that organizational field. Future levels of mobilization by potential beneficiaries—and the policy decisions that will be made by institutional elites—will thus vary, based on how individual and organizational actors interpret the adoption of innovation by particular players in the surrounding environment.

New institutional theorists, emphasizing a cognitive approach to organizational change, have made similar arguments about the social construction of organizational fields (Scott 1995a, 1995b; Scott and Christensen 1995). Empirical studies have found, for example, that the policy decisions of elites rest in part on whom they consider to be their competitors and whether the initial adopters of an innovation are seen as high- or low-prestige organizations (Porac, Thomas, and Badden-Fuller 1989; Porac and Thomas 1990; Galaskiewicz and Burt 1991; Burns and Wholey 1993; Lant and Baum 1995). I extend the logic of this framework by arguing that potential beneficiaries undergo a similar interpretive process. The "need" for institutional activism, in other words, is socially constructed. In deciding whether or not to mobilize in their own places of work, lesbian and gay employees look not simply at the number of companies that have instituted equitable benefits but also at the organizational identities of adopters, and what they "see" is influenced by the reputation those companies have in the wider gay, lesbian, and bisexual community.

Unlikely Adopters: "Oversignification" and the Meaning of Corporate Policy Change

Although numerous employers had already adopted domestic partner benefits before 1995, in that year the decisions of 2 of the Fortune 1000 adopters—the Coors Brewing Company and the Walt Disney Corporations, both corporate giants—came as a great shock to many. The significance of their policy announcements rests not simply in their big-name status but in their previous reputations in the lesbian and gay community. Coors had been the target of a gay boycott for almost twenty years. After the company adopted equitable benefits, Christian fundamentalists called for a boycott of their own (Mathews 1995). Disney likewise was targeted with a boycott after losing its most-favored status among conservatives, who charged the company with abandoning its "family values" foundation.

To counter the Right's campaign against Disney, lesbian and gay activists organized a "buy-cott," whereby consumers were encouraged to express support for Disney's decision by spending two-dollar bills at Disney stores and theme parks. With a tongue-in-cheek reference to the old "queer as a two-dollar bill" phrase, the buy-cott inflamed the antigay American Family Association (AFA), which urged its members to contact Disney stores during the buy-cott. Having already issued a boycott against the company, the AFA declared that "the time is right for another reminder that Disney's pro-family legacy is gone" (quoted in GLOBES 1998).

Coors's decision to adopt equitable benefits was likewise a surprise to many on both the left and right. Coors, founded and still majority-owned by an archconservative family, had long raised the ire of gays and lesbians. After word got out in 1977 that the company was asking applicants their sexual orientation and using lie detector tests to root out gay employees, lesbian and gay activists issued calls for a boycott (Adam 1995). Although decades have passed since then, many still refuse to buy the beer because of the long-standing reputation of the Coors family as key contributors to the New Right. As one journalist put it, "The family foundations—the Castle Rock Foundation and the Adolph Coors Foundation—remain crucial backers of a who's who of antigay politics" (Bull 2001). The Castle Rock Foundation gives the largest of its grants to antigay groups such as the Heritage Foundation, founded by Joseph Coors, and the Free Congress Foundation, chaired by Jeffrey Coors (Mirken 1997b, 1997c; Wilke 2002). The latter organization is "generally credited with demonizing the 'gay agenda,'" a homophobic rhetorical strategy that has become a highly successful "political and fund-raising [tool] for the far right" (Mirken 1997a, 6).

The decision to offer domestic partner benefits at Coors was, thus, truly astonishing. As one vice president of a benefits-consulting firm put it, "It's hard to think of a company that has a more conservative image than Coors" (quoted in Hoback 1995). Nevertheless, with corporate executives making bottom-line decisions and hoping to "grow the brand's estimated tiny 2%–3% share in the gay market's competitive beer category" (Wilke 2002), Coors not only adopted the benefits but also began to aggressively publicize that fact to the lesbian and gay community in an attempt to win back gay dollars. Even in statements to the mainstream press, corporate spokespersons were careful to point out that the company's policies were separate from those of the Coors family and its foundations (Gilpin 1995).

As part of the corporation's gay-inclusive policy shift, the CEO of Coors publicly endorsed ENDA, and some gay rights groups began receiving donations from the company. Others in the lesbian and gay community nevertheless continue to protest the acceptance of such money, arguing that the boycott should remain in effect since corporate profits, placed in the hands of the Coors family, end up funding antigay politics (Mirken 1997a, 1997b, 1997c; Wilke 2002). For the purposes of the present discussion, the significance of the boycott controversy lies not so much in its impact on Coors as in its impact on gays and lesbians who had not mobilized in other places of work at the time Coors changed its policy. In the gay press and in mainstream media, coverage of Coors's benefits adoption highlighted the company's negative reputation in the lesbian and gay community; likewise, follow-up stories reported on divisions within the community over ending the boycott (see, e.g., Gilpin 1995; Hoback 1995; Mathews 1995; Mears 1995; Mirken 1997a, 1997b, 1997c; Bull 2001; Wilke 2002). Thus, even those who previously had been unaware of the acrimonious relationship between Coors and the gay rights movement would, given the media visibility, see the company's policy change in a drastically different light than policy shifts by other employers. This was not simply another company adopting domestic partner benefits; this was a company that for decades had been equated with antigay hatred.

Why, then, in 1995, when two of the most unlikely organizational candidates embraced gay-inclusive policy change, did the pace of new corporate organizing suddenly decline? Perhaps when Coors's decision hit the news, gay and lesbian employees located in other companies "oversignified" the importance of the policy change by assuming that, because this notoriously antigay employer had adopted equitable benefits, others would follow suit in quick order. Likewise, although Disney had no such antigay record, it seems equally plausible that its reputation as *the* "traditional family values" company led to a similar process of oversignification in the lesbian and gay community. Disney's policy change, which generated a great deal of media attention, may have convinced many that if the family-values giant could expand its definition of family to embrace gay men and lesbians—having held out as the last major player in the entertainment industry to do so (Deibel 1996)—then widespread policy change was sure to occur in the rest of corporate America.

The fact that press coverage rarely mentioned the presence of gay employee groups in these companies only reinforced this oversignification. Both companies had faced strong internal pressure by lesbian and gay employees who mobilized for equitable benefits. Even though the vast majority of early benefits adopters were persuaded by organized groups of gay and lesbian workers (see the introduction to this book), media accounts rarely noted the existence, let alone the impact, of these institutional activists. David, in other words, is left out of the story of Goliath. Even today the mainstream press may be quick to cover benefits adoption by the corporate giants, but the story they convey is often incomplete.

Media Representations of Corporate Policy Change

To explain how an innovation becomes widely adopted, new institutional theorists have emphasized isomorphic processes in the wider environment, whereby organizations facing the same environmental pressures come to resemble one another in structure and policy and hence achieve legitimacy (DiMaggio and Powell 1991b). This focus on the diffusion of innovation, as critics within the field have pointed out, leaves unexplained the origin of change and downplays the role of conflict in generating institutional trans-formation (DiMaggio 1988; Brint and Karabel 1991; Suchman 1995; Chaves 1996, 1997; Hirsch 1997; Hirsch and Lounsbury 1997; Rao 1998). Institu-tional scholars have especially ignored the role of mobilized constituencies as agents of organizational change (Chaves 1996, 1997).

I argue that media accounts of gay-inclusive policy adoption suffer from the same weaknesses. This is not surprising, since, as William Gamson (1995a, 98) has found, although journalistic attention to collective agency varies by issue, "the normal assumption in media discourse [is] that citizen action is irrelevant." Likewise, news reports rarely, if ever, describe *how* equi-table benefits came to be or *who* was behind their adoption. Thus, the public is likely to see benefits adoption as an apparently seamless process that, once instituted by enough leading innovators, will ultimately diffuse widely to the rest of the business world. Institutionalization of an innovation appears inevitable, guided by the invisible hand of the market as employers play follow-the-leader. Indeed, media references to the mythical domino effect abound. Reading about the rapidly growing pace of corporate change, many people may simply assume that their company will eventually follow suit.

Not realizing the movement processes behind most companies' bene-fits adoption, potential beneficiaries in other companies may be lulled into complacency. As William Gamson and David Meyer (1996, 285) argue, media access is not simply a key component *of* political opportunity; media attention also plays a role in defining political opportunity *for* movements. Likewise, media representations define the process of policy change in such a way that the general public, straight and gay alike, may come to see bene-fits adoption as a fait accompli. Inaction on the part of gay and lesbian em-ployees therefore seems justified.

Of course, the media is not solely to blame for this faulty perception. I suspect that, even when lesbian and gay employees have pushed long and hard for equitable benefits, corporate spokespersons, whether responding to a reporter's questions or issuing a press release, rarely identify the impact of gay employee groups on the decision-making process. In many cases, for example, the vice presidents I interviewed downplayed the role of employee activists in effecting policy change even in the face of evidence that proved otherwise. But it is not just the media, corporate elites, or public relations professionals who present an incomplete or inaccurate picture of how policy change comes about in the corporate world.

Movement Discourse and the Mythical, Market-Driven Domino Effect

Leaders in the wider gay and lesbian rights movement—as opposed to the workplace wing itself—often adopt what I refer to as "domino discourse" when discussing the corporate adoption of equitable benefits. When issuing press releases or when asked by the media to comment on the most recent adoption, spokespersons for HRC, for example, frequently portray the policy change in market-based terms: once enough business leaders adopt the benefits, it is only a matter of time until others follow suit.

Although leaders in the wider gay rights movement often acknowledge, where applicable, the role of lesbian and gay employee groups, they regularly refer either implicitly or explicitly to "the domino effect," popular terminology for what institutional theorists call mimetic isomorphism (DiMaggio and Powell 1991b). This explanation of policy change emphasizes that once a few leaders have adopted equitable benefits, others in the field will eventually do the same to remain competitive or to achieve legitimacy. In other words, once enough big players have adopted an innovation, others feel pressure to adopt the newest "best practice."

A 1999 press release by HRC (1999c) provides a clear illustration of this domino discourse. Kim Mills, who, as education director, oversees HRC's workplace project, called WorkNet, commented on the rapid succession of benefits adoption by three major carriers in the airline industry. Until that point no one in the industry had instituted equitable benefits. After United Airlines announced, on July 30, 1999, the extension of benefits to domestic partners, six days later American Airlines did the same. Responding to a similar policy change by US Airways, which came four days after the announcement by American Airlines, Mills commented, "This is another instance of how domestic partner benefits cascade through a market sector. It happened first in the information technology sector in the early 1990s and it's happening now in the oil industry, in the Big Five accounting firms, in banking and elsewhere."

When movement leaders utilize domino discourse, it is often a strategic decision. They are framing the situation as largely a "market process" so as to convince other employers to follow suit. This paints the adoption of domestic partner benefits as a rational, profits-oriented move that will enhance an employer's position in a competitive labor market: "With unemployment running at a rock-bottom 4 percent," its lowest level in decades, Mills explained, "employers have discovered these benefits are a tool for attracting and keeping the best employees" (HRC 1999c). Although Mills went on to describe benefits adoption as "a step toward equal pay for equal work" and, at the tail end of the press release, mentioned the role of gay employee groups at both United and American Airlines, the dominant frame running throughout the piece was not one of justice or equal rights but of markets and profit.

In fact, the domino, or "cascade," effect that Mills described had been set in motion not only by the efforts of lesbian and gay employee groups and the larger gay rights movement but also by wider changes in the legal environment. In June 1997, San Francisco adopted the Equal Benefits Ordinance, which requires any employer with a city contract to provide the same benefits to domestic partners as those available to the spouses of heterosexual employees. In an attempt to overturn the ordinance, United Airlines joined in a lawsuit brought by the Air Transportation Association. Gay and lesbian activists quickly issued calls for a boycott, and "United against United" buttons and stickers soon appeared throughout San Francisco. On July 30, 1999, a federal judge ruled that the company must provide at least "soft" benefits, such as bereavement leave. It was on that same day that United announced it would instead offer full domestic partner benefits, including health insurance (E. Epstein 1999).

Thus, the "domino effect" that Mills portrayed as largely market-driven was in fact the result of movement processes that included both internal mobilization and external pressure by lesbian and gay activists. Policy changes stemming from both the United Airlines boycott and the Equal Benefits Ordinance serve as examples of what institutional scholars refer to as coercive isomorphism (DiMaggio and Powell 1991b). Indeed, many companies now appear to be adopting equitable benefits not (or not simply) because of market pressures or mimetic isomorphism, or even employee mobilization, but rather (or also) because of external coercive forces (HRCF 1999b) (a point that I will address further in chapter 4). For example, statistics gathered by the San Francisco Human Rights Commission show that, by the end of fiscal year 2001, over 3,100 employers with city contracts had instituted equitable benefits in order to comply with the Equal Benefits Ordinance (Goldstein 2001).

In the 2001 *State of the Workplace* report, published by HRCF (HRCF 2001b), authors Daryl Herrschaft and Kim Mills acknowledge the complexity of institutional change mechanisms, issuing a reminder that employers extend benefits "in reaction to different stimuli" (18). They discuss the impact of coercive pressures stemming from San Francisco's equitable-benefits mandate and from similar laws that have since been adopted by a handful of other cities (15, 18). Nonetheless, the report emphasizes competitive advantage as the driving force behind policy change—"[F]or the most part . . . these changes are happening because they are good for business" (7); "[T]he overall trend seems to be attributable to sheer market forces" (31)—with the authors highlighting mimetic processes in a section called "Following the Leader" (20–21). Unlike in the previous year's *State of the Workplace* report (HRCF 2000a), nowhere in the 2001 edition do the authors address internal mobilization and the crucial role that lesbian and gay employee activists have played in effecting widespread change in the corporate world. Thus, the domino effect remains the dominant explanation not only in media stories but in many of HRC's and HRCF's own publications.

New institutionalists Erin Kelly and Frank Dobbin (1999) also found the market being afforded primacy in many accounts of the adoption of maternity-leave policies among U.S. employers. While they criticize such accounts for ignoring the role of the state—namely, administrative orders and laws regarding maternity leave—their arguments can also be applied to the case of domestic partner benefits if one substitutes "employee activism" for the words "state" or "public policy" in the following passage:

> Commentators argue that employers created maternity leave policies in response to a change in the labor market. . . . This claim reinforces the idea that, in the United States, the market is powerful and the state is not. That idea becomes self-fulfilling when even the advocates of social change come to believe it. We view the pattern we have documented, of a public policy inducing new business practices and then being forgotten, as evidence of the remarkable rhetorical power of the market in the United States. The inclination to see social practices as driven by market mechanisms . . . appears to have blinded many to the role of the state in improving opportunities for disadvantaged groups. (487–88)

Even when leaders of the wider gay rights movement do acknowledge, where applicable, the impact of employee activism and/or external coercive pressure from the state, they still tend to emphasize market forces when commenting on the spread of equitable-benefits policies. This is most likely an intentional discursive strategy to allow potential adopters, who often fear right-wing backlash, to publicly rationalize benefits adoption not so much as "the right thing to do" but as simply "good business sense." Indeed, the latter phrase appears frequently in corporate-issued press releases and in media accounts that quote organizational decision makers.

But when movement leaders themselves rely too heavily on a discourse that emphasizes institutional or market processes, they may play an unwitting role in fostering complacency. Domino discourse obscures the role of social movements and agency generally. Thus, while this framing may seem a reasonable tactic for influencing potential *adopters*, it can reinforce inaction on the part of potential *beneficiaries*. In other words, emphasizing the institutional processes of mimetic isomorphism (or even coercive isomorphism) can negatively affect future success, since nonactivist gays and lesbians may come to see employee mobilization as unnecessary for policy change.

William Gamson and David Meyer (1996, 285–86) argue that, to counter the "rhetoric of reaction" that casts activism as either futile or too risky, movement leaders must adopt a "rhetoric of change" that "systematically overestimates the degree of political opportunity." My research shows that leaders in the wider gay rights movement sometimes adopt a rhetoric of change that overestimates the role of institutional processes, which unintentionally justifies inaction by gay and lesbian employees. This paradox stems not from carelessness on the part of leaders but from the conflicting requirements that challengers face. Activists must engage in strategic framing efforts that are directed not simply at winning adherents and constituents but also at influencing various policy targets (Einwohner 1999a, 1999b). I argue that, because activists must reach multiple audiences—both potential beneficiaries and potential adopters—and because those targets are differentially positioned in terms of power, resources, and interests, framing efforts that seem to resonate with one audience (corporations) may have an unintended effect on other audiences (nonactivist employees).

Summary

After taking into account the complexity of the sociopolitical and institutional environments, including the ironic effect of partial success and the way that media and movement accounts portray policy change, the third-wave decline in new corporate organizing appears far less mysterious. The decisions of lesbians, gay men, and bisexuals are shaped by a complex mix of factors. Whether seen as political opportunities or institutional opportunities, these factors defy strictly objectivist determination. Opportunities are not merely structural; they are "processual" in that environmental conditions are always mediated by the interpretations of potential challengers, current activists, elites, and media professionals, to name but a few.

One other factor may help to account for the apparent decline in gay network formations. It is possible that the level of mobilization during the third wave was actually higher than current measures indicate. It is difficult to determine the true extent of workplace mobilization, since I lacked the resources to survey all 1,000 companies in the Fortune 1000. Even if I were able to contact every corporation, it would sometimes be impossible to determine whether a company had a gay employee group. When I lacked an activist contact, I had to rely on corporate decision makers to tell me whether a gay network existed. This approach proved problematic, since corporate elites are reluctant to participate in studies on this subject. Aside from the difficulties posed by a low response rate, relying on elites to document the existence of challengers is unreliable, since some gay employee groups intentionally start out with a low profile. Given the methodological limitations of this study, therefore, it may be safer to issue a caveat: what appears to be a decline in third-wave mobilization may be, at least in part, only *apparent* quiescence.

Moreover, since my data collection on gay network formations ended in 1998, it is also possible that there has been an upswing in employee mobilization since then. Indeed, lesbian, gay, and bisexual employees may be mobilizing in the Fortune 1000 at a rate that matches or even exceeds that of previous waves. It could be that these younger gay employee networks, still trying to get on their feet, are less "hooked in" to the larger workplace movement. Not connected with networks in other companies, and uninvolved in workplace conferences, for example, these new groups would not appear on the contact lists that circulate via print and electronic media. They would thus remain invisible to outside observers. Future research is therefore needed to trace the trajectory of workplace organizing in the new millennium in relation to changes in the sociopolitical environment, the actions of the broader gay and lesbian rights movement, and the variable conditions present in other institutional spheres, particularly the media and the workplace.

Whether the drop in new organizing is real or artificial, leaders in the workplace movement have helped to build a considerable infrastructure that provides information, resources, and motivation for the ongoing efforts of employee activists across the country. This infrastructure bodes well for the future of workplace organizing, since new and experienced employee networks—linked together through the Internet, lesbian and gay workplace conferences, and regional or national umbrella groups—can not only share strategies and tactics but also offer emotional support to each other as they take up the hard work that lies ahead. In the next chapter I trace the development of these dense interorganizational connections and discuss their importance in sustaining workplace activism through both the peaks and valleys of mobilization.

3

Building and Benefiting from the Movement

In this chapter I examine the connections, both formal and informal, that arose among gay employee networks in the early to mid 1990s, and I trace the growth and development of this infrastructure up to the present day. The discussion has a dual focus: to explain the institutional and movement processes by which widely dispersed workplace activists became linked to one another; and to highlight the resources, structures, and strategies that arose from these same interorganizational linkages.

Before the rise of such cross-network connections, most lesbian and gay employee activists had little or no knowledge of the struggles being waged by their sisters and brothers in other corporations. Beginning in the early 1990s, however, numerous ties developed among workplace activists from a wide variety of settings. In a short period of time these connections grew more dense and overlapped, creating a strong movement infrastructure. At the informal level these linkages constitute a diffuse but extensive social movement community (Buechler 1990). As ties among employee networks multiplied, some interorganizational linkages became more formalized, leading to the creation of local, regional, and national umbrella groups.

In the first half of the chapter, I examine the institutional and movement processes that fostered such extensive connections among individual activists and employee networks across the country. In particular I consider the facilitative role of three key factors and emphasize their continued importance for the success of the workplace movement: (1) newly available communication technologies, namely, expanded access to e-mail and the Internet, which I conceptualize as "virtual opportunities"; (2) workplace conferences focused on lesbian, gay, bisexual, and transgender issues; and (3) the work-place projects of national organizations in the wider gay rights movement.

In the second half of the chapter, I address the formation of local, re-gional, and national umbrella organizations. Growing from favorable move-ment and institutional terrains, these coalitions unite gay employee networks across a wide variety of workplace settings. I examine the important role that umbrella groups play in strengthening the movement and sustaining em-ployee activism despite the decline in new organizing that I documented in chapter 2. Functioning as abeyance structures (Taylor 1989), umbrella groups help to ensure the survival of the workplace movement amid harsh climate changes in the wider sociopolitical environment. On a more inter-mediate institutional level, they help employee networks weather any storms that appear on their own particular corporate horizons.

The Rise of Interorganizational Linkages and the Impact on Resources, Structures, and Strategies

Virtual Opportunities: The Impact of New Communication Technologies

Just as popular culture began to echo with lively exchanges about the mere "six degrees of separation" between any two individuals in the world, e-mail and the Internet helped to narrow that gap in "virtual," if not spatial, terms. The expanded availability of these electronic forms of communication, which constitute what I call *virtual opportunities,* helps to account for both the surge of new workplace organizing in the early 1990s and the rise of intercorporate networking during the same period.

Referring to the "information society," the "network society," or the "communication age," new social movement theorists also highlight the ways that new forms of communication have facilitated collective action in the late modern era (Giddens 1991; Melucci 1996; Castells 2001). Citing vari-ous forms of electronic communication that allow groups with a common identity to mobilize across vast distances, Verta Taylor (2000) mentions fax machines, copying equipment, e-mail, chat rooms, Listservs, and other resources on the World Wide Web. In his analysis of the civil rights move-ment, Aldon Morris (1999) likewise comments on the favorable mobiliza-tion impact of new communication technologies. The spread of television in the 1950s and the launching of communications satellites in the early 1960s brought galvanizing images of African American protest into the family rooms of millions of households.

Unlike television, whose access depends on the ability of protesters to catch the eye of the broadcast media, the Internet and e-mail bring instant publicity and facilitate rapid diffusion of information that remains unmediated by the constraints and distortions of externally controlled media outlets (see Schock 1999). Electronic mail and the Internet thus constitute a far more accessible and stable institutional opportunity, in that challengers have direct access to free or relatively inexpensive communication venues. Although the Internet was originally developed and used by the government in the late 1960s, at the start of the 1990s availability spread briskly through corporations and to individual computer owners, aided tremendously by the creation in 1991 of World Wide Web technology (Federer 1995; Guthrie 1999; IT Network 1999; DiMaggio et al. 2001).

Electronic Technologies as Mobilizing Structures

Serving as easily co-optable communication networks, which constitute a significant resource for movement recruitment and growth (Freeman 1975, 1979; McAdam 1982; Morris 1984), e-mail and the Internet helped the workplace movement mobilize far more rapidly than was otherwise possible. Lesbian and gay employee groups could use intercorporate communication channels to compare notes, share strategies, and spread news of gay-inclusive policy changes. After Lotus, the first major corporate adopter of equitable benefits, announced its policy change in late 1991, "[w]ithin minutes computer bulletin boards flashed the news to offices and companies across the country" (Stewart 1991, 50). "I got it from ten different people," commented one gay employee group member (quoted on 50), reflecting the degree to which widely dispersed activists were becoming well connected through the diffuse webs of the Internet.

Gay and lesbian employee groups also co-opt corporate e-mail for internal mobilization purposes. For instance, in my findings some networks use electronic communication to provide upper management with up-to-the-minute news of gay-inclusive policy change in the wider business world. When possible, networks use their companies' electronic bulletin boards, accessible to any interested employees, to post announcements of meetings or upcoming events (see also Hayden 1993, 2), although this latter strategy sometimes elicits a backlash from employees who object to receiving gay-related postings. Moreover, a few networks have been successful in winning support from the editorial staff of their companies' electronic newsletters, which are sent to all employees. These allies then publish articles about the gay network, for example, or celebrate Gay Pride Month by sponsoring trivia contests about lesbian and gay figures in history or popular culture.

Whether gay and lesbian employees were communicating with others inside or outside their companies, the expanded access of electronic information sharing represented a pivotal institutional opportunity that was quickly seized upon by the workplace movement. Even the simple electronic circulation of contact lists helped word travel fast about gay employee groups that were forming in and outside of the corporate sector. Several interview respondents noted that they were motivated to organize in their own places of work after learning online about other networks. Activists also set up electronic discussion lists where they could share strategies or seek external encouragement in the face of hostile internal reactions.

Some employee networks set up their own electronic forums that employees could participate in, but activists also established external lists that linked individuals and networks across the country and the globe. One such discussion list, referred to as "glbt-workplace" (accessible today via majordomo@queernet.org), included threads on coming out at work, interacting with colleagues and managers, effecting change through activism in the workplace, and publicizing the activities of gay employee groups in the wider community. Those interested in even more lively interaction could also join real-time chat rooms dedicated to lesbian and gay employment issues.

Previously isolated lesbian and gay employees thus became linked to one another through the use of intra- and intercorporate e-mail, Usenet newsgroups or discussion lists, and postings to gay-related Listservs on the Internet. By early 1993, for example, the Usenet newsgroup called "Soc.motss" (social group for people attracted to members of the same sex) had grown to over forty thousand subscribers, and America Online had numerous lesbian, gay, and bisexual forums, including one focused on corporate issues (Hayden 1993, 2). Those who were interested could even join a discussion list focused on domestic partner benefits.

Existing before the Internet became widely available in the early 1990s, and awkwardly named to serve as a code word for *gay,* the Soc.motss discussion list operated through the Netnews Association, one of the earliest public bulletin boards. The obfuscation of the name Soc.motss was necessary at the time, since many servers prohibited use of the words *gay* or *lesbian* in the titles of newsgroups. Despite this obstacle, lesbians and gay men found each other online, and early workplace activists began using the discussion list in support of their mobilization efforts. To illustrate the mobilizing power of these electronic technologies, I will briefly discuss how members of one of the earliest gay employee networks in the country used Soc.motss and intracorporate e-mail to reach out to other lesbian and gay employees both in and outside of their company.

In 1987, in a major telecommunications corporation, a founding member of "GLUE" (Gay and Lesbian United Employees) used Soc.motss to publicize her group's intention to meet with someone in upper management about the newly formed network. She expressed trepidation over outing herself to such a high-level executive, whom she had never met. Seeking some advice and bravery-boosting solidarity, her posting to Soc.motss read, "I'd particularly like to know of other groups who have organized within their work locations or who are considering such action. And I'd *really* appreciate encouraging words with soothing overtones!"

With news of GLUE's formation spreading far and wide, soon other networks emerged. Indeed, e-mail helped word travel fast, such that other GLUE chapters quickly sprang up in numerous locations within the corporation. At first a tiny group operating within a telecommunications giant, GLUE had expanded to thirty chapters by the mid-1990s, with membership exceeding two thousand. Often considered by others in the workplace movement to be the network that "started it all," GLUE is still the largest gay employee network in the country. In the absence of e-mail and the Internet, it is unlikely that the seeds planted by GLUE would have blown very far. In fact, in the history that is provided on the network's Web site, leaders acknowledge the role that electronic resources played in the organization's rapid growth and diffusion. The rather extensive Web site, unveiled in 1997, is itself a testament to the continued use of the Internet by gay employee networks, many of whom have Web pages of their own that, like GLUE's, provide links to other lesbian and gay workplace sites.

In movement terminology, electronic bulletin boards, discussion lists, chat rooms, and Web sites all function as informal mobilizing structures (Tarrow 1994; McCarthy 1996). As the "collective building blocks of social movements," mobilizing structures serve as the "seedbeds in which framing processes and strategies germinate" (Gotham 1999, 335–36). The virtual networks that arose from e-mail and the Internet thus spurred the growth of workplace activism and diffused the strategic frames born of such struggles. With the spread of new communication technologies, individual activists and employee networks soon became linked to each other. Able to easily compare tactics, share information on victories and setbacks, and build solidarity, these virtual networks have helped connect, inspire, and inform activists in even the most remote locations.

The workplace movement resembles the loose structure of many of the other so-called new social movements (Tarrow 1998). Composed of "decentralized, segmented, and reticulated" social networks (Gerlach and Hine 1970), employee groups function autonomously but are connected through intersecting circles of friends, acquaintances, and discussion list members. These cybernetworks can be seen as "social movement communities"

(Buechler 1990) or "submerged networks" of politicized actors who practice acts of resistance in their everyday lives, not simply through formal organizations (Melucci 1989, 35). Regardless of their category, these virtual communities provide activists with essential resources, both tangible and intangible.

As access to the Internet spread, the number of electronic resources that were focused on gay and lesbian topics grew exponentially. Today the popular Web site PlanetOut draws over a half-million visitors each month (*Gay People's Chronicle* 2001). Topping the charts, Gay.com attracts more than 2.3 million users per month (GLOBES 2000). If adrift in a sea of information and looking for workplace-related sites, Internet users can conduct an online search of the twenty-five thousand files contained in the Queer Resources Directory (Herscher 2000). A long-standing Internet site, the directory provides an indexed compilation of gay Listservs and Web pages. Other navigating tools include books such as *The Harvey Milk Institute Guide to Lesbian, Gay, Bisexual, Transgender, and Queer Internet Research* (Ellis et al. 2002).

To assist those searching the Internet for gay-related information, the Web site of the Human Rights Campaign provides a link to a PowerPoint presentation on how to maximize Internet searches. HRC refers to the PowerPoint resource as an "advocacy tool [that] is provided to you through a technology access grant from IBM Corporation." This message, which appears in the "Take Action" resources section of the site, reflects not only the success of activists in winning corporate donations but also the now firmly established strategy of using the Internet and other electronic resources as "advocacy tools," a connection that was fostered by groups such as Digital Queers. Realizing early on the power of these new communication technologies, activist-minded "techies" founded Digital Queers back in 1992 to help the lesbian and gay community get online and mobilize via the Internet (GLAAD 1999b). Highly regarded for its spearheading efforts in this area, the group has provided technical assistance to countless individuals and gay rights organizations, from the local to the national level.

Cyberspace as Free Space

Whether through electronic mail, Listservs, or the World Wide Web, cyberspace offers to gay employees a virtual and literal "free space," to use the term coined by movement scholars Sara Evans and Harry Boyte (1986). Similar to the free spaces of women-only consciousness-raising groups that facilitated the spread of the women's liberation movement (Evans 1979; Freeman 1979; Buechler 1990), gay-oriented discussion lists and chat rooms allow activists to interact with each other apart from dominant groups and to gain valuable information and support for their mobilization efforts. Scholarly literature on the workplace likewise documents the importance of solidarity-building activities that provide "an independent social space for workers' individual or collective identities" (Hodson 1996, 723).

Leaders of gay employee groups in my study frequently mentioned that even those who are closeted and too afraid to come to meetings can nevertheless maintain contact with the group by subscribing to a confidential e-mail list (see also Hayden 1993, 2). In fact, in most cases joining the network is as simple as signing up to receive e-mail postings. Confidential electronic communication can thus provide closeted employees with a safe environment where they can interact with other gays and lesbians without fear of negative repercussions.

The Contributions of Virtual Members

Reflecting on the significance of these free spaces, network leaders commonly reported two different numbers when asked about the size of their groups. One number consisted of those who would come to meetings and/or events, whether regularly or not, and the other included those who limited their participation to e-mail contact or electronic discussion lists. I use the term "virtual members" to refer to the latter group. Virtual members are sometimes a source of frustration for network leaders who wish for a more active and visible membership or, at the very least, a greater number of people to share the workload.

Looked at from this perspective, virtual members appear to resemble free riders, who choose to reap the benefits of collective action without actually joining in the cause (Olson 1965; Fireman and Gamson 1979). But such a conclusion, grounded in rational-choice assumptions, fails to capture the contradictory nature of gay and lesbian politics. In this particular form of identity politics, individuals cannot free ride on others' successes without first laying public claim to a lesbian, gay, or bisexual identity (see Raeburn and Taylor 1994).

Moreover, while closeted gays and lesbians could choose virtual membership and simply reap "solidary" benefits (Fireman and Gamson 1979) from participating in confidential e-mail or discussion lists, many virtual members, whether closeted or openly gay, do in fact contribute to the group through various forms of behind-the-scenes work. Some provide what Jo Freeman (1979, 173) has called specialized resources, such as expertise, access to key decision makers, and connections to other networks. Others provide "insider knowledge," which organizational scholars have shown to be "a powerful tool for workers" in their struggle for change in the workplace (Hodson 1996, 724). Simply by virtue of their positions in the company, other virtual members provide resources to the group in the form of status (Freeman 1979). Several network leaders in my study emphasized the importance of having high-level managers, often heterosexual, join the gay employee group even if their participation was limited to virtual membership. These highly visible allies, merely by joining the network, offer symbolic support for the cause and hence signal to others that discrimination is unacceptable.

There is another significant way in which virtual membership differs from free riding. Even if they offer no specialized resources, virtual members do in fact join the movement, if only electronically. Resembling "paper members" who donate money but not time to social movement organizations (McCarthy and Zald 1973, 1977), virtual members make "numeric" contributions by adding to the size of the membership base. Just by signing up to receive network e-mail, even the most inactive virtual members can bring tangible benefits to the larger group. For example, in some of the companies that provide resources to employee groups, management allocates budgets based on the number of members in each network. Even in corporations in my study where this was not the case, activist leaders were quick to acknowledge the importance of virtual membership, since they believed that larger networks carried more symbolic weight than smaller ones, an assumption I will put to an empirical test in a later chapter.

Electronic Resources: The Internet as Informational Clearinghouse

Resource mobilization theorists have clearly demonstrated the importance of resources such as publicity, money, space, time, commitment, organizing skills, and substantive expertise (McCarthy and Zald 1977; Tilly 1978; Freeman 1979; McAdam 1982; Jenkins 1983; Morris 1984; Katzenstein and Mueller 1987; Rupp and Taylor [1987] 1990; Tarrow 1989; W. Gamson 1990). Today electronic forums such as e-mail and the Internet make many of these resources accessible with a touch of the keyboard or the click of a mouse, and with much speedier results and far less costly investments of money or time than those associated with traditional communication channels. These new informational and communication technologies represent what Jo Freeman (1979, 174) has called institutional resources. While existing independently of the movement, such resources can be co-opted by challengers in their pursuit of social change.

Indeed, the Internet is now full of Web sites that focus specifically on gay, lesbian, bisexual, and transgender workplace issues. In October 1997, for instance, I easily located nearly seventy-five such sites, many of which were hyperlinked to each other. The numbers have grown tremendously since then. These links, along with the availability of powerful search engines, greatly facilitate both casual and scholarly research. Internet users can quickly access lists of lesbian and gay employee groups, some of which have Web pages of their own. The information contained on these and other workplace-related sites ranges from general advice on starting an employee network and building coalitions to more specific details such as the wording of affidavits, which many corporations require of employees wishing to access domestic partner benefits. Internet users can also access lists of employers that have already adopted equitable benefits. Most of these lists resulted from the early "benchmarking" activities of lesbian and gay employee groups.

Many workplace activists began to document the rise of gay-inclusive nondiscrimination policies and, later, equitable benefits in large part to convince their own employers to do the same. An enormously time-consuming task, these early benchmarking endeavors were sometimes undertaken voluntarily by gay employee networks. More often, however, activists went in search of such information at the request of upper management. Many network leaders today view this request, as early organizers did, as a diversionary tactic used by the corporate elite, who sometimes ask for not only a list of adopters but also the projected cost of adoption and "proof" of favorable financial impact in terms of enhanced recruitment and retention. The latter piece of information, of course, is virtually impossible for employee networks to obtain.

Nonetheless, countless hours of research by employee activists eventually resulted in the compilation of lists containing the names of adopters and, notably, empirical evidence documenting the negligible costs of adoption. Figures gathered by activists have since been substantiated by numerous studies conducted by research institutes, consulting firms, and professional associations of human resource managers and benefits specialists. Summarizing the results of such research, M. V. Lee Badgett, a professor of economics at the University of Massachusetts, Amherst, and research director of the Institute for Gay and Lesbian Strategic Studies, explains that, on average, employers offering equitable benefits will "see an enrollment increase of 1%, even when same-sex and opposite-sex partners are covered," which is the practice for 65 percent of adopters. Correspondingly, these participation rates "generate cost increases that are roughly the same . . . approximately 1%" (2000, 7).

More specifically, according to a survey of 570 large U.S. employers in 2000, the range of employees electing coverage for a domestic partner was between 0 and 10 percent, with an average of 1.2 percent of eligible employees enrolling. Among the companies that extended their policies, 85 percent found that equitable benefits made up less than 1 percent of total benefit expenditures, while 14 percent of adopters said the benefits made up between 1.0 and 2.9 percent of total benefit costs (Hewitt Associates 2000, 27). Low enrollment stems in part from the costly tax consequences borne by employees and their partners. Since under federal law a domestic partner is not considered a spouse, the employer's contribution for the partner's coverage is treated as taxable income. In addition, many partners already have coverage through their own employers, and in other cases gay and lesbian workers fear coming out to an employer, which is, of course, necessary if one is to elect coverage for a same-sex partner (Winfeld and Spielman 1995).

In any case, before these studies and before the rise of the Internet and the interorganizational linkages it helped to create, most gay employee groups were isolated from each other and would therefore have to reinvent the wheel each time management requested such data. Benefiting from early and ongoing benchmarking endeavors, today's employee activists can, with the touch of their fingers, have instant access to the fruits of their predecessors' labor. Individuals in the privacy of their own homes or offices can now find these studies as well as ever-expanding lists of gay-inclusive employers by visiting the Web sites of gay rights organizations such as HRC. These resources are supplemented by a small number of Web pages maintained by lesbian and gay consultants or by dedicated individuals who early on began to compile their own lists of gay-inclusive employers as well as other pieces of information relevant for workplace activists.

HRC's WorkNet Web Resources: Virtual Exemplar

To sample the extensive organizing and policy information contained on the Internet, one need only access the online resources provided by HRC. The "Work Life" section of the HRC Web site is exclusively devoted to WorkNet, a workplace project that is supported by the Human Rights Campaign Foundation. This WorkNet page, accessible through http://www.hrc.org/, provides an excellent compilation of the types of informational resources scattered throughout the Web. Rather than one's having to browse numerous sites maintained by smaller organizations or by individual activists, WorkNet significantly reduces search time by assembling vast amounts of data in one convenient location. The page also includes information not found anywhere else on the Web.

Browsing through the virtual resources provided by WorkNet as of early 2004, one finds a plethora of useful material: a searchable database containing information on employers in the private, public, educational, and nonprofit sectors, including whether or not they have gay-inclusive—and, most recently, transgender-inclusive—nondiscrimination policies, diversity training, domestic partner benefits, and/or lesbian, gay, bisexual, and transgender employee groups (and, if so, contact information); how-to guides for starting employee networks, establishing an "allies program," and winning equitable benefits or other inclusive policies; and biweekly editions of *HRC WorkNet News,* which provides e-mail updates on employer policies, employment legislation, and related court rulings. With the *Corporate Equality Index,* a new addition to HRC's employer database as of August 2002, visitors to the site can compare the numeric ratings of companies or entire industries based on whether they meet various criteria for ensuring workplace equality. I discuss this index in more detail in chapter 4, where I consider such benchmarking tools as important sources of mimetic isomorphism.

As a means of publicizing antigay bias and mobilizing support for federal passage of the Employment Non-discrimination Act, the WorkNet page also offers advice on how to persuade employers to endorse ENDA and provides updates on the status of the legislation, including endorsements by corporations and other organizations. The page invites those who have experienced workplace bias to share their experiences with HRC's *Documenting Discrimination* project, which has a secure online submission form that includes several questions and space for in-depth comments.

In addition to a searchable database of laws, legislation, and ballot initiatives that affect the rights of lesbian, gay, bisexual, and transgender people in and outside of the workplace, WorkNet publicizes the policies of U.S. senators and representatives regarding the employment of gays and lesbians as members of their staff. For those interested in contacting their legislators about workplace issues, WorkNet provides a link to HRC's online Action Center, which offers summaries of key legislative issues along with suggested talking points. Visitors to the page can modify sample correspondence or compose their own letters, which can be faxed for free to the appropriate parties by simply clicking *Send.*

Alternatively, one can access WorkNet to find out whether any boycotts are being waged against particularly hostile employers. Users can also read about the annual Out and Equal workplace conferences on gay, lesbian, bisexual, and transgender issues and other such events across the country. Other resources include a bibliography of books and magazine or journal articles on sexual orientation in the workplace, a listing of diversity trainers who specialize in gay issues, contact information for organizations providing lesbian and gay legal services, links to job search engines and workplace rating systems that focus on gay-friendly employers, and links to a wide variety of other workplace-related Web sites. These links are divided into categories such as news and general information, marketing, investment information, shareholder activism, gender issues, and business and professional associations. WorkNet also provides access to press releases and publications by HRC and HRCF, including the annual *State of the Workplace* and *Corporate Equality Index* reports and various organizing manuals, all of which can be downloaded for free.

Along with a brief description of HRC's corporate-focused Business Council, discussed later in this chapter, the WorkNet section on marketing features a link to the Commercial Closet, a nonprofit education and journalism project described as "the world's largest collection of gay advertising." Tracking sexual orientation issues in marketing within both mainstream media and the gay press, this site raises consciousness about how the lesbian, gay, bisexual, and transgender community has been represented by companies worldwide in approximately 750 advertisements over the last thirty years. Reflecting recent attempts by the larger movement to include transgender people and to seriously address discrimination on the basis of gender identity and gender expression, the WorkNet page also includes information on transgender issues and transitioning at work. The latter addresses how employers can accommodate those individuals who are undergoing a transition from male to female or vice versa. Finally, in addition to providing answers to a list of frequently asked questions, WorkNet contains an "Ask the Experts" section, where Internet users can submit questions on any workplace-related issue. Answers to these inquiries are then posted and divided into topics such as discrimination, domestic partner benefits, diversity issues, employee networks, shareholder activism, marketing and advertising, and advocating within companies for gay rights legislation.

Serving as an informational clearinghouse, the Internet offers crucial resources to employee activists on a twenty-four-hour basis. Without ever leaving their homes or cubicles, individuals can learn about the latest strategies, tactics, networking opportunities, and successes of the workplace movement. Before the rise of e-mail and the World Wide Web, gay and lesbian employees were far more likely to labor in relative isolation. They were therefore unable to capitalize on the lessons learned by activists who had mobilized in other workplace settings. As electronic mail and Internet access spread, so too did the sharing of strategic information. A virtually inexhaustible resource, cyberspace thus facilitated the mobilization and continued success of the workplace movement.

As new communication technologies diffused rapidly through the corporate world and then to individual computer owners, lesbian and gay employees quickly took advantage of the institutional opportunities they afforded. The virtual networks these activists built brought together formerly isolated individuals within companies, connected separate employee organizations across corporations and other employment sectors, and provided vast informational resources in a matter of seconds to anyone with a computer and modem.

While these communication innovations helped members of the workplace movement become more densely interconnected, activists did not depend on virtual networking alone. Staring at a computer screen is no substitute for the power of human contact. Anyone who has ever attended an activist-led event can testify to the profound impact of being with people who seem to live and breathe the tenets and promise of a movement.

The Birth of the Workplace Conference: The Great Mobilizer

Leaders of the workplace movement realized the importance of face-to-face interaction for stimulating interest, sharing strategies, celebrating successes, and maintaining commitment despite repeated setbacks. Thus was born the workplace conference. As mentioned in chapter 1, amid widespread press coverage of the Cracker Barrel firings in 1991, activists organized the first two conferences in the country on gay, lesbian, and bisexual workplace issues. These conferences, one on each coast, were a powerful mobilizing force for the movement. They energized individuals who had been previously inactive, deepened the dedication of employee activists, and extended the reach of the movement by catching the eye of the mainstream business press. Both conferences, preceded by a suddenly publicized grievance, served to educate corporate decision makers and activists as well as link previously secluded employee networks. Just as significant, the conferences whetted the appetite of individuals who had not yet mobilized in their places of work. Hungry for change, many returned to their companies and formed networks of their own.

The success of these early workplace conferences soon inspired employee activists to organize similar events at more local or regional levels. A few networks even began hosting what they call "professional development conferences" in their own companies, with workshops geared toward educating all employees about sexual orientation issues in the workplace. These events are a highly effective means of winning allies throughout a company. Organizers focus particularly hard on convincing executives to attend, some of whom become such strong supporters that they are featured speakers at future professional development conferences. Most workplace conferences, though, are targeted to a much wider audience consisting of employee activists and organizational decision makers from the corporate, nonprofit, and government sectors. Though organized predominantly by employee activists from corporate settings, these conferences both reflect and strengthen the interorganizational linkages that undergird the workplace movement.

The Workplace Conference as a Key Diffusion Mechanism and Local Movement Center

Borrowing from neoinstitutional theory, I view workplace conferences as key "diffusion mechanisms" or "central conduits" for the spread of organizational and tactical innovations (Strang and Meyer 1993, 498). Through their attendance at workplace conferences, activists acquire specialized knowledge and crucial organizing skills, such as how to effectively construct and deploy collective action frames in a corporate environment (Snow et al. 1986; Snow and Benford 1992). In a later chapter I will discuss the central importance of framing strategies for movement success. For now, it simply bears mentioning that workplace conferences play a central role in dispatching frames that are then carried into multiple organizational fields.

As movement scholars have pointed out, "personal and organizational networks provide mechanisms for harmonizing frames across institutional spheres" (Haydu 1999, 319). Thus, in bringing together individual activists and employee networks from various types of organizations, workplace conferences can be seen as "organizational transmission belts," with attendees serving as "carriers for isomorphic frames" (323). Bearing the seeds of change, conference participants return to different work sites across the country and carefully cultivate policy innovations that, while often strategically portrayed as being rooted in corporate "best practices," nevertheless stem from movement ideology.

Drawing on Aldon Morris's research that documents the importance of indigenous resources for mobilization (1984), I also view workplace conferences as "local movement centers" that bring activists and organizations together to articulate goals, develop tactical innovations, and provide training for both leaders and rank-and-file members. Emphasizing the significance of movement centers, Morris argues that "[t]he pace, location, and volume of protest in various communities are directly dependent on the quality and distribution of local movement centers" (284). Relatedly, I would posit that the effectiveness of challengers depends in part on whether they are connected to such movement centers. For example, I found that 58 percent of employee networks that attended workplace conferences (26 out of 45) were successful in their fight for equitable benefits, versus only 39 percent of nonattending groups (7 out of 18). Bearing in mind the far-reaching political, cultural, and mobilization outcomes (Staggenborg 1995) of these workplace conferences, I turn now to a more in-depth look at their origin, development, and content.

The Emergence and Development of the Workplace Conference

In the midst of the Cracker Barrel fury, in the fall of 1991, the Human Rights Campaign Fund (now HRC) and the New York City Lesbian and Gay Community Services Center cosponsored a national conference with the theme "Invisible Diversity: A Lesbian and Gay Corporate Agenda" (Freiberg 1991, 11). Organizers had sent invitations to the CEOs and human resource directors of 9,400 companies but received a disappointing number of responses (Stewart 1991, 56). Nonetheless, attendees included representatives from over 100 major corporations (Freiberg 1991, 11). In his brief descriptive look at workplace organizing, Wallace Swan (1997c, 27) noted how press coverage of the East Coast event helped to fuel the growth and diversification of the movement: "The power of the mass media to cover the activities of gays, lesbians, and bisexuals in workplace groups has been truly astonishing. The fact that the Human Rights Campaign Fund held a dinner where leading corporate representatives were invited to meet with hitherto closeted gays and lesbians from their workplaces resounded like a shot throughout the gay community nationwide, providing much of the impetus for workplace groups to begin throughout the country."

Also in the fall of 1991, but on the opposite coast, members of several gay employee networks in northern California organized the first annual Out and Equal in the '90s workplace conference. The brainchild of employee activists from major corporations in Silicon Valley and the San Francisco Bay area, this event likewise issued a resounding call for workplace activism. Held at San Francisco City College in October 1991, the first Out and Equal conference was a daylong affair that drew over 150 attendees from approximately thirty companies (Bain 1992c).

The event prompted several lesbian and gay employee activists in the San Francisco Bay area to organize an informal intercorporate network, which in 1992 became "formally constituted as an arm of NGLTF [the National Gay and Lesbian Task Force] and the nucleus of the NGLTF Work Place Initiative." In 1992 members of the initiative organized two workplace sessions at NGLTF's annual Creating Change conference, where plans were made for an early 1993 meeting during which activists considered the formation of a national organization of gay, lesbian, and bisexual employee networks that, if realized, would have fallen under the auspices of NGLTF (Bain 1992c, 4).

Reflecting both the rapidly expanding ranks of the workplace movement and the networking success of the Bay Area's intercorporate umbrella group, San Francisco's 1992 gay and lesbian Freedom Day Parade included a sizable number of gay employee networks. The "corporate contingent" of the march was 250 people strong, representing approximately sixty companies both within and outside of the Fortune 1000 (Bain 1992a). This sudden and highly visible increase in the number of workplace activists reveals the profound impact that the 1991 Out and Equal conference had on the movement.

Indeed, that first Out and Equal conference was considered such a success that it soon garnered the financial support and organizational resources of the larger gay rights movement and powerful players in the university and corporate sectors. In both 1992 and 1993, NGLTF cosponsored the conference with Stanford University (Bain 1992c). The 1992 conference, a two-day event held on Stanford's campus, was attended by 330 people from some ninety organizations, mostly corporations. At the 1993 conference, a highly successful fund-raiser for the NGLTF Workplace Organizing Project was held on the grounds of Apple Computer.

In 1994, NGLTF moved the conference to Denver in an attempt to increase attendance and broaden geographic representation. San Francisco was home to the next Out and Equal event, in 1996, and included a well-attended preconference, the Human Resources Institute, for executives and other personnel specialists. The following conference, in 1998, took place in Rochester, New York. By then responsibility for the event had passed to COLLEAGUES, an umbrella organization made up of gay employee networks from across the country. COLLEAGUES itself had originated during an earlier movement conference.

Reflecting the expanded interorganizational leadership of the workplace movement, the 1999 Out and Equal conference was a joint venture between COLLEAGUES and PROGRESS, another major umbrella organization focused on gay and lesbian workplace issues. Held in Atlanta, Georgia, the national conference bore the theme "Workplace Equality in the New Millennium." Attendees had a choice among three different "tracks," with sessions targeted to individual activists, gay employee networks, or human resource professionals. Seattle was home to the 2000 Out and Equal conference, and the following year's event took place right outside Cincinnati, a city that had received much media attention back in 1993, when voters passed a measure that barred the locale from enacting nondiscrimination protection for gays and lesbians. The conference organizers' decision to meet near but not in the city itself was meant as a form of protest against the antigay amendment and as a sign of support for the lesbian and gay community in the region.

Choosing Orlando as the site of the 2002 Out and Equal conference, organizers wanted to pay tribute to the Walt Disney Corporation's commitment to workplace equality and send a message to the mayor urging inclusion of sexual orientation in the city's nondiscrimination ordinance. Expanding the reach of the conference, organizers also began to make recordings of the annual summit available on compact disc. As further testament to the success of these conferences, in October 2002, HRC's WorkNet Web page listed not one but five workplace-related events scheduled over the next seven months. Each sponsored by a different organization, the events were slated for Dallas, Chicago, Columbus, Los Angeles, and New York. In 2003 the Out and Equal conference took place in Minneapolis, where the three-day event broke previous attendance records by attracting approximately six hundred people, who chose from sixty workshops. Tempe, Arizona, will host the 2004 summit, which is expected to be even larger.

The Workplace Conference as Movement Training Ground

The annual Out and Equal conference and similar gatherings foster dense linkages among previously isolated employees and activist networks. But, more than merely structural conduits for the emergence of interpersonal and interorganizational networks, they also function as conveyors of substantive and tactical information that challengers and sympathetic elites take home with them and put into practice in their own places of work. With workshop topics ranging from starting a gay employee group and creating allies to building coalitions and convincing executives of the need for gay-inclusive policies, the Out and Equal conferences provide information, training, and networking opportunities for individual activists, gay and lesbian employee groups, and human resources professionals from a wide variety of business, nonprofit, educational, and governmental organizations.

A sampling of the sessions offered at the 1996 Out and Equal conference, which I attended in San Francisco, reveals the specialized knowledge that these movement centers provide for both gay employee activists and corporate decision makers. At the preconference Human Resources Institute, executives and personnel professionals had a choice among morning sessions focused on domestic partner benefits, gay-inclusive diversity training, AIDS education, and a workshop called "Everything You've Always Wanted to Know about Sexual Orientation as a Diversity Issue But . . ." At lunch, attendees were educated and entertained by aha!, a group of professional performers who depicted heterosexist, sexist, and sexually harassing behaviors in the workplace. The afternoon lineup included sessions on working with a gay employee group; making lesbian, gay, and bisexual issues an integral part of all diversity programs; and "finding the words" to use in gay-inclusive diversity training (a train-the-trainer workshop).

Attendees also had the opportunity to view two videos useful for "teaching tolerance," one about parents of gays and lesbians and the other on the impact of homophobia on African American communities. Use of the latter video reflects the workplace movement's determination in recent years to acknowledge and challenge the interlocking nature of systems of oppression (P. Collins 1990, 2000). In response to the call of black feminists especially (see, e.g., Dill 1983; King 1988; P. Collins 1998), the lesbian and gay movement has begun to pay far greater attention to the "simultaneity" of penalty and privilege based on race, class, gender, and sexuality. Striving to overcome the tendency of many social movements to prioritize oppressions (Barnett 1999), the expanded focus of the workplace movement represents a conscious attempt to avoid an "exclusionary solidarity" (Ferree and Roth 1998, 629). This more integrative approach also bodes well for those employee activists engaged in coalition building, which scholars have argued is an important contributor to movement success (Ferree and Roth 1998; P. Collins 2000; Kurtz 2002).

In addition to numerous workshops, attendees at the Human Resources Institute gained valuable information from plenary sessions, which featured speakers from both human rights and corporate organizations. Reflecting what neoinstitutionalists would call the normative role of the sociolegal environment, which constructs certain organizational policies and practices as ethical and legitimate (Edelman and Suchman 1997), a representative from the San Francisco Human Rights Commission gave a speech titled "Preventing Sexual Orientation, AIDS/HIV, and Gender Identity Discrimination." Given the sometimes hostile reaction of corporate elites to the more coercive side of the legal system (Edelman and Suchman 1997), conference organizers made sure that the rest of the Human Resources Institute did not focus on legal arguments for gay-inclusive policies. Moreover, reliance on legal frames is an unreliable strategy, given the gaps and shifts in the law and the fact that numerous corporations operate in localities not covered by nondiscrimination ordinances.

Realizing the effectiveness of having an elite "insider" or powerful ally deliver the message of the movement, organizers of the Human Resources

Institute selected the vice president of human resources at Xerox Corporation to give the keynote address. His presentation was preceded by a videotaped message from the CEO of the company, whose words echoed the strategic framing of Xerox's own successful gay employee group: "Diversity is more than a moral imperative; it's a business necessity. It improves the bottom line." The vice president's talk heavily emphasized the profit-oriented reasons to adopt gay-inclusive policies, as summarized by the title of his keynote address, "A Total Pay Strategy to Support Workforce Diversity."

The next two days of the general Out and Equal conference included workshops for both human resource professionals and gay employee activists, some of the sessions repeating offerings from the preconference institute. With sessions too numerous to list here, I select only a few to illustrate the diversity and complexity of the issues covered. The first day included workshops on creating and strengthening employee networks; using e-mail and the Internet for workplace activism; and gaining corporate support for ENDA. Other workshops focused on how Disney's gay network won equitable benefits; how to build coalitions with unions and other workplace organizations; and how to mobilize organized labor to help fight the New Right. Another session concentrated on the workplace struggles faced by gays and lesbians of color, transgender employees, and lesbians in male-dominated fields. Having begun with keynote speaker Frank Kameny, a pioneer of the gay rights movement and of workplace activism, the day ended with a closing plenary session on coalition building.

The final day of the conference opened with a plenary address called "Same-Gender Marriage and Domestic Partner Benefits" and continued with another wide array of sessions. Some of the topics included career management advice for gays and lesbians; mentoring and preparing future leaders in the workplace movement; dealing with closeted people in positions of power; and using a database called the Lavender Screen. Developed by investment adviser Howard Tharsing, the Lavender Screen assesses the "gay-friendliness" of companies in terms of their nondiscrimination policies, diversity training, benefits policies, and other related criteria.

Serving as a potentially powerful diffusion mechanism (Strang and Meyer 1993), benchmarking tools such as the Lavender Screen are likely to facilitate mimetic isomorphism (DiMaggio and Powell 1991b). Aware of the comparisons that investors and consumers can now easily make by using these tools, corporate elites may feel increasing pressure to mimic the leaders in order to remain competitive. In the next chapter I will discuss such isomorphic processes in more detail, but what warrants emphasis here is the fact that workplace conferences not only serve as movement centers for the spread of tactical innovations (Morris 1984) but also play a role in larger institutional processes, since attendees, whether activists or corporate decision makers, acquire tools for tracking and interpreting changes in the wider organizational field (DiMaggio and Powell 1991b). What participants do with that knowledge once they return to their own organizations—and the transformations in policy that may result—changes the very organizational fields in which they and others act.

With each passing year, the Out and Equal conference has won the support of additional corporate sponsors and has drawn greater numbers of organizational decision makers as well as lesbian, gay, bisexual, and transgender activists. Since its inception, this annual event has contributed greatly to the size, strength, and diversity of the workplace movement. In addition to the strategic training that attendees gain, these conferences give activists a chance to come together in a safe space where they can seek solace in the face of setbacks and draw motivation from the victories won by others.

Serving as "organizational midwives" (McAdam 1994, 44), early workplace conferences also ushered in the birth of new employee groups and fostered the development of intercorporate networks at the local, regional, and national levels. The visible increase in employee mobilization, in turn, convinced leaders of the wider lesbian and gay movement to commit more resources to workplace activism. I now consider the launching of workplace-organizing projects by the two largest gay rights organizations in the United States and examine their impact on the workplace movement.

Workplace Projects: The Expanded Focus of the Larger Gay and Lesbian Rights Movement

The success of early conferences and the dedication of key leaders in the workplace movement led NGLTF and HRC to institute workplace-organizing projects in the early to mid-1990s. These projects expanded the resource base of the burgeoning workplace movement. They also brought greater publicity to the efforts of employee activists and to the willingness or resistance of employers to grant equality to their lesbian and gay workers. Given the well-recognized standing of NGLTF and HRC in the broader movement, these national projects were both indicators of and contributors to the institutionalization of the workplace movement.

NGLTF's Workplace-Organizing Project

Initiated in the early 1990s, NGLTF's Workplace Project, as it was officially called, was conceived by California activist George Kronenberger, who founded one of the earliest gay employee networks in the country and the first such group in the utilities industry, back in 1986. With his finger on the pulse of the movement and his eye on the political landscape, this central activist figure correctly predicted that the next frontier for lesbian and gay rights would occur not in the legislature but in the workplace, with the pioneering efforts of gay employee groups leading the way (Vaid 1995, 10). Although Kronenberger died of AIDS-related complications in late 1994, he left behind a strong foundation on which the workplace movement continues to build. To honor his legacy, NGLTF established the George Kronenberger Memorial Award, which is bestowed on a gay and lesbian employee organization or workplace activist during the annual Out and Equal conference.

At the urging of Kronenberger and other core activists in the workplace movement, NGLTF initiated its workplace-organizing project to determine how "influence [could] be brought to bear on corporations so that they would see equal treatment for their gay employees as a matter of urgent concern" (D. Baker, Strub, and Henning 1995, x). As one of its earliest project-sponsored activities, NGLTF mailed a survey to Fortune 1000 companies in 1993 inquiring about the existence of gay employee networks and gay-inclusive policies and practices.

These efforts resulted in the publication of the book *Cracking the Corporate Closet: The 200 Best (and Worst) Companies to Work For, Buy From, and Invest In if You're Gay or Lesbian—and Even If You Aren't* (D. Baker, Strub, and Henning 1995). Because the book was published by HarperBusiness, a division of HarperCollins, it reached a much wider audience than a movement-issued document would have. In the book's appendix, the authors included contact information for almost forty gay and lesbian employee groups located in Fortune 1000 companies. The visibility that the book generated for the workplace movement furthered the density of connections among employee networks.

As part of the Workplace Project, NGLTF also began to sponsor the annual Out and Equal workplace conference. In addition, the organization instituted several sessions on the workplace at its annual Creating Change conference. While that conference covers a wide variety of gay rights issues not limited to employment, it is telling that in the mid-1990s organizers decided to offer separate workplace-related tracks, one for beginners and another for advanced attendees. The message of the workplace movement thus spreads further as attendance at Creating Change increases each year. The record-breaking turnout of 2,500 at the 1999 conference portended an even wider audience in the years ahead (NGLTF 2000).

In addition to providing support for workplace conferences and for workplace sessions at general conferences, NGLTF publishes various items that are of direct use to employee activists. For example, in 1999 the NGLTF Policy Institute released the 140-page *Domestic Partnership Organizing Manual for Employee Benefits* (Kohn 1999), an update of a 1992 version by Ivy Young. Other national lesbian and gay rights organizations, including the National Center for Lesbian Rights and the Lambda Legal Defense and Education Fund, have published similar manuals (Roberts and Dettmer 1992; LLDEF 1994).

WorkNet: HRC's Workplace Project

Established in 1995 and commonly referred to as WorkNet, the workplace project of HRC was inaugurated by Elizabeth Birch with the support of HRCF. As executive director of HRC, Birch headed the largest gay rights organization in the country. Birch earned some of her activist stripes in the workplace movement. As corporate legal counsel for Apple in the early 1990s, she decided to join efforts with the gay and lesbian employee network, which had been trying to persuade the company to offer domestic partner benefits. The network succeeded in 1993, making Apple one of the earliest corporate adopters of equitable benefits. Significantly, that year marked a shift in the locus of policy change, as the majority of adopters ever since have been companies rather than universities or municipalities. Having been part of the upper ranks of corporate America, Birch was known for her ability to speak the language of the business elite without pulling any punches. Her experience and skills informed the ongoing activities of WorkNet, which provides assistance to hundreds of individuals and corporations each year (HRC 1998).

Announcing the foundation of WorkNet, then called the Workplace Project, in the fall of 1995, an article in *HRC Quarterly* (HRC 1995c) summarized its main objectives:

> To enlist leading companies and employers to endorse ENDA, or adopt "sexual orientation" as a specific category under their written non-discrimination guidelines. To recruit corporate executives, gay and non-gay, to publicly endorse ENDA, and to cooperate with HRC in delivering congressional testimony and support. To document and reveal verifiable accounts of job discrimination. To significantly expand HRC's data and relationships concerning gay and lesbian employee groups, and enlist their aid as allies. To co-sponsor and facilitate workplace organizing conferences involving gay and lesbian support groups as a direct means of building grassroots support.

Overseen by HRC's education director, Kim Mills, and WorkNet's deputy director, Daryl Herrschaft, the WorkNet project offers valuable assistance to employee activists and to corporate management. For many of the individuals seeking HRC's help, the first point of contact is through WorkNet's Web page (HRC 1998). As discussed earlier, this page serves as an informational clearinghouse for workplace-related materials. Compared to other workplace sites, WorkNet is unparalleled in scope and accessibility. Even those without Internet access can benefit from at least some of the virtual resources provided by WorkNet. By signing up for e-mail alerts from HRC, individuals receive, among other announcements, *WorkNet News,* an online newsletter that provides biweekly updates on gay-related workplace issues. This newsletter covers setbacks and successes in the private and public employment sectors, in local, state, and federal legislatures, and in the courts. The final segment of each report lists the employers that have recently adopted domestic partner benefits.

HRC also spreads the message of the movement by including workplace features in its membership publications. For example, in a 1999 *HRC Quarterly* article (Cromwell and Harris), two members of HRC's Business Council highlighted the successful efforts of lesbian and gay networks at Hewlett-Packard Company and BankBoston. In response to employee activism, both companies adopted gay-inclusive nondiscrimination policies and extended benefits to domestic partners. At the end of the article, the authors enumerate goals and strategies that can be adopted by gay employee networks. They also provide a list of policies and practices that employers can institute to ensure an inclusive, equitable, and profitable environment. Serving as a diffusion mechanism (Strang and Meyer 1993) for the spread of workplace activism, these types of articles alert a half-million HRC members to the possibilities and promise of employee mobilization.

Another contribution of WorkNet can be found in the publication of its annual report *The State of the Workplace for Lesbian, Gay, Bisexual and Transgender Americans,* the 2001 version of which contained forty single-spaced pages (HRCF 2001b). This resource, which can be downloaded without charge, is replete with useful charts and tables. The text centers on several key areas: nondiscrimination laws that include sexual orientation; laws prohibiting discrimination on the basis of gender identity; laws on domestic partner benefits and domestic partner registries; right-wing attempts, whether through the courts or at the ballot box, to overturn employment protections and equitable-benefits laws; nondiscrimination policies and/or domestic partner benefits implemented by employers in the corporate, educational, and government sectors; shareholder activism; and court rulings on lawsuits

brought by lesbian and gay plaintiffs, laws that prohibit employment discrimination, and laws that address domestic partner benefits.

While WorkNet clearly offers a plenitude of informational resources
via its Web page, e-mail distribution service, and hard-copy publications,
the workplace project extends far beyond the virtual and textual realms.
WorkNet staff provide individualized assistance to employee activists and
to corporate executives who are considering inclusive policy changes. As
WorkNet's deputy director, Daryl Herrschaft, explains, "For many workplace
advocates, being able to find out what other companies in their industry
or state are doing is often critical to making a compelling case for change.
We can help tailor information for individuals, gay and lesbian employee
groups or human resources departments." WorkNet also provides sample
proposals for domestic partner benefits, data on policy-adoption costs,
news articles on inclusive policy changes, and lists of insurance carriers
that will write policies for employers wishing to cover domestic partners.
In some cases, requests for assistance are referred to the HRC Business
Council, "whose members have expertise in this area and can advise employers and employees" (HRC 1998).

The Advocacy Work of the HRC Business Council

HRC established its Business Council in 1997 in an attempt to exert a more
direct influence on corporations. The volunteer group meets at least twice
a year and consists of "25 leaders from corporate America" who have been
highly active in the workplace movement (HRC 1999a; 2001). Members
include seasoned employee activists; leaders of regional or national umbrella
organizations; diversity professionals, financial consultants, and marketing
experts who specialize in lesbian, gay, bisexual, or transgender workplace
issues; and others with a wide range of experience in the business world.
Besides its advocacy work inside particular companies, where members work
with executives and, when applicable, gay employee groups, the Business
Council serves as a brain trust that helps HRC decide on such key issues as
whether to support a boycott or join a shareholder campaign (HRC 2001).
The council also works to secure corporate endorsements of ENDA; in
2001, for example, members succeeded in winning support from fourteen
companies.

At a meeting in February 1999, council members decided to "conduct
direct advocacy in at least 10 companies in selected industries or market
sectors." The Business Council chose its targets on the basis of a system
that members had created "to rate companies' readiness to adopt more inclusive policies toward gay and lesbian workers." After selecting the corpo-

rations, "council members then volunteered to be the point person for key industries and to develop strategies for working within those industries" (HRC 1999a).

To better prepare volunteers for this advocacy work, the Business Council dedicated the first half of its two-day meeting to a training session conducted by Brian McNaught. Probably the best-known and most highly respected diversity consultant in the workplace movement, McNaught has worked with numerous corporations. He conducts employee workshops on homophobia in the workplace and meets directly with executives about the need for and profitability of gay-inclusive policies. As an openly gay man and independent diversity professional with ties to both corporate and activist networks, McNaught resembles what Belinda Robnett (1997) has called a "bridge leader." In her study of African American women in the civil rights movement, Robnett defines bridge leadership as "an intermediate layer of leadership, whose tasks include bridging potential constituents and adherents . . . to the movement" (191).

Particularly adept at such bridging work, McNaught is highly acclaimed for his ability to win allies and to create outspoken supporters out of even some of the most reluctant heterosexuals. Workplace activists praise his gift for convincing—indeed, inspiring—executives to institute gay-inclusive policies. It is thus no surprise that HRC invited McNaught to train members of the Business Council before they headed out to the corporations they had decided to target. HRC's then executive director, Elizabeth Birch, who attended both days of the Business Council meeting, commented on the purpose of McNaught's session: "His carefully crafted presentation helped to sharpen members' skills and abilities so that when they have to meet with a CEO or a gay employee resource group, they will make the best case for fairness" (HRC 1999a).

Business Council members were thus well trained for the advocacy work that awaited them. One of the sectors in which members first put this new strategy into practice was the airline industry, where not one company had adopted equitable benefits. Hoping to change the industry's intransigence, Business Council members and WorkNet staff worked directly with United with Pride and GLEAM, the gay employee networks at United Airlines and American Airlines, respectively (HRC 2000b). These networks had been trying for years to convince their employers to extend benefits coverage to domestic partners. In the fall of 1999, both companies finally agreed to do so, joining the ranks of over 2,800 other U.S. employers in the corporate, university, and public service sectors.

United Airlines was the first in the industry to adopt the benefits.

Illustrating a pattern of mimetic isomorphism (DiMaggio and Powell 1991b), American Airlines quickly followed suit, with US Airways close behind. The companies' announcements came within days of each other and brought the total number of Fortune 500 adopters to 71. As discussed in chapter 4, United Airlines' decision was also influenced by a boycott in the gay community and a federal court ruling. Nonetheless, it seems likely that HRC's Business Council, in partnership with employee activists, played an important role in effecting these groundbreaking changes in the industry. As part of its strategic targeting of particular market sectors, the council also helped to win policy transformations in the Big Five accounting firms (HRC 2001).

Sometimes corporate elites themselves approach HRC for assistance. "People at all levels of corporate America have learned to trust HRC's research and counsel with regard to GLBT workplace issues," explains education director Kim Mills. "From line workers to CEOs, they come to us when they are thinking about domestic partner benefits, non-discrimination policies, marketing to the gay community—the whole range of workplace issues that impact GLBT employees" (HRC 2000c). HRC has also helped companies defend against right-wing attacks. In March 2000 the New Mexico Christian Coalition filed a document with the state's Public Regulation Commission arguing that US West could charge telephone customers cheaper rates if the company did not provide domestic partner benefits. The group called the benefits, which were adopted at the urging of the company's lesbian and gay network, a "social experiment" that "contributes to a civil health hazard" by promoting the spread of AIDS and other sexually transmitted diseases (HRC 2000c). The filing, which also argued that the gay community is prone to violence and child molestation, requested that the commission investigate "the social implications of this heinous US West policy." "The partners of homosexuals shouldn't have the right to get benefits from a monopoly when I have no other choice [for service]," argued the group's executive director (gfn.com 2000d).

Thus, besides trying to reverse the legal gains that gays and lesbians have achieved, and in addition to targeting inclusive employers with boycotts or other forms of protest, the New Right has begun to ask the state to intervene directly in order to prevent companies from adopting gay-affirmative policies. Commenting on this strategy, HRC's Daryl Herrschaft noted, "It was an avenue of attack on a domestic partner policy that I hadn't before seen. My reaction was to call the company [US West] immediately and see what help HRC could provide them." His efforts were facilitated by connections that had already been established by HRC's Business Council during a period when US West was being considered for acquisition by two companies that had not adopted equitable benefits. Accepting HRC's offer of assistance, US West asked the organization to "file testimony rebutting the Christian Coalition's falsehoods and detailing the evidence that domestic partner benefits are actually good for business" (HRC 2000c). After drafting supportive testimony, Herrschaft worked in concert with US West attorneys and HRC's general counsel and legal director to file the document. Two months after the struggle began, the Public Regulation Commission threw out the Christian Coalition's case.

In sum, responding to many employee activists, in the early to mid-1990s national gay rights organizations began to focus more of their attention on workplace issues. Through their workplace organizing projects, NGLTF and HRC contributed time, money, space, organizational expertise, and publicity to the workplace movement. And by supporting early conferences, both of these national organizations helped lesbian and gay employees meet face-to-face, where they formed lasting connections and solidified their commitment to equality at work. As organizational mid-wives (McAdam 1994), the workplace conferences inspired the uninitiated to form networks of their own and encouraged more experienced employee activists to build umbrella groups at the local, regional, and national levels. Activists thus became more densely interconnected as they attended conferences and built coalitions of workplace groups that spanned the corporate, university, and government sectors.

While workplace conferences were the birthplace of many umbrella groups, additional coalitions were born from national movement events not related to the workplace. Conferences served as key mobilizers and provided important networking venues for activists, but they failed to reach individuals and employee networks that were not already hooked into such movement centers. Wanting to bring more of these isolated groups into the fold, a few leading activists in the workplace movement developed a new strategy. They decided to take advantage of the enormous networking opportunity afforded by a national march and cultural events in the wider gay and lesbian community.

Capitalizing on National Events in the Larger Gay and Lesbian Movement

In 1994 a few friends who were active in the gay employee networks at their New York– and Connecticut-based companies began discussing the upcoming Gay Games and Stonewall 25 March, scheduled to coincide in Manhattan later that year. The Gay Games, held every four years, serve as the Olympics of the gay community and are intended to showcase its world-class athletes. The Stonewall 25 March was organized to honor the twenty-fifth anniversary of the riots that erupted on the night of June 27, 1969, outside the Stonewall Inn, a Greenwich Village gay bar that had been raided one too many times by police. Considered a watershed event, the rebellion gave rise to the modern gay liberation movement (Adam 1995).

Realizing the vast networking potential that Stonewall 25 and the Gay Games held for workplace activists, this small circle of friends began strategizing jointly. As one of the activists explained to me in an interview, "We said this is a *great* opportunity where there will be a million gay, lesbian, and bisexual people, but we knew we needed a space where people could exchange business cards and talk about what their companies were doing regarding gay and lesbian issues." The friends decided to rent the gym of the Gay and Lesbian Community Center in Manhattan. They called the *Advocate,* a national newsmagazine for the lesbian and gay community, which agreed to provide refreshments. The activists sent about a hundred promotional flyers to those companies that, they had heard, had either a gay employee group or a diversity office. They also contacted NGLTF and posted announcements to various organizations and Listservs on the Internet.

Based on the response they received before the networking event, organizers expected about forty people and so planned to charge ten dollars a person to cover the cost of the rental space. Much to their surprise and delight, over four hundred people showed up, from over 170 companies. Organizers had asked two people to give a five-minute introduction: Ed Mickens, author of *The 100 Best Companies for Gay Men and Lesbians* (1994a) and editor of a newsletter on gay issues in the corporate workplace called *Working It Out*; and Karen Wickery, cofounder of Digital Queers. Some employee networks also tried to set up information booths in the gym, but the size of the crowd made it difficult. One of the organizers explained, "It was a madhouse. People were standing on chairs and tables, and others were lined up outside the door because there wasn't enough room. It was a beautiful thing!" Commenting on the geographic diversity of the attendees, she continued, "We met gays, lesbians, and bisexuals from companies across the country. . . . It was incredibly empowering."

Staff members from NGLTF asked people to fill out cards listing their contact information so that they could build a database of employee activist networks. Unfortunately, the cards were lost, but the informal connections that activists made at the event ensured that the networking continued. As one of the coordinators explained in our interview,

> We as individuals had exchanged business cards and made so many contacts that, through informal networks and e-mail, we could let people know about the next NGLTF workplace conference. As a result, the

conference got bigger and more diverse, and companies that normally wouldn't be represented there started coming. And local and regional umbrella groups started forming after that in places that didn't have them before. . . . Through these regional organizations, we [workplace activists] gained some power and authority. Plus [the umbrella groups] help with job contacts!

Thus, from the vision of a few activist friends grew coalitions of employee groups that drew wider circles of activists into local movement centers (Morris 1984). Boosting attendance at workplace conferences and generating a greater number of umbrella groups, this Manhattan event increased the size, diversity, and organizational connectedness of the workplace movement.

Given the declining organizational birthrate among the Fortune 1000 in the late 1990s (see chapter 2), some might question the future stability of the workplace movement. But this stance ignores the movement's extensive infrastructure, which consists of not only the workplace projects of the nation's two largest gay rights organizations but also numerous umbrella groups. These support systems help buttress the workplace movement, thereby ensuring its staying power in the decades to come.

Umbrella Organizations: Opening Up Networking Opportunities and Strengthening Movement Infrastructure

By umbrella groups I mean coalitions of gay employee networks from multiple institutional settings. Some of these interorganizational networks began as informal get-togethers and largely remain such, while others are structured more formally. Whether local, regional, or national, these umbrella groups provide open channels for the exchange of information and the sharing of strategies and tactics. They also build solidarity among widely dispersed activists, offering a space where individuals can meet outside of their workplaces and develop a sense of connection to the larger workplace movement.

Expanding Umbrellas: From Local to Regional to National

As already discussed, workplace conferences played a big part in establishing connections among employee activists. But because they have typically occurred just once a year, conferences have provided only a narrow window for networking. Useful as these temporal opportunities are, their time-bound nature revealed the need for more frequent and geographically rooted means of connection. In their search for more routinized opportunities for networking, activists began to form umbrella groups. These coalitions brought gay employee networks together at the local, regional, and national levels. Local umbrella groups provide the most frequent avenues for face-to-face networking, since they consist of networks located in the same city or surrounding municipalities. There are numerous local umbrella groups scattered across the country.

One of the most active and highly visible of these local coalitions is AGOG (A Group of Groups), which formed in the San Francisco Bay area in June 1994. Leaders of AGOG were instrumental in establishing a wider alliance of workplace groups called the Pride Collaborative. Signaling the further institutionalization of the workplace movement, the Collaborative won the financial support of the United Way. Members of AGOG also became active in PROGRESS, which began in California in 1995 as the first statewide coalition of gay employee groups.

More than seventy workplace networks attended the first annual PROGRESS Leadership Summit in 1995, where activists decided that PROGRESS would be, as its informational materials now note, "dedicated to making the American workplace safe and equitable for lesbian, gay, transgender, and bisexual people." To allow for more frequent and more personal interaction among members, leaders established chapters, referred to as regionals, in places such as San Diego, Los Angeles, Sacramento, and San Francisco. Activists from several smaller cities joined forces to establish regionals in other areas, such as Orange County, the Central Coast, and the Lower Central Valley. Leaders described regionals as "the backbone of the organization."

In the "PROGRESS Packs" that the organization distributes, a brochure lists some of the resources available to individuals, networks, and interested employers: "Documents on starting and running a network of les/bi/gay/trans coworkers in [the] workplace. Examples of corporate non-discrimination policies and how they were achieved. Diversity Training Curricula. Manuals and examples of Domestic Partners Benefits organizing. A Quarterly Newsletter and pamphlets on timely issues. Website including domestic partner database and reference library. A library of information including: articles and books on les/bi/gay/trans workplace issues." Other resources include a speakers' bureau and, as a brochure describes, a mentoring program that "links emerging Employee Resource Groups with well-established ones to assist in their development and growth." A referral service provides lists of diversity and benefits consultants, community and legal service organizations, and other regional and local employee networks.

Leaders of PROGRESS have been particularly proud of the Leadership Summit, which publicity materials tout as an opportunity for activists to "network with representatives from other employee resource groups, learn management and leadership skills, and explore models of working together and building bridges." Attempting to expand the geographic reach of PROGRESS and to tap an "underorganized" region of the country, organizers chose Dallas, Texas, as the site for the third annual Leadership Summit, in March 1998. By then conference attendance had grown so large and so organizationally diverse that leaders instituted two tracks to accommodate "both the novice and experienced leader."

As additional umbrella groups emerged at the local and regional levels, key activists in the workplace movement began to discuss the formation of a national umbrella organization. Seeking wider input, they decided to hold a daylong organizational and brainstorming meeting at the NGLTF Creating Change conference in the spring of 1996. While the conference itself was not focused on the workplace, the "workplace room" was packed with over fifty people and eventually moved to a larger space as others dropped in throughout the day. At the meeting, representatives of gay employee networks from across the country debated the feasibility and purpose of a national federation. Those present eventually agreed that, aside from increasing the visibility of the workplace movement, a national organization would be taken more seriously by corporate and government elites. Reconvening after splitting into smaller brainstorming groups, activists then came to a consensus about mission, structure, and strategies.

Choosing the name COLLEAGUES, organizers quickly drew up a letter announcing the establishment of the organization. They distributed the letter to all conference participants and attached a survey to tap the interest of attendees and to gather recommendations for the resources that COLLEAGUES should provide. Noting that lesbian, gay, bisexual, and transgender employee groups "are appearing everywhere . . . and making an impact far beyond the workplace," the letter explained the motivation behind COLLEAGUES: "We believe the time is right for one organization to service the needs of all LGBT employee efforts to end discrimination in the workplace."

Although a cause for much heated debate, organizers made a strategic decision to structure the organization on the basis of a corporate model, which they believed would bring them greater legitimacy in the eyes of elites. Describing the purpose and form that the national umbrella group would take, the letter read:

> COLLEAGUES is more than another national organization. Our vision
> is to have this organization be a "For Profit" venture that incorporates

and sells shares to LGBT groups and individuals. As the organization
succeeds, so [do] its customers and shareholders. COLLEAGUES will
offer many products and services, such as kits on "How to start a LGBT
employee group, tips to writing your constitution and bylaws, and holding National Professional Development conferences." Our desire is to fill
a gap in the services and products needed to insure the success of achiev-
ing a fair and SAFE workplace for everyone!

Such mirroring of corporate discourse and practices, while rare in degree,
is a manifestation of what Frank Dobbin (2001) has called "the business of
social movements."

In 1998 COLLEAGUES took over responsibility for the annual Out
and Equal national workplace conference, which had previously been coordinated under the auspices of NGLTF. Deciding to combine the Out
and Equal conference and the PROGRESS Leadership Summit, organizers
held the first annual Out and Equal Leadership Summit in October 1999.
In 2000, leaders of several umbrella groups voted to join forces, calling
the new national collaborative Out and Equal Workplace Advocates, commonly referred to as simply Out and Equal. The organization's title reflects
the powerful mobilizing momentum that the very first Out and Equal
conference generated, back in 1991. The annual conference, now referred
to as the Out and Equal Workplace Summit, is organized by Out and
Equal Workplace Advocates. That new umbrella organization drew together
several preexisting umbrella groups, including COLLEAGUES and the
Pride Collaborative, which had formed in 1998 and consisted of still other
umbrella groups, such as AGOG, PROGRESS, and Building Bridges, an
organization that offered gay and lesbian sensitivity training to agencies
funded by the United Way.

While many other local and regional umbrella groups have formed
across the country, the cases I have selected here document a typical devel-
opmental process. They also provide a good sample of the types of resources
and services that workplace coalitions provide to individual activists, networks, and employers. Whether employee groups join local, regional, or
national coalitions, survey data show that such participation significantly
improves their chances of winning gay-inclusive policies. For example, as of
late 1998, when data collection on gay employee groups ended, 58 percent
of the corporate networks that belonged to one or more umbrella groups
had succeeded in obtaining equitable benefits (33 out of 57), compared
to only 36 percent of the networks that were not coalition participants
(4 out of 11).

Umbrella Groups as Social Movement Abeyance Structures: Weathering Storms in the Political Arena and Other Institutional Environments

In addition to facilitating favorable policy outcomes, umbrella groups provide ongoing support to those networks that have been less successful in their fight for equality at work. As abeyance structures (Taylor 1989), umbrella groups help employee activists persevere against the forces of corporate inertia and internal backlash. They also help challengers withstand hostile conditions in their wider institutional environments, including the relevant organizational field and broader sociopolitical context. Thus, as employee networks join forces across cities, states, and wider geographic regions, they strengthen the infrastructure and safeguard the survival of the workplace movement as a whole.

Verta Taylor's conceptualization of abeyance structures (1989) has expanded scholarly understandings of social movement continuity. Drawing on her and Leila Rupp's study of the American women's rights movement during the "doldrum" years (Rupp and Taylor [1987] 1990), Taylor explains how abeyance structures help mass movements survive amid "a nonreceptive political and social environment" ([1989] 1993, 436). Although usually applied to movements that face tightened political opportunities at the macro level, Taylor's framework can be fruitfully extended to meso-level restrictions that challengers face in their more immediate institutional surroundings. Taking both of these levels into account, I argue that umbrella groups function as abeyance structures in two spheres of contention: they shelter employee networks in the face of a hostile corporate or institutional climate; and they sustain the workplace movement as a whole during bouts of stormy weather in the wider sociopolitical environment.

Umbrella groups keep hope alive even among gay employee networks whose struggle for equitable policies has stretched over the course of a decade with nary a victory in sight. As Taylor explains, abeyance structures help movements endure by "promoting the survival of activist networks, sustaining a repertoire of goals and tactics, and promoting a collective identity that offers participants a sense of mission and moral purpose" ([1989] 1993, 436). Fulfilling all of these functions, umbrella groups assure that the workplace movement will carry on despite repeated disappointments and setbacks.

In addition to offering activists specialized skills, these multinetwork organizations serve another important abeyance function. Through their participation in umbrella groups, activists build a social movement culture that provides meaning, ideological justification, and affective support for their social change efforts (Taylor 1989). Though largely intangible, these cultural resources are crucial for sustaining activist commitment (McAdam 1994).

They help individuals continue with the hard and risky work of challenging the status quo, even when the established order seems impervious to change.

Participants in umbrella groups engage in a wide variety of culture-building activities. Depending on the geographic scope of the workplace coalition, members might meet for happy hour, hold "pride power breakfasts," host holiday parties with humorous skits and celebratory awards, or use workplace conferences as opportunities for renewing long-distance friendships or rekindling old flames. Although many individual networks also create strong activist subcultures in their own companies, umbrella groups help to construct a diffuse yet cohesive movement culture that spans a wider social movement community (see also Buechler 1990; McAdam 1994). By strengthening the bonds among and between individual activists and employee networks, and by fulfilling important symbolic and expressive functions (Taylor 1989), this culture nourishes the lifeblood of the workplace movement. In so doing, it extends the movement's longevity and fortifies its power to effect change in workplaces across the country.

Summary

As the interorganizational linkages among employee activists multiplied and grew increasingly dense in the early to mid-1990s, the workplace movement gained a stronger foothold on the institutional landscape. Drawing on the resources and tools provided by newly available communication technologies, early workplace conferences, and the workplace projects of national gay rights organizations, activists built a sturdy infrastructure consisting of expansive virtual networks as well as local, regional, and national umbrella groups. This infrastructure has helped to sustain the movement amid hostile conditions in the corporate and sociopolitical climates. Of course, the environment does not simply pose obstacles for organizational challengers; it can also provide considerable aid.

I thus turn now to the contextual conditions that constitute favorable institutional opportunities for workplace activists. In chapters 4 and 5, I present what I call a multilevel "institutional opportunity framework." Focusing on the multiple and nested environments in which activist networks are embedded, I highlight the beneficial impact of various elements in corporatations, their surrounding organizational fields, and the wider sociopolitical arena. While I have concentrated thus far on the emergence and development of the workplace movement, the remainder of the book focuses on the institutional and movement processes that facilitate policy success, particularly the adoption of equitable benefits.

4

Winds of Change outside Corporate Walls:
External Factors Influence Gay-Inclusive Policies

In the next two chapters I delineate the elements of a multilevel *institutional opportunity framework* to highlight the contextual conditions that facilitate favorable policy outcomes for institutional activists. Born from the fruitful synthesis of a neoinstitutional perspective on organizational change and a political opportunity approach to social movements, the theoretical model I present offers a systematic framework for understanding how the multiple and heterogeneous environments of challengers can aid and/or constrain the fight for institutional transformation.

To explain organizational change, neoinstitutionalist Neil Fligstein (1991), although not focused on activism, directs attention to the multiple arenas in which power relations get played out. He posits three "institutional spheres" that either constrain or facilitate organizational actors: the current structure and strategy of the *target organization*; the *organizational field* comprising those actors that the focal organization deems relevant to its sphere of activity, such as competitors, suppliers, and consumers; and the *state* (see also DiMaggio and Powell 1991b).

Taking into account these "nested" institutional spheres (see also D. Meyer 2003), I examine the *sociopolitical, field,* and *organizational settings* of activist networks. For each of these spheres, I lay out the key structural and processual elements that operate as institutional opportunities for challengers and thereby facilitate gay-inclusive policy change, particularly the adoption of domestic partner benefits. This chapter focuses on macro-level opportunities in the sociopolitical and field environments, while the next chapter concentrates on meso-level opportunities present in challengers' more immediate organizational settings, meaning targeted corporations themselves.

With an eye on external pressures, new institutional approaches prove useful for understanding how a policy innovation, such as a gay-inclusive benefits package, diffuses across various organizations and eventually becomes institutionalized. A focal concern of new institutional theory centers on how organizations come to resemble each other in form and policy, or, more specifically, "how groups of firms develop shared beliefs, structures, practices, strategies, and networks of relations" (Lant and Baum 1995, 16). Institutional scholars attribute this "homogenization" outcome to *isomorphism,* which Paul DiMaggio and Walter Powell (1991b, 66) define as "a constraining process that forces one unit in a population to resemble other units that face the same set of environmental conditions."

In this chapter I discuss the role that isomorphic processes play in the diffusion of equitable benefits among Fortune 1000 companies. These isomorphic processes function as favorable opportunities, in that challengers are more likely to succeed when their target organization faces external pressures that encourage inclusive policies. Adapting DiMaggio and Powell's model of isomorphic change mechanisms (1991b; see also Scott 1995b), I conceptualize the following processes as *macro-level institutional opportunities*: *coercive isomorphism,* which stems from legal and political pressures such as nondiscrimination statutes, lawsuits, boycotts, and shareholder activism; *mimetic isomorphism,* which originates from field-level influences such as competitive benchmarking, interlocking directorates, and intercorporate employee transfers; and *normative and cognitive isomorphism,* which results from the publications and consulting work of diversity professionals, particularly those who focus on lesbian and gay issues, and from the wider cultural diffusion of change-oriented frames and discourses.

In chapter 5 I adapt Sidney Tarrow's state-centered political process approach (1996, 1998) and the new literature on cultural opportunities (McAdam 1994; Johnston and Klandermans 1995; Taylor 1996) to delineate the proximate or *meso-level institutional opportunities* that exist within the immediate environment of institutional activists. More specifically, I focus on the facilitative impact of four key elements in the target organization itself (here, the corporation), which, if present, promote the adoption of gay-inclusive policies. These components constitute challengers' *organizational-level opportunities*: *structural templates* that provide access to decision makers and to institutional resources; *organizational realignments* that bring more receptive elites or organizations into the issue domain; *allies* who provide assistance as individuals or as coalition partners; and *cultural supports* such as a diversity-embracing corporate culture or, among elites, preexisting personal ties and "punctuating experiences" that foster empathetic understanding of challengers. Providing a brief visual summary of this multilevel institutional opportunity framework, Figure 3 in the conclusion of this book lists the key dimensions of institutional opportunity that exist for challengers within both the macro and meso levels of their environment.

Sociopolitical and Field-Level Opportunities: The Impact of Isomorphic Change Mechanisms

Drawing from DiMaggio and Powell's work on isomorphic change mechanisms (1991b), which have also been called "institutionalization mechanisms" (Lant and Baum 1995), I turn now to a consideration of the coercive, mimetic, normative, and cognitive processes that constitute favorable macro-level institutional opportunities for gay employee networks. In each case, before conducting my interviews I predicted that challengers would be more likely to win equitable benefits when their employers were also facing isomorphic pressures emanating from the sociopolitical and/or organizational field environments.

Coercive Isomorphism as Institutional Opportunity: Legal and Political Pressures

Coercive isomorphism refers to formal and informal pressures that are placed on organizations by the state and by expectations in the wider sociopolitical and cultural arenas (DiMaggio and Powell 1991b). With regard to the struggle for worker rights, the legal and political environment can exert direct or indirect influence on organizations. Subjected to such pressures, organizations may adopt new policies to demonstrate compliance or good faith and thus obtain legitimacy in the eyes of the state, other organizations, and the public (J. Meyer and Rowan 1977; Dobbin et al. 1993; Chaves 1997; Guthrie and Roth 1999; Kelly and Dobbin 1999; Knoke 2001). For example, institutional scholars have found that organizations closer to the public sphere, such as companies with federal contracts or firms located in heavily regulated industries, are more vulnerable to governmental scrutiny and hence more likely to have been early adopters of due process, equal employment opportunity, and affirmative action policies (Tolbert and Zucker 1983; Dobbin et al. 1988; Edelman 1990, 1992; Sutton and Dobbin 1996; Dobbin and Sutton 1998).

The adoption of domestic partner benefits, however, presents an interesting theoretical and empirical challenge to this body of work, in that companies have instituted these changes in the *absence* of any federal, state, or local legislation that would mandate equitable benefits. The first of only a handful of exceptions to this pattern is San Francisco's 1997 Equal Benefits Ordinance, which I will discuss presently. Moreover, other forms of gay-inclusive policy change, such as protections against employment discrimination, are also diffusing far more rapidly in the corporate world than in the state arena. As of mid-February 2004, gay men and lesbians had no legal protections against private-sector job discrimination outside of 14 states (California, Connecticut, Hawaii, Maryland, Massachusetts, Minnesota, Nevada, New Hampshire, New Jersey, New Mexico, New York, Rhode Island, Vermont, and Wisconsin), the District of Columbia, and 153 cities or counties. In contrast, nearly 75 percent of Fortune 500 companies have included sexual orientation in their nondiscrimination policies (HRCF 2004). Later, in the conclusion of the book, I consider various explanations for this apparent paradox.

In any case, the results of my study clearly contradict institutionalist arguments that locate the source of organizational change in exogenous shocks, such as new government mandates or shifts in regulatory enforcement (Fligstein 1991; Powell 1991; Kelly and Dobbin 1999). In the early to mid-1990s, major corporations began extending benefits to domestic partners in the absence of any direct legal pressure whatsoever. Nonetheless, the first exception to this pattern clearly demonstrates the strong influence that coercive pressure can have on corporate policies.

The Impact of the Country's First Equal-Benefits Mandate

In June 1997, San Francisco's Equal Benefits Ordinance took effect. Breaking ground as the first such law in the country, the ordinance requires employers with city contracts to provide to domestic partners the same health-care benefits already offered to married couples (Curiel 1997). As documented in the 1999 *State of the Workplace* report published by the Human Rights Campaign Foundation, San Francisco's 1997 ordinance had a "profound impact on the spread of domestic partner benefits" (1999a, 19). By the end of 1996, only 287 employers in the corporate, university, and government sectors had adopted equitable benefits (HRCF 1999b). In 1997 that number shot up to over 1,500, the vast majority of new adopters being employers with city contracts (HRCF 1999a).

As noted by the authors of the HRCF report, San Francisco's law accounted for "1228 of the 1281 employers that added benefits in 1997, 882 of the 964 employers that added benefits in 1998 and 58 of the 98 employers adding benefits [as of early August] 1999" (1999a, 19). In proportional terms, legal mandate accounted for 96 percent of new adoptions in 1997,

91 percent in 1998, and 59 percent in the first seven months of 1999. As of April 20, 2000, of the 3,402 total employers that offered equitable benefits, 2,612, or 77 percent, did so in order to comply with the ordinance (HRCF 2000b). It is important to keep in mind, however, that many of the complying organizations are small firms located in California (HRCF 1999a). According to a survey of 570 large U.S. employers conducted in the year 2000, only 17 percent of equitable-benefits adopters initiated the change to comply with local government mandates (Hewitt Associates 2000, 10). However, this figure may underrepresent the actual influence of such mandates, given the fact that, in media accounts and in interviews for this study, elites tended to downplay the role of coercive pressures, whether external or internal (see also Kelly and Dobbin 1999).

Regardless of the proportion of small to large firms, those major corporations that extended their policies in response to San Francisco's law began to have a ripple effect in their industries. For example, in late July 1999, following a partial loss in its court battle over the ordinance, United Airlines became the first company in its industry to offer equitable benefits to the partners of gay and lesbian employees. In less than a week American Airlines did the same, followed four days later by US Airways (HRC 1999c). A few months later, Continental Airlines extended its policy to the partners of flight attendants. Within two years of United's decision to offer equitable benefits to its employees, nine of the top ten airlines had come on board, with the tenth, Trans World Airlines, announcing it would do so in 2002, when nonmanagement employees would be granted the benefits that had already been given to management (HRCF 2001b).

Even when coercive pressures are applied to only one company, that organization's response can soon have mimetic effects in the wider organizational field as others adopt equitable benefits not by force of law but to remain competitive with the original adopter. As explained by Kim Mills, the education director of the Human Rights Campaign, "Even without the San Francisco law, we were seeing an average of two employers a week instituting domestic partner coverage, up from one a week in the first half of the 1990s. . . . [But] the San Francisco law has led to a rapid acceleration of this trend, and a domino effect across market sectors and industries" (HRCF 1999a, 4).

Of course, firms do not simply respond passively to coercive pressures. Industry and trade associations, corporate lobbyists, and political action committees all represent collective efforts to effect legislation, regulatory policies, and mechanisms of enforcement (Wilson 1980; Miles 1982; Noll 1985; Kaplan and Harrison 1993, cited in Scott 1995b). Companies also use the courts to fight measures that corporate elites see as threatening to their interests (Edelman and Suchman 1997). For example, United Airlines, represented by the Air Transport Association, balked at San Francisco's Equal Benefits Ordinance and filed a lawsuit against the city (Holding 1997), which was only partially successful (E. Epstein 1999), a point that I will address later in the chapter.

Being the first jurisdiction in the United States to mandate equitable benefits for employers with city contracts, San Francisco also drew heavy fire from conservatives for its ordinance (HRCF 2001b). In 1998, U.S. Representative Frank Riggs introduced an amendment to a Veterans Affairs–Housing and Urban Development appropriations bill that proposed to prohibit funding to any locality that required contractors to provide health-care benefits for domestic partners. Had the Riggs Amendment passed the Senate (having already been approved in the House by a two-vote margin), San Francisco would have been faced with the choice of repealing its law or losing $260 million in federal funding (NGLTF 1998a, 1998b).

Aside from this congressional battle, the city's ordinance also faced conservative attacks in the courts. The American Center for Law and Justice, for instance, which is the legal wing of televangelist Pat Robertson's Christian Coalition, represented an Ohio electrical company that lost its contract with the City of San Francisco after refusing on religious grounds to abide by the law. The company sued the city and argued that the law interfered with interstate commerce, but in June 2001 the U.S. Court of Appeals for the Ninth Circuit, in San Francisco, rejected those arguments, thereby delivering an important legal victory for the city and clearing the way for other locales that had been considering similar ordinances (HRCF 2001b). By mid-February 2004, eight other localities had passed their own benefits mandates: Berkeley, Los Angeles, Oakland, and San Mateo County, California; Minneapolis, Minnesota; and King County, Seattle, and Tumwater, Washington (HRCF 2002h, 2004). By mid-August 2001, just three municipalities alone (San Francisco, Los Angeles, and Seattle) had led 3,087 employers with city contracts to extend benefits to domestic partners (HRCF 2001b, 18).

Despite the wide-reaching impact of such local mandates, the authors of HRCF's 2001 *State of the Workplace* report (2001b, 18) were careful not to overstate the role of coercive forces: "[T]he pace at which employers have been adding the benefits as a result of local contracting requirements has declined since 1997, when the San Francisco law first went into effect, while the pace at which employers are adding them independent of city laws has risen. So far in 2001 [as of August 15], the Human Rights Campaign has identified more employers that have added the benefits independent of city contracting laws requiring them to do so than in any year since it has tracked the trend." Nonetheless, the impact of coercive forces may heighten if cities currently considering such mandates, such as Atlanta, decide to enact laws of their own. In an interesting variation on the mandate approach, in 1999 Broward County, Florida, enacted a provision that gives preference in bidding to companies that provide equitable benefits to their employees (Goldstein 2001). With California becoming the first state in the country to require that state contractors provide equitable benefits, the number of inclusive employers should increase significantly when the law takes effect in 2007 (Salladay and Schevitz 2003).

The Softer Side of Coercive Isomorphism: Normative Impacts of the Legal Environment

The exponential increase in the number of benefits adopters clearly reveals the power of coercive isomorphism. But outside the reach of the handful of cities and one state with such laws, lesbian and gay employees struggle for equitable benefits without the aid of government mandates, albeit assisted by mimetic processes. Nonetheless, new institutionalists predict that other, more diffuse changes in the legal environment can have a strong impact on organizational policies (J. Meyer and Rowan 1977; Scott 1995b; Kelly and Dobbin 1999). As Lauren Edelman (1990, 1403) explains, "The legal environment can engender significant change in the protection of employees' rights, even in the absence of any legal rules that directly mandate such change." This is because, as Edelman and Mark Suchman (1997) argue, the legal environment consists not simply of court rulings or specific laws that regulate the policies and practices of organizations; it also encompasses broader and more symbolic shifts in the sociolegal arena.

Rather than focusing solely on coercive aspects of the law, neoinstitutionalist perspectives point to the wider normative impact of the legal environment. It is in this sense that "organizations look to the law for normative and cognitive guidance, as they seek their place in a socially constructed cultural reality" (Edelman and Suchman 1997, 482). This approach, known as the normative cultural alternative, highlights "organizations' subtle but profound responsiveness to legal ideals, norms, forms, and categories" (493).

Drawing on this normative cultural approach, I draw out three elements in the legal environment that, while not requiring private employers to adopt equitable benefits, nonetheless provide normative and symbolic support for doing so. In particular I focus on the impact of gay-inclusive antidiscrimination laws, city or state laws that provide domestic partner benefits to government employees, and city- or statewide domestic partner registries. Because these measures signal that gays and lesbians are deserving of equal rights and that their relationships are worthy of recognition, I conceptualize them as institutional opportunities for employee activists. Before gathering my data, I hypothesized that challengers would be more likely to succeed if their corporations were headquartered in geopolitical locales that had adopted any of these measures.

Employment Nondiscrimination Laws

As mentioned earlier, by mid-February 2004, 14 states and 153 localities had prohibited antigay employment discrimination in the private sector (HRCF 2004). Findings for my Fortune 1000 sample show that such laws have a significant impact on corporations' willingness to adopt equitable benefits. While 66 percent of companies located in gay-inclusive jurisdictions adopted domestic partner benefits (43 out of 65), only 22 percent of corporations in noninclusive jurisdictions did so (7 out of 32). This difference is especially striking given the fact that nondiscrimination laws do *not* apply to benefits packages. These findings would seem perplexing from a rational materialist theoretical perspective, which views organizations as "rational wealth maximizers" that "instrumentally invoke or evade the law, in a strategic effort to . . . bring the largest possible payoff at the least possible cost" (Edelman and Suchman 1997, 481–82).

In contrast, new institutional theorists who adopt a normative cultural approach to the law would find nothing surprising about my findings. As Edelman and Suchman explain, "[C]ulturalist theories of the regulatory environment place less emphasis on the role of legal sanctions . . . and more emphasis on the role of legal symbols in evoking desirable normative commitments. Regulatory law, in this view, is less a threat than a sermon." In other words, from a culturalist approach the law is seen "as a source of symbol and meaning, rather than as a source of coercive constraint" (495). Thus, gay-inclusive nondiscrimination laws, though lacking any legally mandated provision for benefits, nonetheless facilitate favorable policy outcomes. By signifying that lesbians and gay men are worthy of equal treatment, these laws provide normative challenges to dominant cultural codes and to the "other-creating" processes that construct gays and lesbians as pathological or threatening and thus outside the "universe of obligation" (W. Gamson 1995b, 17).

Since nondiscrimination laws and equitable benefits may both be products of progressive local environments, some might consider the positive relationship between the two variables as potentially spurious. Addressing this possibility in their neoinstitutional analysis of maternity-leave policies, Doug Guthrie and Louise Roth (1999, 57) provide a cogent response that acknowledges the complexity of institutional and societal transformations:

> We do not discount the idea that a culture of liberalism matters for the issues we explore. Regional attitudinal differences may significantly affect the likelihood that organizations will adopt policies that are in line with a progressive reading of equal employment opportunity legislation and workplace policies. . . . Cultural and institutional perspectives are not mutually exclusive. Regional cultures and institutional environments are reciprocally related systems, mutually dependent on one another. More liberal or progressive regions or states tend to construct more progressive institutional environments, and these progressive institutional environments have an impact on the culture and ethos of the state or region.

Laws Granting Equitable Benefits to City or State Employees

Another indicator of a favorable institutional environment for organizational challengers is the passage of local or state laws that grant domestic partner benefits to government employees. As of mid-February 2004, 10 states and 130 localities had such laws on the books (HRCF 2004). Culturalist approaches would expect these laws to have a positive effect on corporate benefits adoption for the same reason that nondiscrimination laws do. Results from my sample of Fortune 1000 companies bear out this prediction. Of those corporations headquartered in cities or states that provide domestic partner benefits to government employees, 66 percent (31 out of 47) followed suit for their own employees. In contrast, among firms located in regions that lacked such laws, only 43 percent (21 out of 49) adopted the benefits.

City- or Statewide Domestic Partner Registries

A final indicator of a supportive normative environment for gay employee activists is the existence of city- or statewide domestic partner registries, which allow gay men and lesbians to officially record their relationships as committed partners. By mid-February 2004, four states (California, Connecticut, Hawaii, and New Jersey) and sixty-six municipalities provided registries (HRCF 2004; NCLR 2004). Registering as domestic partners at the city or county level can sometimes bring a few tangible benefits, such as hospital visitation rights or access to family discounts in local establishments, but such registries function primarily as symbolic recognition, since they do not grant lesbian or gay couples access to the multitude of legal, financial, and tax benefits that accompany heterosexual marriage. The state-level registries vary in how much further they extend the rights of domestic partners; some, for example, ensure the ability to make medical decisions or to inherit property. California's groundbreaking Domestic Partners Rights and Responsibilities Act, which takes effect in January 2005, will entitle registered domestic partners to the same rights and benefits currently bestowed upon married spouses at the state—though not the federal—level. However, none of the city- or statewide registries require private-sector employers to provide equitable benefits (HRCF 2004; NCLR 2004). Nonetheless, findings from my Fortune 1000 sample show that the presence of registries has a significant impact on corporations' willingness to adopt inclusive benefits policies. Companies located in cities or states with domestic partner registries were far more likely to extend their policies than were firms in other locales, with 76 percent of the former (32 out of 42) versus only 35 percent of the latter (19 out of 54) offering the benefits.

City- or statewide domestic partner registries clearly constitute a favorable institutional opportunity for gay employee activists. This makes sense once we examine the rationalistic decision-making process of companies that are considering equitable benefits. According to my interviews, a frequent concern of reluctant corporate elites is how to determine eligibility so as to avoid fraudulent abuse by employees who are not truly involved in committed relationships. Although companies rarely ask heterosexual employees for their marriage licenses, a recent study found that the vast majority of equitable-benefits adopters (87 percent) require "proof" from domestic partners, such as a signed and notarized affidavit verifying that an employee and her or his partner are in a financially interdependent, intimate, and committed relationship and that they have shared a residence for a minimum amount of time, typically from six months to a year (Hewitt Associates 2000, 15, 21–25; see also Winfeld and Spielman 1995, 112). Since domestic partner registries can help alleviate elite concerns about fraud by providing a legally centralized means of documentation, it is not surprising that companies located in registry jurisdictions are far more likely to adopt equitable benefits.

While this interpretation seems to favor a rational materialist stance rather than a normative cultural one, I argue that both accounts offer important insights. Domestic partner registries clearly provide companies with a clear-cut mechanism for the determination of benefits eligibility. At a more diffuse and symbolic but equally important level, registries also represent a wider cultural renegotiation that has resulted in expanded definitions of family. Thus, while many lesbian and gay activists have long argued that "love makes a family," they are far more successful in winning tangible benefits from employers when the law provides a formal means of recognition for gay and lesbian couples.

Acting Up and Waging Boycotts: External Activists as Agents of Coercive Isomorphic Change

With regard to coercive isomorphism, institutionalists have traditionally focused on the influence of the state and various regulatory agencies, but more recently scholars have pointed to the "political costs" that firms may suffer as a result of "the increasing organization of ordinary citizens and the creation of networks of collective interest" (Mezias 1995, 176; see also DiMaggio 1988). Stephen Mezias (1995, 174) mentions that firms face internal pressure from employees and unions and external pressure from consumers as well as politicians and government bureaucrats. Companies are highly cognizant of the negative "political visibility" that can be generated by boycotts, lawsuits, or vocal employee demands.

While it is an important step forward for neoinstitutional scholars to acknowledge the role of mobilized constituencies as both internal and external agents of change, they offer no theoretical framework for understanding organizational transformation when the source of change is internal rather than external to the firm (for an exception, see Chaves 1996, 1997). In chapters 5 and 6, I correct this blind spot by focusing on internal organizational opportunities and the role that employee activists themselves play in effecting policy shifts. For the purposes of the present discussion, however, I confine my focus to coercive pressure originating from activists outside the corporate walls.

A Queer Turn of Events

As discussed in chapter 1, gay employee groups often distance themselves from their radical peers on the streets. In some cases, however, corporate-based networks benefit directly from the more aggressive tactics of queer activists. In one rather interesting turn of events, for example, a West Coast–based utility company sought help from its gay employee network after hearing that ACT UP (the AIDS Coalition to Unleash Power), known for its in-your-face direct-action strategies, might target the corporation for alleged homophobia. Not long before, employee activists had requested that the company endorse a gay rights bill that was pending in the state legislature. The corporation refused, but officials did authorize the use of a company truck in the local gay pride parade. At the request of the employee network, the company's weekly newsletter covered the pride events. Appearing small and hazy but still visible in one of the photos was a poster supporting the gay rights bill, which network members had placed on the hood of the company truck for the parade. After the newsletter went out to every employee in the country, members of the gay network were barraged with hate mail on the company's electronic bulletin board.

Although the vice president of human resources promised to discipline the harassing employees, he nevertheless emphasized that the network was not to engage in "unauthorized political activities," such as displaying a poster endorsing gay rights legislation. But the actions of the network suddenly appeared rather benign once corporate officials caught wind of ACT UP's possible plans to target the company. In an ironic twist, management turned to the gay employee group for help in avoiding negative publicity. Afterward, according to one of the group's founders, the company was far more open to the concerns of the network. Soon, for example, employee activists finally won gay-inclusive diversity training.

The Impact of Boycotts on Corporate Policy

Another source of coercive pressure that can facilitate favorable policy outcomes stems from boycotts of companies perceived to be antigay. After United Airlines filed a lawsuit against San Francisco's Equal Benefits Ordinance in 1997, lesbian and gay activists launched a major boycott. San Francisco–based Equal Benefits Advocates, which organized the campaign, created a Web site to spread the news. Buttons, stickers, and flyers emblazoned with the words "United against United" appeared in numerous shops throughout the Castro, the city's famed gay and lesbian mecca. As part of the boycott, many burned their frequent-flyer membership cards outside the corporation's San Francisco offices (Raine 1999). In July of that year, demonstrators were arrested as they blocked the entrance to a downtown ticket office while dressed from head to toe in purple Tinky Winky costumes. The latter action was a flamboyant attempt to both criticize United and poke fun at Jerry Falwell's recent claim that the popular character featured in the children's television program *Teletubbies* was in fact gay because of his purple color, triangle-shaped antenna, and purse, which producers explained was a "magic bag."

After a two-year boycott, United announced in late July 1999 that it would offer the full range of domestic partner benefits. Some would argue that the decision came solely in response to a U.S. Court of Appeals ruling, which held that the company must offer soft benefits such as family and bereavement leave (E. Epstein 1999). Indeed, United announced its policy change on the same day that the decision was handed down. However, the ruling did not require the extension of health-care benefits, so it seems that activists can take at least partial credit for the company's decision to provide them anyway. While a corporate spokesperson claimed that the San Francisco boycott "had no measurable impact on . . . tickets sold or number of flights," he acknowledged that the company "obviously . . . suffered in the community locally" (quoted in Raine 1999).

Having pushed for the benefits from the inside for several years, United's gay employee network thus finally succeeded, but only after the company faced external pressure from both the courts and lesbian and gay consumers. Tellingly, the company now places full-page ads in both national and local gay publications, where it proudly proclaims that it was the first airline to adopt a gay-inclusive nondiscrimination policy and the first to implement domestic partner benefits. Asked about the ads, a corporate spokesperson explained, "We recognize that the gay and lesbian community is a large market and there is a huge opportunity to market to them" (quoted in Raine 1999).

Gay activist Jeff Sheehy, who helped draft the Equal Benefits Ordinance, was a co-organizer of the United boycott. Responding to questions about the boycott and the company's new advertising campaign, Sheehy commented, "Our goal was to demonstrate to the airline industry that we deserve to be treated equally. The fact that United is spending tens of thousands of dollars to trumpet the fact that they [now] treat their employees equally shows that there is some value in doing that" (quoted in Raine 1999). Clearly, then, coercive pressure from the outside can provide tremendous aid to challengers on the inside. United's gay employee network can now celebrate its long-fought, hard-won battle and the impact that victory has had on others in the industry who quickly began to follow suit.

Did Someone Say "Boycott"? Two Can Play That Game

While activist successes create opportunities for later challengers, they can also spark the mobilization of countermovements (D. Meyer and Staggenborg 1996; Dugan 1999). From attempts to withdraw tax abatement—an unsuccessful strategy used against Apple Computer, for example (D. Baker, Strub, and Henning 1995)—to the threat or use of boycotts against inclusive companies, right-wing groups are seeking to undo the gains made by lesbian and gay workers. For example, through its occasional publication of *The Homosexuality Report,* the explicitly antigay American Family Association has helped its members keep close tabs on the adopters of gay-inclusive policies. The organization calls for boycotts of various employers and provides information on targeted companies. Using the Internet to publicize the campaigns to a wider audience, the AFA Web site sometimes features a special section called the "Boycott Box" (La Salle 1997).

In March 1997, a coalition of groups on the religious Right and other conservative organizations, including the Southern Baptist Convention, the Family Research Council, Focus on the Family, and Concerned Women for America, announced the formation of a "corporate accountability project" aimed at reversing "pro-gay" policies (Data Lounge 1997). Using data compiled by HRC that detailed the ever-growing number of U.S. employers with gay-inclusive policies, the conservative coalition said it would target Fortune 500 companies that have adopted nondiscrimination policies, domestic partnership benefits, diversity training, and marketing efforts directed to the gay and lesbian community. Coalition members indicated that they would use the threat of large-scale boycotts and letter-writing campaigns to achieve their goals.

Key informants in my telecommunications case study believe that their company's long-standing refusal to adopt equitable benefits was due in large part to a right-wing boycott issued against the company for the gay-inclusive policies it already had. After the gay employee network convinced the company to sponsor the 1994 Gay Games, James Dobson, president of the right-wing Focus on the Family, urged members to call the CEO's response center to complain. Requesting a meeting with the CEO but instead winning an audience with the vice president of human resources, Dobson attacked not only the company's sponsorship of the Gay Games but also its support of "GLUE," the gay employee network, and its gay-inclusive diversity training, which some business units made mandatory. Flexing his organizational muscle, Dobson cited Focus on the Family's membership figures and the large number of radio stations belonging to his avowedly antigay organization.

Later, the head of human resources flew to Colorado (where Focus on the Family is based) to meet with Dobson. Despite an "agreement" that the executive thought he had reached with Dobson, on a religious television network Dobson subsequently urged viewers not to use the company's long-distance services because of its gay-inclusive record. Donald Wildmon, president of the AFA, also called on his members to boycott the company. As explained by a former national cochair of GLUE, it was "pretty scary there for several of the HR people" staffing the phones who had to listen to "radical right people calling in and sending in their torn up calling cards."

Tellingly, Wildmon issued the boycott in conjunction with the launching of AFA's Lifeline, which was marketed as a Christian long-distance service. Advertisements for the service specifically criticized the gay-inclusive employer for calling itself "a company without closets" and for supporting the gay employee network. At that point, GLUE had been struggling for equitable benefits for approximately five years. After the boycott, it took another four years—and a new CEO—before lesbian and gay employees finally won their fight.

Of course, the impact of boycotts can be felt far beyond the walls of a targeted corporation. As is hoped for by those waging a boycott, news of such campaigns can also affect other companies by altering elites' perceptions of the apparent costs and benefits of inclusive policy change. Many of the executives I interviewed mentioned the highly publicized Disney boycott, which was issued by the fifteen-million-member Southern Baptist Convention after the company instituted equitable benefits in late 1995 (Adams and Solomon 2000). While several executives were quick to add that the boycott had no effect on Disney's profits, which in fact hit record-breaking levels (Price 2000), such a backlash can nevertheless plant fear in the hearts of corporate elites. This is true even though the vast majority of adopters in my study faced no organized opposition, either internal or external. In fact, based on media reports of such policy change, very few employers ever face such a backlash. Indeed, as the pace of benefits adoption continues unabated, the boycott threat is quickly becoming a dusty weapon in the right-wing arsenal. Nevertheless, based on my interviews in the late 1990s, elites' apprehension of boycotts was palpable in several companies and hence served to slow the progress of lesbian and gay challengers.

At one internationally known corporation, for example, the gay employee network had to fight hard even to keep its officially recognized status. After hearing that the southern-based employer had granted corporate recognition to the group, several members of the company's Christian employee network complained, and the AFA threatened a boycott. In response the company decided to withdraw its recognition of the gay network, whose members then requested help from Elizabeth Birch, then executive director of HRC. A founder of the gay employee group explained Birch's successful plan to save the network and avoid a boycott: "Elizabeth Birch came in and spoke to senior management. She came up with an out for them: develop a diversity council that includes all the employee special interest groups, including us [the gay network], African Americans, other employees of color, and Christians. Because the Council became an umbrella group for *all* diversity groups, the company wasn't endorsing gays and lesbians." In chapter 6 I examine another corporation with gay-inclusive policies that likewise faced organized opposition, both internal and external, but in that case management stood its ground, defending the policies—adopted in the absence of a gay employee network—as a business imperative.

In any case, in the company currently being discussed, Birch's strategy to save the gay employee group worked. And later, when leaders of the network presented their proposal for equitable benefits to senior management, members of the Christian employee network did not oppose it, since the resolution was endorsed by the entire Diversity Council. The proposal nevertheless stalled when it reached the corporate board of directors. Employee activists once again sought the aid of Elizabeth Birch. She offered to ask Coretta Scott King, a strong supporter of gay rights, to call a particular board member who they thought might be an ally. The plan was abandoned, however, after the gay employee group learned the reason for the holdup. As explained to the network by senior management, "The Southern Baptists told the company, 'We *will* boycott you if you do this.'"

Commenting on the gay network's previous emphasis on the profitability of inclusive policies, one of its founders lamented, "The business case gets complicated when you're talking about a boycott." As a result of the boycott threat, management told members of the gay network, "We'll not be the first [in the industry] to adopt the benefits, but we will be the second." The company remained true to its word, extending benefits to domestic partners less than a week after a competitor did so first.

Taking the Plunge Together:
The Rise of Coordinated Policy Change

Aware of the fact that a boycott is more likely targeted against the first company in an industry to adopt equitable benefits than against companies that subsequently do so, gay employee networks at General Motors, Ford Motor Company, and DaimlerChrysler tried to persuade their Big Three employers to institute the benefits simultaneously. If the policy changes were announced at the same time, the networks argued, the likelihood and effectiveness of a boycott would be drastically reduced. In fact, the automakers did just that, issuing a joint press release with the United Auto Workers (UAW) on June 8, 2000. As explained in the *Detroit News*, "The timing of [the] announcement was tactical. All three companies waited until after their annual shareholder meetings to prevent opponents from having a public forum to politicize the move" (Phillips and Truby 2000).

The automakers had already granted same-sex partner benefits to their Canadian employees back in 1996—and the following year Ford vice-chairman Allan Gilmour made national news after coming out as gay—but fear of backlash had prevented the Big Three from extending the benefits to their U.S. workforce (Phillips and Truby 2000). Their decision to do so in June 2000 made automotive manufacturing the first and thus far only market sector to see major players extending their benefits simultaneously. The policy change brought equitable coverage to 465,000 employees.

This landmark move came after years of prodding by gay employee activists in all three companies (Phillips and Truby 2000). After network leaders worked to win strong union support for the benefits, the UAW began pushing in earnest for the policy change. During negotiations with the UAW and other unions in fall 1999, all three companies signed a memorandum of understanding that they would study the issue. Bargaining jointly with the Big Three, the UAW won equitable benefits less than a year later. Notably, the June 2000 announcement came only one month after Subaru of America had extended its benefits coverage, following years of heavy marketing to the lesbian and gay community (HRCF 2000a).

While no other industries have since witnessed this type of coordinated policy change, some industry analysts and labor experts viewed the automakers' move as signaling an important step forward on the road toward institutionalization, wherein equitable benefits will become standard practice among mainstream companies. "When you get an industry announcing this jointly with a union, it's [a] sort of bellwether of what you'll see elsewhere," explained Dale Brickner, professor emeritus at Michigan State University School of Labor and Industrial Relations. Greg Tarpinian, executive director of the Labor Research Association, likewise predicted that the Big Three's policy shift would encourage "a lot of the [other] mainline, Old Economy companies" to follow that same path (both quoted in Hopgood 2000). Mimetic forces do seem to have come into play rather quickly in a related industry, as Delphi, the world's largest auto-parts manufacturer, and Visteon Corporation, another auto-parts supplier and Ford spin-off, extended equitable benefits to their workers within months of the Big Three's announcement. A third supplier, ArvinMeritor, is currently studying the issue (Truby 2000).

Lawsuits as Institutional Opportunities

While fear of a boycott can delay for several years the extension of equitable benefits, other external factors can influence executive decision making as well. As a coercive isomorphic pressure, lawsuits brought against companies also affect elites' willingness to adopt gay-inclusive policies. In my study the human resources director at a consumer services corporation emphasized the fear of lawsuits as a driving force behind her employer's decision to adopt equitable benefits. While acknowledging the work of the gay employee network, she rated the threat of potential lawsuits as more important: "[The company] is concerned with what employees are going to say. They could sue us, and we're concerned with publicity. We don't want gays and lesbians to picket us at headquarters." After being asked to rate a list of internal and external factors as to their importance in influencing her company's decision, she commented as follows: "I realize now that it's not so internally driven. We're worried about what the outside world will say and do to us. If one person says, 'You don't offer domestic partner benefits, so I'll sue,' the dollars can get big. We don't want the world to say we did not do this for gay and lesbian employees. We realize that bad press affects the bottom line."

Interestingly enough, however, her company did not adopt the benefits until merging with another consumer services corporation that had already done so, at the urging of its own gay employee network. Lesbian and gay employees at her company were very aware of the fact that their merger partner had already instituted equitable benefits, so her company's failure to do the same would been seen by some as fertile grounds for a lawsuit. Another facilitating factor was the location of the merger partner's head-quarters in an East Coast city with a very large lesbian, gay, and bisexual community. As explained by the director of human resources, "Like San Francisco, [this city] has a loud voice regarding gays and lesbians." Placing that statement in a larger context, she added, "We're big and visible, so we're sued at the drop of a hat."

Her company's high level of concern about the threat of litigation makes sense given its prior experiences with a highly publicized class-action lawsuit. More than twenty years ago, a group of women employees sued the company when it was still part of a much larger consumer services corpo-ration. Commenting further on why her company decided to adopt gay-inclusive policies, the director referred explicitly to this case: "There was a consent decree in the 1970s where [the company] paid millions and millions of dollars. We can be sued. And we don't want our shareholders to feel that that's a potential. Plus, a lot of our shareholders are employees."

Shareholder Activism as Coercive Pressure

While the preceding quotation alludes to the indirect role that shareholders can play, sometimes their influence is far more direct. As a result of orga-nizing work by lesbian and gay investors, shareholder activism has become an important source of coercive pressure that can facilitate favorable policy outcomes for internal challengers. Referring to "a new breed of activist: the pro-gay shareholder," a 1994 *Advocate* cover article entitled "Waging War on Wall Street" traced the beginnings of this tactical innovation (Mickens 1994b). Although shareholder activism has been a strategy of socially con-scious investors since the 1960s, it was not until the infamous Cracker Barrel incident that gays and lesbians adopted this tactic to fight for equality in corporate America (see also Alpern 1999).

The Equality Project and Gay-Affirmative Shareholder Activism

As discussed in chapter 1, in 1991 Cracker Barrel announced its blatantly antigay employment policy. Around the same time, activist-minded investors formed the Wall Street Project, a national organization that encourages gay-affirmative shareholder activism among individual and institutional investors. Commenting on the impact of the restaurant chain's widely publicized move, the director of the Wall Street Project explained, "We didn't set out to target [Cracker Barrel]. But just as we were forming the group, Cracker Barrel, as if on cue, gave us the perfect issue to mobilize support" (quoted in Bain 1992b, 8). Unlike the divestiture model used in the early antiapartheid movement but mirroring the tactical shift that was successfully adopted by that movement in its later days, the Wall Street Project recommended that investors keep or purchase Cracker Barrel stock in order to lend support to inclusive shareholder resolutions (Mickens 1994b).

Now called the Equality Project, the organization monitors corporate policies on sexual orientation and gender identity or expression, conducts workshops on bringing about corporate adoption of inclusive policies, disseminates information to the media, sponsors shareholder actions, and holds public demonstrations against particularly recalcitrant employers (Equality Project 1999, 2002). The Equality Project aims for companies worldwide to sign on to its "Equality Principles," which can be summarized as follows: company-wide distribution of written nondiscrimination policies that include sexual orientation, gender identity or expression, and perceived health status or disability; equal recognition of all employee groups; diversity training that covers sexual orientation and gender identity or expression; equitable benefits for domestic partners; marketing policies that prohibit negative stereotypes and avoid discrimination on the basis of sexual orientation and gender identity or expression; policies against discrimination in the sale of goods and services; and nondiscrimination in charitable contributions (Equality Project 2002).

As explained on the Equality Project's Web site, available at http://www.equalityproject.org/, shareholder activism refers to a wide range of strategies that include letter-writing campaigns, meetings with upper management, attendance at shareholder meetings, and the filing of shareholder proposals or resolutions that, if placed on the proxy ballot, are voted on by those who hold stock in the company (Equality Project 2002). Following mounting pressure from shareholder activists, in 1998 the Securities and Exchange Commission (SEC) reversed the "Cracker Barrel rule," which had allowed companies to exclude employment-related resolutions. Since then, shareholder proposals have become "an increasingly important tool in compelling corporations to add sexual orientation to their non-discrimination policies" (HRCF 2001b, 27). Because the SEC does not allow shareholder resolutions that address wages or benefit issues, activists cannot submit proposals calling for domestic partner benefits (Equality Project 2002). Nevertheless, proposals calling for nondiscrimination policies are important not only in their own right but also because gay employee networks usually find it necessary to achieve such policies before trying to win equitable benefits.

The Measure of Success

While shareholder proposals are rarely successful in actual passage, typically capturing no more than 10 percent of the vote (HRC 2001b, 27), activists consider the mere placement of their issue on the proxy ballot as a positive outcome, given the visibility and awareness that it generates (Proffitt and Sacks 1999). Even if a shareholder resolution were to pass with a majority vote, such proposals are merely considered "advice" to the board of directors and thus in no way obligate a company to comply (Mills 2001). Success is often measured in terms of whether the proposal garners enough votes to qualify for resubmission to the ballot the next year, with SEC minimum thresholds requiring 3 percent of the vote the first year, 6 percent the following year, and 10 percent in subsequent years (Equality Project 2002). As described in the aforementioned *Advocate* cover story, "[T]he strategy is to keep shareholder dissent growing and in the public eye in order to embarrass management" (Mickens 1994b, 42).

At times shareholder actions bring tangible policy changes. These victories can be accomplished in various ways. Since shareholder proposals spark discussions within upper management as soon as they are filed, sometimes executives decide to make a requested change before the resolution can even appear on a ballot (Mickens 1994b; Equality Project 2002). While some companies may expand their policies because particular elites are convinced that it is the right thing to do, other corporations have changed their policies to avoid a "divisive" shareholder vote (HRCF 2001b) or to avoid being seen as antigay given the large majority of the public that supports nondiscrimination in the workplace (Mills 2001). In any case, the Equality Project has withdrawn proposals at several companies after executives implemented the requested policies. Even when resolutions are ultimately withdrawn, they are often covered by the media, so they have "far-reaching educational value" as well. Success can also come through actual dialogue between corporate decision makers and advocates for equality. Shareholders have often partnered with activist organizations and arranged meetings between activist leaders and corporate elites, who are sometimes moved to amend their nondiscrimination policies even after a resolution has been defeated in the proxy vote (Equality Project 2002).

Thus, shareholder activism should be seen as a process in which policy change can be effected at several points along the way: before a full-fledged proxy campaign; after the proposal is filed but before the vote; or after the proxy vote, even if the numbers fall far short of a majority. Shareholder activists have filed resolutions calling for gay-inclusive equal employment opportunity policies at numerous companies, including American Home Products Corporation, American International Group, Cracker Barrel, DaimlerChrysler, General Electric Company, the Home Depot, Johnson & Johnson, Lockheed Martin Corporation, McDonald's Corporation, Alltel Corporation, Emerson Electric Company, and ExxonMobil Corporation (HRCF 2001b, 2002d; Equality Project 2002). All but the latter three eventually opted to add sexual orientation to their nondiscrimination policies (Mills 2001; Equality Project 2002). Here I highlight a few of these campaigns in order to reveal the diversity of circumstances surrounding the policy changes or lack thereof.

In 1999 shareholder activists succeeded in convincing McDonald's to amend its nondiscrimination statement (HRC 2000a). The fast-food empire's gay employee network had been fighting for inclusion of sexual orientation since 1995. McDonald's agreed to the policy change in order to avoid a shareholder proxy initiative by the Seattle-based Pride Foundation, which had joined with the Equality Project in targeting General Electric (GE) as well. In response to the latter shareholder resolution, GE announced in March 2000 that it would add sexual orientation to both its nondiscrimination policy and its diversity training program even though the proposal was defeated in the proxy vote (HRC 2000a; Equality Project 2002). Responding to a shareholder campaign launched by the Unitarian Universalist Association (UUA), Home Depot agreed in May 2001 to amend its nondiscrimination policy in order to avoid having the issue come to a vote at its shareholder meeting. In return the UUA withdrew the proposal (HRCF 2001b). The compromise came after several longtime employees questioned management's opposition to the resolution (HRCF 2001a).

Even more recently, in 2002 defense contractor Lockheed Martin faced a shareholder resolution calling for a gay-inclusive nondiscrimination policy (HRCF 2002d). Lesbian and gay employees had been pushing for change from the inside for several years. Making no headway, in 2000 they began working with the WorkNet staff of HRC and with HRC's Business Council. After these combined efforts failed to persuade the company, Swarthmore

College business students filed a gay-affirmative shareholder proposal. Lockheed Martin's board of directors actively opposed the resolution, contributing to the company's zero score in HRCF's *Corporate Equality Index*. Unveiled in August 2002 and based on the Equality Project's Equality Principles, the index provides numeric ratings of companies and industries based on whether they have met various criteria for ensuring equal rights in the workplace. Of the 319 employers that were rated in 2002, only 2 other companies earned scores of zero: Cracker Barrel and Emerson Electric (HRCF 2002b).

In October 2002, Elizabeth Birch, then executive director of HRC, requested a meeting with Lockheed Martin's upper management to discuss how the company could improve its rock-bottom performance rating, which had been publicized in highly visible media reports on the new corporate index. The following month the company adopted not only a gay-inclusive nondiscrimination policy but domestic partner benefits as well. Three of its competitors in the defense industry had already instituted both of these policies: Boeing Company, Honeywell, and Raytheon Company, all of which had faced mobilization by gay and lesbian employee networks. Lockheed Martin's decision thus illustrates how coercive and mimetic pressures can facilitate policy success for internal challengers.

If at First You Don't Succeed . . .

Shareholder activists try especially hard to persuade large investors, such as pension funds, to "[use their] huge holdings for their voting power" (Mickens 1994b, 41). Such was the case with the New York City Employees Retirement System (NYCERS), which sponsored the country's first gay-affirmative shareholder action. In 1992 the pension fund filed a proposal calling on Cracker Barrel to adopt a gay-inclusive nondiscrimination policy, the first of what would end up being years' worth of resolutions targeting the company. In response to management's request, the SEC not only allowed the company to omit the proposal from its 1992 proxy ballot but also issued a ruling that flew in the face of long-standing agency policy: corporations could now exclude from their proxy ballots any shareholder resolutions that addressed employment concerns (Bain 1992e; Alpern 1999).

While the "Cracker Barrel ruling" was being fought in court, NYCERS was able to place its proposal on the 1993 ballot, where it garnered 16 percent of the vote. Although unsuccessful in changing corporate policy, that figure "well exceeded the typical 11% margins that persuaded other companies to adopt anti-apartheid policies just a decade [earlier]." This significant showing convinced many institutional investors to support the gay-inclusive campaign. Beforehand, "many big shareholders had routinely sent in their votes in advance, siding as they usually do with management," explained the vice-chair of the Wall Street Project, but "[a]fter they heard about the debate . . . many changed their minds" (Mickens 1994b, 42–43).

A court loss in 1995 regarding the Cracker Barrel ruling forced activists to devise some creatively worded resolutions, such as the two proposals sponsored in 1995 and 1996 by stockholder Carl Owens, a member of Queer Nation, who called on Cracker Barrel to assess the cost of the ongoing boycott and to appoint a more diverse board of directors; and the resolutions sponsored in 1996 and 1997 by NYCERS and the Interfaith Center on Corporate Responsibility, which urged the company to make executives' pay dependent in part on their progress in recruiting diverse employees "without respect to race, color, creed, gender, age, or sexual orientation" (Alpern 1999). Like each gay-affirmative proposal that had appeared on the ballot in the years prior, these resolutions received enough support to qualify for resubmission the next year. After the SEC reversed its Cracker Barrel ruling in 1998, freeing activists to file shareholder proposals addressing employment discrimination, such resolutions continued for another half decade.

Finally, in perhaps the most stunning victory yet for shareholder activists, the notoriously antigay Cracker Barrel added sexual orientation to its nondiscrimination policy in 2002, after facing ten years of shareholder actions calling for change. Although the corporation once again recommended that shareholders oppose the gay-inclusive proposal, arguing that "it would be impossible to list every group which has the potential to be discriminated against in some way," the board of directors nonetheless voted unanimously to amend its policy after its annual shareholder meeting on November 26, 2002 (HRC 2002e). Although a formal shareholder vote was not held, since no sponsor was present to introduce the resolution, a company official told HRC that the proposal would have received a majority (58 percent) of the votes cast. Such strong support is unheard of in the history of shareholder activism.

While it is impossible to gauge the impact of recent press coverage surrounding Cracker Barrel's zero rating in HRCF's *Corporate Equality Index,* it seems likely that the negative publicity played a key role in the policy shift. Cracker Barrel's top brass had obviously remained unmoved in the face of boycotts and bad press following their 1991 adoption of an explicitly antigay employment policy. And perhaps they would have remained obstinate even in response to the recent media attention to their zero rating. The company's shareholders, however, were apparently persuaded that it was, at last, time for a change.

Like Oil and Water

While the previously discussed cases reveal how shareholder actions can result in favorable policy outcomes, lesbian and gay activists continue to face a long, uphill battle with ExxonMobil, the world's largest publicly traded oil company. In November 1999, the newly merged Texas-based corporation nullified Mobil's gay-inclusive nondiscrimination policy and stopped any future enrollment in its domestic partner benefits program (HRCF 2001b). The reversal earned ExxonMobil the ignominious distinction as the first and only corporation to have rescinded a gay-inclusive nondiscrimination policy and one of only two companies (Perot Systems Corporation is the other) to have terminated equitable benefits. As word spread about the oil giant's decision, public outcry ensued. Customers of Exxon and Mobil returned their credit cards, and a letter-writing campaign generated over thirty-five thousand letters, including one signed by twenty-eight members of Congress and three state attorneys. In addition to the written correspondence, ExxonMobil's public relations office received approximately three thousand phone calls condemning the company's move (HRCF 2000a, 31).

Although the Equality Project and other cosponsors have yet to win their fight to reinstate sexual orientation in the nondiscrimination statement—in fact, the company told HRC that the only reason it has any written nondiscrimination policy at all is to retain eligibility for federal government contracts (HRC 2000c)—activists have succeeded in garnering enough votes to have their shareholder resolution placed on the ballot five years in a row, beginning with the first effort in 1999, which was aimed at Exxon prior to its merger with Mobil. That proposal drew 6 percent of the votes cast, with support increasing to 8 percent the following year (Equality Project 2002). In 2001 the measure garnered 13 percent of the vote, more than any other shareholder resolution on the ballot (HRCF 2001b, 27).

Given ExxonMobil's continued refusal to reestablish employment protection and equitable benefits for lesbian and gay workers, in the summer of 2001 HRC called for a nationwide boycott. "While ExxonMobil is free to discriminate, it will soon learn that discrimination is not free," explained Elizabeth Birch. "Prejudice does, indeed, come with a price" (quoted in Smith 2001). Nine national and forty-five statewide gay rights organizations have since joined the Coalition to Promote Equality at ExxonMobil (HRC 2002f), which was launched in fall 2001 at the eleventh annual Out and Equal workplace conference. Shareholder activism remains an instrumental part of the coalition's diverse strategies. Support for the gay-inclusive nondiscrimination resolution rose to 24 percent in a May 2002 shareholder vote and to a record-breaking 27 percent at the May 2003 meeting (Coalition to Promote Equality at ExxonMobil 2002, 2003). In the face of mounting protests, executives nevertheless continue to turn a deaf ear. ExxonMobil's intransigence is especially perplexing given the policies of its competitors: Sunoco, Texaco, Atlantic Richfield, BP Amoco, Chevron, and Shell all prohibit antigay discrimination, and the latter three also provide equitable benefits (HRCF 2000a). Moreover, Shell and BP have both submitted testimony or letters to Congress urging passage of the Employment Non-discrimination Act (HRCF 2002b).

The Rise of Antigay Shareholder Activism

While lesbian and gay activists and their allies have not always been successful in using the proxy ballot to push for change, they have brought increased visibility not only to the struggle for workplace equality but to the strategy of shareholder activism itself. In fact, conservatives have begun to use the shareholder process in their fight against gay and lesbian rights. In May 2001, marking a first in the history of shareholder activism, AT&T stockholders were faced with a proposal to remove sexual orientation from the corporation's nondiscrimination policy. The board of directors urged shareholders to vote against the initiative, a recommendation strongly backed by the company's lesbian and gay employee network. The antigay resolution failed, garnering fewer votes than any of the other proposals on the ballot, although support among 7 percent of shareholders qualified it for resubmission the following year, when it failed again with even less support (HRCF 2001b).

In 2002 the Right targeted Boeing with a shareholder action seeking to overturn the company's gay-inclusive nondiscrimination policy. The sponsors listed domestic partner benefits among their complaints, although they could not directly call for rescission of benefits, given SEC rules. Quoted at length here, their statement in support of the antigay proposal, which ultimately failed, combined fundamentalist religious discourse with an inversion of the profits frame typically used by gay and lesbian employee activists:

> The decision to include sexual orientation in the Company's written diversity and equal employment opportunity policies interjects the Company into one of the most controversial and divisive social issues of our day. Although the policies may be popular among some of the Company's customers, employees and shareholders, the policies are offensive to others due to their deeply held moral and religious beliefs. The Proponent believes the Company's diversity policy offends some current Boeing employees, and has contributed to eroding employee morale. The Proponent

believes potential employees also may be deterred from seeking employment with the Company . . . [and] potential customers may choose not to buy products from the Company because they are offended by the policies . . . [and] potential investors may be discouraged from acquiring Boeing shares. The Proponent of this Shareholder Proposal believes that the Company should not take sides in this controversial issue, and instead should leave this issue to elected officials who can adopt laws to define discrimination policies that are appropriate for a given community.

Whether the sponsors failed to recognize or intentionally wished to obscure the fact that omitting sexual orientation from nondiscrimination policies *is* "taking sides" on the issue, their call for a reliance on the law in deciding such matters is not surprising. As already discussed, lesbians and gay men lack legal protection from employment discrimination in the vast majority of states and localities. Clearly, conservatives seeking to prevent or overturn gay and lesbian rights have been far more successful in the legislative arena than in the corporate domain. Nevertheless, Boeing's board of directors cited a legal rationale in its proxy statement urging shareholders to vote against the antigay proposal, noting that the company "abides by applicable federal, state, and local laws" (Equality Project 2002). Most of the board's argument, however, relied on a profits frame, which will be discussed in more detail in chapter 6. Tellingly, Boeing also has a gay and lesbian employee network that had worked for years to secure gay-inclusive policies.

In sum, coercive isomorphic pressures can serve as important institutional opportunities for internal challengers. Employee activists have a far greater chance of winning equitable policies when their companies are subject to gay-inclusive nondiscrimination statutes, boycotts, lawsuits, or shareholder actions. Nonetheless, it was a rarity for the executives I interviewed to acknowledge the impact of coercive pressures. They were far more likely to rationalize the adoption of gay-inclusive policies as "good for the bottom line." Even when companies change their policies clearly in response to legislation, their stated rationale typically draws on efficiency arguments. For example, when a West Coast bank adopted equitable benefits only after it was mandated to do so by the San Francisco Equal Benefits Ordinance of 1997, a corporate spokesperson claimed, "We feel the San Francisco ordinance was a factor in our decision-making process, but only one factor." Moreover, he emphasized that "the benefits package is also expected to boost worker morale and productivity."

This tendency is in line with the findings of neoinstitutionalists Frank

Dobbin and John Sutton (1998), who report that human resource professionals began to justify the creation of corporate departments for affirmative action, equal employment opportunity, safety, and benefits not as a measure of compliance to civil rights laws but as rationalized structures that would be economically beneficial, given their potential for increasing employee productivity and loyalty. Dobbin and Sutton describe this shift in rationale as a "drift toward efficiency" (443). What institutionalists have failed to investigate, however, is the role that activists themselves play in convincing corporate elites that inclusive policies are rationally beneficial. In the case of gay-inclusive policy adoption, the drift toward efficiency in elites' justifications is often a reflection of activists' own strategic framing, a point that I will return to later in the chapter.

Mimetic Isomorphism as Institutional Opportunity: Competitive Pressures

Mimetic isomorphism refers to a process of imitation or modeling whereby organizations mimic the policies, practices, and structures of other organizations (DiMaggio and Powell 1991b). This source of change stems from the "tendency of administrators to emulate apparently successful forms" (Brint and Karabel 1991, 343). Neil Fligstein (1991, 316–17) argues, for example, that firms engage in extensive monitoring of each other "by reading the business press, which is usually quick to note major organizational changes, attending trade meetings, and using other sources of information."

Heather Haveman (1993) has found that large firms look especially to other large firms but that all organizations, regardless of size or profitability, rely on highly profitable organizations as role models. The adoption of a particular practice by certain firms can therefore have "spearheading effects" on others (Thornton 1995, 210), who may then follow suit either to remain competitive or to be seen as legitimate (DiMaggio and Powell 1991b; Fligstein 1991; Borum and Westenholz 1995). In playing follow-the-leader (Haveman 1993), waves of later adopters both reveal and contribute to a "bandwagon effect" (Thornton 1995, 210). Fligstein captures the duality of this process when he states, "What is an effect at one time point can be a cause at another" (1991, 317; see also Powell 1991).

In considering the sources of mimetic isomorphic change, institutionalists attend to benchmarking, whereby organizations keep tabs on the policies and practices of their competitors and others in the wider business world, and to other field-level influences, such as industry associations, consulting firms, interlocking corporate directorates, and intercorporate career mobility (DiMaggio and Powell 1991b). These factors encourage organizations to model their structures and policies after leaders in the field. Emphasizing the importance of benchmarking, a diversity consultant and manager of employee networks at an East Coast financial services provider in my study commented on the factors that led her company to adopt equitable benefits. She explained that, in addition to facing internal pressure from the gay employee network, her company "conducts a lot of benchmarking to stay ahead of the pack." In fact, her employer was not the first in the industry to institute the benefits, but it was one of the earliest.

Clear evidence of mimetic effects can be found in multiple industries. For example, in addition to the previously discussed adoption wave among passenger airlines, mimetic processes are apparent in the banking industry. After Wells Fargo and Bank of America adopted equitable benefits in 1998 to comply with San Francisco's Equal Benefits Ordinance, soon Bankers Trust Company, BankBoston, and Chase Manhattan extended their policies as well, although they were not obligated to do so by law. This same pattern held in the oil industry, with Chevron extending benefits in compliance with the city's ordinance, followed by Shell, Mobil, and BP Amoco, which were not legally required to do so (HRCF 1999a). As mentioned above, Mobil's policy was later rescinded after the company merged with Exxon in November 1999. Nonetheless, these examples show that the response of particular companies to coercive pressures can soon have ripple effects throughout an industry.

Mimetic processes can, of course, come into play even without an initial coercive influence, as seen in the waves of adoption that have rippled through the accounting and telecommunications industries (HRCF 2001b). In April 1999, KPMG was the first of the then Big Five accounting firms to institute equitable benefits, followed later that year by PricewaterhouseCoopers and the next year by Deloitte & Touche and Accenture, with the last of the five, Ernst & Young, doing so in February 2001. Likewise, announcing domestic partner benefits in December 2000, BellSouth joined all of the other former Baby Bells, which had implemented the benefits prior to their mergers with other telecommunications corporations. As the authors of the 2001 *State of the Workplace* report conclude, "Some other industry sectors are not as far along, but policy changes are occurring" (HRCF 2001b, 21). They cite the aerospace industry as an example.

Mimetic effects are readily apparent in Figure 2. From 1993 to 1996, the Fortune 500 averaged only 5.25 new adopters per year. In 1997, the year that San Francisco's equitable-benefits ordinance took effect, the number of new adopters shot up to 16. That number rose to 24 new adopters the following year, as competitors of the complying companies began to jump on board even in the absence of legal mandate. With 1999 bringing 18 new adopters, the pace of adoption then quickened; equitable benefits were announced by 30 companies in 2000, 36 in 2001, and 37 in 2002. While 2003 brought just 25 new adopters, the first month and a half of 2004 alone saw 12 companies announcing extended benefits. Overall, in the years following San Francisco's 1997 enactment, the Fortune 500 has averaged 28 new adopters per year. While many of these employers had faced pressure from gay employee networks, it is telling that some apparently changed their policies without any internal prodding.

The Power of Benchmarking in the Absence of a Gay Employee Network

Some decision makers also keep a close eye on the policies and practices of their corporate customers (DiMaggio and Powell 1991b). My transportation case study provides a good example. When asked in our interview why her conservative, southern-based company adopted gay-inclusive diversity training in the absence of any gay employee network, the director of corporate diversity explained: "It was a sign of the times. . . . Other companies were doing it. There was just conversation about it going on. . . . Our focus has always been more around what are other companies doing. . . . When you look at some of our [corporate] customers . . . you [need to] know where they stand on issues like this [because] you don't want to be totally off-center, so to speak." The corporate customers this executive referred to were a high-tech firm and an imaging company, both of which have outstanding records with regard to gay-inclusive policies.

The campaign for equitable benefits at this transportation company provides a powerful example of the importance of benchmarking. In the absence

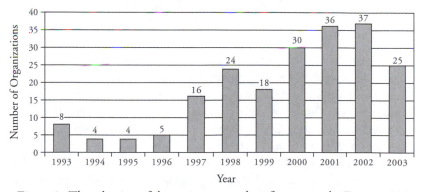

Figure 2. The adoption of domestic partner benefits among the Fortune 500 by year. Data adapted from the WorkNet employer database of the Human Rights Campaign (HRCF 2004).

of a gay employee network, the director of corporate diversity dedicated herself to the issue of equitable benefits. She was joined by a gay manager who, without knowing of her commitment, told her that he had "decided to take a stand" to see if he could persuade the company to adopt the benefits. The manager contacted the National Gay and Lesbian Task Force and HRC for information on the number of companies with equitable benefits and prepared a spreadsheet detailing the expected costs. With data in hand, the two of them approached the vice president of benefits. He was very supportive, given the low projected cost, and agreed to help them develop a presentation for the executive vice president of human resources.

In preparation, they each took responsibility for benchmarking a certain number of companies. The manager used the data he obtained from NGLTF and HRC, while the diversity director consulted the Corporate Advisory Council, an organization that provides research and benchmarking services. The three of them paid close attention to companies that were, in the words of the diversity director, "sort of conservative like [our company], especially oil companies and financial institutions." Although they did end up including some entertainment and high-tech companies, they tried to avoid them, "because they've already been sort of ahead of the curve on these issues."

Choosing to gather in-depth information on fourteen corporations, the team found that ten of them had equitable benefits while four did not. Using the benchmarking data they had gathered, they were able to allay concerns over cost by showing that enrollment was, as the director of diversity explained, "typically less than 1 percent of the employee population." Their research also made clear that, except for Disney, no company experienced an organized backlash following the announcement of equitable benefits.

Interlocking Corporate Directorates

Intercorporate ties also factored highly in the team's choice of benchmarking targets. They were particularly interested in companies represented on the board of directors and those corporations for which their own CEO was a board member. "I've learned here . . . that benchmarking is *very* important," explained the corporate diversity director. "Our CEO *loves* benchmarking," especially with those firms that are linked to the company via interlocking corporate directorates. These ties, which she described as "off the charts" in their level of importance, ended up playing a critical role in the process (see also Useem 1979; DiMaggio and Powell 1991b).

In the spring of 1998, the diversity director presented the team's argument to the board's three-member Committee on Directors in Corporate Responsibility, which consisted of a man who was serving as a close adviser to President Clinton, the CEO of a publishing company that had already adopted equitable benefits, and a woman from a high-powered law firm in Washington, DC. When the diversity director told them that the company was "moving aggressively toward domestic partner benefits," the reaction from the two men on the committee was, "I can't believe you guys haven't already done that." In retrospect, the director commented, "*That* I think was what *really* helped me." Shortly thereafter, during the last stage of the process, the CEO raised this same point in discussions with his "cabinet." He explained to the members of the executive management committee that the board's committee on corporate responsibility was "*more* than supportive" of equitable benefits.

That summer the corporation decided to extend its policy to domestic partners, the first in the industry to do so. Placing the policy change in a larger context, the corporate diversity director explained, "The transportation industry is *very* conservative and *very* male-dominated, so this is a big deal." Indeed, she pointed to the "macho" environment of the company as the reason that the two high-level gay employees she knew remained closeted at work. To further underline the significance of her company's decision, she cited the reaction of the noontime prayer group she belongs to at work, whose disapproval of equitable benefits mirrored that of the general employee population. An earlier survey of employees had revealed, in her words, "overwhelming opposition" to benefits for both gay and unmarried heterosexual couples. "They'll get over it," the diversity director quipped. "This is just such a macho organization, and I know it's going to take us a long time to get there, but I feel that we just have to start making steps toward making this a more inclusive environment."

The Mimetic Impact of Intercorporate Career Mobility

Aside from benchmarking and interlocking directorates, another source of mimetic isomorphism stems from personnel flows, or intercorporate career mobility (DiMaggio and Powell 1991b). Stephen Mezias (1995, 172), for example, has found that personnel turnover is a significant source of diffusion for organizational innovations and that isomorphism is more likely in "highly professionalized sectors." My findings also suggest that in highly competitive environments and in industries in which career tracks entail movement from one firm to another, once an industry leader grants domestic partner benefits, many others follow suit in order to compete for the best talent in the field. This was the case in the high-tech and entertainment industries. As Paul DiMaggio and Walter Powell (1991b, 73–74) explain, "Organizational fields that include a large professionally trained labor force will be driven by status competition. Organizational prestige and resources are key elements in attracting professionals. This process encourages homogenization as organizations seek to ensure that they can provide the same benefits and services as their competitors."

Many point to the high-tech industry's "tremendous staffing crunch" as the key reason it leads other sectors in offering equitable benefits (Bond 1997). Other contributing factors, according to the Employee Benefits Research Institute (EBRI), are the average age and politics of the employee base. The high-tech industry, as one EBRI analyst notes, "usually employs a more liberal, youthful group" (Mason 1995). Even among firms not located in that industry, companies that recruit a sizable number of specialists from within the field appear more likely to offer domestic partner benefits. In the telecommunications industry, for example, reliance on advanced technology brings intense competition for information-technology professionals, computer engineers, and programmers. Similarly, several of my informants located in firms outside the high-tech industry commented that, during their job interviews with prospective employees of their firms, "techies" frequently ask for and expect equitable benefits.

As the earliest adopters of domestic partner benefits, the high-tech and entertainment industries still remain the most thoroughly gay-inclusive fields in the corporate world. It is important to remember, however, that this swift adoption wave—or rapid mimetic isomorphism—was initiated by lesbian, gay, and bisexual employees who mobilized either within their companies (in the high-tech case) or across the industry (in entertainment). In the latter case, leading gay figures in the entertainment industry formed an organization called Hollywood Supports.

In the early 1990s Hollywood Supports began to disseminate information on why equitable benefits should be adopted and how to do so. Although it was primarily focused on the entertainment industry in its early years, Hollywood Supports now provides resources to companies across corporate America. The organization has a task force that concentrates on educating corporate decision makers. As explained in informational literature, members of the task force set up meetings with executives "to explain and discuss the issues involved in implementing [domestic partner] coverage." Reflecting the widespread support for gay rights in the entertainment industry, the organization's board of trustees numbers approximately 150. The names of board members, which appear on all organizational letterhead, include such well-known figures as David Geffen, Whoopi Goldberg, Goldie Hawn, Spike Lee, Bette Midler, Jack Nicholson, and Steven Spielberg.

Supplementing the internal activism of several gay employee networks, Hollywood Supports was highly successful in the entertainment industry, winning equitable benefits among virtually all of the major players. The fact that the organization has been less persuasive in generating a similar wave of rapid adoptions in other industries may be due in part to the factors I have outlined here. If these other fields are less competitive or intercorporate career mobility in them is less common, then mimetic isomorphic change would proceed more slowly. Future investigations should put this institutionalist argument to empirical test.

The Structuration of Organizational Fields

Attending to variability in the extent and pace of institutionalization, new institutional scholars argue that innovations will diffuse most rapidly among those organizational fields that are more highly "structurated." Driven by competition, state processes, and professionalization, the structuration of an organizational field entails the establishment of frequent interaction among organizations and a widely recognized status hierarchy between leading firms and peripheral ones (DiMaggio and Powell 1991b, 65).

Patricia Thornton (1995) has found, for example, that new policies and practices spread more quickly in those fields where "status competition" is more evident. Trade newsletters and other industry publications heighten awareness of such status hierarchies by focusing on "competitive discourse among dominant players in the field" (221). These publications fuel mimetic isomorphism because they facilitate and encourage benchmarking.

The Internet's Impact on the Salience of Benchmarking

While neoinstitutional scholars have not focused on the impact of the Internet on the structuration of organizational fields, I argue that this new communication technology greatly facilitates benchmarking and thus should contribute to mimetic change. The Internet can contribute to the structuration of a field and to the diffusion of innovations across fields by facilitating "mutual awareness" (DiMaggio and Powell 1991b) among organizations as to the policies and practices that each is adopting. As an example, I turn now to a consideration of a new financially oriented Web site focused on gay, lesbian, and bisexual issues, the first of its kind, and I discuss its potential impact on the importance that corporate elites place on benchmarking.

The Gay Financial Network, the "gfn.com 500," and the "gfn.com 50"

Created in April 1998 by the Gay Financial Network, the gfn.com Web site provides a wide variety of tools, including online trading and banking, financial information, and investment services (Chalfant 1998). It also contains a database, complete with search capabilities, for the "gfn.com 500," which focuses on companies listed in the S&P (Standard and Poor's) 500, although the site is currently shifting to the use of the Fortune 500 list. What makes gfn.com unique among financial Web sites is that it allows users to compare and contrast these corporations on the basis of their gay-related policy records, including areas such as nondiscrimination policies, diversity training, domestic partner benefits, and marketing to the lesbian and gay community. It also includes the name of the company's gay and lesbian employee organization, if applicable.

This at-your-fingertips benchmarking engine, catered to socially concerned and financially savvy users alike, not only provides an invaluable (and free) resource but also lends "empirical credibility" (Snow and Benford 1988, 1992) to the profits-oriented framing strategies of workplace activists. The mere existence of the site makes clear that many individuals do indeed consider a company's record on gay and lesbian issues when choosing where to spend and invest their money, time, and talent. In addition to providing detailed financial information on each company, the site publicizes major corporations' commitment (or lack thereof) to gay-inclusive policies in order to inform the decisions of investors and consumers, not to mention prospective job seekers and workplace activists. The site also allows corporate executives to keep close tabs on the personnel, training, benefits, and marketing policies of the nation's top companies generally and their competitors in particular.

To honor those corporations that particularly stand out for their dedication to lesbian and gay rights in the workplace, the site features an annual "gfn.com 50" list. Drawn from the Fortune 500, the list recognizes the fifty "most powerful and gay-friendly publicly traded companies," with selection criteria including not only the adoption of equitable benefits and other inclusive policies regarding sexual orientation and HIV issues but also those gay-affirmative corporations' rank in "revenues, growth, and economic power" (gfn.com 2000c). As explained in the list description, gfn.com experts chose to focus on the Fortune 500 because of "the considerable influence that these companies exercise in shaping not only American corporate policy, but public perceptions, as well."

Given the free and easily accessible benchmarking services provided by gfn.com, this financially oriented Web site has the potential to increase the importance that elites place on other companies' policies. My survey and interview data reveal that corporate elites vary in how much weight they place on the policy stances of other employers when making decisions about their own policies. This weighting in turn affects the willingness of firms to adopt equitable benefits. Firms that rate the policies of their competitors as very important in their decision-making process are far more likely to institute equitable benefits than companies that rank the policies of their competitors as only somewhat or not at all important. The proportion of adopters in the first category is 86 percent, compared to only 44 percent in the latter. Similarly, companies that rate the policies of other Fortune 1000 companies as very important are more likely to extend benefits than firms that rank the policies of the Fortune 1000 as only somewhat or not at all important. The proportion of adopters across these categories is 75 percent and 58 percent, respectively.

In light of the ease with which gfn.com users can compare policies across companies, this comparison tool should increase the salience of benchmarking among corporate decision makers. This is because the site makes highly visible to both elites and outsiders a company's place along the "adoption curve"—that is, how far ahead or behind a corporation is compared to competitors and others in the wider business world. The gfn.com site should thus augment the importance of benchmarking, because now investors, consumers, and job seekers can easily benchmark, too. Targeting both the financially sophisticated and the gay and allied communities, the site is a tangible manifestation of the ideology of profits, which posits that gay-inclusive policies are good for the bottom line. As such, to borrow terms from David Snow and Robert Benford (1992), gfn.com should add to the "resonance" of the activist-generated profits frame and increase its "potency" in the minds of the corporate elite.

National publicity about the site will most likely increase its impact. Featured in a July 1999 issue of the industry newspaper *American Banker*, gfn.com's founder, Walter B. Schubert, "became the first openly gay man to grace its cover" (Wockner 1999, 1). With the recent advent of a six-million-dollar advertising campaign, gfn.com is even more likely to enhance the salience of benchmarking among corporate decision makers. On February 18, 2000, gfn.com made history as the first "gay-specific" company to be advertised in the *Wall Street Journal*. The eye-catching, half-page ad uses humor to comment on "the often uncomfortable way the financial world has reacted to members of the gay and lesbian community" (gfn.com 2000a). Most of the ad space is filled by a large photo of a balding, cigar-chomping businessman clutching at his lapels as though they were suspenders, saying, "You're GAY!!! . . . Well, I'm feeling quite happy myself." Beneath the photo, the text reads, "Log on for a more welcoming financial world," followed by a list of the financial services and information available at gfn.com.

The ad also ran in *Entertainment Weekly,* with other appearances slated for *Time, Newsweek, U.S. News and World Report, Fortune, Business Week, Money,* and a variety of other business publications. In addition to placement in national gay and lesbian magazines such as the *Advocate, Out,* and *Hero,* an online advertising campaign targeted both financial and gay-related Web sites. As word spreads about gfn.com and its benchmarking search engine, it seems likely that corporate elites will pay even closer attention to the policies and practices of other employers, knowing that lesbians, gays, and their allies are doing the same. Such Web sites should thus facilitate mimetic isomorphism, as companies mimic the policies and "best practices" of others in the field in order to remain competitive.

Gay-focused Internet sites are no longer the only ones to track the adoption of gay-inclusive policies. As further evidence that equitable benefits have hit the mainstream, in an October 2000 *Boston Globe* article about online career resources, Donna Milmore listed sites where people could find answers to common questions, such as which Fortune 500 companies offered domestic partner benefits. For readers interested in such information, Milmore recommended Vault.com, which features human resource specialists who address a wide range of career-related questions.

WorkNet's Newest Benchmarking Tool: The *Corporate Equality Index*

While the gfn.com 500 focuses on the gay-inclusive records of companies included in the S&P 500 (but soon Fortune 500) list, the WorkNet page of the HRC Web site (supported by HRCF) provides searchable databases that allow users to conduct several different types of searches. Among the many options available, visitors to the page can research a particular employer, choose an employment sector (private, public, educational, or nonprofit), compare industries, focus on the Fortune 500, or see complete lists of all employers for which information is available.

The newest addition to HRCF's database offerings is the *Corporate Equality Index (CEI),* mentioned earlier in the chapter. HRCF adapted the index from a tool it acquired in 2001 called the Gay and Lesbian Values Index (glvIndex). Based on the Equality Project's Equality Principles, the glvIndex was designed in 1993 by author Grant Lukenbill and financial adviser Howard Tharsing. After some modifications, HRCF introduced the *Corporate Equality Index* in August 2002, when the first *CEI* report and corporate rankings were released. Along with publishing a twenty-four-page report, available online, WorkNet staff added *CEI* data to their Web page's search capabilities, thereby providing Internet users with the ability to compare the scores or ratings of companies or entire industries based on how many gay-inclusive criteria they have met. The WorkNet page describes the new benchmarking tool as "a simple way to evaluate whether America's biggest employers are treating their GLBT employees and consumers equitably."

The index rates companies on a scale of 0 to 100 percent depending on whether they have adopted the following seven criteria, which are weighted equally: a written nondiscrimination policy that includes sexual orientation; a written nondiscrimination policy that includes gender identity or expression; domestic partner benefits; equal recognition and support of employee resource groups; diversity training that includes sexual orientation and/or gender expression; respectful marketing and/or corporate donations to the lesbian, gay, bisexual, and transgender community or AIDS-related organizations; and avoidance of overtly hostile corporate action that would undermine equal rights. Having drawn widespread coverage in both print and broadcast venues—including at least twenty-five different newspapers, CNN Headline News, and almost twenty other television stations from across the country (HRC 2003d)—the *CEI* serves as another important virtual resource that will likely facilitate mimetic isomorphism. As media attention brings greater visibility to these benchmarking tools and to the policies of the country's largest corporations, even elites who were not apt to give much weight to the diversity policies and practices of other companies will most likely begin to do so, knowing that socially concerned consumers, investors, and potential employees can so easily make these comparisons themselves now.

As HRC's then executive director Elizabeth Birch explained in a press release announcing the debut of the index, "The HRC Corporate Equality Index is a tool that can help fair-minded Americans decide what products to buy, where to work and how to invest. At the same time, we hope the index inspires those companies that fell short to take the next step and change their policies, not merely to improve their scores but because fairness is good for business" (HRC 2002j). Indeed, while some executives may not believe that fairness is good for business, they nevertheless recognize that public perception of blatant *un*fairness can be bad for business. As previously discussed, Lockheed Martin and Cracker Barrel, after remaining recalcitrant for years, finally added sexual orientation to their nondiscrimination policies—with the former also adopting equitable benefits—only after news reports publicized the fact that they had scored a zero in the *CEI*. Benchmarking tools such as the *CEI* should thus push an increasing number of employers to initiate at least some gay-inclusive policy changes so as to avoid negative publicity surrounding a zero or near-zero rating. In fact, perusing the WorkNet employer database (an interim *CEI*) in mid-February 2004, one would find no companies with a zero score (HCRF 2004).

Raising Consciousness and Raising the Bar

Aside from a stick, these benchmarking resources offer a carrot as well, in that companies that have already embraced some measure of equality can gain favorable media attention and other forms of public recognition if they adopt increasingly inclusive policies. For example, press coverage of the 2002 *CEI* ratings included the names of employers earning a perfect score, an achievement attained by only 4 percent of companies (13 out of 319). Only a year and a half later, the number of companies with a perfect score—a select group that will be discussed in the conclusion of this book—had more than doubled, reaching 34 by February 2004 (HCRF 2004). With HRC now issuing yearly *CEI* reports, in addition to providing updated rankings on an ongoing basis via its WorkNet employer database, increased media visibility will surely follow and may spur other corporations to improve their standings in order to earn distinction in the months and years ahead. Indeed, according to an *HRC Quarterly* article aptly titled "Corporate Catch-Up?" (HRC 2002c), as soon as the *CEI* was unveiled, in 2002, WorkNet staff began receiving "dozens of calls . . . from U.S. corporations, asking how to get better ratings," some of which, including IBM and PG&E Corporation, quickly added new policies, bringing their scores to 100 percent. Other companies called to announce that they had adopted one or more of the gay-inclusive measures tapped in the report. "The index is having exactly the effect that we had intended," explained Daryl Herrschaft, deputy director of WorkNet. "It acknowledges best practices and sets clear goals for companies to strive toward" (quoted in HRC 2002c).

Even before the index was released, corporate officials at Pfizer, one of the world's largest drug companies, and SBC Communications, the giant provider of phone and wireless services, contacted WorkNet staff to be sure that their companies would be rated in the *CEI* report. "This is just one more sign of the progress we're making in some of America's biggest workplaces," commented Kim Mills, HRC's education director. "Companies are actively seeking to be rated, and many want to know what they need to do to earn the highest score possible because many are looking for bragging rights in their market sector" (quoted in Budisatrijo 2002). Similarly, gfn.com provides opportunities for inclusive employers to toot their own horns in a section of its Business Forum called "Profile of LGBT-Friendly Companies," where "[p]articipating companies have two pages to insert text and photos concerning their policies, a more integrative approach than traditional advertising." The purpose of the feature is to "provid[e] an opportunity for companies to promote their gay-friendly initiatives to key gay and lesbian stakeholders, including employees and consumers" (gfn.com 2003).

Workplace activists are also aided in their pursuit of equality by mainstream business publications that highlight particularly affirming employers. Magazines such as *Fortune* and *Working Woman,* for example, function as important legitimators of diversity best practices by publishing lists such as "America's Best Companies for Minorities" or "The Top 25 Public Companies for Women," which symbolically reward those employers that are judged to be particularly cutting-edge with regard to diversity. These and numerous other lists appear online as well, bringing additional visibility to the issues and to the "most desirable" employers.

Professional associations focused on diversity likewise provide public recognition of inclusive employers by issuing reports such as the annual *Best of the Best: Corporate Awards for Diversity and Women.* Compiled by Diversity Best Practices and the Business Women's Network, the second annual *Best of the Best* report, published in 2002, was based on a meta-analysis of sorts, with assessments made by examining thirty-eight of the latest "best company" lists that ranked employers with regard to their opportunities for people of color, women, older workers, individuals with disabilities, and gay men and lesbians (Business Wire 2002). Tellingly, the authors of the report included at least four gay-themed lists among the thirty-eight consulted: HRCF's *CEI,* the "gfn.com 50" list, *Advocate* magazine's "Best Gay-Friendly Firms in the Country," and the "Top 10 Lesbian Places to Work" list published by *Girlfriends* magazine.

Such significant inclusion of gay-inclusive policies in determining the "best of the best" reflects not only the mainstreaming of gay and lesbian rights in the workplace but also the wider cultural and institutional impact of the benchmarking tools provided by HRC and HRCF, gfn.com, and other organizations and publications. With widespread media coverage accompanying their unveiling, these tools have not only raised public consciousness of lesbian and gay workplace issues, they have also raised the bar for companies interested in earning or maintaining a reputation as "employers of choice" (see also Elswick 2001). As gay-focused benchmarking resources get incorporated into various "metalists," thereby helping to constitute gay-inclusive policies as best practices, other employers will be encouraged to institute such changes as companies compete with one another not only for "the best and the brightest" but for recognition as "the best of the best."

Although he has not focused on challenging groups, Joseph Galaskiewicz (1991, 300) has examined the impact that awards can have on corporate policy, especially when those mechanisms for public recognition become institutionalized. In his study of corporate philanthropy in the Twin Cities, Galaskiewicz commented on the favorable effects of an annual awards luncheon sponsored by the Chamber of Commerce, which publicly recognized particularly generous corporations. With members of the press and high-level political officials in attendance, the ceremony helped companies gain stature in the public eye and hence encouraged other corporations to join the "philanthropic elite" (301).

Mimetic Isomorphism and the Need for Legitimacy

While I have focused on competitive pressures, it is important to keep in mind that mimetic isomorphism also derives from the need for organizations to obtain legitimacy (J. Meyer and Rowan 1977; DiMaggio and Powell 1991b; Christensen and Molin 1995). Once a particular practice starts to become established among certain organizations, pressures toward conformity increase. Thus, organizations will "model their own structures on patterns thought to be, variously, more modern, appropriate, or professional" (Scott 1987, 504, quoted in Mezias 1995, 177). As DiMaggio and Powell (1991b, 65) explain, "As an innovation spreads, a threshold is reached beyond which adoption provides legitimacy rather than improves performance (Meyer and Rowan 1977). Strategies that are rational for individual organizations may not be rational if adopted by large numbers. Yet the very fact that they are normatively sanctioned increases the likelihood of their adoption."

In other words, while early adopters may institute an innovation in order to obtain a competitive advantage, once the practice becomes more widespread, that advantage dissipates. Later adopters may simply be following suit in order to be seen as legitimate. Illustrating this process, several respondents in my study explained that, while their individual companies did not want to be among the first adopters in their field, they eventually offered equitable benefits to avoid being seen as "behind the curve."

Normative and Cognitive Isomorphism as Institutional Opportunity: Discursive Activists and the Business Press

In addition to mimetic and coercive pressures, new institutional theorists focus on professionalization as a key mechanism that promotes the diffusion of policy innovations (DiMaggio and Powell 1991b; Scott 1995b). This source of normative isomorphic change derives from the credentialing standards, knowledge frameworks, and intercorporate networks of various professionals who seek "to establish a cognitive base and legitimation for their occupational autonomy" (DiMaggio and Powell 1991b, 70). University training programs, professional networks, intra- and interindustry councils, and formal associations of human resource managers, diversity specialists, and other management professionals serve as channels for the diffusion of organizational innovations and for the legitimating rationales that define them as best practices. Thus, DiMaggio and Powell (76) hypothesize that the more involved organizational managers are in trade and professional associations, the more likely each one's organization will come to resemble others in its field. Additional mechanisms of diffusion include organizational consultants, professional conferences or seminars, professional newsletters or magazines, and journals for human resource professionals, diversity specialists, and other management personnel (Edelman, Uggen, and Erlanger 1999).

Institutionalists would predict human resource professionals and diversity specialists to be particularly relevant channels for the diffusion of gay-inclusive policies in the corporate world. This is because, according to new institutionalists Frank Dobbin and John Sutton (1998), human resource professionals were responsible for developing and diffusing the idea that diversity is a business imperative. In analyzing the rise and spread of equal employment opportunity (EEO) and affirmative action (AA) departments, for example, Dobbin and Sutton have found that human resource professionals were responsible for "retheorizing" these offices. Human resource professionals argued that, rather than seeing the new departments as compliance measures that emerged in response to federal policy enacted in the wake of the Civil Rights Act, corporate elites should see them as economically rational means of increasing employee productivity and loyalty. Dobbin and Sutton refer to the rise of this framework, which views diversity as a business imperative, as part of the "new human resources management paradigm."

While companies originally instituted EEO and AA offices to signal compliance with the law, beginning in the 1980s middle managers in human resources began to frame these departments in ways that decoupled them from their original source of inspiration. Rather than acknowledging the influence of the "rights revolution" in the employment sector, human resource professionals began to justify new EEO and AA offices "in purely economic terms" (441). Dobbin and Sutton argue that this "drift toward efficiency" occurred because state intervention in the private sector is seen as illegitimate, and because this rhetoric served the professional interests of human resource personnel by expanding their role as specialists.

Likewise, through content analysis of personnel journals, Lauren Edelman, Christopher Uggen, and Howard Erlanger (1999) reveal the role of personnel professionals in framing EEO grievance procedures as rational practices. Employing "ideologies of rationality," these professionals argue that grievance procedures increase employee morale and reduce the risk of lawsuits, union mobilization, and liability. Thus, personnel experts have played a key part in the diffusion of grievance procedures in workplaces across the country.

The Locus of Theorization

The framing work described here exemplifies a cognitive process that neo-institutionalists call "theorization," whereby actors purposefully construct accounts that legitimize particular innovations "in terms of standardized notions of efficiency or justice or progress" (Strang and Meyer 1993, 497; see also Suchman 1995). While attention to theorization acknowledges the role of agents in effecting organizational change, institutional scholars nevertheless tend to emphasize "culturally legitimated theorists," such as academics, policy analysts, and other professionals (Strang and Meyer 1993, 494). This approach pushes activists to the sidelines, portraying them as mere supporters in the diffusion of already theorized accounts rather than as active players in the theorization process itself. Note, for example, how the following neoinstitutionalist account gives short shrift to the role of activists in the diffusion process: "[D]iffusion obviously requires *support* from . . . state authorities, large corporate actors, [and] grassroots activists. In some way, models [or frames] must make the transition *from* theoretical formulation *to* social movement *to* institutional imperative" (495; emphasis added).

In contrast, my theoretical synthesis broadens the reach of the spotlight to illuminate the active role that challengers play in the theorization process. Workplace activists are not simply supportive cast; indeed, they frequently write the script that human resource professionals and other corporate elites use to legitimize new policies to others within and outside of their companies. Contrary to the arguments of new institutionalists (J. Meyer and Rowan 1977; DiMaggio and Powell 1991b; Dobbin and Sutton 1998; Edelman, Uggen, and Erlanger 1999), my results indicate that the primary agents of rationalization are not always located in the professions.

While the "new human resources paradigm" rationalized diversity by framing it as a business imperative (Dobbin and Sutton 1998), it was gay workplace activists who pushed for an expanded definition of diversity that would include lesbian, gay, and bisexual issues. In the case of domestic partner benefits, for example, the original promulgators of the "efficiency argument," which I refer to as an "ideology of profits," were gay employee activists themselves, accompanied by others in the larger workplace movement. The profits frame was then further diffused via the workplace projects of NGLTF and HRC, lesbian and gay diversity consultants, and a small number of heterosexual diversity professionals who were allies of the movement.

I therefore argue that (heterosexual) human resource professionals and diversity consultants who now include gay men, lesbians, and bisexuals in their definitions of diversity—and who paint this expanded definition as profitable—are best seen as the trailing rather than leading edge of such reframing. In other words, the motivation for this "frame extension" (Snow et al. 1986) does not stem from the professional interests of human resource managers who, in the case of EEO and AA, were seen as desiring to expand their domain as specialists (DiMaggio 1991; Dobbin and Sutton 1998); instead, the impetus behind the frame expansion derives from the collectively constructed interests of lesbian, gay, and bisexual employees who wish to secure equitable treatment. Co-opting corporate discourse, these workplace activists utilize a profits frame to gain access to a set of institutionalized employee rights that they are denied.

Once it was developed and honed by early employee activists, the profits frame began to spread rapidly through the infrastructure of the workplace movement, eventually diffusing to the pages of the business press. How did this transfer take place? How did the framing strategies proffered by locally embedded gay networks become established elements of the larger institutional environment? The answer to these questions lies largely in the fact that the workplace movement consists not simply of gay and lesbian employee networks but also of a cadre of gay, lesbian, bisexual, and gay-allied consultants, speakers, researchers, and writers. Functioning as what Mary Katzenstein (1998) would call "discursive activists," this cadre helps to package and publicize the framing efforts of gay employee groups. These discursive activists create opportunities for employee activists as the former's publications, workshops, and seminars diffuse through the business world. Once the work of discursive activists began to be featured in the business press, employee networks could draw on these publications to help legitimate their claims. Before discussing the impact of such publicity on equitable-benefits adoption, it is first necessary to provide a brief sketch of the framing processes themselves, which I will discuss in more detail in chapter 6.

Doing the Right Thing and Increasing the Bottom Line: Ideologies of Ethics and Profits

As part of their strategic repertoire, workplace activists tend to utilize two different "collective action frames" (Snow et al. 1986): what I call an *ideology of profits*, which is part of corporations' claimed domain; and an *ideology of ethics*, which is generally drawn from wider notions of equality and justice promulgated by progressive social movements. The profits frame, on the one hand, *rationalizes*—literally, in terms of cost-benefit analysis—the adoption of equitable benefits by characterizing them as "good for the bottom line." The ethics frame, on the other hand, *justifies*—in the literal sense—the extension of benefits by describing them as "the right thing to do" or as a matter of equal rights. The profits frame co-opts corporate values by arguing that inclusive policies improve employee recruitment and retention, heighten productivity, and expand customer markets. The ethics frame, in contrast, draws on what social movement scholars refer to as a civil rights master frame (Snow and Benford 1992; McAdam 1994).

These two frames constitute the ideological repertoire of gay employee activists. Most networks use the two in tandem, but challengers rely far more heavily on an ideology of profits to legitimate their call for policy change. Employee groups discovered early on that exclusive reliance on an ethics frame met with very little success. This is not surprising, since the profits frame "resonates" (Snow et al. 1986) more deeply with the capitalist values of the corporate world. Some activists even downplay or avoid altogether an ideology of ethics. This is because arguments such as these can incite or exacerbate internal and external backlash by fundamentalist Christian groups. Given activists' reliance on the profits frame, it is important to examine how larger institutional processes help to diffuse this frame throughout the wider business world, thereby increasing the legitimacy of challengers' claims.

The Diffusion of the Profits Frame via the Business Press

Since normative isomorphism refers mainly to the influence of professionalization, it seems more appropriate to view the diffusion of the profits frame as an instance of what I would consider *cognitive isomorphism*. Much of what is "new" in new institutionalist approaches revolves around attention to the influence of "cognitive-cultural processes" (Scott 1998), such as wider belief systems, cultural frames, discourses, and cognitive scripts, that lead to the adoption of similar policies and practices across organizations (Scott 1995b; see also DiMaggio and Powell 1991a). Taking both cognitive and normative processes into account, I see the following as constituting favorable institutional opportunities for employee activists: the increasing coverage of lesbian, gay, and bisexual issues in the business press; and the additional diffusion of the profits frame via business networks, conferences, and professional associations such as the Society for Human Resources Management.

Breaking the Silence of the Business Press

As discussed in chapter 1, a 1991 story in *Fortune* magazine broke the longstanding silence of the business press regarding gay and lesbian issues. On December 16, Thomas Stewart's article "Gay in Corporate America" was featured on the cover of this widely read business magazine. Scattered generously throughout the article were references to the healthy returns that companies could reap from gay-inclusive policies. This emphasis reflects the diffusion of movement discourse onto the pages of mainstream business publications. Mirroring an ideology of profits, the article presented the bottom-line rationale for creating a gay-affirming workplace. Pointing to the high price that companies paid for noninclusive or hostile environments, Stewart cited a study by academic James Woods (later published; see Woods 1993), who documented a phenomenon that he called "entrepreneurial flight." Fearful of a glass ceiling, tired of an unwelcoming environment, or frustrated by unfair treatment, many talented gay professionals ended up leaving companies to start their own businesses (Stewart 1991, 46).

Stewart also raised the issue of productivity, quoting corporate consultant Brian McNaught: "My basic premise is that homophobia takes a toll on the ability of 10% of the work force to produce" (44). This statistic, an implicit reference to the well-known Kinsey study that found 10 percent of respondents clustered toward the "exclusively homosexual" end of the sexual continuum (Kinsey, Pomeroy, and Martin 1948, quoted in Rubenstein 1993, 10), is commonly used by gay employee activists to emphasize the institutional costs of hostile environments and heterosexist policies.

Stewart's decision to interview Brian McNaught is notable, given the key contributions this discursive activist has made to the workplace movement. Although the article does not make explicit his activist connections, McNaught, who is openly gay, holds an esteemed place within the movement. My interviews with employee activists reflect a deep respect and admiration for the man. Over a decade ago he developed corporate workshops on homophobia in the workplace. Having been fired from his job back in 1975 after his employer learned of his sexual orientation, McNaught speaks from experience. Considered the country's leading corporate diversity consultant on gay issues in the workplace and dubbed "the godfather of gay sensitivity training" by the *New York Times,* he has written three books, has produced or been featured in several educational programs that have aired regularly on PBS, and has presented talks at hundreds of companies across the country, sometimes for senior management and other times for employees at large.

Moving Up in the Hierarchy of Prestige

Although movement discourse began to appear in the business press and in personnel journals in 1991, it took a couple of additional years to hit the more prestigious business journals. In part because of the work of discursive activists, who succeeded in publishing a flurry of articles and books in 1993, coverage of gay issues in the workplace finally appeared in academically affiliated business journals. In the summer of 1993, the *Harvard Business Review* published an article entitled "Is This the Right Time to Come Out?" Written by Alistair D. Williamson, an editor at Harvard Business School Press, the article was organized around a case study based on a compilation of real-life experiences, although corporate names and individual identities had been changed. Following the presentation of the case study, meant to provoke discussion of the perils and promise of coming out at work, seven experts responded.

Helping to establish the "respectability" of the topic, the article included photographs of the seven experts along with brief biographies listing their related publications and affiliations. The variety of institutional spheres represented is telling, since it conveyed that gay-inclusive thinking is advocated not only by gay activists but also by high-level professionals in the world of business and law and by academics and consultants who have studied the issue. The panelists included a former Fortune 500 executive who had become president and CEO of the Society for Human Resource Management (to which, according to my survey results, many human resource vice presidents belong); three professors from departments of law, cultural anthropology, and communications, the latter of whom wrote *The Corporate Closet: The Professional Lives of Gay Men in America* (Woods 1993); a management consultant and an attorney, who came out as a couple in their response and had recently coauthored an article on sexual orientation in the workplace for the journal *Compensation and Benefits Management* (Colbert and Wofford 1993); and a lawyer (the only woman on the panel) who was board cochair for the Lambda Legal Defense and Education Fund, a national gay rights organization.

Engagingly well written, the case study resembles a popular role-playing or discussion-based strategy used by gay employee groups and/or outside consultants during diversity workshops. The article presents the case of a "star employee" who is gay and who tells his manager, an assistant vice president of a financial advisory firm, that he intends to bring his partner of five years to the company's silver anniversary dinner. The employee will be featured as a guest of honor at the dinner for his recent success in closing a highly lucrative deal. Also in attendance will be top clients of the firm, including some conservative military contractors, and several influential business and political leaders. Although many colleagues of the employee know that he is gay and have met his partner, who is a corporate attorney, his manager expresses shock that he is gay and asks questions that appear ignorant but not necessarily homophobic ("Why do you want to mix your personal and professional lives?"). The manager receives calm and well-reasoned responses ("For the same reason that you bring your wife to company social events"). After trying to discourage the associate from bringing his partner to the event, the manager says that he needs time to think about what he has been told.

At this point in the article, the case study ended and the seven experts offered commentary on the gay man's actions and on how his manager should respond next. While acknowledging both the risks and benefits of coming out, all of the commentators made a strong case for the bottom-line advantages of gay-affirming environments. Reflecting coercive sources of isomorphism (DiMaggio and Powell 1991b), two of the experts emphasized the legal rationale for adopting inclusive policies, citing the number of states and municipalities that outlaw discrimination on the basis of sexual orientation. One panelist also raised the issue of domestic partner benefits, framing them as a matter of compensation equity. Others framed gay-inclusive policies as both ethically desirable and financially profitable. As two of the experts concluded, "[I]n the long run, the moral choice will be the lucrative one as well. When major changes in cultural values take place, it pays to be leading the trend rather than running behind making excuses" (Williamson 1993, 24).

Activist discourse had thus finally diffused to the pages of a widely read, highly prestigious business journal aimed at corporate decision makers. Even more significant, the burst of gay-related workplace publications in 1993 appears to be related to a jump in the number of equitable-benefits adopters. Until 1993 only 2 Fortune 1000 companies had instituted domestic partner benefits, but by the end of that year the number had increased to 11 (see Figure 2). In a similar vein, neoinstitutionalists Erin Kelly and Frank Dobbin (1999) found that press coverage of new maternity-leave standards stimulated employers to adopt such policies.

Discursive Activists and the Explosion of Gay Workplace Titles

The groundbreaking coverage of gay workplace issues in *Fortune* magazine and the *Harvard Business Review* was soon followed by an explosion of related books published between 1993 and 1996. The titles alone reveal common themes in the new literature, whose intended audience includes not simply lesbian and gay employees but corporate decision makers as well: *Gay Issues in the Workplace* (McNaught 1993), *The Corporate Closet: The Professional Lives of Gay Men in America* (Woods 1993), *Homosexual Issues in the Workplace* (Diamant 1993), *The 100 Best Companies for Gay Men and Lesbians—Plus Options and Opportunities No Matter Where You Work* (Mickens 1994a), *Sexual Orientation in the Workplace: Gay Men, Lesbians, Bisexuals, and Heterosexuals Working Together* (Zuckerman and Simons 1994), *Cracking the Corporate Closet: The 200 Best (and Worst) Companies to Work For, Buy From, and Invest In If You're Gay or Lesbian—and Even If You Aren't* (D. Baker, Strub, and Henning 1995), *Straight Talk about Gays in the Workplace: Creating an Inclusive, Productive Environment for Everyone in Your Organization* (Winfeld and Spielman 1995), *A Manager's Guide to Sexual Orientation in the Workplace* (Powers and Ellis 1995), *Untold Millions: Positioning Your Business for the Gay and Lesbian Consumer Revolution* (Lukenbill 1995), *Straight Jobs/Gay Lives: Gay and Lesbian Professionals, the Harvard Business School, and the American Workplace* (Friskopp and Silverstein 1995), *Out in the Workplace: The Pleasures and Perils of Coming Out on the Job* (Rasi and Rodriguez-Nogues 1995), *The Gay Male's Odyssey in the Corporate World: From Disempowerment to Empowerment* (Miller 1995), and *Sexual Identity on the Job: Issues and Services* (Ellis and Riggle 1996).

The contents of the books clearly reflect movement discourse, providing strong arguments for the ethical and especially the profit-oriented reasons for adopting equitable policies. All of the books include a discussion of gay and lesbian employee networks, some providing specific information such as how to form a new network or how particular groups have won gay-inclusive policies. A few include partial lists of gay employee networks, along with contact information (Mickens 1994a; D. Baker, Strub, and Henning 1995; Friskopp and Silverstein 1995; Powers and Ellis 1995). Most of the authors also list other resources, such as gay-related organizations, consultants, books, articles, newsletters, and videos.

The efforts of these discursive activists, whose publications and presentations disseminate ideologies of profits and ethics, resemble what Eric Abrahamson and Charles Fombrun (1992, 176) call the "mass media production of macro-culture" (quoted in Thornton 1995, 221). New institutional scholars have stressed the role of human resource professionals and academics in producing macro culture, and they have focused on professional journals, trade newsletters, and other business publications in fueling the spread of organizational innovations (Thornton 1995). My research demonstrates that discursive activists can also be important producers of macro culture and thus a key source of isomorphic change. As the publications of discursive activists were reviewed in the business press, the profits frame undoubtedly reached the desks of more and more corporate elites. The work of gay employee networks was thus made a bit easier, as the message of the movement, reflected now in the pages of respected business journals, gained a degree of external legitimacy.

Summary

This chapter has highlighted the ways that isomorphic pressures in the sociopolitical and organizational field environments can promote the diffusion of gay-inclusive policies. Conceptualizing these isomorphic change mechanisms as *macro-level institutional opportunities,* I documented the favorable policy impacts of three institutional processes. Focusing first on *coercive isomorphism,* I discussed the positive effects of San Francisco's Equal Benefits Ordinance, the first of only a few such mandates in the country. I also investigated the "softer" side of coercive isomorphism, uncovering the normative impact of the legal environment. Though not mandating equitable-benefits coverage, each of the following local and/or state-level measures facilitated favorable policy outcomes: nondiscrimination statutes that prohibit antigay bias in private employment, ordinances that grant equitable benefits to government employees, and domestic partner registries that provide mostly symbolic recognition of lesbian and gay relationships. I also revealed the effects of boycotts, lawsuits, and shareholder activism.

Turning next to *mimetic isomorphism,* I discussed the importance of field-level influences such as benchmarking, interlocking corporate directorates, and intercorporate career mobility. Directing attention to the new benchmarking tools available on the Internet, I also considered the impact that such virtual resources are likely to have on corporate decision makers. Relatedly, I addressed the introduction of the *Corporate Equality Index* and its probable role in inducing even some of the most hostile employers to adopt gay-inclusive policies. Even in the absence of gay employee networks, mimetic forces can exert powerful pressures on companies. Once a few leaders adopt equitable benefits, others may follow suit to remain competitive. And once enough companies jump on the bandwagon by mimicking the best practices of these leading organizations, pressures toward conformity increase all the more as slower-moving companies, seeking legitimacy, eventually join in to avoid being seen as "behind the curve."

Finally, I revealed the positive effects of *normative and cognitive isomorphism*, including the emergence of a new human resources paradigm that framed, or "theorized," diversity as a business imperative. Correcting for new institutionalists' tendency to posit the locus of theorization in the professions, I emphasized the role that discursive activists play in expanding this diversity frame to include lesbian, gay, and bisexual issues. As discursive activists succeeded in getting their work published and reviewed in the business press and in the more prestigious journals, corporate elites were increasingly exposed to the profits frame that employee activists themselves had originated. Reflected in the pages of the business press and personnel journals, their message gained legitimacy and thereby facilitated the adoption of gay-inclusive policies.

As important as these macro-level institutional opportunities are for challengers, they are not the only contextual factors that help to account for inclusive policy change. It is also necessary to examine the crucial role of opportunities and constraints in the more immediate environment of activists, namely, the corporation itself. I thus turn in the next chapter to a consideration of *meso-level institutional opportunities,* referred to more simply as *organizational opportunity,* delineating its key dimensions and documenting the impact of each dimension on the adoption of equitable benefits.

5

Corporate Windows of Opportunity: The Impact of Internal Factors on Gay-Inclusive Policies

As shown in the previous chapter, factors outside corporate walls influence the adoption of gay-inclusive policies. But what about the more immediate environment of workplace activists, namely, the targeted corporation? And what about the role of organizational challengers themselves? If the power of institutional analysis lies in the significance granted to large-scale contextual factors, both normative and structural, in explaining the diffusion of organizational innovations, its blind spot has been the failure to identify the agents of change within organizations, whether elites or mobilized constituencies (Chaves 1996; DiMaggio 1988). Even with more recent attempts to address agency and power, scholars in the field acknowledge that neoinstitutionalists lack a clear understanding of "the conditions under which actors in a given organization who do not have power, come to gain power, and bring about shifts in strategy" (Fligstein 1991, 335). In other words, new institutionalism leaves us empty-handed when trying to understand both the meso-level conditions that challengers face within their own companies and the movement strategies that activists use to alter those conditions.

Social movement approaches clearly provide a much-needed complement to institutional perspectives on organizational transformation. Social movement theory directs our attention to the role of activist networks in social change and to the mobilization processes and political opportunities that contribute to movement success (McAdam 1982; McAdam, McCarthy, and Zald 1996a). Students of social movements view activist outcomes as resulting from the interplay between structural constraints and opportunities in the larger political environment and internal organizational, strategic, and cultural factors (Morris 1984; W. Gamson 1990; McAdam 1994; Staggenborg 1995; McAdam, McCarthy, and Zald 1996a; D. Meyer, Whittier, and Robnett 2002).

Researchers in the resource mobilization and political process traditions treat political opportunity primarily in reference to state structures and political alignments (Jenkins and Perrow 1977; Tilly 1978; McAdam 1982; Katzenstein and Mueller 1987; Staggenborg 1991; McAdam, McCarthy, and Zald 1996a; W. Gamson and Meyer 1996; Jenkins and Klandermans 1995a; Tarrow 1998). Pulling from this body of literature, Sidney Tarrow (1998, 76–77) defines the structure of political opportunity as "consistent—but not necessarily formal or permanent—dimensions of the political environment that provide incentives for collective action by affecting people's expectations for success or failure." In addition to focusing on variation in state repression, Tarrow highlights four key dimensions of political opportunity: increased access to the polity, electoral realignments, divided elites, and influential allies (77–80).

While political process theory provides a powerful explanatory model for understanding the emergence and trajectory of state-centered challenges, it needs some fine-tuning in order to fit the needs of scholars interested in institutional activism. When we shift the focus from the state to the workplace, for example, it becomes necessary to examine the elements of opportunity and constraint that exist inside particular corporations. In this chapter I offer such a framework. Adapting Tarrow's political process model (1998) and the new literature on cultural opportunities (McAdam 1994; Johnston and Klandermans 1995; Taylor 1996), I delineate the *meso-level institutional opportunities,* which I also refer to as *organizational opportunities,* that exist within the immediate environment of institutional challengers. In particular, I examine four key elements in the targeted corporation itself. These dimensions of organizational opportunity facilitate favorable policy outcomes or, if absent, constrain activists' chance of success.

I first focus on the impact of *structural templates* that signal at least a minimal level of legitimacy for previously excluded groups and that provide access to decision makers and to institutional resources. Second, I discuss the significance of *organizational realignments* that bring more receptive elites or organizations into the issue domain, thereby altering the balance of power in the corporation. Third, I consider the importance of *allies,* whether influential individuals or other organizational challengers, who serve as coalition partners. Finally, I examine the impact of *cultural supports* such as a diversity-embracing corporate culture and, among elites, preexisting personal ties or "punctuating experiences" that "humanize" challengers and foster empathy with their struggle.

Opportunities as a Dynamic Process of Contestation

In her utopian essay on progressive politics in the twenty-first century, Verta Taylor (2000, 221) emphasizes that movements depend on the ability of challengers "to identify and translate conditions, circumstances, and events in the wider society into protest opportunities." She points out that sometimes opportunities appear "ripe for the plucking," but at other times challengers must work hard to cultivate their own opportunities (221–22). For example, many gay employee groups push to be included in corporate nondiscrimination clauses and then, once successful, use those policies to argue for inclusive diversity training and equitable benefits. Likewise, when elites prove hesitant or unwilling to effect change, activists focus on winning allies who, in turn, help create a more favorable corporate climate.

Given this degree of play and malleability in the opportunities of challenging groups, Taylor argues that opportunities "should be considered not a fixed commodity but a dynamic process of contestation" (222). Similarly, in a section called "Making Opportunities," Sidney Tarrow (1996, 58) explains that an activist network "can experience changes in its opportunity structure as a function of its own actions." By expanding their tactical repertoires, for example, challengers can open up new possibilities (Tilly 1993; McAdam 1982, 1983; W. Gamson 1990). Craig Jenkins and Bert Klandermans also argue that social movements can "[set] in motion changes that often create new opportunities for further action. Hence, opportunities both *exist* and are *made*" (1995a, 7; emphasis in the original). In other words, aggrieved groups do not simply wait for more favorable conditions, they help create them. Through mobilizing structures, framing processes, and strategic deployment of collective identities, challenging groups take aim not only at their immediate target but also at the set of conditions that constrain them (McAdam 1996; McAdam, McCarthy, and Zald 1996b).

Comparative approaches reveal that dimensions of political opportunity vary across political systems, issue domains, groups, and time (Dalton 1995; McAdam, McCarthy, and Zald 1996a; Tarrow 1996). Scholars have also focused on the relative malleability of opportunity structures, some dimensions being more stable and others more volatile (W. Gamson and Meyer 1996). Pointing to the more volatile end of the continuum, Tarrow (1996) refers to "dynamic" opportunities. Likewise, my comparative approach reveals that institutional opportunities and constraints vary not only within but also across companies, with some dimensions being more open to change and others appearing relatively impervious.

Organizational Opportunities: Creating and Capitalizing on Favorable Corporate Conditions

Taking seriously the argument that opportunity is a dynamic process rather than a fixed structure, this chapter has a dual focus: to examine the impact of meso-level institutional opportunities present in the target organization itself; and, where appropriate, to highlight the role of activists in creating these favorable conditions if they do not already exist. I turn now to the immediate site of contention for workplace activists. With the corporation as the focal terrain of struggle, I draw out the dynamic interplay between structures of constraint and opportunity on the one hand and movement processes on the other. I delineate and discuss variations in each of the four key dimensions of organizational opportunity: structural templates, organizational realignments, allies, and cultural supports.

Structural Templates as Organizational Opportunity

The first dimension of organizational opportunity refers to the presence of structural templates that signal at least a minimal level of legitimacy for previously excluded groups and that allow access to key decision makers and institutional resources. Indicators of such templates include the following: preexisting employee resource groups, such as those for women and people of color; mechanisms for official corporate recognition of networks; access to a budget; the presence of a diversity office; and a diversity council or task force that includes representatives from the various employee networks.

Early Risers as Structural Templates

As Tarrow's comparative research (1998) has shown, "early risers" can provide effective models of collective action for new challengers. In many cases nascent gay and lesbian employee groups were able to draw from and expand on the mobilizing structures and collective action frames of their officially recognized sister networks. These diversity groups for women and people of color had already convinced at least some executives that diversity-embracing policies were profitable. Not only can the mere existence of such employee groups signify an important opening for new challengers, but preexisting networks can also express vocal support for newcomers, turning symbolic institutional opportunities into more tangible ones as early risers become allies of those who follow.

Such was the case with the emergence of "GLUE," still the country's largest gay employee network. As mentioned in chapter 1, a small group of friends who worked at a telecommunications company began talking in 1987 about the need for a lesbian and gay employee organization like the other diversity networks that already existed in their corporation. Their employer had adopted a gay-inclusive nondiscrimination policy over a decade earlier in response to external pressure by gay rights activists. Nevertheless, the friends felt that the company did not enforce the policy. Fearful of coming out to top management, they decided to ask someone in the diversity office to serve as a go-between. After the liaison "tested the water," the group decided, with much trepidation, to request a meeting with upper management. As one member of the steering committee put it, "I [was] really leery of talking about this to someone who doesn't know me and who is four levels above me in the hierarchy."

At the same time and halfway across the country, two gay friends who worked in the company's research-and-development site on the East Coast noticed bathroom graffiti targeted against "faggots." One of the two served on the company's Diversity Council, and although "gay issues weren't on the list then," this man explained that he saw the company putting "a big emphasis on equal opportunity and diversity." Testing the depth and breadth of their company's commitment, the two decided to complain to management and the Affirmative Action Council, which included representatives from the women's employee group and the African American network.

Functioning as structural templates and potential allies, or at the very least as symbolic markers of normative support for diversity and inclusion, the preexisting employee networks as well as the diversity office and Affirmative Action Council constituted important organizational opportunities for these gay employees. After hearing the employees' concerns, members of the council expressed their support and invited the gay employees to form a network of their own. Thus, the second chapter of GLUE was born.

It was this East Coast chapter of GLUE, located close to headquarters, that established a working relationship with corporate management and won official recognition for the network in 1988. The head of the facility where the group formed, however, encouraged the group to remain low profile, since "he knew [its] existence would be controversial," explained GLUE's informal historian. Nonetheless, on account of increased access to the company's e-mail system, a "co-optable" communications network in the most literal sense of the word (Freeman 1979, 170), news spread quickly about GLUE, and soon other chapters sprang up across the country.

GLUE's leaders also helped gay employee groups that began to materialize in other companies, a responsibility they still take seriously. Acknowledging

GLUE's advisory role and its status as one of the earliest gay networks in the country, many organizations in the workplace movement consider GLUE to be the "grandmother" of all lesbian and gay employee groups. Members are rightfully proud of their organization's reputation. At an Out and Equal workplace conference in 1996, GLUE members wore buttons that included the group's name and emblem—with pink and lavender overlapping triangles, symbols of gay pride—and that read, "It started with us! 1987–1997 . . . Workplace Pride." In fact, GLUE's reputation extends well beyond the movement itself: as its Web site notes, the national network has even been hosted at the White House.

Mechanisms for Official Corporate Recognition

As an institutionalized form of acceptance, official corporate recognition is a successful outcome in and of itself. Indeed, corporate recognition represents an early goal of most gay activist networks. "Acceptance," in William Gamson's classic movement outcomes study (1975, 1990), entails formal recognition, by the challenging group's target, that the group is a valid representative for a legitimate set of interests. Paul Burstein, Rachel Einwohner, and Jocelyn Hollander (1995) call this form of success "access." Another type of success Gamson calls "new advantages," or benefits granted by the target that meet at least some of the challengers' demands.

The mechanisms of recognition, or the process by which networks achieved official status, can be seen as a form of institutional opportunity. This is because, in most instances, previous employee networks for women and people of color had already won this institutionalized form of access, which in turn made it easier for the gay employee groups who followed. In other words, the success of early risers in establishing procedures for official corporate recognition, which represents a favorable policy outcome, also functions as an important mobilization outcome, in that these institutionalized mechanisms facilitate the formation and success of later challengers. As Suzanne Staggenborg (1995, 341–42) puts it, "One type of success may have a bearing on another type, and outcomes occurring at one point in time affect future outcomes."

Access to Institutional Resources

As a structural template, official corporate recognition of employee networks can also provide access to institutional resources such as a budget. Roger Friedland and Robert Alford (1991, 254) speak to the importance of institutionalized access to resources for those seeking organizational transformation: "The success of an attempt at institutional change depends not simply on the resources controlled by its proponents, but on the nature of power and the institutionally specified rules by which resources are produced, allocated, and controlled. The institutional nature of power provides specific opportunities for not only reproduction, but transformation as well."

Although official corporate recognition did not always come with a budget, 57 percent of gay employee networks in my study (40 out of 70) received some sort of monetary support from their corporations. For most groups the funding came from centralized sources such as a diversity office or human resources department. For others money came in the form of "elite patronage" (Jenkins and Eckert 1986) from influential allies who allocated part of their departmental budgets to the gay network. Overall, funding ranged anywhere from a few hundred dollars to over one hundred thousand dollars a year.

Regardless of the dollar amount, groups that had access to a budget were more successful in winning domestic partner benefits than networks that lacked such monetary support. Sixty percent of groups with a budget (24 out of 40), compared to 43 percent of those without (13 out of 30), won extended policies. At first glance the relationship between budget access and policy success may appear spurious, because both variables can be explained by a supportive corporate culture. The willingness of companies to spend money on employee networks, for instance, reflects a corporate culture that already views diversity as a "business imperative" (Dobbin and Sutton 1998)—that is, as an investment that brings both symbolic and monetary returns to the corporation. This component of institutional opportunity, which I refer to as cultural support, will be discussed in more detail later on. But clearly not all diversity-embracing companies have adopted equitable benefits, so it is safe to say that the financial support of employee networks has a positive policy effect that is operating independently of cultural support for diversity generally. This is not surprising, since the granting of a budget allows networks to hold educational events, bring in outside speakers, organize professional development conferences, and produce awareness-raising materials such as flyers, buttons, and magnets. As will be shown in the following chapter, these tactics play a crucial role in winning allies and convincing elites to institute gay-inclusive policies.

In any case, my results mirror those of John McCarthy and Mayer Zald (1973, 1977), who found that "institutional funding" facilitated favorable outcomes for challengers. Likewise, following William Gamson (1990), I found that "sponsorship" of challengers by elite patrons increased the likelihood of success. However, while Gamson found that these positive effects were limited to groups with small numbers, my findings show that funding is beneficial for groups regardless of the size of their membership.

The higher success rate of budgeted groups also seems to indicate that institutional funding and elite patronage do not lead to co-optation (W. Gamson 1990). Nor does such funding typically serve as a means of social control (McAdam 1982), whereby challengers abandon their goals or strategies in order to maintain elite support. However, I did find evidence of "channeling" (Jenkins and Eckert 1986; Jenkins 1998), in that some networks felt pressure to avoid making public endorsements of gay rights legislation.

Representation on a Diversity Council

Another structural template, representation on a company's diversity council or diversity task force, also makes a significant difference for organizational challengers. In my study, 86 percent of gay networks (60 out of 70) reported that their companies had such a body, made up of representatives from various employee groups. While 57 percent of gay networks (24 out of 42) who sat on these councils succeeded in their fight for benefits, only 33 percent of those lacking such representation were able to effect policy change (6 out of 18). These structures aid challengers not only because they provide regular channels of communication with decision makers, who expect representatives to voice their concerns and ideas, but also because they offer a formal means of interacting with other diversity groups, who may eventually become allies of the gay and lesbian network. A good example of this can be found in chapter 4, where I discussed the gay employee group that was able to overcome opposition by the Christian network after all employee resource groups were brought into an overarching diversity council.

In contrast, at least one gay network saw its company's lack of a diversity council as helpful in the long run. A leader of the network, formed within a well-known scientific and photographic company, explained why her corporation did not have a task force and described the ironically beneficial effect that resulted: "We had an inept diversity officer for quite some time, so we'd go directly to senior management, which was a good thing probably." Indeed, the network won equitable policies across the board and is seen as a role model in the larger workplace movement.

While this particular network benefited from the lack of a diversity council, this finding does not challenge the importance of structural templates. In fact, it underlines the significance of access to key elites. The employee network obviously had direct access to senior management, which meant that its arguments for equitable benefits did not have to be filtered through multiple levels of management or through a diversity task force. In the vast majority of cases, however, findings clearly show that structural templates facilitate favorable policy outcomes. Whether these templates come in the form of early risers, institutionalized mechanisms for official recognition, institutional resources such as a budget, or diversity councils that provide access to decision makers, such organizational opportunities increase the likelihood that challengers will win equal rights in the workplace.

Organizational Realignments as Organizational Opportunity

Various scholars have documented the importance of electoral realignments in encouraging collective action and facilitating legislative victories (Jenkins and Perrow 1977; Piven and Cloward 1979; McAdam 1982; Morris 1984; Costain 1992; Tarrow 1996, 1998). When the focus of contention is the corporation rather than the state, the appropriate counterpart to electoral shifts is organizational realignments. Focusing on the organizational opportunities and constraints that stem from these realignments, I pay particular attention to the impact of the following factors: elite turnover that results in a new CEO; changes in the composition of the board of directors or in the policy status of the organizations represented on the board; and acquisitions of or mergers with other companies. Each of these organizational realignments can bring more receptive elites or organizations into the issue domain and hence can shift the balance of power in ways that benefit activist networks.

The Impact of Elite Turnover

Organizational scholars have found that a very low turnover of administrators can lead to rigidity of company values and behavior; hence, new corporate policies and strategies often depend on a "change of personnel at the top" (Pfeffer 1983, 325). In his institutional analysis of organizational transformation, Stephen Mezias (1995) found that high turnover among top managers is a significant source of diffusion for organizational innovations. While Mezias's findings demonstrate that high-level personnel change can fuel isomorphism at the macro level (DiMaggio and Powell 1991b), here I focus on elite turnover not as a mimetic diffusion mechanism but rather as a meso-level opportunity that offers hope for challengers inside particular corporations. A change in CEO, for example, can bring new ideas and attitudes that effect changes in corporate culture. Organizational realignments can also exert a more direct influence on corporate strategy. For instance, a new CEO can decide to adopt policies that his or her predecessor opposed.

The importance of a change in CEO is powerfully illustrated in my telecommunications case study. The gay network there struggled for nine years before winning its fight for domestic partner benefits. In looking back at GLUE's struggle, every network leader whom I interviewed concluded that the main reason for the company's refusal to adopt equitable benefits was the CEO's personal objection. In a meeting with the network back in 1993, the CEO, whom I will call Michael Smith, brought up his religious beliefs. In the words of GLUE's national cochair, "We knew we were in trouble [then]."

It is telling that although Smith attended professional development conferences organized by other employee networks in the company, he refused every invitation to GLUE's annual conferences. This angered GLUE leaders so much that they decided not to invite him to their 1997 conference even though it was held at corporate headquarters. They instead invited Smith's heir apparent, who attended the conference and received a standing ovation for making it clear that, as one national cochair put it, "he got the issues and understood us." Although this man did not end up taking over as CEO, his willingness to express support for GLUE stood in marked contrast to Smith's refusal even to attend GLUE conferences.

As GLUE's national copresident, "Jane" repeatedly requested meetings with Smith, only to be turned down. "Finally, after all [those] years," Jane commented in our interview, "right before he retired, he agreed to meet with me." Although Jane had to cancel the meeting, in a letter to Smith gay network members pleaded with him: "Grant domestic partner benefits before you leave, or get us access to the decision makers." Smith retired in 1997 without granting the benefits. He had been CEO for nearly ten years, almost as long as GLUE had existed. Commenting on the timing of Smith's retirement and the adoption of benefits shortly thereafter, in 1998, the other national copresident of the gay network stated, "It was absolutely critical that [Smith] was out of the picture. I'm convinced in my soul that he was the reason [the benefits didn't come sooner,] because *everyone*, including people reporting directly to him, came out and supported domestic partner benefits." Indeed, the CEO's resistance was especially glaring given the vocal support for equitable benefits expressed by the company's chief financial officer, the chief legal officer, and the executive vice president of consumers, among others.

In preparation for the changing of the company guard, GLUE leaders did their homework on the new CEO, "Jay Thomspon," in the hopes that he would be supportive of benefits adoption. Although Thompson came from a company that was a major defense contractor, one of GLUE's national co-presidents heard from sources who knew Thompson that he had organized a "Republicans for Feinstein" event. This signaled a potentially receptive attitude, since U.S. Senator Dianne Feinstein, a Democrat representing California, had a pro-gay voting record. Network members also drew hope from a photo that was sent to all company employees in which Thompson smiled astride his Harley-Davidson motorcycle. From outside sources, GLUE's copresident learned that Thompson had dropped out of college for a year to ride his Harley across the country. The copresident laughingly commented, "So I knew he *had* to have met some lesbians along the way."

Thompson did in fact express a receptive attitude toward lesbian and gay concerns during a get-to-know-you session with employees. One of the people in attendance asked the new CEO what he thought of domestic partner benefits. Thompson responded, "To be honest, I don't know that much about it, but I'm willing to learn." In early 1998, shortly after Thompson came on board, all the employee networks met and had lunch with him. Three months later, the company adopted the benefits as part of its negotiations with the unions. As it turned out, by the time the company came to the negotiating table, top management had already decided to grant the benefits. The network copresident explained, "I was very close to the company's chief negotiator. We had lunch right before she went into the negotiating meeting, and she told me that [the benefits] were coming."

It seems clear, then, that elite turnover is an important dimension of organizational opportunity. My interview with the company's director of corporate diversity lends further credence to this interpretation. Using a four-point scale ranging from "very important" to "not at all important," I asked him to rate thirty different factors, both internal and external, as to the role each played in the company's decision regarding equitable benefits. The only factor that he rated as very important was the opinion of the CEO.

Shifts in the Composition or Policy Balance of the Board

Another key organizational opportunity exists in the form of organizational realignments that shift the composition of the corporate board of directors in ways that favor gay-inclusive policy change. This shift can stem from the addition of a new member whose own employer has equitable policies or from the timely adoption of benefits by an organization already represented on the board. My discussion of the transportation case study in chapter 4 reveals the decisive role that supportive interlocking directorates can play in the adoption of equitable benefits, which in that instance occurred in the absence of a gay employee group.

The telecommunications case study provides an illustration of how board members can help lesbian and gay challengers directly. After years of pushing for domestic partner benefits, with the only sign of hope eventually coming in the form of cryptic messages about needing to be patient, GLUE learned that one of the company's recent spin-offs had decided to adopt the benefits. When their own employer failed to do the same, leaders of GLUE sent letters to three of the corporation's board members whose companies or universities had already instituted equitable benefits. In response, as GLUE's national copresident explained, those three board members "went to the head of HR and said, 'Fix this,'" which she said also meant "Make them go away," since they did not want any more letters from GLUE members. Thus, by the time the new CEO met with the corporate board of directors, there were already strong voices of support for equitable benefits among its ranks.

However, sometimes board members pose nearly insurmountable obstacles for challengers. Although several of the vice presidents of human resources I interviewed said that if the CEO supports partner benefits, approval from the board of directors is usually pro forma, in some cases the board prevents inclusive policy change. At an East Coast insurance company, for example, after persistent pressure from the gay employee network, board members finally agreed to at least consider the issue of equitable benefits. But this consideration came only after the endorsement by a yearlong official research team that consisted of representatives from the gay network, human resources, the benefits department, the legal department, and the tax department. Despite strong support from every member of the research team—and from the senior vice president of human resources, everyone in the benefits department, and the CEO—the board of directors chose not to adopt equitable benefits. It took two additional years of mobilizing before the board finally issued its approval.

While shifts in the composition of the board can open up opportunities for challengers, they can also create formidable constraints. For example, in one of the major airlines, the gay employee network had succeeded in winning support for equitable benefits throughout the corporate hierarchy. After informal talks with individuals in human resources, including the vice president, the network prepared a formal proposal and presented it to the senior vice president of human resources and then to the Executive Management Committee, including the CEO. All signaled their support for the proposal, which was then sent to the board for final approval. There it stayed.

Members of the gay network waited interminably for an answer but never received any official response at all. They eventually learned from insiders that the prospect of domestic partner benefits made two of the board members "very unhappy." A founder of the network explained, "For one of them it was a 'moral decline thing' as a Christian. And the other one had been appointed to the board of the National Boy Scouts of America, so he was concerned that [equitable-benefits adoption] would besmirch him." Tellingly, the Boy Scouts argued successfully in front of the U.S. Supreme Court for the right to exclude gays as troop leaders, a decision that allows the organization to keep out gay Scouts as well (Lounsberry 2000).

Mergers and Acquisitions

Acquisitions or mergers, another type of organizational realignment, can also have a significant impact on policy change. The year before the afore-mentioned telecommunications company adopted equitable benefits, one of its industry peers did so after merging with a leading phone company that already had the benefits. Likewise, a late-adopting high-tech firm on the East Coast finally extended benefits to domestic partners after acquiring another high-tech company that had done so a half decade earlier in re-sponse to employee mobilization. Prior to the acquisition, the gay employee network at the East Coast firm had struggled for the benefits for approxi-mately four years.

Additional evidence revealing the importance of organizational realign-ments can be found in the annual *State of the Workplace* report published by the Human Rights Campaign Foundation. For example, BankAmerica, which adopted equitable benefits in 1997, in compliance with San Fran-cisco law, later merged with Nations Bank, which did not have the benefits. Although the newly formed Bank of America Corporation is now head-quartered in North Carolina, where only one other company has adopted equitable benefits, the corporation decided to extend domestic partner bene-fits to all of its employees. Likewise, in the spring of 1999, BankBoston, which had already adopted equitable benefits, announced its upcoming merger with Fleet Financial Group, which had not extended its policy to domestic partners. That fall the combined FleetBoston Financial Corpora-tion offered equitable benefits to all employees (HRCF 1999a). Typically, then, mergers with and acquisitions of gay-inclusive companies offer notable organizational opportunities for challengers.

In the age of conglomerate corporations, acquired subsidiaries are often compelled to adopt the same policies and procedures as the parent company (DiMaggio and Powell 1991b). In the case of mergers, though, the situation can get complicated. For example, the vice president of human resources at a pharmaceutical, agricultural, and food sciences corporation explained in our interview that her employer had originally adopted equitable benefits in response to numerous individual requests that she had received from gay and lesbian employees and friends. However, a company that it was merging with at the time of our interview was balking at the benefits. Testifying to how "against the mainstream" this policy move was—indeed, her employer was the only major corporation in its midwestern state to have adopted equitable benefits—the vice president said two people at her company had resigned in protest, and many other employees had contacted her to say that the company was "breaking down nuclear families and breaking sodomy laws." While the corporation faced no external backlash, she received so many e-mails from outraged employees that, in her words, "I thought my computer screen would melt with animosity."

She explained that when the corporation had acquired four other companies in previous years, it was simply "assumed that they'd adopt our benefits," which they had done. But the current merging partner, another pharmaceutical company, was "adamant about *not* doing domestic partner benefits." Commenting on the impact that the merger would have, she added, "They're two times our size, though it will be an equal merger. I'm not sure how it will work. [Our company] will no longer exist; it will be a whole new company starting from scratch, [with] 60,000 employees."

As far as I could determine from my surveys and data acquired from the WorkNet project of the Human Rights Campaign, there has been only one case in which a merger resulted in the reversal of equitable benefits. Indeed, only two major companies have ever rescinded their benefits policies. As noted in chapter 4, Mobil's equitable-benefits program was terminated after the company was purchased in November 1999 by Texas-based Exxon, which was the far larger of the two firms that now make up ExxonMobil. The other case, though not the result of a merger, clearly reveals the impact of another kind of organizational realignment, namely, a change in leadership.

In April 1998, high-tech Perot Systems went down in history as the first major company in the United States to rescind its equitable-benefits policy. The corporation had adopted the benefits while H. Ross Perot was away from the helm during his campaign for the U.S. presidency. Upon his return, in late 1997, he announced in *Business Week* that he might reverse the policy even though very few companies in the high-tech industry lacked equitable benefits. The executive director of HRC, Elizabeth Birch, then wrote to Perot, asking him to reconsider. Although he told her that he would think carefully before making a decision, gay employees later notified HRC that the benefits were "surreptitiously terminated" (HRCF 1999a, 21). Tellingly, the other company Perot created, Electronic Data Systems, adopted equitable benefits in early 1998 after Perot sold off his controlling shares in the firm.

As demonstrated in the preceding examples, organizational realignments can serve as powerful institutional opportunities for workplace challengers. Whether through elite turnover, shifts in the composition or policy balance of the board, or mergers and acquisitions, gay employee networks can find their fortunes suddenly turning in response to such realignments. While employee activists obviously have no control over organizational realignments, other organizational opportunities are far more malleable and may be opened up in response to the actions of networks themselves. In the following sections I discuss both the impact of these malleable opportunities and the strategies that activists use to create them if they are not already present.

Allies as Organizational Opportunity

A third key dimension of organizational opportunity entails the availability of allies, which can be influential individuals, groups from within or close to the elite, or other organizational challengers who serve as coalition partners. The latter includes other diversity networks in the company and, if applicable, unions. Some companies also provide "executive sponsors" or "management champions," although more typically employee networks actively seek them out. These individuals advise the group and have the ear of key decision makers. If the company does not already fund employee networks, some sponsors use part of their own discretionary budget to support the group. This form of elite patronage (Jenkins and Eckert 1986) can make a key difference in the network's chance of success, as discussed earlier. Regardless of funding, the mere presence of a management champion has a significant impact on policy outcomes.

Management Champions

I focus here on those companies that, according to gay network leaders, have some form of executive sponsorship, whether informally sought by diversity networks or formally instituted by the company, usually through human resources or a corporate diversity office. Lesbian and gay networks are often joined by their sister diversity groups in pushing for the institutionalization of executive sponsorship, since formal mechanisms make it far easier to win influential allies. Of the 70 gay employee groups that I surveyed, 53 (or 76 percent) worked in companies where at least some diversity groups had executive sponsorship, whether formal or not, although not all gay networks were able to secure a sponsor of their own.

The presence of a management champion can make an enormous difference for gay employee groups. While 60 percent of networks with an executive sponsor (18 out of 30) succeeded in their push for equitable benefits, only 25 percent of those without a sponsor (10 out of 40) were able to effect a change in policy. My case study of an East Coast financial services company provides a clear illustration of the importance of management champions.

At this company, sponsors are senior-level executives who support diversity networks in various ways, including the securing of a budget. In 1995, after discussing the need for a well-recognized and well-respected sponsor for their newly formed organization, "LGB" (Lesbians, Gays, and Bisexuals), members of the employee network at corporate headquarters came up with names of executives they had either worked with or felt comfortable approaching. From the list they chose the president of a very visible corporate division who had also been on the company's diversity council. According to one of the founders of LGB, this president had been very active in diversity initiatives and had established "a track record of being somewhat enlightened and supportive." A network member who had previously worked with the executive asked him to be the group's sponsor; he quickly accepted.

For his first action as executive sponsor, he wrote a memo, sent to every U.S. employee in the company, in which he announced LGB's formation, communicated its importance to the company, and identified himself as the network's executive sponsor. In his memo he included an 800 number for anyone interested in joining LGB, and he encouraged support for the organization. In a separate communication the executive sponsor urged senior managers to utilize the gay employee group as a resource for reaching out to the lesbian and gay market. Three months later the CEO also sent a memo about LGB's formation, in which he discussed the importance of all employee networks. As a result of the corporate-wide communication, LGB grew quickly. All of the people who called the 800 number were sorted by location and then introduced to each other. Today the gay employee network has over seven hundred members in fifteen chapters across the country. Each chapter has an executive sponsor, as does the national coordinating body that links the local chapters.

Roadblocks to Winning Benefits

After the memo was sent by their executive sponsor, LGB members at the financial services company rolled up their sleeves and got right to work on the issue that had motivated them to form the network in the first place:

domestic partner benefits. Their strategy was carefully thought out, and their proposal was well researched. Members knew they had to find a way around a roadblock that had surfaced before the network formed. In 1994, the year before LGB was established, three gay employees who belonged to a "satellite" of the company's diversity council wrote to the CEO and asked the company to adopt equitable benefits. In response human resources contacted a consulting firm for additional information. Shortly thereafter the company denied the request and prepared a memo citing several concerns. I briefly cover them here, since, according to my interviews with Fortune 1000 executives, they provide a good feel for the mind-set of corporate elites who are faced with a request for equitable benefits.

From a competitive standpoint one of the issues raised was that the benefits were not "mainstream," since at that time (1994) fewer than fifty companies nationwide had adopted them. More importantly, "none of the fourteen companies [that the corporation] uses for compensation/benefits benchmarking" had adopted equitable benefits. The memo also cited "legal/policy" issues, saying the benefits might "conflict with certain state laws" and that the company would have to decide who qualified as a domestic partner, how to document the relationship, and which policies to extend. Under "tax issues," the company cited the fact that employees would be taxed on the value of their partners' benefits, which was not the case for married heterosexuals. Under "cost concerns" the company raised the issue of "additional risk exposure," reflecting the false assumption that costs would increase significantly if gay men signed up partners with AIDS. The memo also mentioned a "timing" concern, fearing "employee relations issues" that might arise over extending benefits at a time when the company was restructuring and when employee contributions for medical coverage had increased.

Removing the Roadblocks

Realizing the need to address each of these issues, LGB members gathered lists of employers that had already granted equitable benefits, and they interviewed over twenty human resource directors and benefits coordinators to obtain more detailed information on enrollment figures and costs (both low to nil), internal and external reaction, concerns of the CEO and other senior management, and so on. They also sought advice from gay employee networks at other companies, a task made relatively easy given LGB's membership in an informal umbrella group that met regularly at a local restaurant.

In anticipation of their first formal presentation to key decision makers, LGB members met with representatives of the company's general counsel, public affairs, and human resources and compensation and benefits departments, who helped them prepare "an extremely thorough cost analysis," explained "Barb," one of LGB's founders. In these preparatory meetings, LGB asked each of these parties to look at its benefits proposal and "surface all the issues that may come out" if they won an audience with senior management. Since their ultimate goal was to present to the Office of the Chief Executive, members "wanted to make sure that by the time [LGB] got to them, every single question, concern, obstacle was removed," according to Barb.

Partly because of the access provided by its executive sponsor at corporate headquarters, who sat on the company's diversity council, LGB was able to make a formal presentation to members of the council, all of whom were supportive. In fact, according to Barb, because of LGB's previous "awareness work," the diversity council turned out to be another "executive sponsor" of sorts. Network members then prepared a series of presentations, all in company-speak, as Barb described it, which they tailored to different senior management audiences, eventually hitting all of the executives who reported directly to the CEO. The presenters were fairly senior-level gay employees who were well respected by executives on the diversity council, to whom they had first presented their proposal.

The presentation, or "deck," as members called it, was accompanied by several pieces of supporting material: a nineteen-page hard copy of the presentation, a ten-page list of equitable-benefits adopters, and thirty-three pages of interview responses from the companies they had benchmarked. The top of the first page served as a good summary of the profits frame emphasized throughout: "Why offer domestic partner benefits? Apart from fundamental considerations of equity, such a program recommends itself because it is in the Company's best interest." The rest of the deck focused on the advantages of equitable benefits for shareholders, customers, and employees; corporations that had already adopted the benefits; and key considerations. Drawing on the benchmarking interviews LGB had conducted with the more than twenty other adopters, presenters carefully addressed all of the points that had been considered concerns the year before, including expected financial impact, legal and policy issues such as eligibility, and internal and external reactions.

Opening the Doors to the Executive Suite

Because of the support it had won from the diversity council and from a high-level executive for whom one of the network leaders worked, LGB was able to gain access to each one of the company's senior executives, namely, the presidents of the fifteen corporate divisions. Various LGB members who worked for these senior managers then "satellited off and went through the presentation" with each one of them. They had received "fairly unanimous support" from the senior managers by the time they presented to the Office of the Chief Executive, which consisted of the CEO and three vice chairmen. Prior to the meeting, all four had been briefed about the issue.

Barb thought the presentation and discussion afterward went "*exceptionally* well." She noted, "[The CEO] was very engaged; he asked the right questions. I think we had the right answers." She described the meeting as "extremely open, very productive, and enjoyable" as well as "intellectually stimulating and emotionally fulfilling . . . a genuine dialogue." One of the things the CEO asked was for presenters to take him through the company's current benefits program and explain exactly how his wife and children benefited from it. This was juxtaposed with what gay and lesbian employees and their families were denied under current benefits policy. As Barb later explained, the inequity was not obvious to most people, so seeing it on paper and then hearing it described in personal terms proved to be quite powerful. Approximately two months after the meeting, the company announced its decision. After only a year or so of formal organizing, LGB had won its fight for equitable benefits. Following the announcement, key decision makers received between 150 and 200 thank-you letters from LGB members.

Coalition Partners

Sister Networks

Just as influential individuals from within or close to upper management can serve as key allies, so too can other employee networks. The presence of these coalition partners has a significant impact on the likelihood of gay-inclusive policy change. Focusing on equitable benefits, the difference in success rates between gay networks with and without coalition support is striking: 64 percent (30 out of 47) versus 33 percent (7 out of 21), respectively. The telecommunications case study illustrates the important role that these organizational allies can play.

Leaders of "GLUE" firmly believed in the fruitfulness of coalition building. Many members made a concerted effort to establish connections with the other employee resource groups in the company, being sure to attend their events and inviting them to attend GLUE's in return. Through their structural embeddedness in multiple systems of oppression (P. Collins 2000), some members of the gay network were dedicated members of other diversity groups in the company. Leaders described this as "seeding," where activists, through overlapping memberships, would actively contribute to other causes and simultaneously educate other networks on the issues of concern to gay employees. With "spillover" working in both directions (D. Meyer and Whittier 1994), feminists in the women's employee group who joined the gay network had a significant influence on some of the gay male members, who began to claim a profeminist identity (Raeburn 1995).

After establishing strong connections with their sister networks in the company, GLUE members asked the leaders of these groups to support their fight for equitable benefits. After a brief period of deliberation, all of the other networks signed off on GLUE's proposal, which requested benefits for the partners of both unmarried heterosexual and gay employees. Thereafter, in quarterly meetings with management (including business-unit presidents, the head of human resources, and the diversity office), leaders from each of the employee networks expressed support for the benefits.

When GLUE wrote a letter to the top corporate decision makers urging them to adopt equitable benefits, leaders of all the employee networks signed it. Representing their respective constituencies, these signatures "sent a message to the company that 25,000 employees support domestic partner benefits," explained one of the national copresidents of GLUE. Although it took at least two more years, GLUE finally won its fight for equitable benefits. As previously discussed, elite turnover played a crucial role in this policy change, but it seems unlikely that the new CEO would have agreed to the benefits so quickly if it weren't for the vocal support GLUE had already won from all of the company's diversity networks as well as from the chief financial officer, the chief legal officer, and the executive vice president of consumers, among others.

Religious Employee Networks as Cooperative Partners

While the relationship between religious employee groups, which are usually Christian, and gay and lesbian networks can sometimes be contentious, with fundamentalist workers mobilizing against the goals or even the mere existence of a gay network (see chapters 4 and 6), I have also found instances where cooperative ties have emerged, especially as a result of outreach work by lesbian and gay employees, as happened in the telecommunications company just discussed. Indicative of the apparent rarity of cooperation between religious employee groups and gay and lesbian networks, the 2002 Workplace Diversity Conference sponsored by the Society for Human Resource Management featured a session called "Sexual Orientation and Spirituality in the Workplace Can Co-exist: Tools and Techniques." The workshop was led by Liz Winfeld, an author and well-known diversity consultant specializing in lesbian, gay, and bisexual workplace issues. Excerpts from the session description provide a telling commentary on the relationship between these two constituencies and the possibilities for collaborative exchange:

> Previously thought to be so diametrically opposed so as to allow for no commonality or cooperation, the facilitator will demonstrate that cooperation and learning can—and is—being done. The workshop will draw from . . . a case study of the cooperative relationship engendered and working well between the Gay Lesbian Bi-Sexual Transgender (GLBT) affinity group and the Spiritual/Christian group at Texas Instruments. Learning outcomes will focus [in part] on . . . how to establish, set goals for and achieve the mission of employee affinity groups in these two areas—separately and in cooperation with one another. Finally, you will learn how to empower management to work effectively with employees who are members of one, or both, affinity groups in order to maximize productivity and profitability and minimize conflict between employees and others.

Such forms of cooperation as those found at Texas Instruments are not as surprising as they might seem. According to the results of a recent study by the Kaiser Family Foundation, which conducts research on issues related to health care and medical coverage, although the majority of people surveyed "consider homosexual behavior morally wrong," 75 percent of the sample said they "support anti-discrimination measures regarding hate crimes, housing, employment and domestic partner benefits" (*Omaha World-Herald* 2001). Likewise, a 1998 Gallup poll found that, while 59 percent of the public viewed "homosexual behavior" as "morally wrong," 84 percent said that "gays and lesbians deserve equal rights in the workplace" (Leonard 1998).

Nonetheless, given that in some companies conservative Christian employees—if not the religious network itself—have voiced opposition to or even actively mobilized against gay-inclusive policies, more than a few lesbian and gay employee groups find themselves searching for ways to foster cooperative relationships with their company's Christian network. My research shows that the establishment of a diversity council can help lay the groundwork for such ties. This is because such a council provides a routinized mechanism for all of a company's employee resource groups to enter into dialogue with management and, not incidentally, with each other. Other mutually beneficial possibilities stem from overlapping memberships; many gay and lesbian employees are quick to point out that "religious" and "gay" are not mutually exclusive identity categories. Future avenues for collaboration may stem, externally, from the growing number of religious bodies—whether Christian, Jewish, or multidenominational, such as the Unitarian Universalist Association and Metropolitan Community Churches—that are establishing themselves as "welcoming" or "reconciling" congregations, a process that entails affirming the rights and dignity of lesbian, gay, bisexual, and transgender people of faith through a wide variety of measures, such as celebrating the history and diversity of the community, performing same-sex union ceremonies, and actively working for equality and social justice at local, regional, and national levels (Unitarian Universalist Association 2001; HRCF 2003a).

Unions as Coalition Partners

Although it happens infrequently, unions can also serve as coalition partners, as when collective bargaining units negotiate for gay-inclusive policies such as nondiscrimination policies or domestic partner benefits. According to a survey of 570 large U.S. employers conducted in 2000, only 2 percent of companies said they began providing equitable benefits "as a requirement of a collective bargaining agreement" (Hewitt Associates 2000, 1). This figure may increase in the years ahead, given the growing strength of Pride at Work, a national organization of lesbian, gay, bisexual, and transgender union members that was formed in 1994 and in 1998 succeeded in gaining recognition as an official constituency group of the AFL-CIO (Sweeney [1999] 2001). Also boding well for the future, in 1999 John Sweeney, the AFL-CIO president, announced a new organizing agenda specifically directed at mobilizing gay and lesbian workers (Krupat [1999] 2001) and issued a call to make domestic partner benefits a "higher bargaining priority" (Sweeney [1999] 2001, 30; see also contributors to Krupat and McCreery 2001).

Of those companies in my study that had both gay employee networks and unions, collective bargaining units got involved in the fight for benefits in approximately one-third of the cases. Gay activist networks were slightly more successful in winning benefits when unions were involved than when they were not: 40 percent (4 out of 10) versus 32 percent (6 out of 19), respectively. I suspect that the reason union involvement appears to make less of a difference than the presence of other allies is that often union support is somewhat superficial. Plus, in many cases, the percentage of employees covered by collective bargaining agreements was rather low. In the previously discussed example of the automotive industry, where the United Auto Workers helped gay employee networks in the Big Three to achieve domestic partner benefits simultaneously, unionized employees represented a significant proportion of the workforce.

The telecommunications case study illustrates the sometimes tenuous nature of union support for equitable benefits. It also appears to represent one of the most organized efforts on the part of gay employee networks to win strong union backing. GLUE's national leaders toiled long and hard to establish a working relationship with the leadership of the Communication Workers of America (CWA) and the International Brotherhood of Electrical Workers (IBEW). GLUE met with the leaders of both unions and asked them to bring up domestic partner benefits in contract negotiations, which they did in 1992 and again in 1995 (contract periods lasted three years). Both times, however, the unions "easily dumped" the benefits early in the negotiating process, because the membership was not fully committed to the issue.

GLUE's national leaders then met to devise a more effective union strategy. They established a union liaison committee and a vice-presidential title specifically for a union representative. Since half of the gay network's membership belonged to the unions, an unusually high proportion compared to other gay employee groups, the union liaison was able, in the words of one of GLUE's national copresidents, to "work it from the bottom up at the locals wherever [GLUE] had members" and from the top down at the national office by arguing, "This is what our members want." Some gay network members also joined the equity committees of the CWA and IBEW and met with the rank and file to build support for the benefits from the ground up. One of the national copresidents commented that it "took a lot of courage for GLUE union members" to stand up and talk to their fellow union members about partner benefits, because most of the union's membership was "rabidly homophobic." Some individual union stewards were supportive though, because, as another national leader explained, "they have had some personal relationship [with gay people] . . . either in the workplace or outside of it, so they kind of get it."

As a result of GLUE's concerted efforts, the CWA ended up extending benefits to the domestic partners of its own working staff around 1995. The union locals also established diversity councils that included lesbian and gay representatives. GLUE's focus on the unions eventually paid off in 1998, when the union membership passed a resolution saying they would seriously push for equitable benefits in their upcoming contract negotiations. As discussed previously, however, by the time the company came to the negotiating table, top management (including the new CEO) had already decided to grant the benefits. A national copresident of the gay network, who was close to the management's top negotiator, learned that the company was simply waiting for the union to ask for the benefits. He commented on the irony of the situation. Three years earlier, while talking with the benefits director in human resources, this activist had suggested a way for the company to adopt the benefits while avoiding potential backlash: corporate officials could simply attribute the decision to the insistence of the unions. As the gay network leader put it, "Why don't you just do it and say that the unions negotiated for it?" At the time, the benefits director had said, "I can't," but three years later, that's exactly what the company did.

Cultural Supports as Organizational Opportunity

As the final dimension of organizational opportunity, cultural supports refer to ideational elements and interpretive frameworks (Taylor and Whittier 1995) in the target organization itself that facilitate gay-inclusive policy change; and experiential components of opportunity that derive from the personal backgrounds of elites. I focus in particular on the impact of a diversity-embracing corporate culture and, among elites, "punctuating experiences" that evoke empathy with challengers.

A Diversity-Embracing Corporate Culture

In his discussion of institutionalization, Richard Scott (1995b) emphasizes the importance of "cultural carriers," which refer to "patterns of meanings" that operate on multiple planes, from the world system and societal level to more specific levels, such as the field environment, the organization itself, or its various subunits. Corporate culture exemplifies the more particularistic level of meaning (Frost et al. 1991; Scott 1995b). In my interviews, several human resource executives commented at length on the importance of building a corporate culture that treated diversity as a "business imperative," which Frank Dobbin and John Sutton (1998) refer to as a "new human resources management paradigm."

At a different telecommunications company than the one discussed earlier, when asked why her employer had added sexual orientation to its nondiscrimination policy and to diversity training before the gay employee network even emerged, the director of human resources acknowledged the impact of this paradigm and the role of the company's diversity manager, who "presented the rationale and business case for diversity, which was one of seven components of culture change" that the manager was promoting. Indeed, commitment to diversity figures prominently in the motivation of equitable-benefits adopters. A survey conducted by a market-research firm in 2000 found that "[s]eventy-one percent of major corporations . . . cited the increased visibility of the company's diversity commitment as the No. 1 reason for adopting the benefits" (HRCF 2001b, 19).

In relation to gay-inclusive policy adoption, I hypothesized before conducting my study that employee networks would be more likely to succeed if their corporate culture embraced diversity as a business imperative. This is because companies that adopt the new human resources paradigm already view at least some inclusive policies, such as those focused on women or people of color, as a means of attracting and retaining employees and securing the loyalty of equality-minded customers. Indeed, if the company does not already view diversity as profitable, gay employee networks often find that their requests fall on deaf ears. As one frustrated activist put it, reflecting on her employer's unwillingness to adopt equitable benefits despite the network's emphasis on their profit potential, "They just don't buy it."

A Company That Buys It

The financial services case study provides strong evidence in support of the claim that culture matters (Laraña, Johnston, and Gusfield 1994; Johnston and Klandermans 1995). As discussed earlier, despite some initial roadblocks, LGB succeeded in winning equitable benefits after only a year or so of organizing. But its journey was made much easier because they were navigating in a corporate culture that already viewed diversity as profitable. Two years before LGB mobilized, for example, the company had produced a forty-three-page document called *Diversity: 1993 Report to Benchmark Partners*. The report was a "major diversity benchmarking effort" that was described as "breaking new ground in this area." After discussing the process by which benchmarking partners were chosen, the document focused on best practices and interview results. The emphasis throughout was on the competitive advantages that came from embracing diversity. Importantly, the definition of diversity included sexual orientation.

When I interviewed the director of the Diversity Resource Center and asked her about the factors involved in her company's decision to grant domestic partner benefits, she credited the work of LGB, but she also emphasized a strong diversity-affirming corporate culture: "The company's culture consists of a strong set of values. If people can't live, feel, and breathe those values, they don't stay around long. . . . It's part of who we are as a culture. We have a corporate culture that [encourages] being open, embracing, and inclusive no matter who the individual is. To be successful here, that's just the way things are."

A Company That Buys It but Doesn't Think Anyone Wants It: A Case of Missed Opportunity

Similarly, a human resources director at a midwestern insurance carrier comments on his company's diversity-as-profitable stance:

> [While] a lot of companies aren't paying attention to leveraging differences, we've had affirmative action since the 1960s, even before we had federal contracts, and we'll keep them no matter what happens elsewhere. . . . Our diversity concept is not just gender and race but also being sensitive to, recognizing, and leveraging people's differences . . . historical differences, physical differences, and so on. [It's about] creating an environment where everyone feels good and included and which lets everyone add in their special parts. And it's about having our employees mirror our market. This is good leveraging.

While this company, which has no gay employee network, seems to "talk a good talk," it nevertheless lacks domestic partner benefits. The director's explanation for this inconsistency reveals the importance of movement processes in bringing about equitable-benefits policies: "According to our benefits department, there are very little requests for [the benefits] from the field. The company is not actively opposed; it's more about 'Do we have enough interest?'" Likewise, research by the Society for Human Resource Management shows that most employers that have not adopted the benefits cite lack of employee interest as the reason (Bond 1997).

Lights Out: When Diversity-Embracing Gestures Ring Hollow

While a corporate culture that embraces diversity can facilitate favorable policy outcomes for challengers, clearly the span of that embrace is wider at some companies than at others. Certainly not all employers who claim to celebrate diversity have included gays and lesbians in the festivities. Indeed, sometimes when elites tout their commitment to diversity while continuing to exclude lesbians and gay men, workers call them on it publicly.

At the Associated Press (AP), for instance, hundreds of writers, photographers, and other employees mailed back the "diversity" flashlight key chains they received from the company during a promotion in early 2003. Printed with the logo "AP Diversity, many views one vision," each key chain came with a letter saying the gift was a celebration of diversity and a symbol of the company's commitment to fair treatment. According to a press release written by the human rights coordinator of the News Media Guild, which is the collective bargaining unit for AP employees, workers across the country returned the tiny flashlights as a spontaneous form of protest against the corporation's long-standing refusal to extend benefits to the partners of lesbian and gay staff even though virtually all of its competitors had done so (HRCF 2003d). AP employees had been pushing for the benefits for over a decade. During recent contract negotiations the guild had again demanded equitable benefits, and management had once again responded with silence—and that's when, in a gesture that evoked a sense of what I would call "policy dissonance," AP mailed the diversity key chains to employees. "The irony of it is simply too much to bear," wrote a New York City staffer in his letter accompanying the returned trinket. Another from a worker in Albany called on the company to "put its money where its mouth is." More than fifty employees from Washington, DC, the AP's largest bureau, handed back their key chains along with a joint letter of protest. "As long as AP's policy is all chain and no key," wrote the signers, "doors remain closed." AP's top executives appear to have heard the message loud and clear. Less than six months later the media company extended equitable benefits to its employees worldwide (U.S. Newswire 2003).

In chapter 4 I discussed the new human resources paradigm (Dobbin and Sutton 1998) as a component of normative isomorphism and conceptualized the "diversity as business imperative" script as an important macro-level opportunity. Shifting down a level to meso-opportunities, this section has provided examples of how diversity discourse, as reflected in particular corporate cultures, becomes embedded in concrete practices and structures. As Joshua Gamson (1998) has argued, discourses are not simply free-floating ideas; they are attached to particular institutional logics and organizational practices. I have thus highlighted whether and how companies embrace the idea that diversity is good for the bottom line. I argue that the further along the curve a company is in accepting this discourse, the more likely it is that gay employee activists will win equitable policies.

As shown in preceding chapters, employee activists themselves, joined by a cadre of discursive activists, can help to create opportunities if they are not already present. Nonetheless, that effort takes considerably more time, energy, resources, and patience. When companies "just don't buy it," gay employee activists and their allies have to roll up their sleeves, set up their charts and graphs, and push hard to sell it. And it can be a hard sell indeed. The negotiations are much easier when elites have had personal experiences that "punctuate" the need for equality. In other words, while some executives may look at gay employees and think they're being sold a bill of goods, others may be more apt to see a bill of rights.

Punctuating Experiences

While institutional scholars have found that the professional background of the CEO influences corporate strategies (Fligstein 1991; Thornton 1995), they have not focused on the impact of elites' *personal* background. I argue that it is not just professional training but also interpersonal experiences that influence the decisions of elites, especially with regard to issues of justice and equality in the workplace. While themes of fairness and equal treatment are now widely accepted cultural frames, individuals clearly disagree over which groups are entitled to such rights. In his work on the politics of exclusion, William Gamson (1995b, 1) describes this division as "an ongoing contest over who is the 'we,' to whom specific moral obligations apply, and who is the 'they,' to whom they do not." With this in mind, I argue for the importance of examining how wider cultural scripts regarding equal rights become embedded in the heads and hearts of elites and, consequently, in the structures and practices of the organizations they run.

While he does not focus on justice frames, neoinstitutional scholar Richard Scott (1995b, 53) emphasizes that cultural beliefs, whether widespread or organizationally specific, "are carried in the minds of individuals." Attempting to capture the impact of such internalization on organizational actors, Scott draws on the notion of *habitus,* which Pierre Bordieu (1977) defines as a "system of lasting and transposable dispositions which, integrating past experiences, functions at every moment as a matrix of perceptions, appreciations and actions" that structure the behavior of individuals (quoted in Scott 1995b, 53). My interviews likewise reveal the importance of past experiences in shaping the beliefs, attitudes, and practices of organizational elites.

In attempting to convince a particular elite of the need for gay-inclusive policies, some employee networks find that empathy and understanding either already exist or can be generated with relative ease. This receptiveness often derives from what I call *punctuating experiences* that humanize challengers and generate empathy for their concerns. The notion of punctuating experiences is similar to James Jasper and Jane Poulsen's term "moral shocks" (1995), which refers to events that outrage people and hence encourage them to join a social movement even in the absence of any preexisting ties with activists (see also Jasper 1997). I see punctuating experiences as similar to moral shocks in that they can evoke empathy from elites even before (or without) direct interaction with gay employee activists. Empathy may derive, for example, from preexisting ties with gay or lesbian family members, friends, or colleagues. Alternatively, heterosexual elites may be supportive of gay causes because they themselves have suffered from discrimination on the basis of race, ethnicity, gender, or religion.

Personal Ties of Elites

Sometimes personalizing connections come from elites' relationships with lesbian, gay, or bisexual family members. According to one of the network founders at a scientific and photographic company, family ties can greatly facilitate policy change. When asked why she thinks her company adopted equitable benefits and several other gay-inclusive practices, she responded that, in part, "it's because people in upper management have this diversity in their families, and they've told us that. That has really helped us be so successful."

In the same industry, another leading company also adopted domestic partner benefits at the urging of its gay employee network. Members attributed the decision to a variety of factors, including the fact that the CEO's secretary had a son who was gay. Perhaps most important, the CEO had become friends with a man who happened to be the leader of the gay network. As "a big Democratic supporter," the CEO was also asked by HRC to testify before Congress in support of the Employment Non-discrimination Act, which he did. This elite's own family background helped him make personal connections with the concerns of lesbian and gay people, as he himself explained to members of the network. He shared with them the story of his Huguenot ancestors who, as French Protestants, "were hunted down and killed, fled here, but also didn't fit in" in this country either.

The gay network's executive sponsor, who had approached the group and offered to be its champion, didn't necessarily have personal ties with gay and lesbian people, but he did share a similar story about his family background: "I'm Hispanic and Jewish, and my family wasn't accepted in the Hispanic community because we weren't Catholic, and we weren't accepted in the Jewish community because we're Hispanic. So I have a deep commitment to treating people fairly. Plus we [company executives] want good quality people."

Elites' Experiences with Discrimination

Personal experiences with other types of discrimination can be a deep source of empathy with gay employees. For example, an African American man who was a division president at a high-tech corporation agreed to speak at a professional development conference that had been organized by two gay employee networks, one from his company and the other from a sister spin-off in the same industry. During his plenary address, with over three hundred employees present, he drew powerful connections between racism and homophobia: "There was blood spilled in Selma, Alabama. Rosa Parks, Martin Luther King Jr. . . . They are part of my heritage. I know I didn't get here by myself. I relate to the Stonewall Riots [a catalyst for the gay liberation movement] as a watershed event. We *all* benefit from those actions." He next shared personal stories of racism that he had experienced in and outside of the workplace. Commenting on the fact that his employer had not yet adopted equitable benefits, this man then explained why gay-inclusive policies should be adopted: because they are good for business *and* "because it's right." Afterward he took questions from the audience. In one of his responses, he encouraged heterosexuals to "not just say you support diversity" but to actually "do it." As part of his closing comments, he challenged heterosexuals with a simple but telling question: "Can you say 'gay and lesbian' without looking down and staring at every hole in your wingtip shoes?" The speech met with thunderous applause.

Another plenary speaker, an African American woman who was the corporate head of affirmative action and equal employment opportunity at the same high-tech company, said that she could relate in some ways to being closeted. "I can't be all of who I am at work," she explained. Discussing a diversity article she had written on the topic, she said, "I turn off my blues and my Marvin Gaye right before going into work and going 'onstage.'" She continued: "And the clone suit—blue and taupe for women—isn't me. . . . I knew I couldn't thrive with sexism and racism, so I decided I was going to be who I am and be comfortable." After discussing the relationship between homophobia and racism, she proudly exclaimed, "[W]hen I was able to hug my very out lesbian friend in the cafeteria at work, I knew I had arrived."

The woman told the story of a little boy who was seen throwing stranded starfish back into the ocean. When someone asked, "What are you doing? There are too many. You can't help; you won't make a difference," the little boy tossed back another starfish and said, "It sure made a difference for that one." The keynote speaker then added, "That's what I do. . . . I have a passion for equality." During the question-and-answer period, she said that she received phone calls from "pretty senior people who are afraid of coming out," and she tried to encourage them to take the risk. She said that if anyone in the audience was trying to decide whether or not to come out at work, they should consider a phrase repeated often in the African American community after Martin Luther King Jr. was shot and killed: "Either you can keep living on your knees or [risk] dying on your feet."

She then turned and, continuing a ritual that had been woven throughout the other plenary sessions, opened one of the closet doors that had been set up onstage. Behind the door was a huge pink triangle. The national leadership of the two gay employee networks that had organized the conference then joined her onstage and turned all of the closet doors around to reveal the colors of the rainbow flag, a symbol of gay pride and the diversity of the lesbian, gay, bisexual, and transgender community. Written across the closet doors was the conference theme, "A Company without Closets," along with the words "Safe Space" and the logos of both gay networks. The room echoed with cheers and applause.

By inviting heterosexuals to speak at the conference and to challenge the cultural code of the closet, which signifies secrecy and shame, these employee activists purposefully sought to win allies and draw elites into the "emotion culture" of the movement (Taylor and Whittier 1995). Verta Taylor and Nancy Whittier's definition of ritual describes perfectly well the symbolic import of breaking down closet doors. Rituals, they argue, "are the cultural mechanisms through which collective actors express the emotions—that is, the enthusiasm, pride, anger, hatred, fear, and sorrow—that mobilize and sustain conflict" (176). Because of their own experiences as "outsiders within" (P. Collins 1990, 2000), these elites "got" the political connections between homophobia and other forms of institutionalized discrimination. By telling personal stories in plenary speeches and by participating in the rituals and emotion culture of the workplace movement, these allies helped other elites in the audience see those connections as well.

Summary

Just as isomorphic processes in the wider sociopolitical and field environments facilitate favorable policy outcomes for challengers, so too do meso-level institutional opportunities inside the corporation. As this chapter has made clear, employee activists are more likely to succeed when their immediate organizational environment contains certain structural and processual elements that favor inclusive policy change. In particular I have examined the impact of four key dimensions of organizational opportunity: *structural templates* that provide access to decision makers and institutional resources; *organizational realignments* that bring more receptive elites or organizations into the issue domain; *allies* who provide assistance as individuals or as coalition partners; and *cultural supports* such as a diversity-embracing corporate culture and, among elites, punctuating experiences that generate empathy with challengers.

Organizational realignments, such as elite turnover and shifts in the composition of the board of directors, seem relatively beyond the control of activists, but other dimensions of opportunity appear more open to change.

I have thus treated institutional opportunities as a "dynamic process of contestation" (Taylor 2000), in that challengers can, through their own actions, create more favorable conditions when none currently exist. In the next chapter I highlight the role that activists play in creating inclusive corporate climates. I focus especially on the importance of two movement processes: the strategic deployment of identity and the mobilization of profits- and ethics-oriented collective action frames.

6

Changing the Corporation from Inside Out: The Power of Employee Activism

The previous two chapters illuminated how institutional opportunities at the sociopolitical, field, and organizational levels facilitate favorable policy outcomes. In this chapter, attending to what Sidney Tarrow (1998) has called "power in movement," I highlight the role that activists play in bringing about gay-inclusive policy change. Throughout the book I have woven examples of the ways that movements matter; here I provide a more thorough discussion of the collective identity and framing strategies that activists deploy in their efforts to create organizational opportunities and to convince corporate elites to grant them equal rights. I focus in particular on the impact of two movement processes: the use of *identity-oriented strategies* that emphasize the visibility of lesbian, gay, and bisexual employees and their allies; and the mobilization of *profits- versus ethics-oriented collective action frames* that rationalize the call for inclusive policies as "good for the bottom line" rather than simply "the right thing to do."

First I examine the impact of various identity tactics deployed in settings ranging from the casual to the highly formalized. I focus especially on the use of personal narratives by both employee and discursive activists, emphasizing the transformative power of emotions in winning allies and persuading elites to embrace policy change. Next I examine the efforts of employee activists to make allies more visible, including the development of "safe space" programs that encourage allies to display tangible markers of support. Closing the chapter with a discussion of framing strategies, I then consider how workplace activists use ideologies of profits versus ethics and delineate the various components that constitute those frames.

The Impact of Identity-Oriented Strategies

Scholars use the term *collective identity* to refer to the ways challenging groups come to define themselves and their shared situation, or how they "make sense of the question of who we are" and how they "draw the circles that separate 'us' from 'them'" (Taylor 1999, 23; see also Taylor 1989; W. Gamson 1992a; Taylor and Whittier 1992; Mueller 1994; Taylor and Raeburn 1995; Whittier 1995, 2002). New social movement perspectives use the concept of collective identity to highlight the fact that people frequently enact their social and political commitments not simply or even primarily as members of formal groups but rather as empowered individuals (Habermas 1981, 1987; Cohen 1985; Melucci 1985, 1989; Offe 1985; Touraine 1985; Klandermans and Tarrow 1988; Giddens 1991; Castells 1997).

The construction of collective identity consists of three key processes: the creation of submerged networks; the development of new collective self-understandings; and the deployment of personalized political resistance, or the politicization of everyday life (Taylor and Raeburn 1995; see also Taylor and Whittier 1992). In this section I focus on the latter component to demonstrate the impact that personalized political strategies can have on others who fall outside the circle of the "we." Through coming-out stories and other personal narratives, gay and lesbian employees strategically deploy collective identity to effect both structural and cultural change in the corporation. Activists use this form of identity expression in their everyday work lives to challenge group invisibility and dominant representations of themselves, to affirm new politicized identities, and to help others see the connections between the personal and the political (J. Gamson [1989] 1998; Melucci 1989; B. Epstein 1990; Taylor and Whittier 1992; Taylor and Raeburn 1995; Lichterman 1996).

While identity expression has been a central dimension of most movements (Morris 1984; Fantasia 1988), new social movement scholars argue that part of what is new about new social movements is the adamant insistence that the formation and expression of collective identity is indeed politics (Breines 1982; Melucci 1985, 1989; Taylor and Whittier 1992, 117–18). As Verta Taylor and Nancy Whittier (1992, 110) argue, drawing on Alessandro Pizzorno (1978), "[T]he purposeful and expressive disclosure to others of one's subjective feelings, desires, experiences—or social identity—for the purpose of gaining recognition and influence *is* collective action" (emphasis added).

Identity Deployment in the Workplace

Lesbian, gay, and bisexual activists use various forms of identity expression, such as coming-out stories and other personal narratives, to help potential allies and elites relate to their concerns. Nonetheless, I found that gay employee networks vary in the extent to which they rely on this form of personalized political resistance (Lichterman 1996). Likewise, Mary Bernstein's work on "identity deployment" (1997) reveals that activists make strategic decisions to either celebrate or suppress their differences from dominant groups. Adapting her framework, I focus on the deployment of identity-oriented strategies that either promote or downplay gay visibility in the workplace and examine the relative impact of these strategies on policy outcomes.

Collective identity strategies that emphasize visibility can be highly effective means of winning inclusive policy change. With regard to domestic partner benefits, I found a striking difference in success rates between networks that highlight versus those that downplay gay identity. Survey data reveal that 67 percent of groups (16 out of 24) in which most members are out at work succeeded in winning equitable benefits, compared to only 11 percent of groups in which very few members had come out (2 out of 18). As further evidence of the positive impact of lesbian and gay visibility, I found that 62 percent of networks (34 out of 55) that celebrated Gay Pride Month in the workplace won benefits, compared to only 27 percent of groups that did not organize such events (4 out of 15). (Typically observed in June, Gay Pride Month marks the anniversary of the Stonewall Riots in June 1969.)

Similarly, while the success rate was 72 percent (26 out of 36) for networks that participated in National Coming Out Day, which is held in October to commemorate the 1987 National March on Washington for Gay and Lesbian Rights, the success rate for groups that did not participate in this or similar events was only 35 percent (12 out of 34). Another indicator of gay visibility is the number of network chapters that exist within a corporation. While particular chapters clearly vary in the extent to which they emphasize gay visibility in the workplace, the sheer number of chapters raises awareness of lesbian and gay issues. It also sends a strong signal to corporate headquarters that the concerns of gay employees are not simply local or limited to a single group of particularly "disgruntled" employees. As expected, in my study those networks that had more than one chapter were more likely to win benefits than those that did not: 62 percent (21 out of 34) versus 44 percent (16 out of 36), respectively.

Doing It Up Big: Celebrating National Coming Out Day

Employee activist networks that choose to emphasize gay visibility in the workplace do so in a wide variety of ways. At a global corporation headquartered in the South, for example, the gay employee group organized particularly elaborate celebrations of National Coming Out Day. This company had already faced a right-wing backlash in response to its support of the gay network, and it was currently under threat of a boycott for its consideration of equitable benefits. Nonetheless, members of the gay network continued to push hard for the benefits. Understating the degree of pressure but acknowledging the face-to-face work of the network, the vice president of human resources explained in our interview, "Fifteen or so fairly high-level openly gay employees met with the CEO [recently] at one of their homes, and domestic partner benefits were mentioned."

The network also used National Coming Out Day to generate support for gay-inclusive policy change among employees throughout the company. During our interview a network leader spoke excitedly about the group's most recent celebration of the day. Members had organized a two-hour lunchtime event that included outside speakers from the local gay and lesbian community center, the lesbian and gay credit union, and the Metropolitan Community Church, a large multidenominational congregation of gay, lesbian, and gay-supportive people of faith. In honor of the event, the company agreed to replace all of the international flags flown at headquarters with rainbow flags, a popular symbol of pride in the lesbian, gay, bisexual, and transgender community.

There was also an exhibit, organized in part by the National Gay and Lesbian Task Force, called "Love Makes a Family," which included photographs showing the diversity of gay and lesbian families. Infusing some humor into the day's events, the network displayed cartoons such as the smartly funny *Dykes to Watch Out For* series by Alison Bechdel, interspersed with "Did you know . . . ?" snippets to educate employees on various gay and lesbian workplace issues, such as, "Did you know that you can be fired in [this state] for being gay?" Indicating commitment, strength, and power in numbers, members from all eight chapters of the company's gay network flew into town to attend the event.

The network also set up information tables and passed out "safe place" magnets as part of a new awareness program. Allies display the magnets in their work spaces as visible indicators of support for gay and lesbian people, to designate the area as free of homophobia. I will discuss "safe place" or "safe space" strategies in more detail later in the chapter. What warrants emphasis here is the fact that the president of the company unveiled the safe-place program at the National Coming Out Day event.

Perhaps this is not surprising, since the network had already convinced upper management to add sexual orientation to the company's nondiscrimination policy and diversity-training program and to begin marketing and donating to the wider lesbian and gay community. Nonetheless, the corporation had yet to adopt equitable benefits. Despite strong support for the network among top management, the company feared the wrath of the Right. At the time of my interviews, when asked whether the benefits were currently being considered, the vice president of human resources responded: "They're always under consideration. We've done research, we know what we would offer and how we would do it. We could do it very quickly. Will it happen? I think it will happen eventually. No one in our industry does it, but enough other big companies will. Then there will be a peer-pressure effect. They will become so commonplace that reactions of employees, customers, and shareholders will eventually be consensus instead of backlash." The company did in fact adopt equitable benefits. Its announcement came less than a week after the first company in the industry took the plunge and extended its benefit plan. Tellingly, that first adopter had also faced years of both internal and external pressure to adopt the benefits.

The Power of Personal Narratives: Winning Allies and Persuading Elites

Another important way that activists deploy identity-oriented strategies is to use *personal narratives,* or stories that help heterosexuals understand what it is like to be gay or lesbian in the workplace (see Taylor and Raeburn 1995). John Lofland discusses "everyday *stories* told and retold with strong positive or negative emotional expression" as an important component of movement culture (1995, 192; emphasis in original; see also Polletta 1998a, 1998b; Polletta and Amenta 2001; J. Davis 2002). Verta Taylor's work on the postpartum-depression self-help movement (1996, 1999) likewise reveals the mobilizing impact of personal stories, whether shared through face-to-face interaction, letters, publications, telephone conversations, or daytime talk shows. Reflecting the insistence of new social movements that "collective self-expression is politics" and highlighting the transformative impact of "emotion culture," Taylor (1999, 20) argues that "activists use the expression of emotions as a deliberate tool for change" (see also Taylor 1995b). Similarly, Darren Sherkat (1999, 17) emphasizes that "narrative identity constructions and other ideological machinations may be used strategically by social movement organizations to appeal to emotive responses from constituents or targets."

Realizing the power of emotional connection, lesbian and gay networks that choose to emphasize gay visibility often use coming-out stories or other personal narratives. Such revelations are in many ways no different from what heterosexuals do on an everyday basis without even thinking—discussing a weekend spent with a spouse, relaying a funny family incident, sharing a painful personal story. But in the context of a heterosexist environment, such acts of sharing by gays and lesbians take on an additional political and emotional significance. Gay employee activists thus utilize personal narratives not simply because that is what heterosexual friends and colleagues do freely in their everyday lives but also because that very act of sharing, when done by members of a stigmatized or invisible group, can have ramifications that echo long after the stories themselves have been told.

Sometimes network members utilize personal narratives on an individual basis with colleagues or supervisors, while other times they organize formal educational events for management or employees in general and include moving testimony that generates empathy for their concerns. These events are typically small-scale occasions held at particular company locations, with formats ranging from diversity workshops, brown-bag speakers, and panel discussions to more focused presentations targeted to midlevel managers or top executives. Some gay employee groups even organize large-scale professional development conferences and send out company-wide invitations.

Strategies that promote gay visibility by establishing personal connections can be highly effective in convincing elites to support policy change. One gay employee group in the high-tech industry used a personalized strategy in its equitable-benefits presentation to upper management. In preparation for the meeting, network members put together a video featuring interviews with gay, lesbian, bisexual, and heterosexual employees in both line and management positions. Each interviewee explained why she or he supported domestic partner benefits. Their company's extension of the benefits made it one of the earliest adopters in the corporate world, though not the first in its industry.

The telecommunications case study offers an example of a particularly innovative identity strategy that demonstrates the power of personal narrative. Leaders of "GLUE" repeatedly emphasized the importance of establishing a personal connection with heterosexuals so that gay, lesbian, and bisexual concerns were "brought home" rather than seen as abstract issues. One way that members put this philosophy into practice was by compiling a "GLUE Family Album" that contained, in the words of the national co-president, "stories of our gay and lesbian lives." Beginning in 1991, network leaders began to compile "a collection of short autobiographical sketches of members, primarily those in long-term committed relationships, to help overcome society's stereotypes."

Over the years, leaders asked fifty members to contribute to the album by writing personal stories about their lives, their partners, and their work. The album included full-color photographs of the contributors and reproductions of their stories—many of which were handwritten on notebook paper, ragged edges and all—to make the album look "even more human," said the national copresident who coordinated the effort. This woman distributed the album to senior management around 1995. In her words, "I gave the book to every executive I could find." She believes that this strategy, by putting "a human face on the issue," was perhaps the most important factor in obtaining domestic partner benefits, which came in 1998 after a nine-year struggle.

The other national copresident of GLUE ranks other factors as more significant, yet he agrees that the album helped GLUE gain additional allies and was hence "a building block along the way." Indeed, while the former CEO was opposed to equitable benefits, GLUE had succeeded in winning vocal support for the benefits from the chief financial officer, the chief legal officer, and the executive vice president of consumers, among others. Thus, by the time the new CEO took office, the skids had already been greased. Shortly after his arrival, the company announced the extension of benefits to domestic partners.

Professional Development Conferences and the Deployment of Personal Narratives

Some workplace activists also organize company-wide professional development conferences to educate executives and win allies throughout the corporation. Employing discursive strategies aimed at legitimizing their call for a gay-inclusive environment, activists use these conferences to diffuse ideologies of ethics and profits, which I discuss in a later section. Equally important, activists utilize these events, which take place at the regional, national, or sometimes international level, as wide-scale arenas for the deployment of personal narratives.

In 1997 I attended a professional development conference that was jointly organized by gay employee networks from two high-tech companies that had recently spun off from a telecommunications corporation. Attended by nearly 250 people, the conference had two tracks, one general and one for management. Although one of the companies had recently adopted domestic partner benefits, the other had not. Shortly after the conference, however, the second company followed suit. The following are some of the ways that gay and lesbian activists used personal narratives to establish a connection with potential supporters.

In one of the management sessions, entitled "Living the Issues: Our Employees' Experiences," a longtime heterosexual ally organized and facilitated a panel of lesbian, gay, and bisexual managers who shared some of their workplace experiences. Some talked about what it was like being closeted, while others talked about the risks and rewards of being out. One of the panelists, "Sandy," explained how she had been "way closeted" as a teacher in the public schools. Finding the secrecy too difficult and draining, she changed careers. Looking for a company with a nondiscrimination policy, she found one in her current employer, but she was still afraid to come out. Sandy would talk about her life partner, "Jacqui," at work but would not identify her as such. One day, Sandy's heterosexual manager approached her and said, "It must be hard for you and Jacqui." As Sandy explained to the workshop audience, that supportive acknowledgment "opened up the world to me." Having found an ally who gave her the courage to come out, Sandy decided to join the gay employee network and eventually became its national cochair. Still actively involved in the network, she has also served on the board of a national gay rights organization.

In another management session, called "Workplace Realities: Fact and Fiction," several gay, lesbian, and bisexual employees shared experiences of harassment, exclusion, and other forms of discrimination. In one story a gay man, who was a member of both the union and the gay employee network, decided to come out at work the day after his company had an all-employee meeting on harassment. He soon began to receive sexually explicit pictures. In addition to a defaced copy of the gay network's informational pamphlet, he was also sent a safe-space magnet that had been cut into pieces.

After some coworkers began making homophobic remarks and he was excluded from his work group, the man finally decided to go to the equal opportunity office. Although in tears when he arrived, he explained that he was "so relieved to see a safe-space magnet on the door of the EO office before walking in." When the office tried to investigate, the union refused to cooperate. Others present at the management session where this story was told said that situations like these, though very upsetting, were "*not* the worst" examples of homophobic treatment in the workplace. Whether through threatening e-mails, vulgar photos, hurtful jokes, or smashed car windows, lesbian and gay employees had received countless messages that told them to remain closeted. Some network members who worked in the factory side of the business literally feared for their lives.

Many of the managers present at the panel discussion seemed truly shocked to hear these stories. The facilitator, a heterosexual ally, next divided the managers into small groups, where they brainstormed ways not simply to prevent harassment but also to create a truly supportive, gay-affirming environment. They responded to the question "What does social justice and equality really look like?" The managers in attendance generated ideas that filled numerous easel-sized pages, which they then posted around the room. Domestic partner benefits figured prominently on the list.

Bringing in Outside Activists: Emotions and the Role of Institutional Bridge Leaders in Revealing the Personal as Political

Sometimes gay employee networks call on discursive activists from outside the company who they feel will do an exceptional job helping heterosexuals relate to the experiences of lesbian, gay, and bisexual employees. At the aforementioned professional development conference, for example, organizers invited Anna Spradlin, a professor of communications from the University of Colorado, to lead a plenary session on the various "passing strategies" that gay men and lesbians often feel forced to adopt. During her session, entitled "The Price of Passing," she shared moving stories about her experiences as a child from a very religious family and as a college student at a conservative university in the 1950s.

After spending what was seen as "too much time with a woman friend" in college, Spradlin was called into the office of the dean, who "accused [her] of being homosexual" and told her to "repent." She looked up the word *homosexuality* in the encyclopedia and learned that it was considered, at that time, a mental illness. "I also learned," she added, "that I would have to hide." Combining humor with pain, she quickly summarized the next chain of events by saying she got married, got divorced, and then "went to a bigger library." There she found more information about homosexuality. "But the messages," she explained, still said, "You'd better hide." And so she did, for over three decades.

Commenting on her role as plenary speaker, Spradlin told the audience, "As a child of the fifties, I never dreamed of a conference like this. This is a great time to be alive." She continued, "After hearing my story, heterosexuals often respond that they had no idea what I had been going through by passing, but it takes two to tango." She then discussed the various ways that heterosexuals consciously or unconsciously urge gays and lesbians to be closeted. She closed by sharing some of the things that prompted her to come out in 1992. Her reasons underline the importance of the wider sociopolitical context and the presence of movement support. Nineteen ninety-two was the year that voters in her state, Colorado, passed the anti-gay Amendment Two, which banned civil rights protection for gay men and lesbians and thus overturned nondiscrimination laws that had been passed in Aspen, Boulder, and Denver (Adam 1995, 133; Dugan 1999). Angered but still afraid to come out, Spradlin came across an old flyer she had gotten years before about the Lavender Caucus, a lesbian and gay organization at her university. Encouraged by the mere presence of this network, she also found support by joining an evangelical group of gay, lesbian, and bisexual Christians.

Offering a tragic illustration of the personal as political, Spradlin then shared the most powerful reason behind her decision to come out to both her family and her colleagues. That year a young lesbian relative of hers shot herself to death. She was found with a Bible in her lap, wearing a sweatshirt from the corporation that had just fired her for being gay. Emphasizing the crucial struggle that employee activists and their allies are engaged in, Spradlin ended by saying, "You in corporations are changing the workplace from 'Don't ask, don't tell' to 'Be all you can be.'" She then turned to the stage behind her and, continuing the conference ritual mentioned earlier, opened a closet door.

Blending Humor and Pain: The Transformative Power of Emotions

Another discursive activist who does an exceptional job at winning heterosexual allies and who is widely admired in the workplace movement is Brian McNaught, introduced in chapter 4. McNaught has been an honored keynote speaker at several workplace conferences organized by lesbian, gay, and bisexual employee networks, and his workshops are widely sought out and imitated by employee activists. I was fortunate to see him in action at the 1997 aforementioned professional development conference, where he led several of the management sessions, all of which I attended. I will focus now on a few of these sessions to provide additional illustrations of how emotion and personal narratives can be mobilized to create committed allies and to persuade elites to institute inclusive policies.

McNaught was truly captivating. Weaving in some of his own painful memories (e.g., being fired from his job for being gay) as well as joyful ones (e.g., his parents' coming to visit him and his partner of twenty years), he was able to draw people in and create allies in the short span of a one-hour session. Comfortably quoting Dorothy singing "Somewhere over the Rainbow" in *The Wizard of Oz,* to emphasize the need for a place of belonging, alongside Edmund Burke ("All that must happen for evil to triumph is for good people to sit by and do nothing"), McNaught easily combined emotionally moving stories with humor. His messages were reinforced in other management sessions throughout the day.

McNaught titled one of his management sessions "A Quick Walk in

Ruby Slippers or Comfortable Shoes," an easily read code in the gay and lesbian community, intended as a humorous nod to the popularity of Dorothy (and drag) among many gay men and to the rejection of Barbie-doll fashion among many lesbians. Indeed, some gay men refer to each other as "friends of Dorothy" (see Vilanch 1998), and lesbians, sometimes called "women in comfortable shoes," have used the phrase to name their organizations, as seen in a recent film-production company as well as an early lesbian group at Ohio State University. Using the session title, McNaught explained these references and briefly discussed the painful as well as playful use of stereotypes, the rejection of narrow gender norms, and, citing a social psychologist, the psychological factors associated with homophobia. Adding another note of lightheartedness, McNaught questioned the rationality of homophobia by commenting, "Some men say, 'I'll kill a gay man if he comes on to me.' Why kill him? Start with 'No, thank you.' If every heterosexual woman killed the men who came on to [her], there'd be so few men left!"

Switching later in the session to a serious tone when discussing what it is like to be gay in the workplace and in society at large, McNaught asked those in attendance to think about examples of internalized racism, sexism, homophobia, and so on. Citing a psychologist, he used the phrase "psychologically homeless" to describe how outsiders feel. This seemed to really "click" with many heterosexual managers, as I heard several repeat the phrase throughout the conference. He continued, "We need to hear people's journeys to be reminded of people's pain. People won't have the incentive to speak out against bias unless we hear those journeys and name the pain." Then he asked people to come up to an easel and write words and phrases that they had heard used against lesbian, gay, and bisexual people. Pages were filled, which he placed all around the room. Afterward, he discussed suicide as the leading cause of death among gay and lesbian youth and showed a video about a mother who had lost her gay son to suicide. He followed this with a video segment of Marlon Riggs's documentary *Tongues Untied,* which drew connections between racism and homophobia.

Later, he discussed a feminist model of building identity and community, applicable to various oppressed groups. Emphasizing the difference that allies can make, he then asked for a volunteer to remove the homophobic words that had been written earlier on the easel pages. Someone quickly jumped up and tore down all of the hate-filled pages. McNaught then approached the easel and, writing his first name on a blank page, said simply, "Now I can say, 'I am Brian.'" He then invited the lesbian, gay, and bisexual managers in attendance to come up and write their names. It was a powerful moment. Afterward, he said, "Now I have and know my community." He then encouraged the heterosexual managers in the session to show their support in the workplace, to not be afraid to speak out against homophobia, and to work for gay-inclusive policies—in short, to be committed allies. Suddenly, straight participants rushed forward and wrote their names on the easel alongside those of their gay colleagues. One man said as he walked toward the easel, "I guess it's time to swim upstream."

McNaught asked how it felt to declare oneself an ally. "It felt good," said one man, "but I wonder if I'll be strong enough to do it in a different group." McNaught responded, "We all have journeys to make." He then closed with a short but moving children's story he had written called "A Frog Is a Frog," which captured the pain and joy of being different and the importance of allies along the way. Afterward several people approached him and encouraged him to publish the story. Many enthusiastically thanked him for the sessions he had led throughout the day.

Diversity Consultants as Information Intermediaries and Institutional Bridge Leaders

McNaught's ability to win allies is legendary in the workplace movement. While I have focused so far on some of the concrete strategies he uses, I turn now to a more theoretical consideration of his role in the movement. Institutional scholars would see McNaught and other independent diversity consultants as "information intermediaries" (Suchman 1995), or "actors whose structural position allows them to observe multiple examples of organizations facing similar sets of problems and attempting varying solutions" (Scott and Christensen 1995a, 306). Diversity consultants and other information intermediaries serve as channels for the mimetic and normative diffusion of gay-inclusive policies. In this light, McNaught can be seen as an isomorphic change agent.

Adapting Belinda Robnett's work on women as "bridge leaders" in the civil rights movement (1997), I also see McNaught as what I would call an *institutional bridge leader*. Robnett argues that because black women were excluded from authority positions in the church and in activist organizations, they served primarily as bridge leaders who connected "potential constituents and adherents . . . to the movement" (191). Similarly, as an independent diversity consultant, McNaught provides sensitivity training and meets with individual executives to convince them of the need for and profitability of equitable policies. He helps bridge gay employee activists with potential adherents in the corporation, aiding networks in their struggle to win allies and create converts out of reluctant elites.

Robnett (1997, 1998) emphasizes how the structural location of bridge leaders, operating outside the constraints of formal civil rights organizations, granted these activists wider latitude than that available to formal leaders. Thus, bridge leaders were able to "act in more radical ways than men, given [the women's] allegiances to the grassroots" (Morris 1999, 536). As a form of charismatic leadership (Morris 1984; Robnett 1998), the responsibilities of bridge leaders often included "emotional work, which increased [the movement's] mobilization capacity and generated greater strategic effectiveness" (Morris 1999, 536).

In a similar way, given his unique structural location as neither an employee activist nor an in-house member of corporate diversity staff, McNaught is freed from the constraints of these positions. Gay employee activists, as well as the internal allies they may have won, often feel pressure to couch their message in profit-oriented language and to conduct "professional" presentations that emphasize the rational, cost-effective basis for gay-inclusive policies. While McNaught incorporates this approach in his seminars, he also relies heavily on personal and emotional narrative. Drawing on feminist models of activism that emphasize the connections between the personal and the political (Whittier 1995; Taylor 1996), McNaught is particularly adept at relating his own and others' painful experiences of homophobia to larger structures of exclusion in the workplace and wider society.

Practicing "Passionate Politics"

McNaught engages in a great deal of "emotion work" or "emotional labor" (Hochschild 1983, 1990; Taylor 1995b, 1996; Whittier 2001) as he attempts to bridge the worlds of gay employees and corporate decision makers. Workshop participants are often visibly affected by his stories. He exudes charisma, far more than would be considered acceptable in employees of the corporation. The behavioral standards of professionalism in the gendered business world reflect the inexpressiveness and cool emotional detachment of hegemonic masculinity (Connell 1987; Acker 1990; Taylor 1996, 1999). But since McNaught is an independent consultant, he is freed from the fear of being discounted by his colleagues or, worse yet, fired from his job.

Capitalizing on the wider latitude this independence affords him, McNaught uses emotion as a social movement strategy (Taylor 1995a, 1995b, 1996; Taylor and Whittier 1995; Whittier 2001). As a gay man, he employs his own subordinated masculinity (Connell 1987) to challenge both gendered and heterosexist norms in the workplace. A similar emotional and political dynamic has occurred in the larger gay and lesbian community as gay men, coping with the tragedy of the AIDS epidemic, have come to "[break] through the strong cultural taboos that suppress intimate caring relationships between men" (Taylor 1996, 176; see also Adam 1995). Learning to value such emotions for both their personal healing effects and their larger political impact, many gay men have joined lesbian feminists in their revaluation of a traditionally feminine "ethic of care" as politically transformative (Taylor and Whittier 1992; Taylor and Rupp 1993; Taylor 1995b, 1996).

Given McNaught's embrace of emotion and his ability to evoke strong emotional responses in others, his approach can be best described as "passionate politics," to borrow from the title of a recent book edited by Jeff Goodwin, James Jasper, and Francesca Polletta (2001a), who, along with their contributors, bring emotions back into the study of social movements (see also Blee 1998b). Following a long tradition in the social sciences in which the false dualism of rationality and emotion has held sway, movement scholars have until recently neglected emotions altogether, assuming that activists as rational actors are not motivated by such messy stuff as anger or compassion, pride or shame, hatred or love. Rejecting the old approaches to collective behavior that had painted protesters as irrational, beginning in the late 1960s movement scholars emphasized the rationality of challengers and focused on the strategic mobilization of resources, followed by a broadened approach that took into account the larger political environment (Goodwin, Jasper, and Polletta 2001b). Hence, while advancing tremendously the understanding of collective action, resource mobilization and political process theories ignored the role of emotions in the emergence, trajectory, and outcomes of movements.

The more recent cultural turn, while directing attention to collective identity and framing processes, has also failed to explicitly address the significance of emotion. As Goodwin, Jasper, and Polletta (2001b, 1) argue, "Even the recent rediscovery of culture has taken a cognitive form, as though political participants were computers mechanically processing symbols. Somehow, academic observers have managed to ignore the swirl of passions all around them in political life." Robert Benford (1997, 419) likewise comments, "[W]e continue to write as though our movement actors (when we actually acknowledge humans in our texts) are Spock-like beings, devoid of passion and other human emotions" (quoted in Goodwin, Jasper, and Polletta 2001b, 7).

After seeing McNaught in action, it would be difficult for anyone to describe his role in the workplace movement without attending to his emotional energy (see R. Collins 2001). Having watched McNaught interact with session participants and seen the impact he had on the managers in attendance—who were moved to tears at times, and moved to speak out and to act—I think it is clear that emotions can play a vital role in effecting change at both the individual and structural levels.

The Importance of Charisma

In many ways, Brian McNaught can be seen as a charismatic leader, a role that has been shown to contribute greatly to movement success (Morris 1984; Robnett 1997, 1998). Lamenting the fact that significant media attention to the 1993 National March on Washington for Lesbian, Gay, and Bisexual Rights and Liberation had "little lasting impact on movement mobilization," Steven Epstein (1999, 69) blames this failure on the lack of any "widely recognized, charismatic leaders." Reflecting on gay rights activism in the 1990s, Epstein argues: "[G]ay and lesbian movements seemed to have difficulty generating or sustaining leaders with the imagination and personal qualities needed to mobilize or redirect collective sentiments in powerful ways, to generate solidarity across divisions within the movements, or to construct coalitions with movements of other kinds" (69). Whether or not Epstein's arguments are an accurate reflection of the larger movement, I agree with the importance he places on charismatic leadership. In fact, I would argue that the mounting success of the workplace movement can be attributed in part to leaders like McNaught, who inspire countless individuals, gay and straight, to work for change both in and outside of corporate America.

In their study of workplace mobilization, organizational scholars Maureen Scully and Douglas Creed (1998) likewise note the importance of charismatic leaders, although they limit their discussion to high-level management champions. They cite one particular company in which a heterosexual ally of the gay employee group delivered a moving speech at an executive forum organized by the group. Commenting on the mobilizing impact of the speech, the authors explain, "The story of the forum is often retold and is itself institutionalized as an important piece of lore or an inspirational opener for subsequent meetings" (22). I found that a similar process has taken place on a much larger scale in the workplace movement, as activists develop institutionalized mechanisms for the public recognition of charismatic leaders.

As mentioned in chapter 3, at the annual Out and Equal workplace conference on gay and lesbian issues, activists recognize an individual or group with the George Kronenberger Memorial Award. This symbol of achievement is named after the inspirational figure who founded one of the earliest gay networks in the country. Activists from across the country speak very fondly of Kronenberger, crediting him with helping to secure the movement's future by organizing workplace conferences and winning the support of national gay rights organizations. Likewise, gay employee activists from coast to coast heap high praises on Brian McNaught. They speak reverently, even lovingly, of his role in effecting change in their own lives and of his gift in creating allies and winning converts among the corporate elite.

When Insiders Come Out

Sometimes lesbian and gay employee networks are delightfully surprised with the fruits of their labor, as when their efforts to win heterosexual allies unexpectedly draw out influential insiders. When activists attempt to convince elites that the corporation should eliminate its closet, every once in a while one of those elites steps out of that closet. At one company in the scientific and photographic industry, for example, the assistant to the CEO approached the leaders of the gay employee network three years after its formation and said she wanted to join. At the time they did not know that this high-level executive was a lesbian. However, at the network's first Educational Event with Management, as the CEO and his wife sat at rapt attention, the assistant decided right then to break her long silence. She came out to the entire audience. She talked about how for years no one had known she was a lesbian and how difficult and painful that had been for her.

Many of the senior executives present were moved to tears. Afterward, this woman became the management sponsor for the gay employee group. Commenting on the importance of the network's educational event in spurring this personal revelation, the founder of the network explained, "[O]nce she saw the management event, and she saw the commitment to what we were doing, she realized that she had an opportunity to [be] a role model." Shortly after this emotional event, "some of the people who [were] in charge of policy got together and decided that it was time to take a serious look at the system."

The following year, the company adopted soft benefits, such as family and bereavement leave, and the year after that, it extended medical coverage to domestic partners of employees. Tellingly, the company adopted the new policy despite the right-wing boycott it had recently faced for sponsoring the Gay Games. Indeed, it was the assistant to the CEO, as the gay network's new management champion, who had convinced the company to sponsor the games, where she herself won a medal. Since coming out, she has joined the boards of several national gay rights organizations and has taken on a leadership role in the workplace movement as a whole. Her contributions to the struggle for lesbian and gay equality both in and outside of her company have earned her national awards.

Noting how openly-gay insiders can serve as key change agents, the authors of the 2000 *State of the Workplace* report (HRCF 2000a, 35), published by the Human Rights Campaign Foundation, write:

> Many of [the workplace movement's] goals are being met, as an increasing number of LGBT people dare to be open about their lives at work and then ask to be treated equally. Openly gay people are breaking through the "lavender ceiling" at many workplaces, meaning they are increasingly being promoted to positions where they can influence policies and benefits. Others are sitting on the boards of major corporations, which again, has an impact on how companies behave, much as the presence of women, African Americans and Latinos in boardrooms has had an impact.

Also recognizing the contributions of insiders who are out at work is the annual "gfn.com 25" list, which honors "the 25 most influential out gay and lesbian executives in corporate America" (gfn.com 2001). These individuals use their "powerful positions . . . to make a difference on a corporate and socially responsible level." The brief write-ups for each recipient show that out executives have played an important part in bringing about various gay-inclusive policies and practices at such big-name companies as American Airlines, Citigroup, First Union Corporation, FleetBoston Financial Corporation, IBM, Miller Brewing Company, J.P. Morgan Chase and Company, and MTV, to name but a few (gfn.com 2000b, 2001).

Aside from the favorable movement outcomes afforded by insiders who are out, workplace activists are quick to point out that companies themselves benefit when employees—executive or not—can be themselves. Indeed, in a particularly strong embrace of the diversity framework so often emphasized in the human resources literature, where talk of "managing diversity" entails "capitalizing" on or "leveraging" differences to achieve a competitive advantage, IBM adopted the rare, if not unparalleled, practice of "actively tracking and encouraging out gay and lesbian executives (increasing from four in 1998 to 16 in 2001)" (gfn.com 2003). The company itself highlights this fact in gfn.com's "Profile of LGBT-Friendly Companies," a Web feature discussed in chapter 4. While I do not wish to downplay the role of openly gay insiders in effecting inclusive policy change at IBM, it bears mentioning that the company's thousand-member gay employee network, EAGLE (Employee Alliance for Gay, Lesbian, Bisexual, and Transgender Empowerment), has been active for several years and boasts over thirty chapters worldwide. In fact, IBM listed all of the chapters that were in existence at the time it submitted its profile to gfn.com and included a link to EAGLE's Web site.

When Outsiders Come In

While the preceding examples reveal that openly gay insiders, often in concert with gay employee networks, can bring about wide-ranging transformations in corporate policies and practices, it is also important to note the occasional role of external movement players, such as the outside speakers that were featured at the professional development conference discussed earlier. Besides using discursive activists who specialize in workplace issues, gay employee networks also call on national leaders in the wider gay rights movement. Such was the case at the aforementioned scientific and photographic equipment company. In addition to the unplanned coming-out testimony of the assistant to the CEO of the company, which served as a powerful punctuating experience for the senior management team, members of the gay employee network were assisted by Elizabeth Birch, then head of the Human Rights Campaign. Leaders of the network had asked Birch to deliver the keynote address at the Educational Event for Management. She shared, among other things, some of her previous experiences as senior counsel for Apple Computer, where she had been involved in the successful campaign for equitable benefits, a move that distinguished her employer as one of the earliest corporate adopters in the country. Referring to Birch's speech in our interview, the national president of the gay employee network noted, "She talked about a number of issues, and domestic partner benefits was one of them. So she gave the managers an education." One of the network founders added, "I think she has a great style about her, and she's a wonderful presenter. She tells you things in a nonthreatening way so that you want to do things. Almost like she calls you to action: 'Here's some information, and now that you have this, what are you going to do with it?'" Another founder, also present at the management event, had a slightly different recollection of Birch's style: "We wanted domestic partner benefits, but we wanted to come off gently. . . . Elizabeth Birch . . . nailed [the CEO] and said, 'You're not the first, you won't be the last. It's the right thing to do.' He sat there shaking his head yes. We couldn't have gotten away with that. This was the first management event we had, and we were, like, 'Come on, Elizabeth, don't kill us before we start.'" In their postevent survey, senior managers rated Birch "very highly," but at the time members of the network were scared that she was pushing too hard. As one of the founders put it, "We were dying!"

Although they acknowledged the role of the larger gay rights movement and national leaders such as Elizabeth Birch, members of the network nevertheless emphasized the crucial impact of internal supporters. Each year at their Educational Event for Management, employee activists have presented key allies with what they call "Visible and OUTspoken Awards," which upper management regards very highly. Recently the awards have gone to the management sponsor, the CEO, and a divisional vice president. The latter was spurred to action after a childhood friend of hers came out as a lesbian. Over time she rebuilt the relationship they had once enjoyed, but her friend died of breast cancer. After seeing the support that other lesbians had given her dying friend, this vice president decided to offer her own support to the lesbian and gay employee network, illustrating again the power of punctuating experiences that personalize gay and lesbian concerns.

Making Allies Visible: Pink Triangles, "Outies," Safe Spaces, and Symbolic Politics

As is illustrated by the Visible and OUTspoken Awards, activists do not engage in identity-oriented strategies simply to increase their own visibility; through rituals of public recognition, they also seek to increase the visibility of their allies. Every year, for example, GLUE members choose an influential ally at their telecommunications company and honor the person with a ceremony and a nicely designed glass plaque. In addition to a written engraving, two overlapping pink and lavender triangles, symbols of gay pride, figure prominently on the award. While these awards are usually given to individuals, GLUE has also recognized an entire business unit for its support of the network. National cochairs also thank allies informally by sending flowers or chocolates. GLUE recognizes allies at the local level as well during gay pride events organized by chapters across the country.

While these awards are genuine gestures of gratitude, they also legitimate gay-affirmative support and encourage others to become allies. Moreover, the awards increase the likelihood that individual supporters will publicly adopt and proclaim their identities as allies to the movement. Thus, identity-oriented strategies work both ways: gay and lesbian employees come out to win allies, and those outspoken and publicly recognized allies in turn construct a new collective identity that inspires them and others to practice personalized political strategies of their own while working for cultural and structural change in the workplace. For example, besides displaying safe-space magnets, some allies wear buttons that read, "Straight but not narrow." Indeed, making allies a more prominent part of the larger gay rights movement was the inspiration for And Justice for All, a national organization formed in 1995 whose mission is to "fight for equality for everyone without regard to sexual orientation" and to "increas[e] the visibility and participation of heterosexuals in the lesbian, gay, bisexual and transgender rights movement" (And Justice for All 2002).

Are You an "Outie"?

The workplace wing of the movement does a particularly good job of publicly recognizing its allies. In fact, employee activists have gone well beyond simply honoring individual allies within their own companies. Each year one ally at the national level is singled out for his or her outstanding contribution to the workplace movement. As described in its national newsletter, Out and Equal Workplace Advocates bestows several different "Outie awards" at its annual Out and Equal Workplace Summit, including

> [t]he Significant Achievement Award for a company that has made the most significant progress toward LGBT equality in the past year . . . the Workplace Excellence Award for companies that have historically supported LGBT employees . . . the Champion Award honoring straight allies who have played a pivotal role in championing equal treatment of LGBT employees . . . the Trailblazer Award for an LGBT person who has made a significant contribution to advancing workplace equity . . . [and] the Employee Resource Group of the Year [Award]. (Out and Equal Workplace Advocates 2001)

As more corporations adopt equitable benefits, and as more influential allies and individual companies are publicly rewarded for helping to effect such change, I expect that other companies will be motivated to follow suit. In other words, to use institutionalist terms, public recognition of allies—and of gay-inclusive companies as a whole—should facilitate mimetic isomorphism as other employers seek the legitimacy and visibility that previous adopters have already obtained (DiMaggio and Powell 1991b).

Encouraging Allies to "Come Out":
The Institutionalization of Safe-Space Programs

First appearing at the 1987 March on Washington, "SILENCE = DEATH," the powerful slogan of ACT UP (the AIDS Coalition to Unleash Power) was soon plastered on the posters, stickers, buttons, and T-shirts of queer activists across the country. The bold block letters were paired with an inverted pink triangle to symbolize the Nazi genocide of known and suspected homosexuals, who were forced to wear the triangle as a visible marker of stigma. ACT UP's inversion of the triangle, according to one of the developers of the visual campaign, was meant to denote a "disavowal of the victim role" (quoted in Soehnlein 1994, 371). The slogan's call to action had a mobilizing impact on countless individuals who were moved by the imagery and urgency of the message (see also Gould 2001). The transformative effects of these symbols serve as a vivid reminder of the power of "discursive politics," a term that Mary Katzenstein (1998, 17) uses to refer to challenges that rely primarily on language and revolve around struggles over meaning.

ACT UP's motto and symbol became widely recognized and were adopted by many advocates of gay rights, including those who otherwise eschewed the group's direct-action strategies. In 1989 GLUE members in the telecommunications case study borrowed from the imagery of ACT UP to develop the safe-space program. During diversity-training sessions, antihomophobia workshops, and various other events, the network passes out educational flyers with magnets bearing the inverted pink triangle surrounded by a green circle to symbolize universal acceptance. Members ask allies to display the magnets to show support for gay rights and to designate their work spaces free from homophobia. GLUE members also distribute the magnets and flyers at external speaking engagements across the country, encouraging allies to "come out" in support of gay and lesbian employees.

Although GLUE formed in 1987, it was not until 1989, after the network launched its safe-space program, that the CEO began to include sexual orientation in his talks on diversity. He even started mentioning the magnets by name. The program was so successful that GLUE now sells the magnets to other gay employee groups and interested corporations. Allies at the telecommunications company where the program was born can also obtain the magnets at the GLUE Store, which sells various items bearing the network's name and logo. Whether T-shirts, hats, mugs, or key chains, these products increase the visibility of lesbian and gay employees and their allies.

Thus, in addition to winning allies, the safe-space program was an attempt to make those allies more visible. Providing a symbolic means of demonstrating support, the magnets began to appear in greater numbers as networks distributed them during internal diversity-training sessions, professional development conferences, and external workplace conferences. Many gay employee networks now participate in safe-space programs or derivations thereof, such as the Open Mind, Open Door program launched by gay activists at another telecommunications company. In the financial services case study, the presence of a pink-triangle magnet in an office or other work space signals that the person displaying it has completed training geared specifically around the Safe Place program. In addition to hearing what it is like to be lesbian, gay, bisexual, or transgender in an unwelcoming climate, participants learn specific ways to foster an affirming work environment, such as not assuming everyone is heterosexual, using inclusive language, and confronting homophobic and transphobic jokes or comments. The distribution of safe-space magnets, visible indicators of support for inclusive policies, significantly increases activists' chance of success. In my study, while 67 percent of networks that instituted such programs won equitable benefits (14 out of 21), only 27 percent of those lacking the programs achieved policy equity (13 out of 49).

As the preceding examples clearly demonstrate, identity-oriented strategies that emphasize the visibility of gay, lesbian, and bisexual employees—and their allies—contribute greatly to movement success. Through coming-out stories and other personal narratives, lesbian and gay activists provide moving testimony that gives a human face to the issues, thereby increasing the likelihood that others will empathize with them. Emotion work thus proves to be an effective part of the workplace movement's "cultural repertoire." Similar to the notion of strategic repertoire (Tilly 1978; Tarrow 1998), the concept of cultural repertoire emphasizes the "strategic dimensions of culture" (Williams 1995).

Constructing and Deploying Ethics and Profits Frames

As important as personal narratives, emotional strategies, and safe-space programs are in effecting change, they comprise only part of the movement's cultural repertoire. Virtually all workplace activists find that identity-oriented strategies must be supplemented by collective action frames that rationalize gay-inclusive policies not simply as "the right thing to do" but also as "good for the bottom line" and hence the most profitable course of action (see also Creed, Scully, and Austin 2002). In the sections that follow, I pull from social movement and new institutional approaches that emphasize the role of such cognitive processes in effecting organizational change. In particular I examine the framing or sense-making accounts of lesbian and gay activists, who draw from the symbols, discourses, and cultural scripts that are available to them in the corporate world and beyond in order to convince elites to extend equal rights.

Collective Action Frames and the Interpretation of "Murky" Environments

Attempting to correct the lack of attention that resource mobilization theorists paid to social psychological processes, more recent social movement approaches have emphasized the importance of framing and other cultural processes (Snow et al. 1986; Snow and Benford 1988; Morris and Mueller

1992; Johnston and Klandermans 1995; W. Gamson and Meyer 1996; Tarrow 1998; Buechler 2000). Collective action frames are cognitive scripts or interpretive schemata that challengers use to legitimate their campaigns (Snow et al. 1986; Snow and Benford 1992). The emergent frames or subjective meanings that actors attach to their circumstances serve as the mediating link between opportunity structures and organizational action (McAdam 1982; McAdam, McCarthy, and Zald 1996b). Thus, William Gamson and David Meyer (1996) have coined the phrase "framing political opportunity" to highlight the ways in which activists influence others' perceptions of opportunity. Organizers "frame" the political context in favorable terms to persuade others that action is needed and that success is possible.

Attempting to "bring the actor back in" to institutional perspectives on organizational change, Neil Fligstein (1991, 1997) likewise emphasizes the cognitive and political role that actors play in interpreting "murky" environments. These sense-making accounts, along with the relative power of particular actors, shape the possibilities for institutional transformation. As my interviews with executives made clear, elites pay close attention to the wider environment when making policy decisions. But the meaning and significance of those external conditions vary, especially since corporations are embedded in multiple environments that often exert contradictory pressures (Scott 1998; Hall 1999). Gay employee activists attempt to influence the subjective judgments of elites by helping them interpret their murky environments in ways that favor change. What this usually boils down to is an emphasis on the competitive advantages that equitable policies can bring vis-à-vis other players in the industry and wider business world.

Ultimately, in institutional spheres beyond the state, it is elite decision makers who determine whether activists' opportunities, resources, and strategies "matter." For, unlike in political systems, the leaders cannot be voted out of office by citizens or overthrown by the masses. Nevertheless, much like the "bargaining" that occurs between challengers and elites in the formal political arena (Burstein, Einwohner, and Hollander 1995), corporate executives weigh employee requests in light of the conditions present in wider institutional environments. As neoinstitutionalists have shown, these conditions, including the very definition of one's competitive reference group, are up for subjective interpretation (Porac, Thomas, and Badden-Fuller 1989; Porac and Thomas 1990). Thus, gay employee networks, though not unionized, can gain bargaining points by framing their requests—and the competitive environment—in ways that reveal how elites themselves can benefit from inclusive policy change.

In his discussion of cultural repertoires, Rhys Williams (1995) empha-sizes the significance of social movement ideologies, conceiving of rhetorical frames as key cultural resources. He discusses the wider political culture of the United States as providing "abundant resources" for activists. Williams's arguments reveal the significance of the context in which challengers mobi-lize: "Actors pull elements from a cultural repertoire and adapt them to their movement's purposes; the relationship between movement cultural resources and the wider cultural repertoire is therefore crucial. Ideologically-driven challenger movements . . . are particularly in need of legitimacy. Drawing on ideological resources firmly established within the cultural repertoire is one way of acquiring legitimacy" (140).

These arguments apply well to the workplace movement. As activists who mobilize inside corporations, gay and lesbian employees operate in a domain that emphasizes profits rather than ethics, rationality rather than rights. Given the need to legitimize their call for equality, gay employee networks must draw on the ideological resources that carry the most "cul-tural currency." In the context of the corporate world, that means relying on a profits frame, a tactic that David Westby (2002, 297) would refer to as "framing which strategically appropriates hegemonic ideology."

Mobilizing an Ideology of Ethics inside the Corporation

In drawing on their strategic repertoire, workplace activists proffer both an *ideology of ethics,* which generally derives from larger movement frames that emphasize equal rights and social justice, and an *ideology of profits,* which is part of the corporation's claimed domain. While employee networks rely on the latter far more than the former, their use of an ethics frame illustrates an important cultural opportunity (McAdam 1994), namely, the availability of a preexisting "master protest frame" that various challengers can appro-priate (Snow and Benford 1988).

Lesbian, gay, and bisexual employee activists draw on the "civil rights master frame" (McAdam 1994) as well as later feminist frames when they argue that domestic partner benefits are a matter of equal pay for equal work, particularly since benefits comprise approximately 40 percent of an employee's compensation, according to the U.S. Bureau of the Census (Woods 1993; Adams and Solomon 2000; City and County of San Fran-cisco Human Rights Commission 2003). This point is emphasized in an equitable-benefits organizing manual published by NGLTF (Kohn 1999, 9) and in how-to guides featured on the WorkNet page of the HRC Web site. In fact, this frame appears to resonate deeply with the wider public, as seen in a recent *Newsweek* poll which found that "83 percent of Americans favor partner benefits just because they provide equal pay for equal work" (Winfeld 2001).

When justifying gay-inclusive policy change as "the right thing to do," sometimes activists draw direct connections to other oppressed groups. For example, the authors of the 2001 *State of the Workplace* report, published by HRCF, argue that employers should ensure equality for lesbian and gay workers "[i]n the same way that most agree women and ethnic minorities should be protected from unfair treatment because of who they are" (HRCF 2001b, 7). Occasionally challengers refer to the lack of equitable benefits as a form of "second-class citizenship."

Adapting the Master Protest Frame: The Constraints of Antiunionism and Right-Wing Backlash

Typically the ethics frame takes a less direct form, however, where arguments about doing the right thing rely less on calls for "equal rights" or "equal pay for equal work" and more on talk of "simple fairness," "dignity," or "respect for all employees." In fact, some employee activists shy away from the former, more pointed framings, because, as more than one respondent explained, if lesbian and gay networks make arguments that sound too much like activist "demands," then management too easily takes an adversarial stance and points out that networks are "not unions." As two employee respondents emphasized during a joint interview, one activist chiming in to finish the other's clearly oft-repeated sentence, "We don't make demands—*we make requests.*"

Thus, many employee networks take up the more diffuse version of the ethics frame, arguing that domestic partner benefits and other inclusive changes are simply about establishing fairness in the workplace, with gay and lesbian workers treated the same as their heterosexual colleagues. Where applicable, activists point out to upper management that denial of equitable benefits for lesbian and gay employees is a violation of the corporation's own gay-inclusive nondiscrimination policy. Several activist networks in my study noted that this line of reasoning alone seemed to make little difference in the minds of elites. Nonetheless, according to a survey of 570 U.S. employers conducted in 2000, 30 percent of corporate adopters cited compliance with a nondiscrimination policy as one of the reasons they extended benefits to domestic partners (Hewitt Associates 2000, 10).

Aside from the antiunion stance of corporate elites, right-wing backlash also helps to account for the fact that many employee activists decide to speak of fairness or respect more frequently than they do of rights or justice. Scholars interested in movement-countermovement dynamics, particularly battles over early gay rights laws as well as more recent debates over same-sex marriage, have documented the ways that antigay opposition affects the frames used by lesbian and gay activists or their supporters (Fetner 2001; Hull 2001; see also Bernstein 2002). Along with the conservative painting of gay rights as "special rights" (Duggan [1994] 1998), the religious Right typically contests or rejects the rights frame altogether by arguing that homosexuality is a chosen and immoral "lifestyle." While workplace activists are quick to explain that keeping all employees free of discrimination is not a "special right," they can often sidestep the morality debates by using rhetorical strategies that rely less on rights discourse and more on appeals to widely held values such as a commitment to fairness, tolerance of difference, or respect for the dignity and worth of each individual.

Conservatives attempt to counter these appeals as well. For example, as part of the wider backlash against multiculturalism and progressive causes in general, a commonly used discursive tactic entails derisively brandishing the label "PC," or "politically correct," to dismiss any embrace of diversity (Perez 1995). Indeed, even some of the most gay-supportive corporate elites try to shield themselves from charges that they are "caving in" to pressure from the "PC police," another derogatory tag used to portray liberals or progressives as infringing upon the freedom and rights of others. A quotation that was featured for a time on the main WorkNet page of HRC's Web site is telling in this regard. Highlighted and labeled as a "Quotable" was a statement made on August 8, 2002, by American Airlines CEO Donald Carty, who was commenting on his company's perfect score on HRCF's 2002 *Corporate Equality Index*: "Taking a stand against discrimination—whether based on race, gender, religion, sexual orientation or anything else—is not politically correct. It is simply correct, and it is the right thing to do."

Government-Forsaken Families: Heightened Awareness of Inequity after September 11

Since the attacks on the United States on September 11, 2001, the public has become increasingly aware of the systemic inequities that lesbians and gay men face. Growing numbers of Americans are condemning as unethical the government's continued denial of equal treatment for gay and lesbian families affected by the attacks. "The September 11th tragedies drove home the sense of urgency about these issues," explained Barbara Menard, HRC's deputy director for legislation. "Our families are now being seen in a whole new way. There's now more of a concrete understanding. And that's largely because families of gay and lesbian victims courageously spoke out, sharing personal stories about their loved ones and urging federal agencies and relief organizations to treat them fairly" (quoted in Hughes 2002, 13).

Even before the attacks, various polls showed that large majorities of Americans favored the extension of various rights to same-sex domestic partners both in and out of the workplace, including hospital visitation (90 percent), inheritance (73 percent), and Social Security benefits (68 percent) (Hughes 2002, 13). Such support appears to be growing, aided in part by the efforts of national gay rights organizations that, along with advocating for the surviving partners of lesbians and gay men who were killed in the attacks, helped to raise public awareness of the fact that same-sex partners were being denied federal, state, and private aid along with other benefits automatically given to heterosexual spouses. In case after case, surviving partners were refused access to relief funds. In but one example, HRC (2002g) publicized the experiences of Peggy Neff, who lost her partner, Sheila Hein, in the attack on the Pentagon. The two had been partnered for over eighteen years and owned a home together. After applying to the State of Virginia's victim-assistance fund, she received a four-sentence letter that explained she was being denied aid because, under state law, only spouses, parents, or dependents were eligible. The letter then offered condolences on the loss of her "friend."

To educate the public about the systematic exclusion of gay men and lesbians from a wide variety of rights, protections, and benefits, HRC placed a full-page ad in the *New York Times* about four months after the attacks (HRC 2002d). The ad, which appeared on Sunday, January 20, 2002, and which also ran in the *New Republic* magazine, showed a woman carrying a young child on her shoulders, photographed from behind while walking in a field. A top caption reads, "Now that her life partner is gone . . ." Side captions pointing to her and the child highlight the numerous rights denied to lesbian and gay couples, some of which read as follows: "Hospital Visitation—right up to the end, she had to fight her way into the room every time"; "Social Security—she can't collect survivor benefits, even though her partner worked her whole life"; "Military and Employer Pensions—her partner served in the Gulf War, but she has no right to her partner's pension benefits"; "Marriage—they never had the right to marry—not in any state. After more than twenty years and a child together, they had fewer protections than a couple married for one hour." Employee activists often highlight this latter point when they meet with top executives in yet-to-adopt companies, arguing that while the corporation would willingly give a slew of benefits to a brand-new hire who just got married, management is essentially turning its back on gay and lesbian workers, many of whom have been with their employer (and their partner) for years.

Other side captions in the ad focused on inequities in health-care benefits, COBRA coverage, inheritance, immigration, and taxation. Appearing at the bottom were brief details about HRC, a call for people to join in the struggle for equal rights, and contact information, including an 800 number and Web site addresses for the organization and two of its focal projects, FamilyNet and WorkNet, both supported by HRCF. With such ads and the ongoing advocacy work of numerous gay rights organizations all helping to heighten public support for partnership rights, employee activists working for equitable benefits are likely to find an increasingly receptive audience in the corporate world as well.

Shifting Demographics and the Push for Equal Treatment

As part of the ethics frame, challengers have also begun to use recently released data from the 2000 U.S. census, which activists interpret as showing a dramatic increase in the number of gay and lesbian families. Again, HRCF's *State of the Workplace* report offers a useful example. In a section called "Changing Makeup of the American Family," the authors describe equitable benefits as a matter of fairness (HRCF 2001b, 7):

> Many states reported seven or eight times the number of same-sex partner households as in 1990—which is still a vast undercount, in HRC's view. . . . Since a key purpose of a benefits program is to provide a safety net for employees and their families, thereby enabling employees to focus better on work, a plan that does not include domestic partner benefits ignores a growing portion of the work force. And since benefits are a form of compensation, it is unfair to restrict some of them to married workers when gay and lesbian workers cannot get legally married.

Activists are not alone in attaching significance to such census data. Publications geared toward human resource professionals also point to shifting demographics as an important factor behind the adoption of domestic partner benefits. One article in *Employee Benefit News,* for instance, cites 1998 census figures showing that "only 25% of America's households mirror the traditional view of the family: a husband and wife living with their children. Meanwhile, the number of unmarried partner households increased 11% from 1994 to 1998" (Elswick 2001, 2)—compared to only a 2 percent increase in married-couple households (Adams and Solomon 2000, 1)—"for a total of 5.9 million Americans living with a domestic partner" (Elswick 2001, 2). Of these domestic partnerships, 28 percent were same-sex couples (Adams and Solomon 2000, 1). Making even longer-term comparisons of census figures, an article in *HR Magazine* (Wells 1999, 68) noted the significant increase in domestic partnerships since 1980, when unmarried couples made up only 1.6 million households. Recognizing these "societal shifts," the author explained, can have a considerable influence on employers' decisions to offer domestic partner benefits.

A Sign of the *Times*

Public awareness of such significant changes in the makeup of American families will surely be heightened in light of a recent and groundbreaking policy change instituted by the *New York Times*. In August 2002, the newspaper of record announced that it was expanding its Weddings column, now labeled Weddings/Celebrations, to include reports of same-sex commitment ceremonies. As the paper's executive editor explained, "In making this change, we acknowledge the newsworthiness of a growing and visible trend in society toward public celebrations of commitment by gay and lesbian couples—celebrations important to many of our readers, their families and their friends" (*New York Times* 2002). By early February 2004, over 220 newspapers had adopted inclusive announcement policies (GLAAD 2004).

These policy changes provide an important form of cultural legitimation for same-sex partners and should thus assist gays and lesbians in their struggle for equitable benefits and the numerous other rights routinely granted to heterosexual spouses. As the number of inclusive newspapers increases, the demographic shifts and census numbers that activists have been citing will eventually seem far less abstract and will take on a more human form in the public eye. While this will certainly aid workplace activists in their call for organizational policies that embrace fairness, lesbian and gay employees will most likely continue, by necessity, to supplement their ethical appeals with arguments that emphasize equality's positive returns for the company.

Frame Blending: The Bottom-Line Benefits of Equality

Whether describing equitable benefits as equal pay for equal work or, in the more diffuse version of the ethics frame, a simple matter of fairness, gay employee groups typically find that, when used alone, arguments about "doing the right thing" carry little weight in the profit-driven corporate world. Indeed, according to the 2000 survey noted earlier, of the companies that have adopted domestic partner benefits only 6 percent said they instituted the change because it "seemed right/fair" (Hewitt Associates 2000, 10). Not surprisingly, then, activists usually end up emphasizing the "bottom-line" advantages of equitable policies. More often than not, employee networks engage in a dualistic rhetorical strategy that I call *frame blending.* Combining an ideology of ethics with an ideology of profits, they argue that doing the right thing *is* good for the bottom line. In short, say activists, equality makes good business sense.

Similarly, neoinstitutionalist Joseph Galaskiewicz (1991, 309), though not focused on activist groups, discusses how corporations in the Twin Cities were persuaded to make substantial contributions to charities. As the "new philanthropic corporate elite" began to hold executive seminars and awards banquets, originally reluctant business executives came to see corporate commitment to philanthropy as "enlightened self-interest," which Joseph McGuire (1963) defines as "a crude blend of long-run profit and altruism" (quoted in Galaskiewicz 1991, 302). As Galaskiewicz argues, analysts should take heed of the fact that "cultural elements that may even run contrary to the dominant ideology of the firm can be consciously introduced into the organization by change agents" (309; see also Silver 2001). His conclusions mirror my own regarding the impact of workplace activists: "[T]his study shows that conscious efforts to institutionalize meanings, values, and norms both within the organization and at the interorganizational field level are effective in changing organizational behavior" (309–10).

Co-opting Corporate Discourse: Key Dimensions of the Profits Frame

In his ethnographic study of corporate culture in a large high-tech firm, Gideon Kunda (1992) discusses organizational ideology and the ways that managers, as "engineers of culture," create and selectively apply particular definitions of reality. Adopting a critical stance, Kunda comments that "the concept of culture is expropriated and drawn into the political fray by culture engineers and their various helpers in the service of corporate goals" (222). Although a useful starting point, this approach ignores the fact that employee groups can and do co-opt corporate discourse in the service of their *own* goals. The profits frame is a case in point.

While I have previously discussed how discursive activists helped to diffuse the profits frame across organizational fields, primarily through the wider business press (see chapter 4), I turn now to the specific ways that employee activists use a profits frame to convince executives that equality for gay and lesbian workers is in the corporation's own best interests. Highlighting the competitive advantages of equitable practices, activists' deployment of a profits frame generally takes three main forms, often used in combination: an emphasis on increased *productivity,* enhanced *recruitment and retention,* and expanded *markets.* The telecommunications case study provides a particularly strong example of how employee activists utilize an ideology of profits.

Increasing Productivity

In all of its presentations to upper management, GLUE stressed that gay-affirmative policies and practices improved employee productivity by freeing up the time and energy that gay employees and their supporters would otherwise expend worrying about or combating harassment and discrimination. The network also attempted to spread this message through internal company publications. For example, in the corporate "yearbook" on affirmative action and equal employment opportunity, which GLUE members fought hard to be included in, one of the sections on the gay network included a photograph and description of a workshop on homophobia in the workplace. The text, written by a GLUE member, noted that the facilitator "effectively presented the cost of homophobia to organizations like [GLUE's employer]." Besides the negative effects on gay employees themselves, "relatives and friends of gays and lesbians are less productive when their loved ones become the target of homophobia."

Likewise, in a section called "Fair Policies Improve Productivity," the authors of HRCF's 2001 *State of the Workplace* report argue, "Maintaining strong policies against discrimination and harassment and providing equal benefits can alleviate personal stress that may keep employees from focusing fully on work" (HRCF 2001b, 7). In 2002, demonstrating elite support for such claims, HRC's WorkNet Web page, in another of its rotating "Quotable" features, highlighted an excerpt from the Senate testimony of FleetBoston Financial's president and CEO, who on February 27 spoke in support of the Employment Non-discrimination Act: "[FleetBoston gay and lesbian employees] remind me of how tiring it can be to stay 'in the closet' and how much energy is wasted, and how focus is diverted from their job, when they feel they must conceal so much of who they are. . . . [O]ur business would be greatly diminished if a gay [or] lesbian employee only brought a piece of themselves, and not their whole self, to work every day because they lived in fear of discrimination."

Expanding on the productivity theme, employee activists also point to increased morale and heightened employee satisfaction as a reason for instituting inclusive policy change. In journalistic accounts of equitable-benefits adoption, many corporate spokespersons acknowledge these favorable impacts as well. For example, at the Discovery Channel, which extended benefits in 1995 after a group of employees requested them from management, the human resources coordinator explained the move as follows: "Part of our decision was to stay competitive, and part was to meet the needs of our employees. . . . We've also seen that it increases morale, which in turn raises productivity. And when recruiters contact me they are aware of the policy because some of the candidates are interested in it" (quoted in Ginsberg 1997; see also Jacobs 2001).

Enhancing Recruitment and Retention

The second type of profits frame argues that adoption of inclusive policies will provide a competitive edge by attracting outstanding employees, both gay and gay-supportive, who expect fair-mindedness from an employer. Assisting employers in this regard, GayWork.com posts jobs available at companies that have domestic partner benefits, nondiscrimination policies, and/or gay and lesbian employee groups. As explained in "Diversity Dot-Com," an aptly titled article appearing in a career-planning magazine distributed on college campuses across the country in the fall of 2000, "niche web sites" targeting the gay and lesbian community, people of color, or people with disabilities help job seekers "hone in on workplaces with welcoming cultures" and assist employers in diversifying the workplace and recruiting the most qualified people (McBride 2000, 32). When emphasizing how equitable policies help companies in the race for top talent, employee activists can now point to such high-profile employers as IBM, Microsoft Corporation, Nike, and Wells Fargo, all of whom use GayWork.com to publicize job opportunities. ProGayJobs.com provides similar services and, along with WorkplaceDiversity.com, also sponsors the Best Companies for Gays and Lesbians at Work Award.

In pushing for gay-inclusive policies, workplace activists also stress that a recruitment advantage is especially critical in a tight labor market (HRCF 2001b, 7). Journalistic accounts likewise point to the connection between labor shortages and equitable benefits. As a 1997 article in the *Washington Post* notes, for example, "The nature of today's tight labor market, with highly skilled workers at a premium, dictates that employers consider workers based on the skills they possess rather than the partners they prefer" (Ginsberg 1997). News coverage of benefits adoption is replete with quotes from corporate executives who use similar arguments when explaining their companies' policy moves.

In addition to playing up favorable recruitment effects, activists emphasize that equitable policies increase employee retention. As argued in HRCF's 2001 *State of the Workplace* report, in a section called "Turnover Is Costly," fostering company loyalty is imperative given the large investment of resources required to replace workers who leave for opportunities available at other companies: "Some studies have put the total cost of recruiting a new employee as high as $75,000. These costs include advertising, interviewing, training, relocation, lost productivity and recruitment incentives" (2001b, 7). In fact, according to an employer guidebook on domestic partner benefits written by attorneys specializing in compensation and benefit plans, research has shown that "it costs five times as much to replace an employee as it does to keep one" (Adams and Solomon 2000, 9).

In an interview that appeared in the aforementioned telecommunications company AA/EEO yearbook, a gay employee, who remained anonymous for fear of his coworkers' reactions, painted the lack of domestic partner benefits at his company as not only discriminatory but also economically irrational: "We will not be able to attract and retain the best people unless this changes. Young people are especially sensitive to these issues and will not tolerate this kind of treatment, especially since they now have so many other alternatives, companies such as Lotus, Microsoft, and Levi Strauss, that do offer equal benefits to gay employees." The comment about workers' having "so many other alternatives" is significant, since it signals an institutional environment where arguments about competitive advantage would be seen as credible. In the earliest adoption wave, when domestic partner benefits were still a rarity, activists found that such talk often failed to convince reluctant elites, since they knew that their benefits packages were just as competitive as the vast majority of employers. As an increasing number of companies started to extend their policies, however, these arguments began to carry more weight. Indeed, results from the 2000 survey of 570 U.S. employers show that 76 percent of adopters cited improved recruitment and retention as a reason they initiated the benefits (Hewitt Associates 2000, 10).

Some gay activist networks have even attempted to show empirical evidence of the economic disadvantages that companies suffer when they retain exclusionary policies and practices. Frustrated after a four-year struggle for domestic partner benefits, one of the leaders of the gay network at a leading company in the scientific- and photographic-equipment industry wrote an internal report on what she called brain drain. In the report she documented how many employees had recently left the company for positions with other employers who already offered the benefits. Shortly thereafter, her company expanded its policy. She attributes the decision not only to the brain-drain report but also to two situations that served as potent illustrations of the report.

Two high-level employees of the company, one a gay man and the other a lesbian, one of whom cochaired the gay network, had been offered promotions that would entail relocation. Both refused, saying that the company's lack of domestic partner benefits made it too difficult for them to move. They explained that their partners, who were both over fifty and well established in their careers, were fearful of their job-market chances in a new city. Without secure positions of their own, their partners would have no health insurance. The man who was offered the promotion emphasized that relocation assistance, which was available only to heterosexual spouses, would have helped alleviate but would not have eliminated this concern. He also mentioned that he was being actively courted by another company that already offered the benefits.

In response to her promotion offer, the other high-level employee explained that her partner had a chronic health condition that did not affect her ability to work but nevertheless made it too risky for her to leave behind a job that guaranteed medical coverage. When this news reached the head of human resources, who was also the executive sponsor of the gay network, he was able to use these concrete examples to convince the company to change its policy. With the promise that the benefits would be adopted in the immediate future, both employees accepted their promotion offers.

Expanding Markets

The third version of the profits frame emphasizes the marketing advantages or expanded customer base that inclusive policies would provide. For instance, GLUE fought hard to convince upper management that instituting equitable benefits and actively targeting the lesbian and gay market would be profitable for the company. As a network member explained in the corporate AA/EEO yearbook, "There are also [telecommunications] companies that are competing with us and are marketing to the gay community. In my opinion, as long as [our company] retains this discriminatory policy [noncoverage of domestic partners], it will be difficult to represent our company to these customers in a positive light. We will lose their money."

In an attempt to provide concrete evidence of the favorable returns that would accrue to gay-affirmative employers, GLUE developed a marketing survey that members distributed at the 1993 National March on Washington for Lesbian, Gay, and Bisexual Rights and Liberation. One of the questions asked how respondents would feel about "a long distance carrier whose marketing efforts specifically recognize lesbian/gay/bisexual people." Another question asked about their willingness to participate in a market-research study. The response was so great and the results so convincing that the company began marketing and donating to the gay, lesbian, and bisexual community. One of its first such moves was a direct-mail campaign, which featured a brochure with photos of same-sex couples and a letter from

GLUE, and corporate sponsorship of the 1994 Gay Games, which immediately drew the wrath of right-wing forces that issued calls for a boycott. Gay-targeted marketing efforts and donations to lesbian and gay causes nevertheless continue at this and a growing number of companies, spurred on by gay employee networks and publications such as Grant Lukenbill's *Untold Millions: Positioning Your Business for the Gay and Lesbian Consumer Revolution* (1995), now in its second edition (1999).

Employee groups pushing their companies to adopt gay-affirmative policies, including marketing to the lesbian and gay community, can also draw on the advertising information provided by the Commercial Closet, a featured link on the WorkNet page of the HRC Web site. A nonprofit education and journalism project that tracks gay-themed marketing campaigns in both gay and mainstream venues, the Commercial Closet is described as "the world's largest collection of gay advertising." As publicity surrounding the Commercial Closet heightens awareness of corporate advertising, companies may be subject to greater mimetic pressures not only to begin similar marketing efforts but also to adopt equitable benefits and other inclusive policies. As gay and lesbian consumers become increasingly aware of corporate standings on these issues, they will most likely see through efforts to win the gay dollar that are not backed by a firm commitment to equality in and outside of the workplace.

As highlighted in a recent *WorkNet News* report, which featured an article by Jean Halliday from *Advertising Age,* public relations and advertising consultants who specialize in lesbian and gay marketing campaigns often point to Subaru of America when discussing the profitability of inclusive policies and targeted advertising (HRCF 2002c). Subaru is well known in the lesbian, gay, and bisexual community for its sponsorship of HRC and its founding sponsorship of the Rainbow Endowment, which uses a portion of the funds generated from the Visa Rainbow Card to donate money to gay and lesbian nonprofits. Subaru's name appears on the credit card, which features a striking aerial photograph taken during the 1993 March on Washington, which drew anywhere from three hundred thousand to one million participants, depending on the estimates used (S. Epstein 1999, 68). In the photo, the marchers and the Washington Monument are shown in black and white, whereas many of the rainbow flags appear in full color.

Subaru became a founding sponsor of the Rainbow Endowment in 1995, the same year it began advertising to the gay community, which proved to be a lucrative move given its rising sales in that segment (HRCF 2002a, 2002c). The automaker initially decided to target lesbians after research showed that "they were among several niche groups with a high propensity to buy its vehicles," but after print ads expanded to the wider community, gay men started to purchase in greater numbers than lesbians (HRCF 2002e).

Tongue in Cheek and Money in the Bank

Many of Subaru's print and billboard ads have featured lines that are wide-ly understood in the gay community but that go over the heads of at least some straight consumers. Company officials have said they never intended the ads as "code," but, as explained in a Commercial Closet report, "When a gay-targeted campaign from Subaru using light hearted license plates began appearing in general outdoor advertising, the news media raced to understand the plates' seemingly 'coded' messages, including 'XENA-LVR,' 'P-TOWN' and 'CAMP OUT'" (HRCF 2002a). Those in the know were quick to explain that the first plate's message alludes to the strong lesbian following that surrounds the television series *Xena: Warrior Princess,* while the second plate references the gay community's commonly used shorthand for Provincetown, Massachusetts, a wildly popular destination for lesbian and gay vacationers. The third plate's triple entendre blends references to "out" gays and lesbians who, putting the car's four-wheel-drive feature to good use, go camping in the rugged outdoors, with "camp" also alluding to the playful (and political) parody of gender roles commonly associated with gay men (see also Rupp and Taylor 2003). When the ads met with rave reviews in many segments of the lesbian and gay community, the company decided to continue the wordplay (HRCF 2002a); recent ads have featured slogans such as "Entirely comfortable with its orientation" and "Get out. And stay out." Even Subaru's mainstream television commercials have "gay overtones," with tennis legend and lesbian activist Martina Navratilova star-ring in an ad for the Subaru Forester (HRCF 2002c).

Most companies that market to the gay and lesbian community rely on print ads and conduct far less direct television campaigns. That may change, though, with lesbian and gay characters appearing in twenty-one network and cable TV programs in starring, supporting, or recurring roles in early 2002 (HRCF 2002c). As explained in the Commercial Closet re-port, "While companies regularly run mainstream ads in gay media, they rarely run gay-targeted ads in the mainstream, since the expense is greater and there is risk of turning off other consumers. Little research exists on how general audiences respond to gay-targeted messages" (HRCF 2002a). However, research does show the profitability of gay-specific marketing campaigns that appear in lesbian and gay media, particularly when done by a company known for its commitment to gay rights. According to a study conducted in 2000, for example, readers of the *Advocate* and *Out* magazines "said they'd be 1.5 times more likely to buy a Subaru than another car brand." The company then doubled the frequency of ads in those publications, and "readers are now 2.6 times more likely to buy a Subaru than non-readers" (HRCF 2002c).

Empirical Credibility and Discursive Strategies

In her social constructionist analysis of the adoption of hate-crime legislation, Valerie Jenness (1999, 548) focuses on the claims-making and discursive strategies of social movement organizations and how they "rendered particular types of violence empirically credible and worthy of federal attention" (see also Jenness and Broad 1997). By documenting, drawing media attention to, and providing legislators with examples of bias-motivated acts of violence, gay and lesbian civil rights groups were able to win gay-inclusive hate-crime statutes in many states.

Likewise, many lesbian and gay workplace activists attempt to establish the "empirical credibility" of the profits frame. David Snow and Robert Benford (1992, 140) define empirical credibility as "the apparent evidential basis for a master frame's diagnostic claims" (see also Snow and Benford 1988). By distributing marketing surveys at gay pride events in the wider community and gathering data on brain drain, for example, activists provide empirical support for their claims that gay-inclusive policies are profitable and their absence costly. Similarly, HRCF's 2001 *State of the Workplace* report (2001b) cites a 1999 survey of human resource professionals conducted by the Society for Human Resource Management (SHRM), which found that equitable benefits "were the No. 1 most effective recruiting tool for executives and the No. 3 most effective recruiting tool for managers and line workers" (38). As an article in the *Denver Post* put it, summarizing the results of the SHRM survey, "[N]othing is as effective as domestic partner benefits for recruitment and retention—not cash, 401(k) plans, perks, bonuses, nothing" (Winfeld 2001). It is not surprising, then, that of the corporations on *Fortune* magazine's 2001 list of the "100 Best Companies to Work For," selection of which was based in part on a survey of over thirty-six thousand workers, almost half (47 percent) offer equitable benefits (Schlosser and Sung 2001, 148).

Authors of the HRCF report likewise interpret the following data as evidence of equality's profitability: while 29 percent of the Fortune 500 offered domestic partner benefits by the end of August 2001, the percentage of adopters increased as the list was narrowed, with 38 percent of the Fortune 250, 49 percent of the Fortune 100, and 54 percent of the Fortune 50 providing such benefits (HRCF 2001b, 21). Commenting on a similar pattern found among the adopters of gay-inclusive nondiscrimination statements, the authors conclude, "The closer a company is to the top of the Fortune 500 list, the more likely it is to [adopt equitable policies], suggesting that the most successful companies in America are those that embrace diversity and work toward providing an inclusive work environment for lesbian and gay employees" (HRCF 2000a, 8).

While I lack data on the number of employee groups that supplement their discursive strategies with "hard" evidence, I expect that networks that do attempt to provide empirical support for the profits frame are more likely to win policy victories than those that rely on discourse alone. I did find indirect support for this hypothesis. As discussed in chapter 3, the dense infrastructure of the workplace movement facilitates communication among employee networks across the country. After activists in particular companies gather empirical evidence to back up their bottom-line arguments, many share the results with other networks via conferences, umbrella groups, e-mail, and the Internet. It therefore comes as no surprise that, in my study, activist groups that were hooked into these communication structures were far more likely to win equitable benefits than groups that were relatively isolated. As previously reported, the success rates for participants versus nonparticipants of workplace conferences were 58 percent and 39 percent, respectively; and for members versus nonmembers of umbrella groups, 58 percent and 36 percent, respectively.

Employee networks wishing to provide tangible support for their profits-oriented arguments can also draw on findings from a survey conducted in 2001 by Harris Interactive and Witeck-Combs Communications, which found that 47 percent of lesbian and gay respondents versus 18 percent of heterosexuals used their awareness of a company's diversity policies to make purchasing decisions (Simanoff 2002). As reported on HRC's WorkNet Web page, the study also revealed that 56 percent of all gay people in the sample agreed, and 41 percent strongly agreed, that they were more likely to trust a brand when the company had adopted progressive policies. Driving the point home, WorkNet staff explain:

> Since corporate America is courting this market, GLBT consumers, investors and employees can play a role in ensuring that they work hard for the money. Increasingly, GLBT consumers are not content to buy a product merely because a company deigns to direct advertising toward them. Many gay consumers use HRC's website and other resources to find out whether a company also has a non-discrimination policy that covers sexual orientation and/or gender identity; whether it offers domestic partner

health insurance; whether it sanctions a GLBT employee resource group; and if it makes contributions to GLBT and/or HIV/AIDS community organizations. (HRCF 2002e)

Using the Profits Frame to Defend against Backlash

In an interesting turn of events, some elites have recently found themselves having to use the activist-generated profits frame to defend against right-wing attacks waged through the proxy ballot. As discussed in chapter 4, the first attempt at antigay shareholder activism was directed at AT&T in May 2001, when conservatives sought to remove sexual orientation from the company's nondiscrimination policy. Undeterred by its loss, the Right targeted Boeing the following year, again unsuccessfully. Like AT&T, Boeing's board of directors recommended that shareholders vote against the resolution.

The Boeing board's proxy statement is striking in that it could have been borrowed directly from any number of gay employee groups' presentations to upper management. Not surprisingly, Boeing has a lesbian and gay employee network whose members helped to secure inclusive policies. Emphasizing how the antigay proposal "would negatively impact [the] workplace environment," Boeing's board of directors reasoned,

> We make every effort to be a leader in the recruitment, development and management of a diverse work force. Our corporate policy is, in part, to attract and retain the best-qualified people. . . . Moreover, Company executives are required to attend courses at the Boeing Leadership Center specifically designed to enable executives to cultivate an inclusive and diverse workforce. Through a diversity policy that focuses on the uniqueness each Boeing employee brings to the workplace, we strive to be the employer of choice, with an inclusive work environment, in which everyone demonstrates respect for differences and feels valued by the enterprise. Boeing believes that an effective diversity strategy provides a wealth of benefits, including increased productivity, global competitiveness and the ability to attract skilled workers in a highly competitive market. (Equality Project 2002)

Largely because of the work of discursive activists, the profits frame has diffused so widely in the corporate sector that even companies without a gay network draw on it when explaining or defending their gay-inclusive policies. Cummins Engine, a Fortune 500 company and the world's largest diesel engine manufacturer, provides a good example. When, in March 2000, Cummins adopted equitable benefits—becoming only the third company in Indiana to do so—a conservative worker voiced religious objections and organized an ad hoc employee group to fight the policy (HRCF 2000a). In late March, approximately 300 people gathered outside corporate head-quarters for a "prayer protest" planned by employee Ben Manring (*Advocate* 2000d), an electrical engineer who summarized the protesters' objections thus: "We don't believe a group of corporate executives has the right to med-dle with what God has established. . . . The Bible contains the definition of marriage as a union between one man and one woman" (*Advocate* 2000b). A counterprotest in support of the company's equitable policies drew about 150 people (*Advocate* 2000d), some of whom held signs that read "The Christian Right Is Wrong" and "Thank God I'm Gay" (HRCF 2000a). As explained by Bil Browning, a Cummins contractor and member of the Indiana chapter of Pride at Work, a national gay and lesbian organization affiliated with the AFL-CIO, "This fight was brought to us by the religious right, and we intend to put a stop to it" (*Advocate* 2000d).

Carried over into a different venue, the battle continued on the stage of the company's annual shareholder meeting, which took place approximately a week after the protests. Speaking in front of an audience of 800, Manring again charged the company with violating his religious beliefs: "I'm a Christian. I challenge you to demonstrate one of these world religions that approves of sodomy or fornication." In contrast, a representative of Indiana's statewide gay rights organization thanked the company for "taking this simple, dignified step toward its employees" (*Advocate* 2000a). Standing firm, Cummins CEO Tim Solso took the podium and announced, "This decision is done. . . . We genuinely feel this is the right thing to do. We need to think of our company as one that welcomes those employees and allows them to grow."

Although this statement framed the extension of benefits as an ethical move, Solso and other executives in the firm also relied heavily on a prof-its frame to defend the policy. As described in HRCF's 2000 *State of the Workplace* report (2000a), "Company officials said the decision to offer the benefits was a business imperative brought on by a need to retain and re-cruit good employees. . . . [The CEO said that] for Cummins to remain the employer of choice, it must provide flexible benefits plans." Moreover, in his public statements to the media, which offer an eloquent example of frame blending, the CEO essentially argued that doing the right thing was good for the bottom line. In writing to the local newspaper to explain Cummins's policy move, Solso cited a 1983 letter from J. Irwin Miller, the company's former CEO and chairman: "In the search for character and commitment, we must rid ourselves of our inherited, even cherished, biases and preju-dices. Character, ability and intelligence are not concentrated in one sex over the other, nor in persons with certain accents, or in certain races or in persons holding degrees from some universities over others. When we indulge ourselves in such irrational prejudices, we damage ourselves most of all and ultimately assure ourselves of failure in competition with those more open and less biased." Describing those words as still true today, Solso added, "We are proud to have taken this step which enables us to grow and to change. It is a change that we believe will make us even stronger" (quoted in HRCF 2000a).

It is interesting that, of all the company statements I was able to locate concerning this policy decision, the CEO never once used the words *gay, lesbian,* or *sexual orientation.* Nevertheless, it is telling that Solso publicly justified equitable benefits by citing an almost twenty-year-old letter that in no uncertain terms condemned sexism, racism, xenophobia, and elitism as economically irrational. In any case, while gays and lesbians may not have been acknowledged in name, the company's commitment to equality was apparently founded on more than just a concern for remaining competitive; the following year Cummins canceled its annual sponsorship of a race that raised money for the Boy Scouts. Management said it withdrew its support because of the Scouts' ban on gay members and troop leaders (*Advocate* 2001).

Summary

As activists in the workplace movement attempted to convince elites to extend equal rights to gay and lesbian employees, they saw that, when used alone, arguments framing equitable policies as an ethical choice carried little weight in the bottom-line world of corporate America. By blending discourses that emphasize fairness and equality with those that focus on dollars and cents, workplace activists found that they had a much better chance of winning inclusive policy change. Gay employee networks thus co-opted corporate discourse and constructed accounts that literally rationalized inclusive policies, weighing their costs (virtually nil) and benefits and concluding that equality was the most profitable course of action. When talk of fairness produced little reaction, activists framed equitable benefits less as a matter of social justice and more as a best practice that would serve the interests of the corporation.

Even without any apparent prodding by organized groups of workers, more and more elites are coming to this same conclusion, adopting domestic partner benefits to remain competitive. But the workplace movement still deserves at least partial credit for these policy changes. If it weren't for the early work of employee activists pushing those first-wave adopters—all of whom faced internal mobilization—domestic partner benefits would not hold the meaning that they do today. Early on, when activists argued that equality would be profitable, most elites believed this frame lacked credibility, given the dearth of adopters, and therefore rejected domestic partner benefits as "too radical," "too costly," or "too risky." Today's executives, even if vehemently opposed to gay-inclusive policy change, cannot legitimately make those claims. On the contrary, research has shown that equitable benefits have moved into the mainstream, cost very little, and in the vast majority of cases bring backing rather than backlash.

As demonstrated in chapters 4 and 5, institutional opportunities at both the macro and meso levels play a crucial part in facilitating policy success. In the absence of favorable conditions in the sociopolitical, field, and corporate environments, some gay and lesbian networks find that their employers seem impervious to change regardless of the strategies and tactics that activists employ. Nonetheless, by utilizing collective action frames that highlight the profitability of equitable policies, by engaging in emotion work, and by deploying identity-oriented strategies that emphasize the visibility of lesbians, gays, bisexuals, and their allies, workplace activists have developed a potentially potent combination. Evidence clearly reveals that most workplace challengers can mobilize resources, identities, emotions, and strategic frames to create at least some opportunities where none currently exist. My study thus points to the usefulness of a theoretical perspective that integrates both movement and institutional processes.

Conclusion

Movement Success, Theoretical and Practical

In the first half of this conclusion, which blends theoretical and practical considerations, I first show how my *institutional opportunity framework,* conceived from the synthesis of social movement perspectives and new institutional approaches to organizational analysis, offers a theory of movement success that can be used to understand the outcomes of institutional activism. Such a framework fills gaps in both scholarly literatures and also provides a useful guide for those challengers whose quest for equality targets not (or not simply) the state but other major institutions of society.

After summarizing the key elements and contributions of a multilevel institutional opportunity approach, which illuminates both the impact of nested environments and the significance of mobilization itself, I then focus on practical implications for the workplace movement. I begin this second half of the conclusion by discussing the perils and promise of profit-centered explanations of policy change, particularly the way that external players in the wider gay rights movement often downplay the role of internal challengers when issuing public accounts of equitable-benefits adoption. I explain the reasons behind such a contradictory stance and the consequences for the workplace wing itself. Next I discuss the lessons that can be culled from combining the empirical findings of the 2002 *Corporate Equality Index,* a benchmarking tool unveiled by the Human Rights Campaign Foundation, with data available on the Human Rights Campaign's WorkNet Web page. Such an examination reveals the crucial role of employee activists in securing not only domestic partner benefits but also several other inclusive policies and practices. Turning then to a cross-sector comparison of equitable-benefits adoption, I show that companies far outpace other types of employers in instituting such policies, and I consider various explanations for this apparent paradox. Finally, I discuss what my findings reveal about the relative effects of institutional processes and internal activist challenges on policy change over time, and I conclude by offering some thoughts on the future course of the workplace movement and the prospects for continued success.

Attending to the Power of Activism inside Institutions

Some twenty-five years ago, Mayer Zald and Michael Berger (1978) issued a cogent yet still seldom-heeded reminder that social movements can take place *inside organizations* and not just in or toward nation-states. Lesbian, gay, and bisexual employee activism is a powerful case in point. Emerging from the intersection of workplace organizations and social movements, the adoption of gay-inclusive corporate policies represents the latest expansion in the definition of workers' rights, yet to date there are virtually no scholarly analyses of this phenomenon (but see Scully and Creed 1998; Foldy and Creed 1999). I argue that to understand both the rise and spread of these policies—indeed, to understand the outcomes of institutional activism in general—requires a synthesis of two previously separate theoretical traditions: social movement perspectives that accentuate the impact of political opportunities and the role of mobilized constituencies as agents of social change; and new institutional approaches that focus on the role that isomorphic processes play in the diffusion of a policy innovation among similarly situated organizations.

Emphasizing the multiple sites of contention in late modern societies, Verta Taylor (2000) echoes Zald and Berger's call by reminding movement scholars that challengers do not always target the state. The struggle for change is waged in a wide variety of institutional arenas, including the workplace, education, science and medicine, religion, and the military (Katzenstein 1990, 1998; D'Emilio 1992; Taylor and Raeburn 1995; Taylor 1996; Taylor and Van Willigen 1996; Chaves 1996, 1997; S. Epstein 1996; McNaron 1997; Scully and Creed 1998; Foldy and Creed 1999; Moore 1999; O'Brien 2002; Creed and Scully 2000; Creed, forthcoming).

Offering similar advice to scholars who study the workplace, Randy Hodson (1996) calls for more attention to the role of internal mobilization in shaping organizational policies and practices. Describing the workplace as "contested terrain," Hodson argues, "Resistance, struggle, and effort bargaining are important components of everyday life in the workplace. Yet workers' strategies of autonomous activity are given little weight in most theoretical models of the workplace." Part of the reason for this oversight is the fact that "workers' strategies are often subtle and situationally specific" (719; see also Hodson 1995, 1999, 2001; Jermier, Knights, and Nord

1994). Institutional activism, then, has been largely neglected by workplace researchers, institutional theorists, and social movement scholars alike. Attempting to correct these gaps in both theory and empirical study, I cast much-needed light on an important form of resistance, namely, the workplace movement for lesbian, gay, and bisexual rights.

Unobtrusive Mobilization, Tempered Radicalism, and Institutional Activism

In her study of progressive activism in the Catholic Church and in the military, Mary Katzenstein (1990, 1998) refers to "unobtrusive mobilization" and "protest inside institutions" as important sources of organizational change. Gay employee groups provide a good example of what she calls "institution-based organizations." Such networks, unlike more autonomous groups, are "beholden" to the "institutions they intend to influence" (1998, 9). Though often invisible to the wider public, these unobtrusive activists can effect significant changes in the institutional landscape.

Highlighting such distinctive activists as "outsiders within" (see P. Collins 1990, 2000), Debra Meyerson and Maureen Scully (1995) coin the term "tempered radicalism." They define tempered radicals as "individuals who identify with and are committed to their organizations, and are also committed to a cause, community, or ideology that is fundamentally different from, and possibly at odds with the dominant culture of their organization" (586). In his brief editorial introduction that appears at the beginning of Meyerson and Scully's article, Peter Frost comments on the motivations and strategic decisions of tempered radicals: "Their radicalism stimulates them to challenge the status quo. Their temperedness reflects the way they have been toughened by challenges, angered by what they see as injustices or ineffectiveness, and inclined to seek moderation in their interactions with members closer to the centre of organizational values and orientations."

These tempered radicals resemble the "institutional activists" described by Wayne Santoro and Gail McGuire (1997), who challenge the widely held view that social movement participants are "necessarily non-institutional actors" (see, e.g., Freeman 1975; McCarthy and Zald 1977; Tilly 1978; McAdam 1982; W. Gamson 1990). Santoro and McGuire define institutional activists as individuals "who occupy formal statuses within the government and who pursue social movement goals through conventional bureaucratic channels." Their research reveals the beneficial policy impact of these "social movement insiders" or "activists who work as insiders on outsider issues" (503; see also Freeman 1975; Eisenstein 1995; Gagné 1996, 1998).

Since the fight for social change takes place in multiple institutional spheres, I have expanded the definition of institutional activism to include mobilization not simply within the government but also within corporations and other supposedly nonpolitical arenas. I have broadened the concept in another important way as well. While Santoro and McGuire describe institutional activists as "polity members," given their "routine, low cost access to decision-makers" (504), I use the term in a wider sense to also encompass challengers who do not—or do not yet—have this routine access. Indeed, many gay employee networks face an uphill battle in obtaining such access.

Toward a Theory of Movement Success

As various scholars have noted, aside from the work underlying William Gamson's classic study (1975, 1990), researchers in the field of social movements rarely direct systematic attention to the outcomes of activism (Burstein, Einwohner, and Hollander 1995; Staggenborg 1995; Giugni, McAdam, and Tilly 1999; D. Meyer 2002). Punctuating this point, Paul Burstein, Rachel Einwohner, and Jocelyn Hollander (1995) cite the fact that Doug McAdam, John McCarthy, and Mayer Zald, in their well-known survey of the literature (1988), "devote less than a page and half of their forty-two-page review to outcomes." Part of this shortfall stems from larger theoretical gaps: "[D]espite great theoretical advances in the area as a whole, we still lack an overall theory of movement success." Burstein, Einwohner, and Hollander then offer a simple yet potent justification of their call for such a theory: "[T]he many studies of movement emergence, participation, and maintenance done since the 1970s mean little if movements never effect social change or if their successes are beyond participants' control" (276).

Pointing to the "extreme difficulty" of trying to understand movement outcomes, Sidney Tarrow (1999) praises contributors to a new book, *How Social Movements Matter,* edited by Marco Giugni, Doug McAdam, and Charles Tilly (1999). Although undoubtedly an important move forward, as Giugni acknowledges in the book's introduction, the volume does not provide "a coherent theoretical framework that will set the pace for future research on the topic" (xxxii). While such an endeavor would prove daunting for any number of reasons, not the least of which is the fact that movements produce several different types of outcomes—policy or other structural changes, mobilization effects, and cultural transformations (Staggenborg 1995)—I offer with hope a useful instrument for the bigger toolbox that is surely required for such a project. My institutional opportunity framework, put to work thus far on understanding the policy outcomes of the workplace movement in particular, makes a theoretical contribution to the study of institutional activism in general, which has itself received very little systematic attention.

The Need for Theoretical Synthesis: Combining Social Movement Perspectives and New Institutional Approaches to Organizational Analysis

Accounting for the success or failure of institutional activists means attending to the multiple embeddedness of organizational challengers. While not focused on activism, neoinstitutionalist Neil Fligstein (1991) asserts that organizational actors are located in three institutional spheres that constrain or facilitate action: the current structure and strategy of the *target organization*; the *organizational field,* comprising the complex of organizations that the focal organization deems relevant to its sphere of activity; and the *state.*

Taking into account these three spheres, which represent "nested" levels of the environment (see also D. Meyer 2003), I have offered a multilevel institutional opportunity framework that delineates the key dimensions of opportunity that challengers face in attempting to transform their organizations' policies and practices. I adapted political opportunity theory to identify the variables in the target organization that explain variation in the adoption of inclusive policies, and I drew from new institutional approaches to understand how isomorphic processes in the larger organizational field and sociopolitical environment affect policy outcomes. Attending to the power of movement actors themselves, I also pulled from framing and collective identity approaches to social movements as well as newer work that brings emotion back into the study of collective action.

In their recently published volume, David Meyer, Nancy Whittier, and Belinda Robnett (2002) highlight a new generation of social movement theory whose practitioners, emphasizing the need to consider both structure and culture, bridge political opportunity and collective identity paradigms. My institutional opportunity perspective expands such bridge-building efforts by synthesizing these paradigms with new institutional approaches to organizational analysis. By combining frameworks used by social movement scholars with those utilized by organizational theorists, I extend the reach of both fields. In the next sections I summarize the theoretical approaches that I have drawn from, and highlight the ways that my synthesis fills gaps in, both literatures.

Expanding the Purview of Social Movement Theory: Shifting the Focus from the State to Other Institutional Arenas

Cultivating Political Opportunity Theory

Taking the state as the site of contention, political process theory highlights how the shifting opportunities and constraints in the larger political environment affect the emergence, trajectory, and outcomes of social movements (Tilly 1978; McAdam 1982; Jenkins 1983; Katzenstein and Mueller

1987; Tarrow 1989, 1998; Jenkins and Klandermans 1995a; McAdam, McCarthy, and Zald 1996b; W. Gamson and Meyer 1996). Sidney Tarrow's definition of political opportunity (1998) focuses on the elements of the political environment that either encourage or discourage mobilization by influencing people's perspectives on the chances of success or failure. Four key dimensions of political opportunity include increased access to the polity, electoral realignments, divided elites, and influential allies (77–80). Comparative studies reveal that these dimensions vary across political systems and issue domains, as well as over time, with some elements exhibiting relative stability and others volatility (W. Gamson and Meyer 1996).

In a heated critique of political process theory, Jeff Goodwin and James Jasper (1999) charge that the political opportunity model retains a structural bias and lacks applicability to movements that do not directly target the state (see also Abrahams 1992; Taylor 1999). While I concur that current conceptualizations are limited in this regard, I do not agree with Goodwin and Jasper's implicit call to abandon political opportunity theory, which arguably has been the dominant perspective on social movements (McAdam, McCarthy, and Zald 1996b; Goodwin, Jasper, and Polletta 2001b). Rather, I have modified the approach to extend its usefulness for analyzing activism in other institutional arenas, including the unobtrusive mobilization of institution-based organizations found in businesses, universities, religious congregations, and the military (Katzenstein 1990, 1998).

Expanding Cultural Opportunities

Other movement scholars have called attention to the cultural or cognitive dimensions of opportunity, including ideational elements in the wider environment such as belief systems, values, political discourse, and media frames (McAdam 1994; Johnston and Klandermans 1995; W. Gamson and Meyer 1996; Taylor 1996; Goodwin and Jasper 1999; Kane 2003). Doug McAdam (1994, 39–43) highlights four types of "expanding cultural opportunities" that are likely to facilitate mobilization: events that reveal inconsistencies between widely held cultural values and actual practices; unexpected events that generate grievances; incidents that dramatize the vulnerability of opponents; and the availability of a "master protest frame" (Snow and Benford 1988) that later challengers can appropriate.

Drawing from and expanding on this work, I attended to the cultural opportunities that aid workplace activists in their fight for inclusive policies. In addition to the elements McAdam identifies, I documented the importance of not only master protest frames but also cognitive scripts in the human resources literature that had already begun to frame diversity as a business imperative (Dobbin and Sutton 1998). I also examined the impact of suddenly *publicized*—rather than suddenly imposed—grievances. Besides these macro-level cultural opportunities, I identified cultural supports that may exist in the target organization itself and that increase the likelihood of gay-inclusive policy change.

Meso-level Institutional Opportunities

Adapting political process theory and the nascent model of cultural opportunities, I have delineated four key dimensions of *organizational opportunity* that facilitate favorable policy outcomes or, if absent, constrain challengers' chance of success (see chapter 5). First is the presence of *structural templates* that allow access to key decision makers and signal at least a minimal level of legitimacy for previously excluded groups. Second is *organizational re-alignment* that brings into the issue domain new elites or organizations that are supportive of or receptive to the goals of challengers. Third is the availability of *allies,* which can include influential individuals or groups from within or close to the elite as well as other organizational challengers who serve as coalition partners. Fourth is the existence of *cultural supports* such as a diversity-embracing corporate culture and, among elites, "punctuating experiences" that humanize challengers and evoke empathetic understanding. Figure 3 provides a more detailed layout of these organizational opportunities as well as the macro-level opportunities present in the wider organizational field and sociopolitical environments.

Mining New Institutional Theory: Conceptualizing Isomorphic Processes as Elements of Institutional Opportunity

New institutional approaches to organizational analysis allow us to understand how variations in the organizational field and broader sociopolitical environments affect policy change. Institutionalists find that many organizational structures and policies reflect external expectations originating from and sometimes enforced by courts of law, legislatures, regulatory agencies, the professions, and public opinion (J. Meyer and Rowan 1977). The more recent focus on culture as constituting organizational repertoires is largely what distinguishes the "new" institutionalism from the "old" (DiMaggio and Powell 1991a). This cognitive approach highlights the more "subtle" influence of the environment, particularly how wider symbolic systems, cultural frames, discourses, and taken-for-granted cognitive scripts "penetrate the organization, creating the lenses through which actors view the world" (13; see also J. Meyer and Rowan 1977; Scott 1995a, 1995b, 1998).

Macro-Level Institutional Opportunities

A central aim of new institutional theorists is to explain institutional iso-morphism, or the processes by which organizations facing the same envi-ronmental pressures come to resemble one another in form and policy and hence achieve legitimacy. Adapting Paul DiMaggio and Walter Powell's model of isomorphic change (1991b; see also Scott 1995b), I have identified three processes that operate at the sociopolitical and organizational field levels to promote the diffusion of gay-inclusive policies. I conceptualized these processes as macro-level institutional opportunities that, if present, aid challengers in their struggle for equal rights (see chapter 4).

These three change mechanisms include *coercive isomorphism,* which entails political and legal pressures such as nondiscrimination statutes, lawsuits, boycotts, and shareholder activism; *mimetic isomorphism,* which stems from benchmarking, interlocking corporate directorates, interorgani-zational career mobility, and other field-level influences; and *normative and cognitive isomorphism,* which originates from the publications and consult-ing work of diversity professionals, particularly those who specialize in gay and lesbian issues, and from the wider cultural diffusion of change-oriented frames and discourses. Figure 3 provides a summary of each of these macro-level institutional opportunities, along with the meso-level organizational opportunities enumerated earlier.

Accounting for Variation in the Extent of Institutional Isomorphism

Organizational scholars have theorized institutionalization not simply as an either/or outcome but as a process entailing variability in the degree to which particular structures and practices become diffused throughout organization-al fields and hence become taken for granted as proper and legitimate (Zucker 1977; DiMaggio 1988; Strang and Meyer 1993; Scott and Christensen 1995a; Tolbert and Zucker 1996; Scully and Creed 1998). Thus, research-ers have attempted to specify the factors, both internal and external, that ac-count for variation in the rate and extent to which organizations in a sector will become homogeneous and hence isomorphic with their environments (Tolbert and Zucker 1983; Edelman 1990; DiMaggio and Powell 1991b; Fligstein 1991; Powell 1991; Scott 1995a, 1995b; Chaves 1996).

Mediating factors include competing external pressures (Fligstein 1991; Mezias 1995) as well as internal characteristics that make some organizations more vulnerable to isomorphic influences (Scott 1995b). For example, schol-ars have focused on the impact of size (Greening and Gray 1994; Mezias

Macro-level Institutional Opportunities

Coercive isomorphism: sociopolitical processes

- Legal statutes: laws on nondiscrimination, benefits, and domestic partner registries
- Lawsuits
- Boycotts
- Shareholder activism

Mimetic isomorphism: organizational field processes

- Benchmarking: traditional sources and virtual tools and reports from outside activist organizations
- Interlocking corporate directorates
- Intercorporate career mobility
- Structuration of organizational fields

Normative and cognitive isomorphism: professional and cultural processes

- New human resources paradigm: diversity as a business imperative
- Outside discursive activists: consultants, speakers, and writers on gay issues in the workplace
- Expanded attention of the business press: diffusion of the activist-generated profits frame

Meso-level Institutional Opportunities: Elements of Organizational Opportunity

Structural templates

- Early risers: preexisting networks
- Mechanisms for official recognition
- Access to institutional resources
- Diversity offices
- Representation on diversity councils or task forces

Organizational realignments

- Elite turnover
- Shifts in composition or policy balance of board of directors
- Mergers and acquisitions

Allies

- Management champions or executive sponsors
- Coalition partners: sister networks and unions

Cultural supports

- Diversity-embracing corporate culture
- Punctuating experiences of elites: discrimination and personal ties

Figure 3. Key components of an institutional opportunity framework: contextual factors that facilitate success for institutional activists.

1995), divisional structure (Thornton 1995), organizational age (Stinch-combe 1965), professional background of elites (Fligstein 1991), com-petitive position (DiMaggio and Powell 1991b), and relational connections such as interlocking board memberships (G. Davis 1991). These internal characteristics do not have consistent effects, however, in part because of en-vironmental complexity. Because any particular organization is embedded simultaneously in multiple and heterogeneous contexts—a situation I refer to as *institutional simultaneity*—it often faces competing external pressures (Fligstein 1991; Mezias 1995; D. Meyer 2003).

Focusing on the interplay of internal and external characteristics, many institutional scholars have examined how organizational susceptibility to isomorphic pressures depends on proximity to the public sphere (Dobbin et al. 1988; Edelman 1990, 1992; Sutton and Dobbin 1996; Dobbin and Sutton 1998). This group of scholars has found that organizations that were closer to the state sector—such as public organizations, companies with fed-eral contracts, and firms in heavily regulated industries—were more vulner-able to governmental scrutiny and hence were more likely to become early adopters of due process, equal employment opportunity, and affirmative action policies (see also Tolbert and Zucker 1983).

I find that the case of domestic partner benefits presents a challenge to this body of literature, in that corporate adoption has proceeded in the *absence* of legislation that would mandate equitable benefits in the private sector. No federal laws require employers to provide such benefits, and only one state and a handful of cities do. Yet companies, often responding to in-ternal mobilization, are leading the way when it comes to instituting lesbian and gay rights. Nonetheless, institutional theory would predict that gay-inclusive nondiscrimination laws and city or state ordinances that provide domestic partner registries and/or benefits to government employees would have a positive effect on corporate adoption of benefits. This is because such pieces of legislation reflect a normative environment that draws at least symbolic attention to inequitable treatment (Edelman 1990). My findings support this prediction. However, I suggest that it is often more accurate to view variations in the legal environment as mediating the impact of internal activist challenges. My results thus challenge institutionalism's tendency to posit the impetus for and locus of organizational change either as exogenous shocks (Fligstein 1991; Powell 1991), such as changes in the law; or as the strategic actions of dominant firms (Fligstein 1991) or, alternatively, periph-eral players in an organizational field (Leblebici et al. 1991; Powell 1991).

Focusing on exogenous shocks as the original source of organizational transformation, Frank Dobbin and John Sutton (1998), for example, discuss how federal policies enacted in the wake of the Civil Rights Act of 1964 spurred the creation of affirmative action and equal employment opportunity offices, which human resource managers eventually began to frame as a business imperative rather than as symbolic markers of compliance with the law, thereby downplaying the influence of the "rights revolution" in the employment sector. This "retheorizing" or "drift toward efficiency" was seen to have served the professional interests of human resource specialists.

My study, however, tells another story and points to a different impetus for gay rights policies in the workplace as well as a different motivation for the adoption of efficiency arguments. In the case of domestic partner benefits, the securing of which can be seen as the new "gay rights revolution" and which represent the latest expansion in the definition of workers' rights generally, the state's role seems far more ambiguous. Indeed, given the antigay backlash that has occurred at the city, state, and federal levels throughout the 1980s, 1990s, and into the current decade, it seems prudent to acknowledge that the state can be a potential inhibitor of—rather than impetus for—equitable benefits adoption in the corporate world. Moreover, while I documented a similar move toward efficiency arguments, which I conceptualized as an ideology of profits, this framing stemmed not from the professional interests of human resource specialists but rather from the collective interests of lesbians and gay men whose employers turned a deaf ear to arguments centered on justice.

Correcting New Institutionalism's Blind Spot: The Role of Internal Activists

By highlighting the role of mobilized constituencies as agents of institutional change, I correct the gaping hole that exists in the vision of neo-institutionalists who focus so intently on the external environment that they often miss the action going on inside organizations. By synthesizing social movement and new institutional approaches, I provide a systematic framework for understanding the origin—and not simply the diffusion—of organizational innovations. Critics from within the institutionalist perspective have long faulted its practitioners for focusing almost exclusively on the isomorphic processes that account for the spread of new organizational practices rather than on the genesis of those innovations (DiMaggio 1988; DiMaggio and Powell 1991a; Brint and Karabel 1991; Fligstein 1991; Suchman 1995; Chaves 1996; Lounsbury 1997). In other words, while neo-institutional theory offers a useful model for understanding how particular policies and practices become institutionalized, it offers little in the way of explaining how those structures arise in the first place.

Calling for a better understanding of the origin of change, or how new organizational forms, practices, and policies emerge, Paul Hirsch and Michael Lounsbury (1997, 416) argue, "The genesis of an innovation must be explained just as much as its diffusion." The lack of focused theoretical attention to both the origin of change and the role of conflict in fueling the transformation process (Chaves 1997; Hirsch 1997; Rao 1998) stems from neoinstitutionalism's tendency to ignore agency and interest (DiMaggio 1988; Chaves 1996; Hirsch and Lounsbury 1997).

As a corrective, a recent symposium of scholars has focused on "bringing actors back in" to institutional analysis (see, e.g., Fligstein 1997; see also Scott and Christensen 1995a). These new institutionalists attend to "the problem of explaining change" at its source rather than merely how innovations, once originated, diffuse across organizations (Leblebici et al. 1991, 335). Appealed for early on by Paul DiMaggio (1988), this investigative turn shifts the spotlight to "the creation of institutions" and to the role of "institutional entrepreneurs" as agents of change. As DiMaggio argues, "New institutions arise when organized actors with sufficient resources *(institutionalized entrepreneurs)* see in them an opportunity to realize interests that they value highly. The creation of new legitimate organizational forms . . . requires an *institutionalization project*" (14; emphases in original).

Nevertheless, in examining the role of institutional entrepreneurs, the vast majority of institutional scholars assume that the change agents are either elites or professional occupational groups working within or across organizations and that these actors are motivated by self-interest to secure or expand their positions as specialists (DiMaggio 1991; Dobbin and Sutton 1998). For example, concentrating on elites, researchers have focused on the institutionalization project of hotel-chain operators (Ingram 1998), community college administrators as "constrained entrepreneurs" (Brint and Karabel 1991), and the role of corporate elites in instituting philanthropic efforts (Galaskiewicz 1991). Other examinations of institutional entrepreneurs focus on the efforts of professional occupational groups, such as the "professional projects" of art-museum directors (DiMaggio 1991) and the role of human resource managers in the creation and diffusion of offices for equal employment opportunity and affirmative action (Dobbin and Sutton 1998).

As is obvious from this brief review, institutional scholars tend to ignore the fact that challenging groups can be important agents of institutional change (for exceptions, see Chaves 1996, 1997; Fligstein 1997; Lounsbury 1997). In contrast, I have emphasized the part that internal activists play in transforming complex organizations. While institutional models prove useful in discerning the impact of isomorphic processes, which I conceptualize as institutional opportunities, social movement approaches are necessary

for understanding the crucial role that challengers themselves play in effecting organizational change. Thus, I turn once again to the social movement
literature, drawing on cultural perspectives that highlight the significance
of strategic framing, collective identity, and emotions.

Framing, Collective Identity, and Emotions in Social Movement Theory: Expanding the Focus to Account for Policy Outcomes

Challengers not only react to but also interactively shape the set of opportunities and constraints they face, creating new opportunities and winning
new advantages through "power in movement" (Tarrow 1998; see also
W. Gamson and Meyer 1996; Gornick and Meyer 1998). While expanded
institutional opportunities create possibilities for change, success depends
as well on the resources, tactical repertoires, mobilizing structures, strategic
framing, and solidarity of challengers (McCarthy and Zald 1977; McAdam
1982; Jenkins 1983; Morris 1984; W. Gamson 1990; Rupp and Taylor
[1987] 1990; Tarrow 1998). In recent years, social movement theorists have
placed increasing emphasis on ideas and beliefs, or the collectively shared
grievances, identities, and unique frames of understanding that people use
to make sense of their situation and to legitimize collective action (Morris
and Mueller 1992; McAdam 1994; Johnston and Klandermans 1995; Taylor
and Whittier 1995; Klandermans 1997). European new social movement
theorists and other contemporary scholars primarily rely upon two concepts
for understanding the cultural dimensions of social movements: *collective
action frames* (Snow et al. 1986; Snow and Benford 1992; W. Gamson 1992b)
and *collective identities* (Cohen 1985; Melucci 1989; W. Gamson 1992a;
Taylor and Whittier 1992; Taylor and Raeburn 1995).

Scholarly perspectives on framing reflect new interpretive approaches
that conceptualize culture as a "toolkit" which people draw from in order
to construct courses of action and to solve various problems (Swidler 1986;
Kunda 1992; Taylor and Whittier 1995). By punctuating an injustice and
identifying its causes and likely solutions, collective action frames serve
as interpretive schemata that activists use to legitimate their campaigns
(Snow et al. 1986; Snow and Benford 1988, 1992). Research on frame-
alignment processes suggests that successful mobilization depends in part
on the degree to which a proposed frame "resonates" with the experiences
and interests of potential supporters (Snow et al. 1986; W. Gamson 1992b;
Babb 1996).

Similar to William Gamson's work on ideological packages (1988) and
Bert Klandermans's research on consensus mobilization (1988), this literature tends to define the success of a framing effort in terms of its ability to

recruit movement participants (Snow et al. 1986; Snow and Benford 1988; see also Jasper and Poulsen 1995). In contrast, I have extended the usefulness of framing approaches by demonstrating their applicability not simply to mobilization but to the very policy outcomes toward which mobilization is directed. In particular, I examined the impact of two different strategic frames that activists deploy in their efforts to win gay-inclusive policies: an *ideology of ethics,* which portrays the adoption of domestic partner benefits as a matter of social justice; and an *ideology of profits,* which frames the extension of benefits as a moneymaking move. Engaging in what I call *frame blending,* employee activists typically end up arguing that doing the right thing is good for the bottom line (see chapter 6).

I also analyzed the strategic uses of collective identity, which refers to a challenging group's emergent understanding of itself and its shared situation (Taylor 1989; W. Gamson 1992a; Mueller 1994; Taylor and Raeburn 1995; Whittier 1995). New social movement theorists propose the concept of collective identity to emphasize that people often practice politics not simply through formal groups but also as empowered individuals (Habermas 1981, 1987; Cohen 1985; Melucci 1985, 1989; Offe 1985; Touraine 1985; Klandermans and Tarrow 1988; Giddens 1991; Castells 1997). A key process in the formation of an oppositional collective identity is the utilization of personalized political resistance (Taylor and Raeburn 1995; see also Lichterman 1996). Aiming for institutional as well as cultural change, activists exercise this form of identity expression in their daily lives to counter hegemonic representations, proclaim new politicized self-understandings, and challenge conventional demarcations between the personal and the political (J. Gamson [1989] 1998; Melucci 1989; B. Epstein 1990; Taylor and Whittier 1992; Taylor and Raeburn 1995; Lichterman 1996; Polletta and Jasper 2001).

Challengers vary, though, in the means by which they practice personalized politics and in the extent to which they rely on this form of resistance (Lichterman 1996). Mary Bernstein's work on "identity deployment" (1997), for example, reveals the strategically oriented decisions that activists make to either highlight or suppress their differences from the majority. Likewise, I focused on the *deployment of identity-oriented strategies* that promote rather than downplay the visibility of gay, lesbian, and bisexual employees and their allies. Extending Bernstein's approach, I examined the relative impact of these identity tactics on policy change. My focus on the policy outcomes of identity strategies provides a useful addition to the scholarly literature on collective identity. As my findings show, coming-out stories and other personal narratives function not simply as identity-building processes for movement participants but also as powerful means of cultivating allies and persuading elites (see chapter 6).

Embracing emotions that are otherwise suppressed in the corporate world, activists use narratives that reveal the pain of exclusion, the yearning for a sense of belonging, and the joy of community. These stories all help to establish a deeper human connection that can move potential allies and elites beyond a cognitive grasp of the issues to what I would call a felt understanding. Whether engaged in by internal challengers or by discursive activists brought in from the outside, such emotional expressions can evoke not simply empathy but also a desire to speak out and to work for change. By examining the policy outcomes of "passionate politics" (Goodwin, Jasper, and Polletta 2001a), my research thus contributes to the most recent advances in social movement theory, particularly a cultural approach that brings emotions back into the study of collective action.

Contextualizing Employee Activism: The Fruitfulness of an Institutional Opportunity Framework

A small but growing number of scholars have begun to apply social movement and new institutional approaches in tandem (Ramírez 1987; Amenta and Zylan 1991; Fligstein and McAdam 1995; Minkoff 1995; Chaves 1996, 1997; Fligstein 1996, 1997; Jenness and Broad 1997; Katzenstein 1998; Lounsbury 1998; McCarthy and McPhail 1998; Strang and Soule 1998; D. Meyer 2003). This move makes particular sense given that "well-established lines of thought in both of these literatures attempt to 'bring culture back in' by highlighting the role of normative and cultural expectations in shaping organizational forms, strategies, goals, and discourse" (Jenness and Broad 1997, 10). Thus far, however, no one has attempted a systematic theoretical synthesis aimed at understanding the impact of both institutional and movement processes on the emergence and diffusion of new organizational policies and practices, particularly those that ensure equality for previously excluded groups. In other words, no one has systematically combined these approaches to offer a theory of movement success.

Taking a first step toward filling that gap, I have offered a multilevel institutional opportunity framework that highlights the impact of the multiple institutional environments in which challengers are embedded and the significance of mobilization itself. I have analyzed the effects of nested environments through attention to isomorphic change mechanisms, and I have examined the impact of movement processes via a focus on identity-oriented strategies, emotions, and collective action frames. My findings show that policy outcomes are not simply determined by environmental conditions; instead, it is more accurate to view various sociopolitical, field, and corporate-level variables as mediating the impact of activist strategies. I thus argue that institutional scholars should recognize social movements as important agents of organizational change, and movement scholars should attend to the dimensions of opportunity that exist for challengers who target institutions besides the state. By providing a theory of movement success that can be applied to mobilization in a wide variety of settings, my institutional opportunity framework, combined with a cultural analysis of the emotional, framing, and identity-oriented strategies of activists, advances scholarly understanding of social movements and institutional transformation.

Aside from the explanatory power of an institutional opportunity approach for analyzing gay-inclusive policy change in particular, the framework I have developed here expands the usefulness of political process theory in general by widening the focus to include multiple terrains of struggle, not just the formal political arena. My study also corrects the tendency of American political process theorists to concentrate on the emergence of movements rather than on their outcomes. My approach more closely resembles European scholars whose comparative focus attempts to explain cross-national variation in the structure and outcomes of the same movements based on different national political contexts (McAdam, McCarthy, and Zald 1996b, 3). Shifting the focus from the state to the workplace, I have compared the policy outcomes of employee activists across various corporate, field, and sociopolitical contexts.

My conceptualization of institutional opportunities thus reflects not simply a shift in terminology but, more importantly, an expansion in theoretical and empirical focus. An institutional opportunity framework directs attention to the opportunities and constraints that challengers face both in and beyond the state. Activists are simultaneously situated in multiple, nested environments that both separately and in combination exhibit variable and at times contradictory conditions (D. Meyer 2003). Social movement scholars have noted that activists sometimes face a conflicting set of political opportunities (W. Gamson and Meyer 1996; Tarrow 1998). This is all the more true for institutional activists, who are embedded in multiple institutional spheres that include not only the sociopolitical arena but also the more immediate site of contention, such as the corporation, and the organizational field in which that target organization is located. Thus, whether utilized to study mobilization inside workplaces, universities, or religious congregations, this framework should prove a fruitful one for understanding the rise and spread of policies that ensure equality to those laboring, learning, or worshiping within a given organization.

Moving Landscapes, Institutional Simultaneity, and Environmental Inconsistency

Institutional scholars have drawn attention to the complexity and heterogeneity of the multiple environments or institutional spheres in which organizations are located (Fligstein 1991; Powell 1991; Mezias 1995; Scott 1995a). Similarly, social movement scholar David Meyer (2003) refers to nested institutions, with actors—whether individuals, organizations, or states—each being embedded within broader social and political environments such that the opportunities of challengers in one arena are shaped by the conditions present in each of the other arenas. Given the complex set of factors that come into play, Meyer aptly describes strategic battles as being waged on a "moving landscape."

The embeddedness of challengers in multiple environments, a situation I refer to as *institutional simultaneity,* means that activists often face a contradictory set of conditions, both within one institutional sphere and across multiple spheres. Some elements of challengers' environments facilitate success, while other elements limit the possibility. This *environmental inconsistency,* as I call it, is an inevitable consequence of institutional simultaneity. In other words, activists rarely face a congruent or consistent set of institutional conditions. Challengers do not encounter *either* a favorable set of opportunities *or* an unfavorable array of constraints; in most cases, institutional activists face *both* sets of circumstances.

Thus, in comparing the likelihood of policy success among employee networks, it is imperative to examine the "specific context of embeddedness" (Karnøe 1995, 247) for each group. Identical tactics, for example, can produce quite different results. To understand why, scholars must take into account the widely varying sets of institutional opportunities that exist both within and across network environments. Different employee groups must traverse quite different institutional terrains. The soil may be relatively rich for some but rocky for others, so the tools and strategies that work in one context may prove futile in another. Likewise, as the political, industry, and corporate conditions change over time for a particular network, previously unsuccessful tactics may finally bear fruit.

Institutional Opportunities as a Continuum

Given such contextual variations, I argue that it is useful to conceptualize institutional opportunities as falling along a continuum, with conditions ranging from highly favorable to highly unfavorable. At either end of the continuum, challengers operate under conditions of environmental consistency. Falling between the two poles are opportunities that present a mixed bag for challengers, who in those situations face environmental inconsistency. I propose that the emergence, trajectory, strategies, resources, and outcomes of challenging groups are all shaped by the intersecting and complex set of environmental conditions—some favorable, some not—within each institutional sphere, namely, the target organization, the wider organizational field, and the sociopolitical arena. Future investigations of institutional activism should therefore attend to the interplay between movement processes and the often complicated array of institutional opportunities that challengers face, noting especially the impact of environmental inconsistency on the likelihood of policy success.

Like the traditional political domain, institutional arenas such as the workplace present openings as well as obstacles, of which some seem more stable while others vary considerably over time and place. These sometimes mercurial climates affect both the emergence and outcomes of mobilization. Activists, however, do not simply react to changes in their environment; through their own actions they can create opportunities for themselves and others (W. Gamson and D. Meyer 1996; Meyer and Staggenborg 1996; Tarrow 1996, 1998; Sawyers and Meyer 1999). In other words, while movements are susceptible to stormy conditions, so too are they partially responsible for improved climates.

Although mobilization inside institutions often remains unseen by the wider public, "unobtrusive activists" can accomplish substantial institutional transformations (Katzenstein 1990, 1998). Indeed, by coming out and organizing inside their places of work, lesbian, gay, and bisexual employees and their allies are winning equitable policies and practices in organizations across the country. A testament to the power of institutional activism, their fight for equal rights reveals how relatively small but committed groups of people can bring about wide-scale social change.

Practical Implications for the Workplace Movement

Unlikely (versus Unsung) Heroes in the Struggle for Equal Rights

At a press conference on August 13, 2002, HRC unveiled the *Corporate Equality Index* (see chapter 4), "a simple and effective tool to rate large American businesses . . . on how they are treating their gay, lesbian, bisexual, and transgender employees, consumers, and investors" (HRCF 2002b, 2). Commenting on the 2002 *CEI* findings, which revealed surprisingly widespread commitment to at least some gay-inclusive policies, HRC's then executive director, Elizabeth Birch, exclaimed, "The truth is, it's corporate America that has been the unlikely hero in the movement for equality for gay and lesbian Americans." Birch's statements aired on CNN Headline

News and nearly twenty other television stations across the country (HRCF 2003c). At least twenty-five different newspapers covered the story as well. Echoing Birch's pronouncement in the headline of one article, the *Los Angeles Times* announced, "In Gay Rights, Private Sector Is 'Unlikely Hero,' Survey Finds . . ." (Fackler 2002).

As I watched the segment on CNN Headline News, I was struck by Birch's choice of words. While her statement was meant to acknowledge the fact that companies were far more likely than other types of employers to have adopted gay-inclusive policies, it occurred to me that, given such "hero" talk, the general public may have been left with the impression that corporate America's rather incredible embrace of gay-inclusive policies stemmed not from internal pressure, or even external competition, but simply from the goodness of executives' hearts. In this scenario the agents of change would appear to be corporate decision makers who, intent on righting some long-standing wrongs, forged a path for others to follow.

While I in no way wish to discount the role of fair-minded elites, my findings reveal that, although some companies are now instituting equitable benefits even in the absence of internal mobilization, it was lesbian and gay employee activists who brought about those early and groundbreaking changes in the business world and who even still play an important role in the ongoing transformation of the corporate workplace. In most cases, moreover, challengers wrought these successes only after convincing elites—who, notably, remained unpersuaded by ethical arguments alone—that policy change would be a profitable move.

Workplace Movement Accounts of Policy Change

Not surprisingly, leaders of the workplace wing of the movement are quick to credit employee activists, as seen in the following account found in the *Knight Ridder/Tribune Business News*, one of few media reports I found that quoted a national leader in the workplace movement itself rather than a spokesperson from the larger gay rights movement:

> "Occasionally you see [the adoption of gay-inclusive policies] as a top-down change, but *usually* you see it because there's been some *push from the employees themselves*," says Selisse Berry, executive director of Out and Equal Workplace Advocates [a national organization] in San Francisco, Calif. "Companies do this because it's the right thing to do, but many gay, lesbian, bisexual and transgendered employees have *created the business cases* to share with their employers and [human resource] managers," she says. (Simanoff 2002; emphasis added)

Wider Movement- and Media-Generated Accounts of Policy Change

The "business case," or profits frame, itself has diffused so widely that it has become the dominant explanation in most public accounts of equitable-benefits adoption. Journalists, leaders of the wider gay rights movement, and corporate executives alike turn to it when commenting on the latest policy announcement or overall adoption trends (see chapter 2). Indeed, in press interviews about the results of the *CEI*, Birch herself emphasized the profit-driven reasons for embracing gay-inclusive policies: "Most successful companies know [that] discrimination is bad for business and that treating all employees fairly returns enormous dividends" (quoted in Krupin 2002; see also, e.g., E. Epstein 2002; *Newsday* 2002).

In searching through media reports on the unveiling of the *CEI* (see also HRCF 2003c), I was able to locate only one newspaper article that alluded to the significance of activism—though not to internal mobilization in particular—and that reference was contained in a single sentence: "Birch said she was not surprised at the [corporate index] results, saying they were the results of a decade's worth of efforts to end discrimination against gays and lesbians" (*Newsday* 2002). Of course, when members of the press seek comments on the latest policy announcement or on the growing number of equitable-benefits adopters in general, national spokespersons from the wider gay rights movement may specifically acknowledge the role of lesbian and gay employee groups. It would not be surprising if such comments ended up on the editing-room floor, given the media's tendency to reduce an argument to "ever shorter sound bites" and catchphrases (W. Gamson 1995a, 93)—thus the "unlikely hero" refrain. In any case, in media coverage of inclusive policy shifts, references to internal mobilization are rare; thus, employee activists remain the unsung heroes. And when workplace challengers *are* mentioned in the press, they are overshadowed by the story line that dominates virtually all media accounts of corporate policy change: namely, companies institute domestic partner benefits and other inclusive practices simply because they make good business sense.

But it is not just the media that emphasize the profit motive while giving short shrift to the impact of employee mobilization. Even in many of their own publications and press releases, when accounting for equitable-benefits adoption and other inclusive policy changes, national leaders in the larger gay rights movement often give higher billing to the role of the market than to the crucial part played by gay employee activists. In fact, in HRCF's own report summarizing the results of the 2002 *CEI*, the impact of internal mobilization is acknowledged only in reference to the small number of companies (seventeen) that had added gender identity to their nondiscrimination policies: "GLBT employee groups and transgender employees themselves have led corporate change in this area" (2002b, 3). A profit-centered explanation is offered for all of the other policy changes documented in the report, including gay-inclusive nondiscrimination statements, domestic partner benefits, diversity training that includes sexual orientation, equal recognition of all employee resource groups, and advertising in and/or corporate donations to the lesbian, gay, bisexual, and transgender community. As noted on the first page of the report's introduction, "Employers have taken these and other steps to attract and retain good employees and to market to the GLBT community (which is seen by some marketers as having a substantial amount of disposable income)" (1).

What such profit-focused accounts of policy change do not reveal is that these now dominant frames of understanding were spearheaded by the meaning-making endeavors of lesbian and gay employees who, after convincing enough companies that equitable policies would be good for the bottom line, essentially made such predictions come true. Now numerous employers *do* offer domestic partner benefits to attract and retain the best talent. And now, to remain competitive, a growing number of corporations are beginning to follow suit even without pressure from organized groups of gay and lesbian workers. This seems a perfect illustration of an oft-quoted social constructionist tenet: if people define situations as real, they become real in their consequences (Thomas and Thomas 1928, 572).

The Power and Peril of Profit-Centered Accounts

There is no doubt that the profits frame facilitates favorable policy outcomes (see chapter 6). It is thus not surprising that, in their public accounts of equitable policy change, which are of course meant to influence potential adopters, national gay rights leaders portray previous adopters as having been motivated (and rewarded) by profit—and indeed they were. The problem comes when external movement players rely too heavily on economically based reasoning to explain policy change—emphasizing the impact of tight labor markets, for example, while ignoring or barely touching on the presence of employee activism. When leaders in the wider gay rights movement neglect to point out the numerous cases in which internal mobilization helped to drive policy change, they may unintentionally generate complacency in potential beneficiaries and thereby have a demobilizing effect on the workplace wing of the movement, which could in turn jeopardize future policy success (see chapter 2).

In other words, whether issued by the media, corporate executives, or leaders in the wider gay rights movement, profit-centered explanations of equitable-benefits adoption treat the process of policy change too narrowly. While these public accounts avoid portraying corporate elites as the heroic protagonists, they typically err too far in the other direction by leaving out protagonists altogether. In such tellings of the story, there appear to be no "live and in the flesh" change agents at all, just the amorphous market and its competitive pressures spurring companies to play follow-the-leader. Left with this impression, many gay and lesbian workers in yet-to-adopt companies may likely decide that mobilizing for equitable benefits is unnecessary. Change, they would reason, is surely on the way. But this is a risky assumption. If market forces alone drive the adoption of equitable benefits, as profit-centered accounts seem to imply, then why are there still so many companies dragging their feet?

As my study of policy transformation in the 1990s has shown, all of the early Fortune 1000 innovators—and a large majority of later adopters—instituted domestic partner benefits only after lesbian, gay, and bisexual workers pushed them to do so. In all, of the 83 Fortune 1000 companies that had adopted equitable benefits by the end of the decade, over two-thirds (67 percent) had faced pressure from mobilized groups of gay and lesbian employees. It is true that the presence of a gay network has become somewhat less necessary over time (see Table 1 in the introduction to this book), and the pace of adoption has accelerated since the end of the 1990s, the number of Fortune 500 adopters alone having climbed to 211 by mid-February 2004 (HCRF 2004). This increase is undoubtedly driven in part by competitive pressures and by the small number of mandates that require companies with city contracts to provide domestic partner benefits (see chapter 4, including Figure 2). But, given the vast numbers of lesbian and gay workers who still lack equitable benefits, clearly these mimetic and coercive pressures are not strong enough. Despite the impressive gains noted here, it bears repeating that, at the start of 2004, nearly 60 percent of the Fortune 500 had yet to adopt inclusive benefit programs (HRCF 2004). While these and other laggards may no longer need the hard push that was required of so many gay employee networks in the past, they must still need at least a little nudge.

Bringing the Activists Back In (or Out): Revealing the Hidden Lessons of the "Corporate Equality Index"

The preceding figures clearly confirm the central role that employee activists have played in the rise and diffusion of domestic partner benefits among the Fortune 1000. The findings of the 2002 *CEI,* when supplemented with data from HRC's WorkNet Web page, likewise reveal the significance of internal mobilization for securing not only equitable benefits but a host of other inclusive policies as well. The 319 companies included in the *CEI* were drawn mostly from the 2002 Fortune 500 list and from the 200 largest privately held firms on the 2001 Forbes Private 500 list. The sample also included other corporations, all with at least five hundred employees, which were either already in the WorkNet database or were included in the *CEI* at their own request (HRCF 2002b, 2). Of the 319 companies that were rated, 129 (40 percent) have lesbian and gay employee groups (4).

With a scoring system based on seven equally weighted criteria (see chapter 4), the *CEI* allowed HRCF to objectively rate employers on a scale of 0 to 100 percent depending on whether they had adopted various gay- and transgender-inclusive policies and practices. Overall, the median score for the 319 companies was 57 percent, or four out of seven criteria (HRCF 2002b, 3). Only 13 companies (4 percent of the total sample) earned a perfect score: Aetna, AMR/American Airlines, Apple Computer, Avaya, Eastman Kodak Company, Intel Corporation, J. P. Morgan Chase and Co., Lucent Technologies, NCR Corporation, Nike, Replacements Ltd., Worldspan, and Xerox Corporation.

By consulting the WorkNet database, I was able to determine something that was noticeably absent in the *CEI* itself: of the 13 companies with a perfect score, 12 (92 percent) had faced pressure from mobilized groups of gay, lesbian, bisexual, and transgender employees. The only top scorer lacking such a network was North Carolina–based Replacements Ltd., the world's largest retailer of crystal, silver, and china patterns. Surprised that a corporation had met all seven criteria with apparently no internal mobilization, I contacted the company to see if the lack of an employee group contact in HRC's database was perhaps a mistake. The staff coordinator confirmed that there was no gay network but then kindly referred me to a local organization for lesbian and gay professionals. In the end, it was the "gfn.com 25" list that helped to solve the mystery (see chapter 6). There, among those honored as the twenty-five most influential gay or lesbian executives in corporate America, was Robert Page, the founder and president of Replacements Ltd., who has received national recognition from HRC as well as from the Gay Financial Network for his role in urging other corporate leaders to support gay and lesbian causes (gfn.com 2000b, 2001). Over 25 percent of the company's employees are openly gay, making Replacements Ltd. an obvious employer of choice in the lesbian and gay community (gfn.com 2000b).

The Driving Force behind the Cutting Edge

Clearly, the corporations that have demonstrated the strongest commitment to equality—those that have blazed a trail for others to follow—have been pushed, encouraged, inspired, or led by gay, lesbian, bisexual, and transgender employees themselves. This acknowledgment is not intended to take away from the truly progressive advances that these employers have made; it is simply meant to give credit where credit is due.

Not just in these top-scoring companies but in numerous other organizations as well, lesbian and gay employee activists deserve recognition as change agents not simply because of the risks they take in coming out at work, nor because of the considerable amount of time they dedicate to the struggle, nor even because of the impressive policy shifts and immeasurable cultural changes they have brought about in workplaces across the country; while these factors are justification enough for public recognition, I argue that these institutional challengers should be a more central part of external movement-generated accounts because, aside from providing a more complete picture of how institutional transformation takes place, such acknowledgment should aid the workplace movement—and the larger gay rights movement as a whole—by inspiring others to mobilize for gay-inclusive changes in their own places of work.

Making Sense of Contradiction: External Movement Players Downplaying Internal Workplace Activism

While I have used media accounts and some of HRC's own documents to show how, in the public eye, the efforts of internal challengers are often either obscured or omitted from sight altogether, I need to make clear that this is certainly not the case in all of HRC's publications or press releases. Moreover, if HRC has been subject to more scrutiny here than have other national organizations in the wider gay rights movement, it is testament to the truly unparalleled contributions that its staff and its foundation have made to the workplace wing of the movement. As seen in numerous examples throughout the book (see especially chapters 3 and 4), HRC's WorkNet project and the volunteer-member Business Council are essential parts of the struggle for gay and lesbian equality in the workplace.

What also warrants emphasis here is that while HRC and other external movement players typically emphasize institutional rather than movement processes in their public accounts of policy change, it is partly because these market-based or profit-centered explanations help to navigate around potential quagmires in corporate and sociopolitical terrains. First, profit-centered accounts provide a ready-made rhetorical defense for corporate executives who fear right-wing backlash. Portraying inclusive policy shifts as being driven by market forces and bottom-line considerations alone—and not by lesbian and gay employee activists—plants the decision firmly within the corporation's claimed domain and thus helps insulate against attacks from the New Right. Second, economically rationalized accounts that describe policy change as being motivated solely by "good business sense" avoid raising the ire of corporate elites themselves, who often see any coercive pressures—whether internal mobilization or external regulation by the state—as threats to their own base of power, encroachments on their professional turf, or illegitimate interference with the "free market" (see also Dobbin and Sutton 1998).

In any case, in the interest of future mobilization and policy success, when issuing public accounts of policy change, leaders in the wider gay rights movement need to keep in mind that the audience includes not simply corporate decision makers who have yet to adopt equitable benefits but also lesbian and gay employees who have yet to mobilize. The challenge, then, is to find ways to balance two equally important movement needs: appealing to potential adopters and motivating potential beneficiaries. The latter seems particularly important given the fact that so many companies still lack equitable benefits *despite* the fact that the profits frame has become the dominant theme in media reports, external movement accounts, and human resource publications alike. In other words, economically rationalized discourse in the wider institutional environment may be a strong facilitator of policy shifts, but it is no substitute for the potential power of even the smallest groups of lesbians and gay men who, by virtue of coming out and working for change inside their own places of work, put a human face on the issues and thus infuse some passion into an otherwise coldly rational cost-benefit analysis.

Why the Corporate Sector Has Been Leading the Way

Despite the incomplete picture evoked by characterizing corporate America as the "unlikely hero" in the struggle for gay and lesbian equality, Birch's statement during the 2002 press conference did hit on what many would see as a glaring paradox: companies far outpace educational, nonprofit, and government-sector employers in adopting gay-inclusive policies and practices. By mid-February 2004, offering domestic partner benefits had become standard practice in 6,909 companies, including 211 (42 percent) of the Fortune 500. In contrast, the same could be said for only 10 state and 130 local governments, 40 unions and other labor organizations, 125 nonprofits and professional associations, and 198 colleges or universities (HRCF 2004). I now consider various explanations for the more rapid diffusion of equitable benefits in the corporate sector.

Higher Levels of Employee Mobilization

I suspect that one of the most important factors accounting for such policy variation is the greater presence of gay employee networks in the corporate world as compared to other employment sectors. While I have recently begun a research project that tracks both the adoption of equitable benefits and the actual rate of employee mobilization in each sector, until such a comparative analysis is completed it is important to keep in mind that levels of internal mobilization may only appear to be higher in the corporate world. In any event, it is certainly the case that the vast majority of attendees at the national workplace conferences I observed were employed in companies, and most of the key players in the workplace movement were based in the corporate sector. Moreover, the employee group contact lists that were circulating at the time I began my research were composed almost entirely of corporate networks. Even if the pace of mobilization in noncorporate workplaces has picked up considerable steam since then, it seems clear that, as an early target, the business world has been subjected to far more extensive internal pressure than have other employment sectors.

Battles over Benefits in the Government Sector

Aside from variations in the level of employee mobilization, institutional context is obviously an important factor in accounting for cross-sector differences in the rate of policy change. With lesbian and gay rights—particularly the recognition of same-sex relationships—being so hotly contested in the formal political arena, the slower pace of equitable-benefits adoption in the public sector comes as no surprise. As one journalist writing for the *Boston Globe* puts it, "[T]he public sector tends to lag [behind] private industry because proposals to provide state or local employees with domestic-partner benefits become political hot potatoes" (Leonard 1998).

Witness, for example, the congressional injunction that for nearly a decade prevented Washington, DC, from implementing a domestic partner benefits law that had been approved by the city's elected leaders in 1992. The measure, aside from offering hospital visitation rights and family and bereavement leave, simply proposed to allow DC government employees, if registered as domestic partners, to purchase—at their own expense—health insurance coverage for their partners. In late September 2001, the House of Representatives finally ended the ban that had prohibited the use of local funds to implement the program (Data Lounge 2001a). Criticizing the prolonged Republican resistance to such a relatively small step, Representative Nancy Pelosi (2001), then House Democratic whip, expressed her strong support for equitable benefits and noted, "Over 4,200 employers around the country, including a third of the Fortune 500, have . . . establish[ed] domestic partnership health programs. Many of these programs go much further [than] the D.C. law."

Another telling illustration of the hostile political climate that constrains equitable policy adoption in the public sector is the so-called Marriage Protection Pledge. This campaign calls on elected officials, candidates, and political appointees to sign a pledge that states in part, "I will protect the importance and uniqueness of marriage between a man and a woman. I believe that awarding spousal-equivalent [domestic partner] rights to non-married couples cheapens the value of marriage" (quoted in California Alliance for Pride and Equality 2002). The pledge campaign is but one tactic in the Right's new and expanded strategic repertoire, which aims to prevent not only gay marriage but the granting of any rights whatsoever to domestic partners (see also chapters 2 and 4).

As part of the antigay backlash, conservatives are also waging legal challenges to statutes that provide equitable benefits for government employees and to laws that prohibit employment discrimination in the private or public sector. Many such cases have been brought by the American Center for Law and Justice (see chapter 4) and the Northstar Legal Center, which focuses its litigation on overturning legal protections that have been won by gay men and lesbians. In 2001 alone, judges heard at least nine separate cases related to equitable-benefits laws for government employees (HRC 2001b, 13).

In their arguments to the courts, conservatives have claimed that "local governments lack the authority to enact [such laws]" (28), that "the local ordinance violates the state's marriage law" (13), and/or that nondiscrimination laws "violate the First Amendment rights of would-be discriminators" (28). While these strategies have brought some limited success to antigay forces, local ordinances have largely been upheld by the courts (28). Case law varies greatly, however, since states differ in how much power they give municipalities to regulate their own affairs (13).

Conservatives are also using ballot measures to fight equal rights for gays and lesbians. Based on their analysis of the tactical or venue-related choices made by gay rights supporters and opponents over a twenty-six-year period (1974–1999), Regina Werum and Bill Winders (2001, 386) suggest that, since the early 1990s, "gay rights opponents increasingly find success through ballot initiatives, a venue based on popular support rather than access to central government arenas." In 1998, for example, right-wing activists in Maine succeeded in winning majority support for a ballot initiative that repealed the state's civil rights protections for gays, which had been signed into law the year before (HRCF 2001b). Two years later, similar efforts to overturn equitable benefits for state employees failed. Antigay forces also attempted to repeal Maryland's nondiscrimination law via voter referendum, but the initiative was defeated in the 2002 elections. Such battles continue across the country at both the state and local levels.

In addition to using the ballot box directly, conservatives attempt to push various state legislatures and city councils to overturn nondiscrimination ordinances and equitable-benefits laws. This strategy may have increasing impact as elections tip the balance toward conservative majorities. Indeed, as a result of such compositional shifts, antigay forces have succeeded even in rescinding union-secured benefits. For instance, in July 2003 public employees in Minnesota lost the domestic partner benefits they had won through labor agreements back in 2001, because the Republican majority in the state house refused to ratify the contracts if the same-sex benefits remained (HRCF 2003b).

The Fickle Nature of the Political Process

Even when gays and lesbians succeed in winning some concessions from the state, then, equality wrought in the formal political arena can be rather tenuous. Whether through voter referenda that rescind equitable benefits for government employees, ballot initiatives that repeal nondiscrimination statutes, elections that tip the legislative balance toward conservatives, or court decisions that overturn previous gains, lesbians and gays cannot count on the state to guarantee equal treatment (see chapter 4; see also Werum and Winders 2001). In the corporate world, however, only three employers, all based in Texas, have ever rescinded gay-inclusive benefits policies or nondiscrimination clauses. At Perot Systems Corporation, H. Ross Perot terminated equitable benefits upon his return from the 1996 presidential campaign trail. At ExxonMobil Corporation, in 1999 postmerger management revoked Mobil Corporation's nondiscrimination policy and also closed any future enrollment in its equitable-benefits program. ConocoPhillips Company removed sexual orientation from Conoco's nondiscrimination statement after merging with Phillips Petroleum Company in 2002, but then moved to restore the category a few months later. The change of heart came just days after HRC issued a press release condemning the corporation (Sixel 2003).

The Relative Advantages of Mobilizing in the Corporate Arena

As noted by Ed Mickens (1994b, 41), who, as book author and consultant, is one of the discursive activists so essential to the workplace movement, "For those used to looking at gay and lesbian issues through a political lens . . . [waging] a war on the economic front while we are still battling in politics may seem a bit daunting." Nonetheless, compared to the formal political sphere, the economic front seems "an ideal arena for lesbian and gay progress," in part because it "doesn't have the standard disadvantage that electoral politics has for gays and lesbians—being the minority, even counting our nongay allies." Likewise, in an editorial in support of gay rights, Ohio State University professor of law Douglas Whaley (2002) notes, "By definition, minorities cannot succeed in any legislative process unless the members of the majority are interested in their issues."

In contrast, in the corporate arena, gays and lesbians can often effect significant change by convincing a relatively small number of elites that inclusive policies are in the best interests of the company. While some employee activists in this study found that months of hopeful efforts dragged into years of struggle, with even the best of efforts being blocked by staunchly antigay elites, most challengers found that even some of the most reluctant or hesitant decision makers grew more receptive when networks emphasized how equitable policies were good for the bottom line. Others found additional assistance from executives who, by virtue of their own experiences of discrimination or their preexisting personal ties, saw gay-affirmative policy change as the right thing to do.

Overall, then, despite inevitable setbacks, the labors of corporate challengers are made easier in some ways because of the terrain on which they struggle. Whereas in the political arena the cause of diversity is subject to attack, in the corporate world it is more likely to be celebrated (at least in theory). The business and professional literature is replete with references to diversity as a "business imperative" or a "corporate best practice," with a myriad of articles touting the competitive advantages of "managing diversity" and "leveraging differences" (see Dobbin and Sutton 1998). In response, numerous companies new to the issue regularly seek the services of outside diversity consultants, while those further along the curve establish in-house diversity offices. Meanwhile, in the sociopolitical sphere, conservatives continue to wage war on diversity—whether discursively, as when any embrace of difference is derisively dismissed as "PC," or structurally, as when right-wing forces mobilize against affirmative action, women's rights, and gay and lesbian equality. To put it bluntly, while hearing the word *diversity* makes many conservatives see red, more and more executives simply see profits.

Jean Hardisty gets at this same dynamic in her book *Mobilizing Resentment* (1999), which traces the emergence and impact of various right-wing movements. In one of her chapters, Hardisty compares the corporate, university, and government sectors in their level of support for or opposition to affirmative action. Her analysis, which captures the importance of institutional context, applies equally well to gay-inclusive policies:

> [M]any . . . corporations now stand out as defenders of [affirmative action], while elected politicians and right-wing activists are successfully dismantling [such] programs in the public sector and in higher education. . . . And, with the majority of public bureaucracies in the hands of conservative state- and local-level Republicans, it is within the corporate sector that there seems to be an appreciation of the value of diversity in the workplace and the advantages of tapping the entire breadth of the U.S. talent pool—pragmatic rather than moral arguments. So long as the moral justification for affirmative action remains muddled in the public's mind and infected with disinformation from the right, it appears that support for [the policy] will hang on most strongly where it is good for business. (158)

Refusing to "Argue with People about God"

Although scholars may debate the usefulness of the term "culture wars" (see, e.g., Williams 1997), clearly certain "morality debates" continue to hold sway in the sociopolitical arena. A *Boston Globe* article on domestic partner benefits, for example, cites Boston University sociologist Alan Wolfe, whose research on middle-class Americans showed that, in his words, "[h]omosexuality is the one area where people still use words like 'sinful, abnormal, wrong, and immoral'" (quoted in Leonard 1998). Placing these findings in a larger context, the journalist notes, "That's why developments in the workplace, with the rapid extension of benefits to nontraditional partners, [are] significant. Businesses are setting aside moral questions and using the bottom line to justify changes in social policy. They also can—and do—politely ignore the organized opponents of gay rights who can paralyze the political process."

Such was the case with the Eastman Kodak Company. After adopting equitable benefits, the company received a handful of complaints, some internal but most external to the firm, which were described as "hate letters" by Renee Brownstein, director of total compensation. Commenting on criticisms by religious conservatives from outside the company, Brownstein stated, "It was none of their business." Nevertheless, she continued, "[w]e [formed] standard responses before we got any hate mail, and that's how we chose to deal with them," she explained. "We did not argue with people about God. . . . We chose to take the high road and say, 'Here's the reason we're doing this. This is why it makes sense for Kodak as a business. Thank you for your input.' You really cannot argue with these people" (quoted in Adams and Solomon 2000, 50).

Political Struggles in Public Universities

While corporations may "politely ignore" right-wing opposition to gay-inclusive policies, public universities operate under a different set of conditions, given their reliance on support from taxpayers, state legislatures, and various government agencies. This institutional vulnerability to outside political influence may help to explain the slower pace of equitable-benefits adoption in the educational sector as a whole. The struggle over benefits at Ohio State University (OSU) sheds light on some of the constraints that activists face when mobilizing in publicly funded institutions. Lesbian and gay faculty, staff, and students have been pushing for equitable benefits at OSU for over a decade. In March 2002, the administration finally granted same-sex partners a limited number of "soft" benefits, such as family and medical leave, life insurance for dependents, financial-planning services, and a doctor-referral service for travelers (HRCF 2002f). While gay faculty and staff now have access to these benefits, many must be purchased by the employees themselves; the university pays nothing for any of the benefits. Unlike most universities that have extended benefits, OSU does not offer health-insurance coverage to domestic partners.

OSU president William "Brit" Kirwin tried to offer as many benefits as he could without having to seek approval from the board of trustees, which, according to university officials, is not open to the issue. "I know that the president is very supportive of offering domestic-partner benefits to our employees," explained a spokeswoman for the university, "but he is aware that the political climate is such in Ohio that he is not going to bring anything to the board any time soon." She then added that the president and the chair of the board of trustees, David Brennan, "have decided to respectfully disagree." A top fund-raiser for the Ohio Republican Party, Brennan commented, "I don't think Ohio State even has the right to extend benefits [just] to same-sex partners. We're a state agency and the state of Ohio doesn't recognize those relationships. I expect to look into it" (quoted in HRCF 2002f).

Whereas some gay rights supporters acknowledged the university's progress while nevertheless criticizing the move as "baby steps," conservative lawmakers and "pro-family" groups immediately attacked the policy as going too far. Such right-wing opposition is exactly what the board had feared, explained OSU law professor Douglas Whaley: "The problem is that the Board of Trustees is worried that the legislature will retaliate in financial ways or some other way." That could indeed happen, according to state senator Jim Jordan, one of the legislature's leading conservatives: "If a private company wants to do it, that's one thing, but this is a taxpayer-supported university. When you have the budget debate, and you're talking about taxpayer-supported universities, I think it's appropriate to have a policy debate about what the universities are doing." Notably, the attack on OSU's policy coincided with the state legislature's consideration of a bill that declared the extension of "certain legal benefits of marriage to same-sex partners [as] 'against the strong public policy of this state'" (HRCF 2002f). Opponents pointed out that the bill, which eventually became law, takes aim at not simply the possibility of gay marriage but also the formal recognition of domestic partnerships.

Clearly, then, employees mobilizing for equitable benefits in public universities and in the government sector can face a nearly overwhelming set of constraints given the strong presence of conservative legislators at the local, state, and federal levels and the formalized channels of political influence available to antigay forces in general. While activism in the corporate sector is certainly not without its obstacles, the considerable progress that lesbian and gay challengers have made in the business world seems attributable at least in part to this structural difference in institutional context.

Working for Change on the Inside, Inspiring Change on the Outside

Aside from the relative advantages of mobilizing in the corporate arena, activism on this front offers the gay and lesbian community important opportunities to effect more widespread social change. This is because, as Ed Mickens (1994b, 41) notes, "corporate policy . . . has considerable impact on social attitudes and politics." In other words, while companies are influenced by numerous forces in the external environment—legislation, judicial rulings, consumers, shareholders, and the court of public opinion (J. Meyer and Rowan 1977)—so too do corporations shape the world outside their walls.

Much of that corporate impact has been detrimental, as pointed out by environmentalists, opponents of corporate globalization, fair-trade supporters, labor and consumer advocates, public interest and public health groups, critics of the military-industrial complex, alternative-media supporters, and campaign finance reformers, to name but a few. These challengers are joined by numerous other social justice groups opposed to the inordinate power that corporations wield in and outside of the economic arena, particularly their influence over the political process as whole, a dominance that critics say has rendered the United States a "corpocracy" (Roth 2002). Nonetheless, largely because of the pushing and prodding of lesbian, gay, and bisexual employees who have been working for change from the inside, companies adopting gay-inclusive policies are beginning to inspire changes on the outside.

According to conversations I have had with employee activists in the educational, nonprofit, and government sectors, and as has been the case with my own participation in campus groups fighting for equitable benefits, institutional challengers working outside the business world often ask their employers why they lag behind corporate America in their commitment to equality. In at least some cases, this question is highly effective in spurring change. Corporate actors are also beginning to play a more direct role in effecting wider institutional transformation, as when companies withdraw advertising from explicitly antigay radio or television programs, such as the heavily criticized *Dr. Laura Schlessinger Program* (*Advocate* 2000c), or when they stop donating to organizations with explicitly antigay policies, such as the Boy Scouts of America (*Advocate* 2001).

Numerous corporate executives have also submitted congressional testimony in support of the Equal Employment Non-discrimination Act (see chapter 2). Many of them reach out to their peers as well in an attempt to win additional corporate endorsements. For instance, at a fall 2002 "breakfast of champions" hosted by HRC and Hewlett-Packard Company, executives from HP and Eastman Kodak joined two congressional representatives from both sides of the aisle to discuss ENDA with corporate decision makers from at least eleven other companies. Shortly after the event, two of those companies, Cisco Systems and Levi Strauss & Co., announced their endorsements of ENDA (HRC 2002a). Notably, all four of the aforementioned corporations have active lesbian and gay employee networks.

Some top executives also work directly with elites in and outside of the business world to encourage them to adopt gay-inclusive policies in their own organizations. I offer the following example to illustrate not only a case of cross-sector influence but also the favorable impact of media attention to equitable policy change, an important institutional opportunity discussed in chapter 1. In early 2001, the CEO of Indiana-based Cummins Engine was asked to speak at Indiana University's Bloomington campus after his company extended benefits to domestic partners in 2000 (Vecchiollo 2001).

The invitation for the speaking engagement came at the prompting of Steve Sanders, who was both assistant to the IU chancellor and, notably, the Indiana state coordinator for HRC. Sanders had begun working a few months earlier to convince the university to adopt equitable benefits. After reading about the Cummins controversy and being highly impressed with CEO Tim Solso's "eloquent and forceful statement" in the newspaper, where he defended his company's policy in the face of highly vocal opposition both in and outside of the firm (see chapter 6), Sanders approached the dean of IU's business school about bringing Solso to campus. Solso's talk, which drew more than one hundred people, got front-page coverage in both the Bloomington and campus newspapers. Shortly thereafter, the university's staff council voted to urge the president of the IU system to institute equitable benefits. The administration adopted the benefits that same year.

As these examples illustrate, the activist-inspired sea change in corporate America has begun to reverberate across multiple sectors of society, effecting transformations in other institutional arenas that, surprisingly or not, have lagged far behind the business world in granting equality to lesbians, gays, and bisexuals. Given the potential for even more widespread societal change, one of the key challenges for the workplace movement is to find ways to generate higher levels of mobilization both in and outside of the corporate sector.

The Relative Importance of Movement versus Institutional Processes over Time

Contrary to the predictions of institutional theorists, the original catalyst for the rise of gay rights in the workplace was not employment legislation but rather employee mobilization. Early corporate adopters of domestic partner benefits instituted these changes only after they had been urged to do so by gay and lesbian employee groups. Thus, while institutional processes clearly play a facilitative role in the diffusion of inclusive policies, it is the groundbreaking efforts of workplace activists that explain the first wave of corporate adoptions. As word got out about these mavericks in the business world, others slowly began to follow suit, eventually triggering more rapid isomorphic change as mimetic, normative, and coercive pressures kicked in.

Once these institutional processes were set in motion, extensive internal campaigns for equitable benefits became somewhat less necessary. To put it differently, whereas in the early years of Fortune 1000 adoption, gay employee networks appeared to be "necessary" (though rarely "sufficient," in that various institutional opportunities also needed to be present), now it appears that institutional processes alone can sometimes persuade a company to institute equitable policies. While the earliest adopters of domestic partner benefits all faced internal pressure from gay employee networks, the presence of such networks became less necessary in later adoption waves (see Table 1 in the introduction to this book). Even with the decline in new corporate organizing since 1995 (see chapter 2), more and more companies are adopting equitable benefits along with several other inclusive policies.

Of course, as mentioned earlier in the book, it is possible that many of the corporations that appear to be adopting such benefits in the absence of a gay network could in fact be instituting these changes at the request of individual employees or informal groups that are not detectable by outside observers. Indeed, given the quickened pace of adoption, lesbian and gay employees may increasingly find that more formal or extensive campaigns are unnecessary. While it is good news for the workplace movement, the ability to effect change in this way may make it harder for researchers to trace the origin of policy shifts. Also invisible to outside observers may be successful networks that disbanded after their victories. In addition, local or statewide gay rights organizations occasionally pressure companies to extend benefits, but, since these efforts rarely get widespread (if any) press coverage, their contributions are largely hidden from public sight. Moreover, HRC sometimes works behind the scenes in certain companies, with its staff or Business Council members quietly urging particularly reluctant elites to adopt inclusive policies. Here again, the role of movement pressure in securing equitable benefits may remain unseen.

In any case, institutional processes have clearly begun to figure more prominently such that formal mobilization is not as necessary as it was in previous waves of adoption. In a similar vein, Pamela Tolbert and Lynne Zucker (1983) found that although city characteristics, including the presence of a political reform movement, were strong predictors of municipal civil service reform in the first adoption wave, those characteristics played less of a role in subsequent waves, eventually having no bearing whatsoever. Likewise, the presence of a gay employee network should *eventually* be unrelated to the adoption of equitable benefits.

Clearly, however, we are still a long way from that point. Indeed, I argue that lesbian and gay workers should not assume that their employers will jump on board the benefits bandwagon in the absence of internal pressure. Employees who are standing idly by, waiting for their companies to adopt equitable policies, should be careful of resting on others' laurels. Silence does not precipitate change, and institutional pressures—whether coercive, mimetic, or normative—are not so strong that most corporations are instituting inclusive policies in the absence of internal mobilization. In other words, these isomorphic pressures, if present, offer no promise of policy change, just promising opportunities. Thus, the slowdown in new corporate organizing beginning in 1995 is risky for the workplace movement, since complacency can result in what Traci Sawyers and David Meyer (1999) have called "missed opportunities."

Even in those circumstances where the organizational field and wider sociopolitical environment offer little in the way of macro-level opportunities, corporations themselves often contain at least some elements that facilitate policy success. Certain of these meso-level opportunities, such as organizational realignments resulting from elite turnover or mergers and acquisitions, are relatively beyond the control of activists. But other dimensions of organizational opportunity, such as structural templates, allies, and cultural supports, if not already there for the seizing, can often be created over time.

Thus gay, lesbian, and bisexual employees who have not yet mobilized in their places of work should neither take for granted the power of isomorphic pressures in the wider institutional environment nor despair over the apparent lack of organizational opportunities in the corporate setting itself. By deploying identity tactics that emphasize visibility, using personal narratives that entail emotion work, and utilizing framing strategies that highlight the bottom-line benefits of equality, workplace activists can win allies throughout multiple levels of a company and can even convince some of the most reluctant elites to adopt gay-inclusive policies. As the stories in these pages have shown, with courage, commitment, and perseverance, lesbian and gay workers can effect remarkable transformations, changing minds as well as policies, corporate cultures as well as corporate structures. And those changes, in turn, alter the wider institutional landscape on which other organizational challengers struggle.

Concluding Thoughts . . . or Utopian Dreams? Shifts in the Cultural Meaning of Equitable-Benefits Adoption

Neoinstitutional scholar Patricia Thornton (1995, 214–15) argues that the "cultural meaning" of particular organizational innovations can vary over time because of both the "evolution of management ideologies" and the level of structuration in an organizational field. As the ideologies that justify new practices diffuse within and across highly structured organizational fields, which exhibit frequent interactions among organizations and a widely recognized status hierarchy (DiMaggio and Powell 1991b), later adopters can rationalize their incorporation of the innovation by using already elaborated discourses and/or by invoking economic motives about remaining competitive. Applying Thornton's arguments to movement rather than management ideologies, it seems clear that once enough firms in a field begin to adopt equitable benefits, employee activists can more effectively mobilize a profits frame, emphasizing the need for employers to keep up with their competitors.

Early in the game, however, workplace activists were constrained in their ability to argue convincingly that equitable benefits would give employers a competitive advantage. Since very few companies were offering the benefits, the empirical credibility of the profits frame was hard to establish. To a degree the same would apply to activist networks located in industries that until recently had virtually no benefits adopters, such as manufacturing, aerospace, engineering, construction, consumer products, and food and grocery enterprises (see HRCF 2002b). Tellingly, these slow-to-adopt industries are market sectors with few, if any, visible gay employee networks. This demonstrates that movements still matter. In other words, to reemphasize the point, lesbians and gay men should not count on isomorphic pressures in the wider environment to effect change in their particular workplaces without simultaneous pressure from the inside.

Nonetheless, new institutional analysis helps to explain why the presence of an activist network has become less necessary for policy change, as compared to the first adoption wave, which was composed almost entirely of corporations facing pressure from gay employee groups. Once a "critical mass" of major companies instituted equitable benefits in response to internal pressure, and once enough people began asking for the benefits at college recruitment fairs and in job interviews, other corporate elites were more likely to mimic the innovators and extend their policies as well, since they could see the competitive advantage of doing so (see Elswick 2001). Hence, even in the absence of a gay network pushing from within, later adopters "got" the profits frame, because they saw it being played out before their very eyes. Thus, as diversity became defined as a business best practice, and as more and more companies began to institute gay-inclusive policies, domestic partner benefits moved from the margins into the mainstream.

Looking ahead, I expect that equitable-benefits adoption will proceed at an increasingly faster pace as companies and other employers, faced with a rapidly mounting list of adopters, begin to feel even greater pressure to conform. This prediction is in keeping with the work of institutionalists who have studied the spread of organizational innovations across time. Attending to waves of adoption on the road to institutionalization, several scholars have found that the diffusion of innovations proceeds more rapidly in later adoption waves (Knoke 1982; Edelman 1990; Chaves 1996; Dobbin and Sutton 1998). Studying the expansion of due-process protections in the workplace, for instance, Lauren Edelman (1990, 1424) found that "the rate at which organizations adopt nonunion grievance procedures increases over time as a function of the prevalence of such procedures in the population."

Casting additional light on this process, Pamela Tolbert and Lynne Zucker (1983) emphasize the changing motivations behind the adoption of innovations across time. Early adopters of municipal civil service reform, for example, instituted the policy changes out of "rational self-interest," while later cities did so "to be in conformity to prevailing beliefs" (Scott 1995b, 87). Tolbert and Zucker explain: "As an increasing number of organizations adopt a program or policy, it becomes progressively institutionalized, or widely understood to be a necessary component of rationalized organizational structure. The legitimacy of the procedures themselves serves as the impetus for the later adopters" (35).

Although domestic partner benefits are far from becoming fully institutionalized and hence taken for granted, I expect that their cultural meaning will eventually shift such that the rationale for adoption will no longer be a primarily economic one. Instead, future adopters will implement the benefits because they are seen as proper and legitimate. At that point, equitable benefits will have reached the stage of complete institutionalization, where nonadoption is seen as not only out of step with "modern" corporate practices but also blatantly discriminatory—for why else would a company refuse to grant equitable benefits when that refusal would discredit the firm in the eyes of the public and hence threaten its own bottom line?

From the perspective of today's lesbian, gay, and bisexual employees who are still fighting tooth and nail for equal rights, this may seem a hopelessly utopian vision. From the standpoint of the New Right, however, full equality for gays and lesbians looms large, a specter right around the corner. Thus, as right-wing forces fill their coffers by painting the "homosexual agenda" as a threat to the sanctity of the home and the security of the nation (Adam [1994] 1998, 1995; Blain 1997; Dugan 1999; S. Epstein 1999), gay and lesbian activists struggle on. Aided in their fight by the rapidly growing number of corporations that are instituting equitable policies in the name of profit, lesbian and gay people should take heart. Who would have thought that the engines of capitalism would provide fuel for social justice?

The Birth of Gay Employee Networks
and the Adoption of Domestic Partner Benefits

Table A.1. Formation and Spread of the Corporate Workplace Movement: Organizational Births by Year, Industry, and Geographic Region

Year(s)	Number of Groups Formed (Percentage of Organizational Population [N = 69])	Number by Industry (and Region)
	1978–89: Slow rise	
1978	1 (1.4%)	1 high-tech (West Coast)
1979	0	
1980	1 (1.4%)	1 high-tech (East Coast)
1981–85	0	
1986	1 (1.4%)	1 high-tech (West Coast)
1987	3 (4.3%)	2 telecommunications (1 each in East and West Coasts) 1 utility (West Coast)
1988	2 (2.9%)	1 aerospace (West Coast) 1 pharmaceutical (Midwest)
1989	2 (2.9%)	1 financial (East Coast) 1 high-tech (West Coast)
Subtotal	10	

Subtotal by region: 6 (60%) West Coast, 3 (30%) East Coast, 1 (10% Midwest)
Percent of organizational population born in this period: 14%
Birthrate in this period: Less than 1 (0.83) new organizations per year

	1990–94: Rapid growth and diversification	
1990	10 (14.5%)	1 apparel (West Coast) 1 automotive (Midwest) 1 financial (East Coast) 1 high-tech (West Coast) 2 insurance (East Coast) 1 paper products (South) 2 scientific/photographic (1 each in Midwest and East Coast) 1 telecommunications (West Coast)
1991	6 (8.7%)	1 aerospace (East Coast) 1 communications (East Coast) 1 entertainment (West Coast) 1 petroleum (West Coast) 1 scientific/photographic (East Coast) 1 utility (Midwest)
1992	9 (13.0%)	1 airline (Midwest) 1 chemical (East Coast) 1 electronics (South) 2 financial (East Coast) 1 retail (Midwest)

		1 scientific/photographic (East Coast) 1 telecommunications (Midwest) 1 utility (Midwest)
1993	17 (24.6%)	2 banking (Midwest) 1 beverage (Mountain) 2 consumer products (Midwest) 1 electronics (Midwest) 1 entertainment (East Coast) 1 financial (West Coast) 3 high-tech (2 East Coast, 1 West Coast) 3 insurance (1 each in East Coast, Midwest, West Coast) 1 office equipment (East Coast) 2 telecommunications (1 each in East Coast, South)
1994	8 (11.6%)	1 airline (South) 1 automotive (Midwest) 2 banking (1 each in Midwest, South) 1 financial (East Coast) 1 high-tech (South) 1 petroleum (South) 1 scientific/photographic (Midwest)
Subtotal	50	

Subtotal by region: 18 (36%) East Coast, 16 (32%) Midwest, 8 (16%) West Coast, 7 (14%) South, 1 (2%) Mountain
Percent of organizational population born in this period: 72%
Birthrate in this period: 10 new organizations per year

1995–mid-1998: Decline in new organizing

1995	3 (4.3%)	1 food service (Midwest) 1 insurance (Midwest) 1 retail (South)
1996	3 (4.3%)	1 automotive (Midwest) 1 insurance (East Coast) 1 scientific (East Coast)
1997	2 (2.9%)	1 petroleum (South) 1 pharmaceutical (East Coast)
Through mid-1998	1 (1.4%)	1 pharmaceutical (East Coast)
Subtotal	9	

Subtotal by region: 4 (44%) East Coast, 3 (33%) Midwest, 2 (22%) South
Percent of organizational population born in this period: 13%
Birthrate in this period: Less than 3 (2.57) new organizations per year

Note: Data are from surveys and interviews with 69 gay, lesbian, and bisexual employee networks in Fortune 1000 companies, conducted primarily between May and October 1998. Subtotal percentages are rounded to the nearest whole percentage.

Table A.2. Growth and Diversification of the Corporate Workplace Movement: The Periodized Clustering of Network Formations by Industry and Geographic Region

Years	n (Percentage of Organizational Population [N = 69])	Birthrate per Year	n (%) Clusters by Industry	n (%) Clusters by Region
1978–89	10 (14%)	<1	4 (40%) high-tech 2 (20%) telecommunications 4 (40%) diverse mix	6 (60%) West Coast 3 (30%) East Coast 1 (10%) Midwest
1990–94	50 (72%)	10	5 (10%) high-tech 5 (10%) financial 5 (10%) insurance 5 (10%) scientific/photographic 4 (8%) telecommunications 4 (8%) banking 22 (44%) diverse mix	18 (36%) East Coast 16 (32%) Midwest 8 (16%) West Coast 7 (14%) South 1 (2%) Mountain
1995–mid-1998	9 (13%)	<3	2 (22%) insurance 2 (22%) pharmaceutical 5 (56%) diverse mix	4 (44%) East Coast 3 (33%) Midwest 2 (22%) South
Total, 1978–mid-1998	69 (100%)	<4	9 (13%) high-tech 7 (10%) insurance 6 (9%) telecommunications 6 (9%) financial 5 (7%) scientific/photographic 36 (52%) diverse mix	25 (36%) East Coast 20 (29%) Midwest 14 (20%) West Coast 9 (13%) South 1 (1%) Mountain

Note: Data are from surveys and interviews with 69 gay, lesbian, and bisexual employee networks in Fortune 1000 companies, conducted primarily between May and October 1998. All percentages are rounded to the nearest whole percentage.

Table A.3. Number of Employers That Provide Domestic Partner Benefits by Sector and by Industry, as of Mid-February 2004

Colleges and universities		198
State and local governments		140
Nonprofit organizations and professional associations		125
Unions and other labor organizations		40
Corporations		6,909
Fortune 500	211	
Other private-sector companies	6,698	
Corporations by industry*		
Advertising and marketing	31	
Aerospace and defense	6	
Airlines	12	
Apparel and department stores	23	
Automotive	11	
Banking and financial services	100	
Chemicals and biotechnology	5	
Computer and data services	26	
Computer software	91	
Computers and office equipment	28	
Consulting	36	
Engineering and construction	7	
Entertainment and electronic media	71	
Food, beverages, and groceries	40	
Forest and paper products	2	
Health care	90	
High-tech/photographic/scientific equipment	33	
Home furnishings	1	
Hotels, resorts, and casinos	19	
Insurance	43	
Law	198	
Mail and freight delivery	5	
Manufacturing	7	
Oil and gas	3	
Pharmaceuticals	29	
Publishing and printing	84	
Retail and consumer products	38	
Telecommunications	28	
Tobacco	2	
Transportation and travel	11	
Utilities	52	
Other	43	
Total number of employers		7,412

*Numbers of corporations by industry do not include employers that adopted equitable benefits to comply with city contracting laws (i.e., Berkeley, Los Angeles, Oakland, San Francisco, and San Mateo County, California; Minneapolis, Minnesota; and King County, Seattle, and Tumwater, Washington), since cities with equitable-benefits mandates do not track compliance by industry.

Source: Adapted from the WorkNet employer database of the Human Rights Campaign and Human Rights Campaign Foundation, current as of February 14, 2004 (HRCF 2004).

Works Cited

Abell, Peter. 1995. "The New Institutionalism and Rational Choice Theory." In Scott and Christensen 1995b, 3–14.

Abrahams, Naomi. 1992. "Towards Reconceptualizing Political Action." *Sociological Inquiry* 62:327–47.

Abrahamson, Eric, and Charles J. Fombrun. 1992. "Forging the Iron Cage: Interorganizational Networks and the Production of Macro-Culture." *Journal of Management Review* 18:487–517.

Acker, Joan. 1990. "Hierarchies, Jobs, Bodies: A Theory of Gendered Organizations." *Gender and Society* 4:139–58.

Adam, Barry D. [1994] 1998. "Anatomy of a Panic: State Voyeurism, Gender Politics, and the Cult of Americanism." In Nardi and Schneider 1998, 467–76.

———. 1995. *The Rise of a Gay and Lesbian Movement.* 2nd ed. New York: Twayne.

Adam, Barry D., Jan Willem Duyvendak, and André Krouwel, eds. 1999. *The Global Emergence of Gay and Lesbian Politics: National Imprints of a Worldwide Movement.* Philadelphia: Temple University Press.

Adams, Joseph S., and Todd A. Solomon. 2000. *Domestic Partner Benefits: An Employer's Guide.* Washington, DC: Thompson Publishing Group.

Advocate. 1970a. "Gays Picket ABC Station." March.

———. 1970b. "Survey Starts Drive on Job Discrimination." July 22–August 4.

———. 1971. "Won't Hire Gay, Says 'Ma Bell,' But . . ." November 10.

———. 1972a. "Bay Area Firms Sign Hiring Pledges." August 30.

———. 1972b. "PT&T Eyes Hiring Policy." July 5.

———. 1973a. "ACLU Suit Will Challenge Northwestern Bell Hiring Ban." October 10.

———. 1973b. "Battle of Ma Bell Spreads to Minnesota." August 29.

———. 1973c. "Honeywell Faces Bias Charge at Minnesota University." April 25.

———. 1973d. "Ma Bell Zapped in S.F." May 23.

———. 1974a. ". . . As Ma Bell Decrees: No More!" August 28.

———. 1974b. "Ma Bell Will Switch, not Fight Law." May 8.

———. 1975a. "Civil Rights Bills in 8 States." April 9.

———. 1975b. "Employment Rights Roundup." January 29.

———. 1975c. "Rights Bill Going to the House." February 12.

———. 2000a. "Cummins Execs Won't Back Down." April 7. http://www.advocate.com/html/news/040700/040700news08.asp (accessed December 29, 2002).

———. 2000b. "Protests over DP Policy." March 25–27. http://www.advocate.com/html/news/032500-032700/032500news08.asp (accessed December 29, 2002).

———. 2000c. "Schlessinger Loses Another Advertiser." July 8–10. http://www.advocate.com/html/news/070800-071000/070800news06.html (accessed July 14, 2000).

———. 2000d. "300 Protest DP Policy." March 28. http://www.advocate.com/html/news/032800/032800news03.html (accessed December 29, 2002).

———. 2001. "Cummins Inc. Cuts Ties to Scouts." September 20. http://www.advocate.com/new_newsarchive.asp?ID=750&sd=09/20/01 (accessed December 29, 2002).

Alpern, Shelley. 1999. "Update: What Is Shareholder Activism? Gay and Lesbian Workplace Rights: An Issue for Investors." http://www.planetout.com/pno/finance/investments (accessed June 15, 1999).

Amenta, Edwin, and Yvonne Zylan. 1991. "It Happened Here: Political Opportunity, the New Institutionalism, and the Townsend Movement." *American Sociological Review* 56:250–65.

And Justice for All. 2002. "And Justice for All." http://www.qrd.org/qrd/www/orgs/aja (accessed December 30, 2002).

Babb, Sarah. 1996. "'A True American System of Finance': Frame Resonance in the U.S. Labor Movement, 1866 to 1886." *American Sociological Review* 61:1033–52.

Badgett, M. V. Lee. 1995. "The Wage Effects of Sexual Orientation Discrimination." *Industrial and Labor Relations Review* 48:726–39.

———. 2000. "Calculating Costs with Credibility: Health Care Benefits for Domestic Partners." *Angles: The Policy Journal of the Institute for Gay and*

Lesbian Strategic Studies 5 (November): 1–8. http://www.iglss.org/media/files/Angles_51.pdf (accessed December 29, 2002).

Bain, C. Arthur. 1992a. "Corporate Focus: Building Community at PG&E." *Gay/Lesbian/Bisexual Corporate Letter*, November–December, 3–6.

———. 1992b. "Cracker Barrel Seeks SEC Dismissal of First Gay Rights Shareholder Action." *Gay/Lesbian/Bisexual Corporate Letter*, September–October, 1–2, 8.

———. 1992c. "Going National." *Gay/Lesbian/Bisexual Corporate Letter*, November–December, 4.

———. 1992d. "A Letter from President Elect Bill Clinton." *Gay/Lesbian/Bisexual Corporate Letter*, November–December, 7.

———. 1992e. "SEC Denies First Gay Rights Shareholder Action." *Gay/Lesbian/Bisexual Corporate Letter*, November–December, 1.

Baker, Daniel B., Sean O'Brien Strub, and Bill Henning. 1995. *Cracking the Corporate Closet: The 200 Best (and Worst) Companies to Work For, Buy From, and Invest In If You're Gay or Lesbian—and Even If You Aren't.* New York: HarperBusiness.

Baker, Peter. 1996. "President Quietly Signs Law Aimed at Gay Marriages." *Washington Post*, September 22. http://proquest.umi.com/ (accessed June 29, 1999).

Barnett, Bernice McNair. 1999. "Social Movements and Race, Gender, and Class." In *Introduction to Sociology: A Race, Gender, and Class Perspective*, ed. Jean Ait Belkhir and Bernice McNair Barnett, with the participation of Anna Karpathakis, 409–36. Southern University at New Orleans Race, Gender, and Class Book Series. New Orleans: Southern University at New Orleans Press.

Benford, Robert D. 1997. "An Insider's Critique of the Social Movement Framing Perspective." *Sociological Inquiry* 67:409–30.

Bernstein, Mary. 1997. "Celebration and Suppression: The Strategic Uses of Identity by the Lesbian and Gay Movement." *American Journal of Sociology* 103:531–65.

———. 2002. "The Contradictions of Gay Ethnicity: Forging Identity in Vermont." In Meyer, Whittier, and Robnett 2002, 85–104.

Berzon, Betty. 1994. "Acting Up." In Thompson 1994, 307–8.

Bjornson, Lars. 1974. "A Quiet Win: Honeywell Yields." *Advocate*, April 10.

Blain, Michael. 1997. "The Politics of Victimage: Power and Subjectivity in Anti-gay Campaigns." Paper presented at the annual meeting of the Pacific Sociological Association, San Diego.

Blee, Kathleen M., ed. 1998a. *No Middle Ground: Women and Radical Protest.* New York: New York University Press.

———. 1998b. "Women on the Left/Women on the Right." Introduction to Blee, 1998a, 1–15.

Blumstein, Philip, and Pepper Schwartz. 1983. *American Couples.* New York: Morrow.

Bond, P. A. 1997. "Money and More: Insuring Domestic Partners; National Trend: As Competition Heats Up for Qualified Workers, Companies Are Broadening the Scope of Their Health Care Packages to Include the Mates of Gay Employees." *Atlanta Journal-Constitution,* September 21. http://www.lexis-nexis.com/.

Bordieu, Pierre. 1977. *Outline of a Theory of Practice.* Trans. Richard Nice. Cambridge: Cambridge University Press.

Borum, Finn, and Ann Westenholz. 1995. "The Incorporation of Multiple Institutional Models: Organizational Field Multiplicity and the Role of Actors." In Scott and Christensen 1995b, 113–31.

Breines, Wini. 1982. *Community and Organization in the New Left, 1962–68.* New York: Praeger.

Brint, Steven, and Jerome Karabel. 1991. "Institutional Origins and Transformations: The Case of American Community Colleges." In Powell and DiMaggio 1991, 337–60.

Budisatrijo, Alice. 2002. "Giving Credit Where It's Due: HRC's New Corporate Equality Index." *HRC Quarterly,* Summer, 16.

Buechler, Steven M. 1990. *Women's Movements in the United States: Woman Suffrage, Equal Rights, and Beyond.* New Brunswick, NJ: Rutgers University Press.

———. 2000. *Social Movements in Advanced Capitalism: The Political Economy and Cultural Construction of Social Activism.* New York: Oxford University Press.

Bull, Chris. 2001. "Out of the Brewing Storm." *Advocate,* November 6. http://www.advocate.com/html/stories/850/850_coors.asp.

Burns, Lawton R., and Douglas R. Wholey. 1993. "Adoption and Abandonment of Matrix Management Programs: Effects of Organizational Characteristics and Interorganizational Networks." *Academy of Management Journal* 36:106–38.

Burstein, Paul. 1991. "Legal Mobilization as a Social Movement Tactic: The Struggle for Equal Employment Opportunity." *American Journal of Sociology* 96:1201–25.

Burstein, Paul, Rachel L. Einwohner, and Jocelyn A. Hollander. 1995. "The Success of Political Movements: A Bargaining Perspective." In Jenkins and Klandermans 1995b, 275–95.

Business Wire. 2002. "Xerox Ranks among Top 10 Companies for Diversity and

Women; New Report Recognizes Companies as 'Best of the Best.'" December 4. http://www.infotrac.galegroup.com/.

California Alliance for Pride and Equality. 2002. "CAPE Commends Governor Gray Davis' Formation of LGBT Working Group." Press release, March 21. http://www.calcape.org/ (accessed March 22, 2002).

Castells, Manuel. 1997. *The Power of Identity.* Malden, MA: Blackwell.

———. 2001. *Internet Galaxy: Reflections on the Internet, Business, and Society.* New York: Oxford University Press.

Chalfant, David. 1998. "Finding His Niche: Walter Schubert Launches Gay Financial Network." *HRC Quarterly,* Fall, 13.

Chaves, Mark. 1996. "Ordaining Women: The Diffusion of an Organizational Innovation." *American Journal of Sociology* 101:840–73.

———. 1997. *Ordaining Women: Culture and Conflict in Religious Organizations.* Cambridge, MA: Harvard University Press.

Christensen, Søren, and Jan Molin. 1995. "Origin and Transformation of Organizations: Institutional Analysis of the Danish Red Cross." In Scott and Christensen 1995b, 67–90.

City and County of San Francisco Human Rights Commission. 2003. "Overview of the Equal Benefits Ordinance." http://www.sfgov.org/sfhumanrights/over12b.htm (accessed January 15, 2003).

Coalition to Promote Equality at ExxonMobil. 2002. "ExxonMobil Shareholder Vote a Huge Boost toward Changing the Company's Discriminatory Policies, Says HRC." http://www.hrc.org/equalityatexxon/newsreleases/2002/index.asp (accessed November 22, 2002).

———. 2003. "New York City Pension Fund Renews Call for Non-discrimination Policy at ExxonMobil." June 2. http://www.hrc.org/ExxonMobilTemplate.cfm?Section=News_Releases1&CONTENTID=15594&TEMPLATE=/ContentMangement/ContentDisplay.cfm (accessed February 11, 2004).

Cohen, Jean L. 1985. "Strategy or Identity: New Theoretical Paradigms and Contemporary Social Movements." *Social Research* 4:663–716.

Colbert, Charles, and John Wofford. 1993. "Sexual Orientation in the Workplace: The Strategic Challenge." *Compensation and Benefits Management,* Summer: 1–18.

Collins, Patricia Hill. 1990. *Black Feminist Thought: Knowledge, Consciousness, and the Politics of Empowerment.* Boston: Unwin Hyman.

———. 1998. "Toward a New Vision: Race, Class, and Gender as Categories of Analysis and Connection." In *Questions of Gender: Perspectives and Paradoxes,* ed. Dina L. Anselmi and Anne L. Law, 35–45. New York: McGraw-Hill.

———. 2000. *Black Feminist Thought: Knowledge, Consciousness, and the Politics of Empowerment.* 2nd ed. New York: Routledge.

Collins, Randall. 2001. "Social Movements and the Focus of Emotional Attention." In Goodwin, Jasper, and Polletta 2001a, 27–44.

Coltrane, Scott. 2001. "Marketing the Marriage 'Solution': Misplaced Simplicity
in the Politics of Fatherhood: 2001 Presidential Address to the Pacific Sociological Association." *Sociological Perspectives* 44:387–418.

Connell, R. W. 1987. *Gender and Power: Society, the Person, and Sexual Politics.*
Stanford, CA: Stanford University Press.

Costain, Anne N. 1992. *Inviting Women's Rebellion: A Political Process Interpretation of the Women's Movement.* Baltimore: The Johns Hopkins University
Press.

Creed, W. E. Douglas. Forthcoming. "Voice Lessons: Tempered Radicalism and
the Use of Voice and Silence." *Journal of Management Studies.*

Creed, W. E. Douglas, and Maureen Scully. 2000. "Songs of Ourselves: Employees' Deployment of Social Identity in Work Encounters." *Journal of
Management Inquiry* 9:391–412.

Creed, W. E. Douglas, Maureen A. Scully, and John R. Austin. 2002. "Clothes
Make the Person? The Tailoring of Legitimating Accounts and the Social
Construction of Identity." *Organization Science* 13:475–96.

Cromwell, Kim, and Kim Harris. 1999. "Beyond Domestic Partner Benefits:
What's Next for Employee Groups?" *HRC Quarterly,* Spring, 14–15.

Curiel, Jonathan. 1997. "The Little City That Could." *Advocate,* March 18.

Dalton, Russell J. 1995. "Strategies of Partisan Influence: West European Environmental Groups." In Jenkins and Klandermans 1995b, 296–323.

Darcé, Keith. 1997. "Companies Offer Insurance to Partners of Gay, Lesbian Workers." *New Orleans Times-Picayune,* November 16. http://www.lexis-nexis.com/.

Data Lounge. 1997. "American Airlines Protest Just the Beginning, Right Vows."
News report, March 17. http://www.datalounge.com/datalounge/news/
record.html?record=1862 (accessed March 18, 1997).

———. 1999a. "Massachusetts High Court Repeals Boston Domestic Partnership
Ordinance." News report, July 9. http://www.datalounge.com/cgi-bin/
dbm/news/record?record=3699 (accessed July 15, 1999).

———. 1999b. "Robertson Targets Massachusetts Domestic Partnership Ordinances." News report, September 8. http://www.datalounge.com/templates/
news/record.html?record=3898 (accessed September 9, 1999).

———. 2001a. "D.C. Domestic Partners Get Benefits." News report, September 26. http://www.datalounge.com/datalounge/news/record.html?record=
16949&searchwords=c,d,domestic,partner (accessed December 29, 2001).

———. 2001b. "Domestic Partner Benefits Sweeping U.S. Firms." News
report, April 16. http://www.datalounge.com/datalounge/news/
record.html?record=14266 (accessed November 15, 2002).

————. 2001c. "Right Pushes Anti-gay Constitutional Amendment." News report, July 12. http://www.datalounge.com/datalounge/news/record.html?record=15801 (accessed July 19, 2001).

Davis, Gerald F. 1991. "Agents without Principles? The Spread of the Poison Pill through the Intercorporate Network." *Administrative Science Quarterly* 36:583–613.

Davis, Joseph E., ed. 2002. *Stories of Change: Narrative and Social Movements.* Albany: State University of New York Press.

DeBold, Kathleen. 1997. Foreword to Swan 1997a, xvii–xx.

Deibel, Mary. 1996. "Boycotted Disney Late on Same-Sex Benefits." *Pittsburgh Post-Gazette,* July 7. http://www.lexis-nexis.com/.

della Porta, Donatella, and Mario Diani. 1999. *Social Movements: An Introduction.* Malden, MA: Blackwell.

della Porta, Donatella, and Herbert Reiter, eds. 1998. *Policing Protest: The Control of Mass Demonstrations in Western Democracies.* Social Movements, Protest, and Contention 6. Minneapolis: University of Minnesota Press.

D'Emilio, John. 1983. *Sexual Politics, Sexual Communities: The Making of a Homosexual Minority in the United States, 1940–1970.* Chicago: University of Chicago Press.

————. 1992. *Making Trouble: Essays on Gay History, Politics, and the University.* New York: Routledge.

Diamant, Louis, ed. 1993. *Homosexual Issues in the Workplace.* Washington, DC: Taylor & Francis.

Dill, Bonnie Thornton. 1983. "Race, Class, and Gender: Prospects for an All-Inclusive Sisterhood." *Feminist Studies* 9:131–50.

DiMaggio, Paul J. 1988. "Interest and Agency in Institutional Theory." In Zucker 1988, 3–21.

————. 1991. "Constructing an Organizational Field as a Professional Project: U.S. Art Museums, 1920–1940." In Powell and DiMaggio 1991, 267–92.

DiMaggio, Paul J., Eszter Hargittai, W. Russell Neuman, and John P. Robinson. 2001. "Social Implications of the Internet." *Annual Review of Sociology* 27:307–36.

DiMaggio, Paul J., and Walter W. Powell. 1991a. Introduction to Powell and DiMaggio 1991, 1–38.

————. 1991b. "The Iron Cage Revisited: Institutional Isomorphism and Collective Rationality in Organizational Fields." In Powell and DiMaggio 1991, 63–82.

Dobbin, Frank. 2001. "The Business of Social Movements." In Goodwin, Jasper, and Polletta 2001a, 74–80.

Dobbin, Frank R., Lauren Edelman, John W. Meyer, W. Richard Scott, and Ann

Swidler. 1988. "The Expansion of Due Process in Organizations." In Zucker 1988, 71–98.

Dobbin, Frank, and John R. Sutton. 1998. "The Strength of a Weak State: The Rights Revolution and the Rise of Human Resources Management Divisions." *American Journal of Sociology* 104:441–76.

Dobbin, Frank, John Sutton, John W. Meyer, and W. Richard Scott. 1993. "Equal Opportunity Law and the Construction of Internal Labor Markets." *American Journal of Sociology* 99:396–429.

Downs, A. 1972. "Up and Down with Ecology—The Issue Attention Cycle." *Public Interest* 28:139–71.

Dugan, Kimberly B. 1999. "Culture and Movement-Countermovement Dynamics: The Struggle over Gay, Lesbian, and Bisexual Rights." PhD diss., Ohio State University.

Duggan, Lisa. [1994] 1998. "Queering the State." In Nardi and Schneider 1998, 564–72.

Dun's Business Month. 1983. "Profits Bottom Out." June.

Edelman, Lauren B. 1990. "Legal Environments and Organizational Governance: The Expansion of Due Process in the American Workplace." *American Journal of Sociology* 95:1401–40.

———. 1992. "Legal Ambiguity and Symbolic Structures: Organizational Mediation of Civil Rights Law." *American Journal of Sociology* 97:1531–76.

Edelman, Lauren B., and Mark C. Suchman. 1997. "The Legal Environments of Organizations." *Annual Review of Sociology* 23:479–515.

Edelman, Lauren B., Christopher Uggen, and Howard S. Erlanger. 1999. "The Endogeneity of Legal Regulation: Grievance Procedures as Rational Myth." *American Journal of Sociology* 105:406–54.

Einwohner, Rachel L. 1999a. "Gender, Class, and Social Movement Outcomes." *Gender and Society* 13:56–76.

———. 1999b. "Practices, Opportunity, and Protest Effectiveness: Illustrations from Four Animal Rights Campaigns." *Social Problems* 42:169–86.

———. 2002. "Bringing the Outsiders In: Opponents' Claims and the Construction of Animal Rights Activists' Identity." *Mobilization: An International Journal* 7:253–68.

Eisenstein, Hester. 1995. "The Australian Femocrat Experiment." In Ferree and Martin 1995, 69–83.

Ellis, Alan L., Liz Highleyman, Kevin Schaub, and Melissa White, eds. 2002. *The Harvey Milk Institute Guide to Lesbian, Gay, Bisexual, Transgender, and Queer Internet Research.* New York: Harrington Park Press.

Ellis, Alan L., and Ellen D. B. Riggle, eds. 1996. *Sexual Identity on the Job: Issues and Services.* New York: Harrington Park Press.

Elswick, Jill. 2001. "Partner Benefits Ground Swell Continues at Steady Clip." *Employee Benefit News,* April 1. http://www.infotrac.galegroup.com/ (accessed December 30, 2002).

Epstein, Barbara. 1990. "Rethinking Social Movement Theory." *Socialist Review* 20:35–66.

Epstein, Edward. 1999. "United Airlines Capitulates on Partners Issue: Full Benefits Worldwide for Gay, Lesbian Couples." *San Francisco Chronicle,* July 31.

———. 2002. "Big Business Less Biased against Gays: National Survey Shows Bay Area Leads the Way." *San Francisco Chronicle,* August 14. http://sfgate.com/cgi-bin/article.cgi?file=/c/a/2002/08/14/MN173686.DTL&type=printable (accessed November 21, 2002).

Epstein, Steven. 1996. *Impure Science: AIDS, Activism, and the Politics of Knowledge.* Berkeley and Los Angeles: University of California Press.

———. 1999. "Gay and Lesbian Movements in the United States: Dilemmas of Identity, Diversity, and Political Strategy." In Adam, Duyvendak, and Krouwel 1999, 30–90.

Equality Project. 1999. "The Equality Project: Gay and Lesbian Consumers, Employees, and Investors Working Together." http://www.equalityproject.org/ (accessed June 14, 1999).

———. 2002. "The Equality Project." http://www.equalityproject.org/ (accessed November 21, 2002).

Ettelbrick, Paula. [1989] 1993. "Since When Is Marriage a Path to Liberation?" In Rubenstein 1993, 401–6.

Evans, Sara. 1979. *Personal Politics: The Roots of Women's Liberation in the Civil Rights Movement and the New Left.* New York: Vintage.

Evans, Sara, and Harry Boyte. 1986. *Free Spaces.* New York: Harper & Row.

Fackler, Lisa. 2002. "In Gay Rights, Private Sector Is 'Unlikely Hero,' Survey Finds; Reform: Businesses Lead the Way in Ending Bias in Benefits, Other Workplace Issues, Advocacy Group Says." *Los Angeles Times,* August 14.

Faderman, Lillian. 1991. *Odd Girls and Twilight Lovers: A History of Lesbian Life in Twentieth-Century America.* New York: Penguin.

Fantasia, Rick. 1988. *Cultures of Solidarity: Consciousness, Action, and Contemporary American Workers.* Berkeley and Los Angeles: University of California Press.

Federer, Christopher. 1995. "Websites and Gophers and E-Mail—Oh My! (Part One)." *Stonewall Journal,* November, 12.

Ferree, Myra Marx, and Patricia Martin, eds. 1995. *Feminist Organizations: Harvest of the New Women's Movement.* Philadelphia: Temple University Press.

Ferree, Myra Marx, and Silke Roth. 1998. "Gender, Class, and the Interaction between Social Movements: A Strike of West Berlin Day Care Workers." *Gender and Society* 12:626–48.

Fetner, Tina. 2001. "Working Anita Bryant: The Impact of Christian Anti-gay Activism on Lesbian and Gay Movement Claims." *Social Problems* 48:411–28.

Fireman, Bruce, and William A. Gamson. 1979. "Utilitarian Logic in the Resource Mobilization Perspective." In Zald and McCarthy 1979, 8–44.

Fligstein, Neil. 1991. "The Structural Transformation of American Industry: An Institutional Account of the Causes of Diversification in the Largest Firms, 1919–1979." In Powell and DiMaggio 1991, 311–36.

———. 1996. "Markets as Politics: A Political-Cultural Approach to Market Institutions." *American Sociological Review* 61:656–73.

———. 1997. "Social Skill and Institutional Theory." *American Behavioral Scientist* 40:387–405.

Fligstein, Neil, and Doug McAdam. 1995. "A Political-Cultural Approach to the Problem of Strategic Action." Unpublished manuscript, Department of Sociology, University of California–Berkeley.

Foldy, Erica Gabrielle, and W. E. Douglas Creed. 1999. "Action Learning, Fragmentation, and the Interaction of Single-, Double-, and Triple-Loop Change: A Case Study of Gay and Lesbian Workplace Advocacy." *Journal of Applied Behavioral Science* 35:207–27.

Foucault, Michel. 1979. *Discipline and Punish: The Birth of the Prison.* Trans. Alan Sheridan. New York: Vintage.

Frase-Blunt, Martha. 2002. "Time to Redo Your Benefits?" *HR Magazine,* December. http://www.shrm.org/hrmagazine/articles/1202/default.asp?page=1202agn-compensation.htm (accessed January 19, 2003).

Freeman, Jo. 1975. *The Politics of Women's Liberation: A Case Study of an Emerging Social Movement and Its Relation to the Policy Process.* New York: McKay.

———. 1979. "Resource Mobilization and Strategy: A Model for Analyzing Social Movement Organization Actions." In Zald and McCarthy 1979, 167–89.

Freiberg, Peter. 1991. "Corporate Officials and Activists Talk Business." *Washington Blade,* October 18.

Friedland, Roger, and Robert R. Alford. 1991. "Bringing Society Back In: Symbols, Practices, and Institutional Contradictions." In Powell and DiMaggio 1991, 232–63.

Friskopp, Annette, and Sharon Silverstein. 1995. *Straight Jobs/Gay Lives: Gay and Lesbian Professionals, the Harvard Business School, and the American Workplace.* New York: Scribner.

Frost, Peter. 1995. Introduction to Meyerson and Scully 1995, 585.

Frost, Peter, Larry F. Moore, Meryl Reis Louis, Craig C. Lundberg, and Joanne Martin. 1991. *Reframing Organizational Culture.* Newbury Park, CA: Sage.

Gagné, Patricia. 1996. "Identity, Strategy, and Feminist Politics." *Social Problems* 43:77–93.

———. 1998. *Battered Women's Justice: The Movement for Clemency and the Politics of Self-Defense.* New York: Twayne.

Galaskiewicz, Joseph. 1991. "Making Corporate Actors Accountable: Institution-Building in Minneapolis–St. Paul." In Powell and DiMaggio 1991, 293–310.

Galaskiewicz, Joseph, and Ronald S. Burt. 1991. "Interorganizational Contagion in Corporate Philanthropy." *Administrative Science Quarterly* 36:88–105.

Gamson, Joshua. 1995. "Must Identity Movements Self-Destruct? A Queer Dilemma." *Social Problems* 42:390–407.

———. [1989] 1998. "Silence, Death, and the Invisible Enemy: AIDS Activism and Social Movement 'Newness.'" In Nardi and Schneider 1998, 334–48.

———. 1998. *Freaks Talk Back: Tabloid Talk Shows and Sexual Nonconformity.* Chicago: University of Chicago Press.

Gamson, William A. 1975. *The Strategy of Social Protest.* Homewood, IL: Dorsey.

———. 1988. "Political Discourse and Collective Action." In Klandermans, Kriesi, and Tarrow 1988, 219–46.

———. 1990. *The Strategy of Social Protest.* 2nd ed. Belmont, CA: Wadsworth.

———. 1992a. "The Social Psychology of Collective Action." In Morris and Mueller 1992, 53–76.

———. 1992b. *Talking Politics.* New York: Cambridge University Press.

———. 1995a. "Constructing Social Protest." In Johnston and Klandermans 1995, 85–106.

———. 1995b. "Hiroshima, the Holocaust, and the Politics of Exclusion: 1994 Presidential Address." *American Sociological Review* 60:1–20.

Gamson, William A., and David S. Meyer. 1996. "Framing Political Opportunity." In McAdam, McCarthy, and Zald 1996a, 275–90.

Gamson, William A., and Gadi Wolfsfeld. 1993. "Movements and Media as Interacting Systems." *Annals of the American Association of Political and Social Sciences* 528:114–25.

Gay and Lesbian Alliance against Defamation (GLAAD). 1999a. "A Brief Introduction to GLAAD." http://www.glaad.org/glaad/history.html (accessed July 28, 1999).

———. 1999b. "GLAAD and Digital Queers Proudly Announce Integration." http://www.glaad.org/media/archive_detail.php?id=121& (accessed November 19, 2002).

———. 2004. "Newspapers That Publish Same-Sex Union Announcements." http://www.glaad.org/action/campaigns_detail.php?id=3297& (accessed February 11, 2004).

Gay Financial Network. *See* gfn.com.

Gay People's Chronicle. 1999. "HBO Film Looks at Lesbian and Gay Workplace Bias." January 1.

———. 2001. "PlanetOut-Advocate Merger Is Off." March 16.

Gerlach, Luther, and Virginia Hine. 1970. *People, Power, Change.* Indianapolis: Bobbs-Merrill.

gfn.com (Gay Financial Network). 2000a. "Gfn.com Makes History with First Gay Ad in the *Wall Street Journal.*" E-mail from gfn.com, February 18.

———. 2000b. "The gfn.com Power 25." December 7, 1999. http:// www.gfn.com/gfn/gfn25_2000.phtml (accessed December 30, 2002).

———. 2000c. "The Most Powerful and Gay-Friendly Public Companies in Corporate America." http://www.gfn.com/gfn/gfn50.phtml (accessed December 30, 2002).

———. 2000d. "N.M. Christian Coalition Complains of Benefits." March 22. http://www.gfn.com/archives/story.phtml?sid=5388 (accessed December 30, 2002).

———. 2001. "The gfn.com 25." http://www.gfn.com/gfn/gfn25.phtml (accessed December 30, 2002).

———. 2003. "Profile of LGBT-Friendly Companies." http://www.gfn.com/ bizforum/pgfc/index.phtml (accessed January 25, 2002).

Giddens, Anthony. 1991. *Modernity and Self-Identity: Self and Society in the Late Modern Age.* Stanford, CA: Stanford University Press.

Gilpin, Kenneth N. 1995. "Benefits Given Coors Workers' Gay Partners." *New York Times,* July 8. http://www.lexis-nexis.com/.

Ginsberg, Steven. 1997. "More Companies Reaching Out with Gay-Friendly Policies: Domestic Partner Benefits Gain Momentum in Tight Labor Market, Despite Risk of Offending Conservative Customers." *Washington Post,* July 6. http://www.lexis-nexis.com/.

Gitlin, Todd. 1980. *The Whole World Is Watching.* Berkeley and Los Angeles: University of California Press.

Giugni, Marco. 1999. "How Social Movements Matter: Past Research, Present Problems, Future Developments." Introduction to Giugni, McAdam, and Tilly 1999, xiii–xxxiii.

Giugni, Marco, Doug McAdam, and Charles Tilly, eds. 1999. *How Social Movements Matter.* Social Movements, Protest, and Contention 10. Minneapolis: University of Minnesota Press.

GLAAD. *See* Gay and Lesbian Alliance against Defamation.

GLOBES (Gay, Lesbian, or Bisexual Employees at Schwab). 1998. "Gay Day at Disney Parks and Stores!" E-mail announcement from GLOBES, May 17.

———. 2000. "Pride Power Breakfast on the LGBT Community and the Media." E-mail announcement from GLOBES, March 15.

Goldstein, Cynthia G. San Francisco Human Rights Commission. 2001. "Fourth

Year Report on the San Francisco Equal Benefits Ordinance." http://www.ci.sf.ca.us/sfhumanrights/fouryear.htm#P206_11372 (accessed November 19, 2002).

Goodwin, Jeff, and James M. Jasper. 1999. "Caught in a Winding, Snarling Vine: The Structural Bias of Political Process Theory." *Sociological Forum* 14:27–54.

Goodwin, Jeff, James M. Jasper, and Francesca Polletta, eds. 2001a. *Passionate Politics: Emotions and Social Movements*. Chicago: University of Chicago Press.

———. 2001b. "Why Emotions Matter." Introduction to Goodwin, Jasper, and Polletta 2001a, 1–24.

Gordon, Rachel. 2004. "Legal Battle Looms: City Hall Ceremonies Spur Constitutional Showdown, Injuncton Threat." *San Francisco Chronicle,* February 13.

Gornick, Janet C., and David S. Meyer. 1998. "Changing Political Opportunity: The Anti-rape Movement and Public Policy." *Journal of Policy History* 10:367–98.

Gotham, Kevin Fox. 1999. "Political Opportunity, Community Identity, and the Emergence of a Local Anti-expressway Movement." *Social Problems* 46:332–54.

Gould, Deborah. 2001. "Rock the Boat, Don't Rock the Boat, Baby: Ambivalence and the Emergence of Militant AIDS Activism." In Goodwin, Jasper, and Polletta 2001a, 135–57.

Gourevitch, Peter. 1986. *Politics in Hard Times*. Ithaca, NY: Cornell University Press.

Greenberger, Scott S. 2004. "Same-Sex Ruling/Reactions; Official, State Legislators Ponder Their Next Moves." *Boston Globe,* February 5. http://www.lexis-nexis.com/.

Greening, Daniel W., and Barbara Gray. 1994. "Testing a Model of Organizational Response to Social and Political Issues." *Academy of Management Journal* 37:467–98.

Gross, Larry. 1993. *Contested Closets: The Politics and Ethics of Outing.* Minneapolis: University of Minnesota Press.

Guthrie, Doug. 1999. "A Sociological Perspective on the Use of Technology: The Adoption of Internet Technology in U.S. Organizations." *Sociological Perspectives* 42:583–603.

Guthrie, Doug, and Louise Marie Roth. 1999. "The State, Courts, and Maternity Policies in U.S. Organizations: Specifying Institutional Mechanisms." *American Sociological Review* 64:41–63.

Habermas, Jürgen. 1981. "New Social Movements." *Telos* 49:33–37.

————. 1987. *Lifeworld and System: A Critique of Functionalist Reason.* Vol. 2 of *The Theory of Communicative Action.* Boston: Beacon.

Haines, Herbert H. 1988. *Black Radicals and the Civil Rights Movement, 1954–1970.* Knoxville: University of Tennessee Press.

Hall, Richard H. 1999. *Organizations: Structures, Processes, and Outcomes.* 7th ed. Upper Saddle River, NJ: Prentice Hall.

Hardisty, Jean. 1999. *Mobilizing Resentment: Conservative Resurgence from the John Birch Society to the Promise Keepers.* Boston: Beacon.

Haveman, Heather A. 1993. "Follow the Leader: Mimetic Isomorphism and Entry into New Markets." *Administrative Science Quarterly* 38:593–627.

Hayden, Ronald. 1993. "Email and Why You Need It." *Gay/Lesbian/Bisexual Corporate Letter,* Winter, 1–2, 8.

Haydu, Jeffrey. 1999. "Counter Action Frames: Employer Repertoires and the Union Menace in the Late Nineteenth Century." *Social Problems* 46:313–31.

Herek, Gregory M., Jared B. Jobe, and Ralph M. Carney, eds. 1996. *Out in Force: Sexual Orientation and the Military.* Chicago: University of Chicago Press.

Herrschaft, Daryl. 1999. "Equality Works: Revamped WorkNet Website Empowers GLBT Workers." *HRC Quarterly,* Fall, 14–15.

Herscher, Elaine. 2000. "Gay and Lesbian: Places to Come Out and Make a Difference." *San Francisco Chronicle,* March 7.

Hewitt Associates. 2000. *Domestic Partner Benefits 2000.* Lincolnshire, IL: Hewitt Associates.

Hirsch, Paul M. 1997. "Sociology without Social Structure: Neoinstitutional Theory Meets Brave New World." *American Journal of Sociology* 102:1702–23.

Hirsch, Paul M., and Michael Lounsbury. 1997. "Ending the Family Quarrel: Toward a Reconciliation of 'Old' and 'New' Institutionalisms." *American Behavioral Scientist* 40:406–18.

Hoback, Jane. 1995. "Coors Wins Praise for Benefits Stance: Company's Swift Action Makes It State's Largest to Provide Health Care for Same Sex Partners." *Rocky Mountain News,* July 8. http://www.lexis-nexis.com/.

Hochschild, Arlie. 1983. *The Managed Heart.* Berkeley and Los Angeles: University of California Press.

————. 1990. "Ideology and Emotion Management: A Perspective and Path for Future Research." In *Research Agendas in the Sociology of Emotions,* ed. Theodore D. Kemper, 117–42. Albany: State University of New York Press.

Hodson, Randy. 1995. "Worker Resistance: An Underdeveloped Concept in the Sociology of Work." *Economic and Industrial Democracy* 16:79–110.

————. 1996. "Dignity in the Workplace under Participative Management: Alienation and Freedom Revisited." *American Sociological Review* 61:719–38.

———. 1999. "Management Citizenship Behavior: A New Concept and Empirical Test." *Social Problems* 46:460–78.

———. 2001. *Dignity at Work*. New York: Cambridge University Press.

Holding, Reynolds. 1997. "Airlines Sue San Francisco over Benefits: Trade Group Balks at Domestic Partner Law." *San Francisco Chronicle,* May 14.

Hollingsworth, Gaines. 1990. "Corporate Gay Bashing." *Advocate,* September 11.

Hopgood, Mei-Ling. 2000. "Automakers to Cover Same-Sex Partners: Insurance Move Steers Policy into Mainstream." *Detroit Free Press,* June 9. http://www.freep.com/money/business/pact9_20000609.htm (accessed November 21, 2002).

HRC. *See* Human Rights Campaign.

HRCF. *See* Human Rights Campaign Fund.

Hughes, Janice. 2002. "Critical 'Kitchen Table' Issues Draw Increased Attention after Sept. 11." *HRC Quarterly,* Summer, 13–14.

Hull, Kathleen E. 2001. "The Political Limits of the Rights Frame: The Case of Same-Sex Marriage in Hawaii." *Sociological Perspectives* 44:207–32.

Humanist. 2002. "A Constitutional Amendment That Would Ultimately Ban Same-Sex Marriages, Civil Unions, and Probably Domestic Partner Benefits Is Quietly Being Pushed through Congress." January–February, 47.

Human Rights Campaign (HRC). 1994. "Employment Non-discrimination Act of 1994 Introduced in House and Senate." *Momentum: The Newsletter for Members of the Human Rights Campaign Fund,* Summer, 1. *Nota bene:* Before August 7, 1995, the Human Rights Campaign was known as the Human Rights Campaign Fund.

———. 1995a. "Jesse and the Out-Laws." *HRC Quarterly,* Fall, 7.

———. 1995b. "1995: Hope and Progress in a Difficult Political Climate." HRC mailing (received February 5, 1996).

———. 1995c. "Support for ENDA Grows." *HRC Quarterly,* Fall, 7.

———. 1996a. "Corporations Endorsing ENDA." Partial list, as of March 14. HRC mailing.

———. 1996b. "Legislative Update: ENDA Hearings Held in House." HRC Action Alert, Summer (received August 1996).

———. 1997. "Human Rights Campaign Unveils Job Discrimination Ad." HRC press release, April 22. http://www.hrc.org/feature1/shoes.html (accessed July 16, 1999).

———. 1998. "Working It Out." *HRC Quarterly,* Fall, 3.

———. 1999a. "Focusing on HRC Business." *HRC Quarterly,* Summer, 3.

———. 1999b. "The State of the Workplace: HRC Report Finds GLBT Workers Made Substantial Gains in 1990s." *HRC Quarterly,* Winter, 4–5.

———. 1999c. "US Airways to Offer Domestic Partner Benefits to Lesbian and

Gay Employees, HRC Learns." HRC press release (received as e-mail on August 9).

———. 2000a. "HRC Applauds General Electric for Amending Non-discrimination Policy to Include Sexual Orientation." HRC press release (received as e-mail on March 22).

———. 2000b. Letter to HRC members, January.

———. 2000c. "Working for Fairness: HRC WorkNet Plays Key Role in Many Corporate Decision[s]." *HRC Quarterly,* Summer. http://www.hrc.org/publications/hrcq/hrcq00sum/pg11.asp (accessed October 24, 2002).

———. 2001. "Volunteer Body Makes a Difference in Corporate America." *HRC Quarterly,* Summer, 25.

———. 2002a. "Breakfast of Champions." *HRC Quarterly,* Winter, 4.

———. 2002b. "Congressional Scorecard: 107th Congress." HRC mailing (received October 20).

———. 2002c. "Corporate Catch-Up?" *HRC Quarterly,* Winter, 5.

———. 2002d. "High Visibility for Equal Justice." *HRC Quarterly,* Spring, 7.

———. 2002e. "HRC Praises Cracker Barrel's Decision to Prohibit Discrimination Based on Sexual Orientation: 10-Year Struggle to Change Policy Ends with Apparent Majority Vote on Shareholder Resolution." HRC press release, December 4 (received as e-mail on December 4).

———. 2002f. "Human Rights Campaign and Coalition Leaders to Denounce ExxonMobil's Discriminatory Policies: Shareholders Urged to Vote for Proposal to Add Sexual Orientation to Equal Employment Opportunity Statement." HRC press release, May 24. http://www.hrc.org/newsreleases/2002/020528exxonmobil.asp (accessed November 21, 2002).

———. 2002g. "On the Road: Ensuring that Gay Survivors of Sept. 11 Attacks Find Equal Justice." *HRC Quarterly,* Spring, 8–9.

———. 2002h. "Public Polling Shows Strong Support for Employment Non-discrimination Act." http://www.hrc.org/issues/federal_leg/enda/background/polling_june2001.asp (accessed November 2, 2002).

———. 2002i. "Talking Points on HJ93, Proposing an Amendment to the U.S. Constitution Relating to Marriage." May 23. http://www.hrc.org/issues/marriage/background/talkpts_hj93.asp (accessed October 31, 2002).

———. 2002j. "13 Companies Earn Perfect Score on First HRC Corporate Equality Index: Demonstrate Leadership with Regard to Gay, Lesbian, Bisexual, Transgender Employees." HRC press release, August 13. http://www.hrc.org/newsreleases/2002/020813cei.asp (accessed November 7, 2002).

———. 2003. "HRC Condemns ConocoPhillips for Rescinding Employee Non-discrimination Policy Following Merger of Conoco and Phillips: Only

Second Company, after ExxonMobil, to Do So." HRC press release, February 6. http://www.hrc.org/newsreleases/2003/030206work.asp (accessed February 8, 2003).

Human Rights Campaign Foundation (HRCF). 1999a. *The State of the Workplace for Lesbian, Gay, Bisexual, and Transgendered Americans, 1999,* coauthored by Kim I. Mills and Daryl Herrschaft. Washington, DC: Human Rights Campaign Foundation.

———. 1999b. WorkNet employer database. http://www.hrc.org/issues/workplac/data.html (accessed July 15, 1999).

———. 2000a. *The State of the Workplace for Lesbian, Gay, Bisexual, and Transgender Americans, 2000,* coauthored by Daryl Herrschaft and Kim I. Mills. Washington, DC: Human Rights Campaign Foundation. http://www.hrc.org/worknet/publications/state_workplace/2000/sow2000.pdf (accessed December 29, 2002).

———. 2000b. WorkNet employer database. April 20. http://www.hrcusa.org/worknet/data.html (accessed April 22, 2000).

———. 2001a. "Home Depot Changes Course, Bans Discrimination against Gays." WorkNet *WorkAlert,* June. http://www.hrc.org/worknet/workalert/0406/0406_06.asp (accessed July 11, 2001).

———. 2001b. *The State of the Workplace for Lesbian, Gay, Bisexual, and Transgender Americans, 2001,* coauthored by Daryl Herrschaft and Kim I. Mills. Washington, DC: Human Rights Campaign Foundation. http://www.hrc.org/worknet/publications/state_workplace/2001/sow2001.pdf (accessed November 4, 2002).

———. 2002a. "Commercial Closet Report: Gay-Coded Subaru Ads Return to Mainstream." WorkNet News, May. http://www.hrc.org/worknet/workalert/2002/0505/article01.asp (accessed January 22, 2003).

———. 2002b. *Corporate Equality Index, 2002.* August 13. Washington, DC: Human Rights Campaign Foundation. http://www.hrc.org/worknet/cei/cei_report.pdf (accessed November 7, 2002).

———. 2002c. "Gay Ride: Targeted Ads and Promotional Efforts Reap Results for Automakers." WorkNet News, February 25. http://www.hrc.org/worknet/workalert/2002/0503/article02.asp (accessed December 13, 2002).

———. 2002d. "Lockheed Martin Changes Policies toward Gay Employees." November 21. http://www.hrc.org/worknet/news/2002/021121lockheed.asp (accessed December 2, 2002).

———. 2002e. "Marketing and Advertising to the GLBT Community." http://www.hrc.org/worknet/marketing/index.asp (accessed December 13, 2002).

———. 2002f. "OSU Offers Services to Gay Workers' Partners." WorkNet

News, March 12. http://www.hrc.org/worknet/workalert/2002/.0503/
article07.asp (accessed March 15, 2002).

―――. 2002g. *The State of the Family: Laws and Legislation Affecting Gay, Lesbian, Bisexual, and Transgender Families.* Washington, DC: Human Rights
Campaign Foundation. http://www.hrc.org/familynet/documents/SoTF.pdf
(accessed October 31, 2002).

―――. 2002h. *The State of the Workplace for Lesbian, Gay, Bisexual, and Transgender Americans: A Semiannual Snapshot.* October 28. Washington, DC:
Human Rights Campaign Foundation. http://www.hrc.org/publications/
sow2002/snapshot.pdf (accessed October 28, 2002).

―――. 2002i. "States with Anti-gay Marriage Laws." http://www.hrc.org/
familynet/chapter.asp?article=195 (accessed October 30, 2002).

―――. 2003a. "Ask the Experts: Religion Experts: Looking for a Welcoming
Congregation." http://www.hrc.org/familynet/chapter.asp?article=261 (accessed January 19, 2003).

―――. 2003b. "Health Benefits to Be Dropped for Same-Sex Partners."
WorkNet News, February 7. http://www.hrc.org/worknet/workalert/2003/
0602/article05.asp (accessed February 8, 2003).

―――. 2003c. "HRC Corporate Equality Index Coverage: HRC in the News."
http://www.hrc.org/pressroom/cei%5Fnews.asp (accessed January 27, 2003).

―――. 2003d. "Hundreds of AP Staffers Return Novelty Key Chains, Saying
Keep the Gift and Give Gay Staffers Benefits Instead." WorkNet News,
January 9. http://www.hrc.org/worknet/workalert/2003/0601/article10.asp
(accessed January 15, 2003).

―――. 2004. WorkNet employer database. February 14. http://www.hrc.org/
Template.cfm?Section=Search_the_Database&Template=/CustomSource/
WorkNet/WorkplacePolicySearchAdvanced.cfm (accessed February 14,
2004).

Ingraham, Chrys. 1994. "The Heterosexual Imaginary: Feminist Sociology and
Theories of Gender." *Sociological Theory* 12:203–19.

Ingram, Paul. 1998. "Changing the Rules: Interests, Organizations, and Institutional Change in the U.S. Hospitality Industry." In *The New Institutionalism
in Sociology,* ed. Mary C. Brinton and Victor Nee, 258–76. New York: Russell Sage Foundation.

IT Network. 1999. "A Little History of the Internet." *Local Source: San Francisco
and Marin Edition,* Fall, 27.

Jacobs, Cherie. 2001. "More Companies Extend Benefits to Same-Sex Partners."
Tampa Tribune, August 12. http://www.lexis-nexis.com/.

James, Krista. 1995. "The Lesbian Avengers" (Vancouver, BC, chapter). September. http://www.ams.ubc.ca/media/Citr/discord/sept95/features/lesbian.htm (accessed August, 9, 1999).

Jasper, James M. 1997. *The Art of Moral Protest: Culture, Biography, and Creativity in Social Movements.* Chicago: University of Chicago Press.

Jasper, James M., and Jane D. Poulsen. 1995. "Recruiting Strangers and Friends: Moral Shocks and Social Networks in Animal Rights and Anti-nuclear Protests." *Social Problems* 42:493–512.

Jenkins, J. Craig. 1983. "Resource Mobilization Theory and the Study of Social Movements." *Annual Review of Sociology* 9:527–53.

———. 1998. "Channeling Social Protest: Foundation Patronage of Contemporary Social Movements." In *Private Action and the Public Good,* ed. Walter W. Powell and Elisabeth S. Clemens, 206–16. New Haven, CT: Yale University Press.

Jenkins, J. Craig, and Craig M. Eckert. 1986. "Channeling Black Insurgency." *American Sociological Review* 51:812–29.

Jenkins, J. Craig, and Bert Klandermans. 1995a. "The Politics of Social Protest." In Jenkins and Klandermans 1995b, 3–13.

———, eds. 1995b. *The Politics of Social Protest: Comparative Perspectives on States and Social Movements.* Social Movements, Protest, and Contention 3. Minneapolis: University of Minnesota Press.

Jenkins, J. Craig, and Charles Perrow. 1977. "Insurgency of the Powerless: Farm Worker Movements (1946–1972)." *American Sociological Review* 42:249–68.

Jenness, Valerie. 1999. "Managing Differences and Making Legislation: Social Movements and the Racialization, Sexualization, and Gendering of Federal Hate Crime Law in the U.S., 1985–1998." *Social Problems* 46:548–71.

Jenness, Valerie, and Kendal Broad. 1997. *Hate Crimes: New Social Movements and the Politics of Violence.* New York: Aldine de Gruyter.

Jermier, John M., David Knights, and Walter R. Nord, eds. 1994. *Resistance and Power in Organizations.* London: Routledge.

Johnston, Hank, and Bert Klandermans, eds. 1995. *Social Movements and Culture.* Social Movements, Protest, and Contention Series 4. Minneapolis: University of Minnesota Press.

Kane, Melinda D. 2003. "Social Movement Policy Success: Decriminalizing State Sodomy Laws, 1969–1998." *Mobilization: An International Journal* 8:313–34.

Kaplan, Marilyn R., and J. Richard Harrison. 1993. "Defusing the Director Liability Crisis: The Strategic Management of Legal Threats." *Organization Science* 4:412–32.

Karnøe, Peter. 1995. "Institutional Interpretations and Explanations of Differences in American and Danish Approaches to Innovation." In Scott and Christensen 1995b, 243–76.

Katzenstein, Mary F. 1990. "Feminism within American Institutions: Unobtrusive Mobilization in the 1980s." *Signs: Journal of Women in Culture and Society* 16:27–54.

———. 1998. *Faithful and Fearless: Moving Feminist Protest inside the Church and Military.* Princeton, NJ: Princeton University Press.

Katzenstein, Mary F., and Carol McClurg Mueller, eds. 1987. *The Women's Movements of the United States and Western Europe: Consciousness, Political Opportunity, and Public Policy.* Philadelphia: Temple University Press.

Kelly, Erin, and Frank Dobbin. 1999. "Civil Rights Law at Work: Sex Discrimination and the Rise of Maternity Leave Policies." *American Journal of Sociology* 105:455–92.

King, Deborah K. 1988. "Multiple Jeopardy, Multiple Consciousness: The Context of a Black Feminist Ideology." *Signs: Journal of Women in Culture and Society* 14:42–72.

Kinsey, Alfred C., Wardell B. Pomeroy, and Clyde E. Martin. 1948. *Sexual Behavior in the Human Male.* Philadelphia: Saunders.

Klandermans, Bert. 1988. "The Formation and Mobilization of Consensus." In Klandermans, Kriesi, and Tarrow 1988, 173–96.

———. 1997. *The Social Psychology of Protest.* Oxford, UK: Blackwell.

Klandermans, Bert, and Sjoerd Goslinga. 1996. "Media Discourse, Movement Publicity, and the Generation of Collective Action Frames: Theoretical and Empirical Exercises in Meaning Construction." In McAdam, McCarthy, and Zald 1996a, 312–37.

Klandermans, Bert, Hanspeter Kriesi, and Sidney Tarrow, eds. 1988. *From Structure to Action: Comparing Social Movements across Cultures.* International Social Movement Research 1. Greenwich, CT: JAI Press.

Klandermans, Bert, and Sidney Tarrow. 1988. "Mobilization into Social Movements: Synthesizing European and American Approaches." *International Social Movement Research* 1:1–38.

Knoke, David. 1982. "The Spread of Municipal Reform: Temporal, Spatial, and Social Dynamics." *American Journal of Sociology* 87:1314–39.

———. 2001. *Changing Organizations: Business Networks in the New Political Economy.* Boulder, CO: Westview.

Kohn, Sally. 1999. *The Domestic Partnership Organizing Manual for Employee Benefits.* New York: National Gay and Lesbian Task Force Policy Institute.

Koopmans, Ruud. [1993] 1997. "The Dynamics of Protest Waves: West Germany, 1965 to 1989." In *Social Movements: Readings on Their Emergence, Mobilization, and Dynamics,* ed. Doug McAdam and David A. Snow, 367–83. Los Angeles: Roxbury.

Korb, Lawrence J. 1996. "The President, the Congress, and the Pentagon: Obstacles to Implementing the 'Don't Ask, Don't Tell' Policy." In Herek, Jobe, and Carney 1996, 290–301.

Krupat, Kitty. [1999] 2001. "Out of Labor's Dark Age: Sexual Politics Comes to the Workplace." In Krupat and McCreery 2001, 1–23.

Krupat, Kitty, and Patrick McCreery, eds. 2001. *Out at Work: Building a Gay-Labor Alliance.* Cultural Politics 17. Minneapolis: University of Minnesota Press.

Krupin, Stephen. 2002. "Local Firms Rate High, Low in Gay Survey." *Atlanta Journal-Constitution,* August 14.

Kunda, Gideon. 1992. *Engineering Culture: Control and Commitment in a High-Tech Corporation.* Philadelphia: Temple University Press.

Kurtz, Sharon. 2002. *Workplace Justice: Organizing Multi-identity Movements.* Social Movements, Protest, and Contention 15. Minneapolis: University of Minnesota Press.

Laabs, Jennifer J. 1991. "Unmarried . . . with Benefits." *Personnel Journal* 70:62–70.

Lambda Legal Defense and Education Fund (LLDEF). 1994. *Negotiating for Equal Employment Benefits: A Resource Packet.* New York: Lambda Legal Defense and Education Fund.

———. 1999. "1999 Anti-marriage Bills Status Report." August 12. http://www.lambdalegal.org/cgi-bin/pages/documents/record?record=319 (accessed September 9, 1999).

———. 2000. "Baehr v. Miike (Hawaii Supreme Court, December 9, 1999)." http://www.lambdalegal.org/cgi-bin/pages/documents/record?record=541 (accessed April 27, 2000).

Lant, Theresa K., and Joel A. C. Baum. 1995. "Cognitive Sources of Socially Constructed Competitive Groups: Examples from the Manhattan Hotel Industry." In Scott and Christensen 1995b, 15–38.

Laraña, Enrique, Hank Johnston, and Joseph R. Gusfield, eds. 1994. *New Social Movements: From Ideology to Identity.* Philadelphia: Temple University Press.

La Salle, Rob. 1997. "Hate Surfer Puts the Spotlight on Bigotry." *Stonewall Journal,* March, 11.

Leblebici, Huseyin, Gerald R. Salancik, Anne Copay, and Tom King. 1991. "Institutional Change and the Transformation of Interorganizational Fields: An Organizational History of the U.S. Radio Broadcasting Industry." *Administrative Science Quarterly* 36:333–63.

Leonard, Mary. 1998. "Corporate Competition Is Leading the Way in Providing Domestic Partners with Dependable Benefits: Gay Rights." *Boston Globe,* April 5. http://www.lexis-nexis.com/.

Levine, Martin P. 1979. "Employment Discrimination against Gay Men." *International Review of Modern Sociology* 9:151–63.

———. 1992. "The Status of Gay Men in the Workplace." In *Men's Lives,* ed. Michael S. Kimmel and Michael A. Messner, 251–66. New York: Macmillan.

Levine, Martin P., and Robin Leonard. 1984. "Discrimination against Lesbians in the Work Force." *Signs: Journal of Women in Culture and Society* 9:700–710.

Lewis, Gregory B. [1997] 2003. "Lifting the Ban on Gays in the Civil Service: Federal Policy toward Gay and Lesbian Employees since the Cold War." In *The Dynamics of Inequality: Race, Class, Gender, and Sexuality in the United States,* ed. Patricia Gagné and Richard Tewksbury, 75–88. Upper Saddle River, NJ: Prentice Hall.

Lewis, Sasha Gregory. 1979. *Sunday's Women: A Report on Lesbian Life Today.* Boston: Beacon.

Lichterman, Paul. 1996. *The Search for Political Community: American Activists Reinventing Commitment.* New York: Cambridge University Press.

LLDEF. *See* Lambda Legal Defense and Education Fund.

Lockhead, Carolyn. 2000. "Gay Unions Win Final Vote in Vermont: Governor to Sign Measure Extending Rights of Marriage." *San Francisco Chronicle,* April 26.

———. 2003. "Gay Rights Affirmed in Historic Ruling; 6–3 Decision: Supreme Court Throws Out Sodomy Law." *San Francisco Chronicle,* June 27.

———. 2004. "Court Says Same-Sex Marriage Is a Right: Massachusetts Judges Pan Civil Unions." *San Francisco Chronicle,* February 5.

Lofland, John. 1995. "Charting Degrees of Movement Culture: Tasks of the Cultural Cartographer." In Johnston and Klandermans 1995, 188–216.

Lounsberry, Emilie. 2000. "Boy Scouts Can Prevent Gays from Becoming Troop Leaders, Supreme Court Rules." Knight-Ridder/Tribune News Service, June 28. http://www.infotrac.galegroup.com/ (accessed November 21, 2002).

Lounsbury, Michael. 1997. "Exploring the Institutional Tool Kit: The Rise of Recycling in the U.S. Waste Field." *American Behavioral Scientist* 40:465–77.

———. 1998. "The Structuration of Work in the U.S. Field of Finance: The Professionalization Project of Money Managers and the Rise of Mutual Funds." Paper presented at the annual meeting of the Pacific Sociological Association, San Francisco.

Lukenbill, Grant. 1995. *Untold Millions: Positioning Your Business for the Gay and Lesbian Consumer Revolution.* New York: HarperCollins.

———. 1999. *Untold Millions: Secret Truths about Marketing to Gay and Lesbian Consumers.* 2nd ed. New York: Harrington Park Press.

Mason, Julie Cohen. 1995. "Domestic Partner Benefits." *Management Review* 84:53–55. http://www.infotrac.galegroup.com/ (accessed December 30, 2002).

Mathews, Jay. 1995. "Two Sides Hit Coors on Gay Rights: Christian Right Foams at Benefit Plan; Gays Attack Lobbying Effort." *Toronto Star,* September 18. http://www.lexis-nexis.com/.

McAdam, Doug. 1982. *Political Process and the Development of Black Insurgency, 1930–1970.* Chicago: University of Chicago Press.

———. 1983. "Tactical Innovation and the Pace of Insurgency." *American Sociological Review* 48:735–54.

———. 1994. "Culture and Social Movements." In Laraña, Johnston, and Gusfield 1994, 36–57.

———. 1996. "Conceptual Origins, Current Problems, Future Directions." In McAdam, McCarthy, and Zald 1996a, 23–40.

McAdam, Doug, John D. McCarthy, and Mayer N. Zald. 1988. "Social Movements." In *Handbook of Sociology,* ed. Neil Smelser, 695–737. Beverly Hills, CA: Sage.

———, eds. 1996a. *Comparative Perspectives on Social Movements: Political Opportunities, Mobilizing Structures, and Cultural Framings.* New York: Cambridge University Press.

———. 1996b. "Opportunities, Mobilizing Structures, and Framing Processes— Toward a Synthetic, Comparative Perspective on Social Movements." Introduction to McAdam, McCarthy, and Zald 1996a, 1–20.

McBride, Pamela. 2000. "Diversity Dot-Com." *Experience,* Fall, 30–32.

McCarthy, John D. 1996. "Constraints and Opportunities in Adopting, Adapting, and Inventing." In McAdam, McCarthy, and Zald 1996a, 141–51.

McCarthy, John D., and Clark McPhail. 1998. "The Institutionalization of Protest in the United States." In *The Social Movement Society: Contentious Politics for a New Century,* ed. David S. Meyer and Sidney Tarrow, 83–110. Lanham, MD: Rowman & Littlefield.

McCarthy, John D., Jackie Smith, and Mayer N. Zald. 1996. "Accessing Public, Media, Electoral, and Governmental Agendas." In McAdam, McCarthy, and Zald 1996a, 291–311.

McCarthy, John D., and Mayer N. Zald. 1973. *The Trend of Social Movements in America: Professionalization and Resource Mobilization.* Morristown, NJ: General Learning Press.

———. 1977. "Resource Mobilization and Social Movements: A Partial Theory." *American Journal of Sociology* 82:1212–41.

McGuire, Joseph W. 1963. *Business and Society.* New York: McGraw-Hill.

McNaron, Toni A. H. 1997. *Poisoned Ivy: Lesbian and Gay Academics Confronting Homophobia*. Philadelphia: Temple University Press.

McNaught, Brian. 1993. *Gay Issues in the Workplace*. New York: St. Martin's.

McPhail, Clark, David Schweingruber, and John McCarthy. 1998. "Policing Protest in the United States: 1960–1995." In della Porta and Reiter 1998, 49–69.

Mears, Jennifer. 1995. "Coors Hit on Benefits for Gays." *Chicago Sun-Times*, October 9. http://www.lexis-nexis.com/.

Melucci, Alberto. 1985. "The Symbolic Challenge of Contemporary Movements." *Social Research* 52:789–816.

———. 1989. *Nomads of the Present: Social Movements and Individual Needs in Contemporary Society*. Philadelphia: Temple University Press.

———. 1996. *Challenging Codes: Collective Action in the Communication Age*. Cambridge: Cambridge University Press.

Meyer, David S. 2002. "Opportunities and Identities: Bridge-Building in the Study of Social Movements." In Meyer, Whittier, and Robnett 2002, 3–21.

———. 2003. "Political Opportunity and Nested Institutions." *Social Movement Studies* 2:17–36.

Meyer, David S., and Suzanne Staggenborg. 1996. "Movements, Countermovements, and the Structure of Political Opportunity." *American Journal of Sociology* 101:1628–60.

Meyer, David S., and Nancy Whittier. 1994. "Social Movement Spillover." *Social Problems* 41:277–98.

Meyer, David S., Nancy Whittier, and Belinda Robnett, eds. 2002. *Social Movements: Identity, Culture, and the State*. New York: Oxford University Press.

Meyer, John W., and Brian Rowan. 1977. "Institutionalized Organizations: Formal Structure as Myth and Ceremony." *American Journal of Sociology* 83:340–63.

Meyerson, Debra E., and Maureen A. Scully. 1995. "Tempered Radicalism and the Politics of Ambivalence and Change." *Organization Science* 6:585–600.

Mezias, Stephen J. 1995. "Using Institutional Theory to Understand For-Profit Sectors: The Case of Financial Reporting Standards." In Scott and Christensen 1995b, 164–96.

Mickens, Ed. 1994a. *The 100 Best Companies for Gay Men and Lesbians—Plus Options and Opportunities No Matter Where You Work*. New York: Pocket.

———. 1994b. "Waging War on Wall Street." *Advocate*, April 19.

Miles, Robert H. 1982. *Coffin Nails and Corporate Strategy*. Englewood Cliffs, NJ: Prentice Hall.

Miller, Gerald V. 1995. *The Gay Male's Odyssey in the Corporate World: From Disempowerment to Empowerment*. New York: Haworth.

Mills, Kim I. 2001. "Taking Stock of Shareholder Resolutions." *HRC Quarterly,* Summer, 22–23.

Milmore, Donna. 2000. "Careers 2000: Go Online for Data on Careers." *Boston Globe,* October 15. http://www.lexis-nexis.com/.

Minkoff, Debra C. 1995. *Organizing for Equality: The Evolution of Women's and Racial-Ethnic Organizations in America, 1955–1985.* New Brunswick, NJ: Rutgers University Press.

Mirken, Bruce. 1997a. "Coors Controversy Explodes Up and Down California: San Francisco Community Center under Fire for Accepting Coors Donation to Capital Campaign." *San Francisco Bay Times,* June 12, 2–6.

———. 1997b. "San Francisco Community Center Project Plays Hot Potato with Coors $$: Passes the Money to P-FLAG." *San Francisco Bay Times,* June 12.

———. 1997c. "SF Community Center Delays Decision on Coors Funding as Anti-Coors Protests Haunt L.A. Film Fest." *San Francisco Bay Times,* June 24.

Molotch, Harvey. 1979. "Media and Movements." In Zald and McCarthy 1979, 71–93.

Moore, Kelly. 1999. "Political Protest and Institutional Change: The Anti–Vietnam War Movement and American Science." In Giugni, McAdam, and Tilly 1999, 97–115.

Morris, Aldon D. 1984. *The Origins of the Civil Rights Movement: Black Communities Organizing for Change.* New York: Free Press.

———. 1999. "A Retrospective on the Civil Rights Movement: Political and Intellectual Landmarks." *Annual Review of Sociology* 25:517–39. http://proquest.umi.com/ (accessed November 10, 1999).

Morris, Aldon D., and Carol McClurg Mueller, eds. 1992. *Frontiers in Social Movement Theory.* New Haven, CT: Yale University Press.

Mueller, Carol McClurg. 1994. "Conflict Networks and the Origins of Women's Liberation." In Laraña, Johnston, and Gusfield 1994, 234–63.

Nardi, Peter M., and Beth E. Schneider, eds. 1998. *Social Perspectives in Lesbian and Gay Studies: A Reader.* New York: Routledge.

National Center for Lesbian Rights (NCLR). 2004. "Same-Sex Relationship Recognition" (section of "NCLR Publications" Web page). January 1. http://www.nclrights.org/publications/index.htm#relationship (accessed February 11, 2004).

National Gay and Lesbian Task Force (NGLTF). 1996a. *Beyond the Beltway: State of the States, 1995.* January. Washington, DC: National Gay and Lesbian Task Force.

———. 1996b. *Capital Gains and Losses: A State by State Review of Gay-Related*

Legislation in 1996. December 5. http://www.ngltf.org/cgintro.html (accessed June 15, 1999).

———. 1996c. *The Record on Gay-Related Referenda Questions.* May 20. Washington, DC: National Gay and Lesbian Task Force.

———. 1997. *Capital Gains and Losses: A State by State Review of Gay-Related Legislation in 1997.* http://www.ngltf.org/97cgal/intro.html (accessed June 15, 1999).

———. 1998a. "National Gay and Lesbian Task Force Action Alert" (on Riggs Amendment). E-mail from NGLTF, July 16.

———. 1998b. "Two Anti-gay Amendments Pass Narrowly on VA/HUD Appropriations Bill: New Poll Shows Latest Right Wing Attacks against Gay People Backfiring." E-mail from NGLTF, July 30.

———. 1999a. *Capital Gains and Losses: A State by State Review of Gay, Lesbian, Bisexual, Transgender, and HIV/AIDS–Related Legislation in 1998.* January 21. http://www.ngltf.org/98CGAL/intro.html (accessed June 15, 1999).

———. 1999b. *Legislative Update.* June 2. http://www.ngltf.org/legupdate99/legup060299.html (accessed June 15, 1999).

———. 1999c. *1999 Capital Gains and Losses: A State by State Review of Gay, Lesbian, Bisexual, Transgender, and HIV/AIDS–Related Legislation in 1999,* by Dan Hawes. December 13. http://www.ngltf.org/downloads/cgal99.pdf (accessed October 30, 2002).

———. 1999d. "Task Force 1999 State Legislative Update: Record Number of GLBT-Related Bills for Session Start Washington, DC." E-mail from NGLTF, January 28.

———. 2000. "Walking the Walk and Creating Change in Oakland." *Task Force Report: The Quarterly Newsletter of the National Gay and Lesbian Task Force Policy Institute,* Winter, 4.

Navarro, Mireya. 1995. "Disney's Health Policy for Gay Employees Angers Religious Right in Florida." *New York Times,* November 29.

NCLR. *See* National Center for Lesbian Rights.

Neuman, W. Lawrence. 2002. *Social Research Methods: Qualitative and Quantitative Approaches.* 5th ed. Boston: Allyn & Bacon.

New York Newsday. 2002. "Survey: Most U.S. Companies Protect Gay Rights." August 14.

New York Times. 1996. "Senate Votes on Marriage and Rights." September 11.

———. 2002. "*Times* Will Begin Reporting Gay Couples' Ceremonies." August 18. http://www.nytimes.com/2002/08/18/fashion/18PAPE.html?pagewanted=print&position=top (accessed November 29, 2002).

NGLTF. *See* National Gay and Lesbian Task Force.

Noll, Roger T., ed. 1985. *Regulatory Policy and the Social Sciences.* Berkeley and
    Los Angeles: University of California Press.

O'Brien, Jodi. 2002. "How Big Is Your God?" Unpublished manuscript, Depart-
    ment of Sociology, Seattle University.

Offe, Claus. 1985. "New Social Movements: Challenging the Boundaries of Insti-
    tutional Politics." *Social Research* 52:817–68.

Olson, Mancur. 1965. *The Logic of Collective Action: Public Goods and the Theory
    of Groups.* Cambridge, MA: Harvard University Press.

Omaha World-Herald. 2001. "Welcome Tolerance." Editorial, November 23.
    http://www.lexis-nexis.com/.

Out and Equal Workplace Advocates. 2001. "'Outies' Recognize LGBT Work-
    place Achievements." *Out and Equal Workplace Advocates Newsletter,* Fall.
    http://www.outandequal.org/newsletter/fall2001/index.htm (accessed
    November 29, 2002).

Out of the Past: The Struggle for Gay and Lesbian Rights in America. 1997. VHS,
    written by Michelle Ferrari and directed and produced by Jeff Dupre. New
    York: Unapix Films.

Pelosi, Nancy. 2001. Letter to constituents, December 3.

Perez, Christina. 1995. "The Politics of Multiculturalism." *Humanity and Society*
    19:79–88.

Pfeffer, Jeffrey. 1983. "Organizational Demography." In *Research in Organization-
    al Behavior,* ed. L. L. Cummings and Barry M. Staw, 5:299–357. Greenwich,
    CT: JAI Press.

Pfohl, Stephen. 1994. *Images of Deviance and Social Control: A Sociological History.*
    2nd ed. New York: McGraw-Hill.

Phillips, David, and Mark Truby. 2000. "Car Firms Insure Same-Sex Partners:
    It's Biggest Extension of Benefits by a Single Industry." *Detroit News,* June 9.
    http://www.detnews.com/2000/autos/0006/09/a01-71911.htm (accessed
    November 29, 2002).

Piven, Frances Fox, and Richard A. Cloward. 1979. *Poor People's Movements.* New
    York: Vintage.

Pizzorno, Alessandro. 1978. "Political Science and Collective Identity in Industri-
    al Conflict." In *The Resurgence of Class Conflict in Western Europe since 1968,*
    ed. Colin Crouch and Alessandro Pizzorno, 277–98. New York: Holmes &
    Meier.

Podolsky, Robin. 1994. "Birth of a Queer Nation." In Thompson 1994, 367–69.

Polletta, Francesca. 1998a. "Contending Stories: Narrative in Social Movements."
    Qualitative Sociology 21:419–46.

———. 1998b. "'It Was Like a Fever': Narrative and Identity in Social Protest."
    Social Problems 45:137–59.

Polletta, Francesca, and Edwin Amenta. 2001. "Second That Emotion? Lessons from Once-Novel Concepts in Social Movement Research." Conclusion to Goodwin, Jasper, and Polletta 2001a, 303–16.

Polletta, Francesca, and James M. Jasper. 2001. "Collective Identity and Social Movements." *Annual Review of Sociology* 27:283–05.

Porac, Joseph F., and Howard Thomas. 1990. "Taxonomic Mental Models in Competitive Definition." *Academy of Management Review* 15:224–40.

Porac, Joseph F., Howard Thomas, and C. Badden-Fuller. 1989. "Competitive Groups as Cognitive Communities: The Case of the Scottish Knitwear Manufacturers." *Journal of Management Studies* 26:397–415.

Powell, Walter W. 1991. "Expanding the Scope of Institutional Analysis." In Powell and DiMaggio 1991, 183–203.

Powell, Walter W., and Paul J. DiMaggio, eds. 1991. *The New Institutionalism in Organizational Analysis.* Chicago: University of Chicago Press.

Powers, Bob, and Alan Ellis. 1995. *A Manager's Guide to Sexual Orientation in the Workplace.* New York: Routledge.

Price, Deb. 2000. "Partnership Benefits Become the Norm." *Detroit News,* October 30. http://www.detnews.com/EDITPAGE/0010/30/price/price.htm (accessed November 29, 2002).

Proffitt, W. Trexler, Jr., and Michael Alan Sacks. 1999. "Hitting a Moving Target: The Receiving End of Social Movement Activism." Paper presented at the annual meeting of the Pacific Sociological Association, Portland, OR.

Raeburn, Nicole C. 1995. "Intermovement Influence in Institutional Settings: Feminism's Impact on Lesbian and Gay Employee Activism." Paper presented at the annual meeting of the American Sociological Association, Washington, DC.

———. 1998. Review of *Out in Force: Sexual Orientation and the Military,* ed. Gregory M. Herek, Jared B. Jobe, and Ralph M. Carney. *Contemporary Sociology* 27:238–39.

Raeburn, Nicole C., and Verta Taylor. 1994. "Discrimination against Lesbian and Gay Sociologists: Coming Out as High-Risk Activism." Unpublished manuscript, Department of Sociology, Ohio State University–Columbus.

Ragin, Charles C. 1994. *Constructing Social Research.* Boston: Sage.

Raine, George. 1999. "Policy Change Benefits United: Gays Applaud Airline's Shift on Domestic Partners." *San Francisco Chronicle,* October 3.

Ramirez, Francisco O. 1987. "Comparative Social Movements." In *Institutional Structure: Constituting State, Society, and the Individual,* ed. George M. Thomas, John W. Meyer, Francisco O. Ramirez, and John Boli, 281–96. Newbury Park, CA: Sage.

Rao, Hayagreeva. 1998. "Caveat Emptor: The Construction of Nonprofit Consumer Watchdog Organizations." *American Journal of Sociology* 103:912–61.

Rasi, Richard A., and Lourdes Rodriguez-Nogues, eds. 1995. *Out in the Workplace: The Pleasures and Perils of Coming Out on the Job.* Los Angeles: Alyson.

Reger, Jo. 2002. "More Than One Feminism: Organizational Structure and the Construction of Collective Identity." In Meyer, Whittier, and Robnett 2002, 171–84.

Richardson, Laurel, Verta Taylor, and Nancy Whittier, comps. 1997. *Feminist Frontiers IV.* New York: McGraw-Hill.

Ridinger, Robert B. Marks. 1987. *An Index to "The Advocate," the National Gay Newsmagazine, 1967–1982.* Los Angeles: Liberation Publications.

Roberts, Patti, and Lisa Dettmer, with Abby Abinanti, Maria Gil de Lamadrid, and Kristin Gulling. 1992. *Recognizing Lesbian and Gay Families: Strategies for Obtaining Domestic Partners Benefits.* 2nd ed. San Francisco: National Center for Lesbian Rights.

Robnett, Belinda. 1997. *How Long? How Long? African-American Women in the Struggle for Civil Rights.* New York: Oxford University Press.

———. 1998. "African American Women in the Civil Rights Movement: Spontaneity and Emotion in Social Movement Theory." In Blee 1998a, 65–95.

———. 2002. "External Political Change, Collective Identities, and Participation in Social Movement Organizations." In Meyer, Whittier, and Robnett 2002, 266–85.

Roth, William. 2002. *The Assault on Social Policy.* New York: Columbia University Press.

Rouilard, Richard. 1994. "Year of the Queer: 1990." In Thompson 1994, 357–58.

Rubenstein, William B., ed. 1993. *Lesbians, Gay Men, and the Law.* New York: New Press.

Rubin, Gayle S. [1984] 1998. "Thinking Sex: Notes for a Radical Theory of the Politics of Sexuality." In Nardi and Schneider 1998, 100–133.

Rupp, Leila J., and Verta Taylor. [1987] 1990. *Survival in the Doldrums: The American Women's Rights Movement, 1945 to the 1960s.* Columbus: Ohio State University Press.

———. 1999. "Forging Feminist Identity in an International Movement: A Collective Identity Approach to Twentieth-Century Feminism." *Signs: Journal of Women in Culture and Society* 24:363–86.

———. 2003. *Drag Queens at the 801 Cabaret.* Chicago: University of Chicago Press.

Ryan, Barbara. 1992. *Feminism and the Women's Movement: Dynamics of Change in Social Movement Ideology and Activism.* New York: Routledge.

Salladay, Robert, and Tanya Schevitz. 2003. "Davis Signs Partner Benefit Bill; Business Groups Say It Will Make It Harder to Operate in the State." *San Francisco Chronicle,* October 13.

Sandalow, Marc. 2004. "Same-Sex Marriage Ban of 'National Importance'; Bush Digs In: He Calls for Constitutional Amendment." *San Francisco Chronicle,* February 25.

Santoro, Wayne A., and Gail M. McGuire. 1997. "Social Movement Insiders: The Impact of Institutional Activists on Affirmative Action and Comparable Worth Policies." *Social Problems* 44:503–19.

Sawyers, Traci M., and David S. Meyer. 1999. "Missed Opportunities: Social Movement Abeyance and Public Policy." *Social Problems* 46:187–206.

Schlosser, Julie, and Jessica Sung. 2001. "The 100 Best Companies to Work For: These Employers Show No Signs of Cutting Back on Their Commitment to Employees." *Fortune,* January 8. http://www.infotrac.galegroup.com/ (accessed December 30, 2002).

Schmidt, Martha A. 1994. "Dahmer Discourse and Gay Identity: The Paradox of Queer Politics." *Critical Sociology* 20:81–105.

Schneider, Beth E. 1984. "Peril and Promise: Lesbians' Workplace Participation." In *Women-Identified Women,* ed. Trudy Darty and Sandee Potter, 211–30. Palo Alto, CA: Mayfield.

———. 1986. "Coming Out at Work: Bridging the Private/Public Gap." *Work and Occupations* 13:463–87.

———. 1988. "Invisible and Independent: Lesbians' Experiences in the Workplace." In *Women Working,* ed. Ann Stromberg and Shirley Harkess, 273–86. Palo Alto, CA: Mayfield.

Schock, Kurt. 1999. "People Power and Political Opportunities: Social Movement Mobilization and Outcomes in the Philippines and Burma." *Social Problems* 46:355–75.

Scott, W. Richard. 1987. "The Adolescence of Institutional Theory." *Administrative Science Quarterly* 32:493–511.

———. 1995a. "Institutional Theory and Organizations." Introduction to Scott and Christensen 1995b, xi–xxiii.

———. 1995b. *Institutions and Organizations.* Thousand Oaks, CA: Sage.

———. 1998. *Organizations: Rational, Natural, and Open Systems.* 4th ed. Upper Saddle River, NJ: Prentice Hall.

Scott, W. Richard, and Søren Christensen. 1995a. "Crafting a Wider Lens." Conclusion to Scott and Christensen 1995b, 302–13.

———. eds. 1995b. *The Institutional Construction of Organizations: International and Longitudinal Studies.* Thousand Oaks, CA: Sage.

Scully, Maureen, and W. E. Douglas Creed. 1998. "Switchpersons on the Tracks of History: Situated Agency and Contested Legitimacy in the Diffusion of Domestic Partner Benefits." Paper presented at the annual meeting of the Academy of Management, San Diego.

Sherkat, Darren E. 1999. "What's in a Frame? Toward an Integrated Social Psychology of Social Movements." Paper presented at the annual meeting of the Pacific Sociological Association, Portland, OR.

Silver, Ira. 2001. "Strategically Legitimizing Philanthropists' Identity Claims: Community Organizations as Key Players in the Making of Corporate Social Responsibility." *Sociological Perspectives* 44:233–52.

Simanoff, Dave. 2002. "America's Corporate Players Institute Gay-Friendly Policies." *Knight Ridder/Tribune Business News,* November 25. http://www.infotrac.galegroup.com (accessed December 30, 2002).

Sixel, L. M. 2003. "Energy Companies Under Fire to Ensure Gay Rights." *Houston Chronicle,* February 14. http://www.lexis-nexis.com/.

Smith, Rhonda. 2001. "HRC Calls for National Boycott of ExxonMobil." Data Lounge news report, June 18. http://www.datalounge.com/datalounge/news/record.html?record=15377 (accessed June 25, 2001).

Snow, David A., and Robert D. Benford. 1988. "Ideology, Frame Resonance, and Participant Mobilization." In Klandermans, Kriesi, and Tarrow 1988, 197–217.

———. 1992. "Master Frames and Cycles of Protest." In Morris and Mueller 1992, 133–55.

Snow, David A., E. Burke Rochford Jr., Steven K. Worden, and Robert D. Benford. 1986. "Frame Alignment Processes, Micromobilization, and Movement Participation." *American Sociological Review* 51:464–81.

Soehnlein, Karl. 1994. "Hitting the Streets with Furious Art." In Thompson 1994, 370–71.

Stacey, Judith. [1987] 1997. "Postindustrial Conditions and Postfeminist Consciousness in the Silicon Valley." In Richardson, Taylor, and Whittier 1997, 510–25.

———. 1996. *In the Name of the Family: Rethinking Family Values in the Postmodern Age.* Boston: Beacon.

Staggenborg, Suzanne. 1991. *The Pro-choice Movement: Organization and Activism in the Abortion Conflict.* New York: Oxford University Press.

———. 1995. "Can Feminist Organizations Be Effective?" In Ferree and Martin 1995, 339–55.

Stewart, Thomas A. 1991. "Gay in Corporate America." *Fortune,* December 16, 42–56.

Stinchcombe, Arthur L. 1965. "Social Structure and Organizations." In *Handbook of Organizations,* ed. James G. March, 142–93. Chicago: Rand McNally.

Stoddard, Thomas. [1989] 1993. "Why Gay People Should Seek the Right to Marry." In Rubenstein 1993, 398–401.

Strang, David, and John W. Meyer. 1993. "Institutional Conditions for Diffusion." *Theory and Society* 22:487–511.

Strang, David, and Sarah A. Soule. 1998. "Diffusion in Organizations and Social Movements: From Hybrid Corn to Poison Pills." *Annual Review of Sociology* 24:265–90.

Suchman, Mark C. 1995. "Localism and Globalism in Institutional Analysis: The Emergence of Contractual Norms in Venture Finance." In Scott and Christensen 1995b, 39–63.

Sutton, John R., and Frank Dobbin. 1996. "The Two Faces of Governance: Responses to Legal Uncertainty in U.S. Firms, 1955–1985." *American Sociological Review* 61:794–811.

Swan, Wallace. 1997a. *Gay/Lesbian/Bisexual/Transgender Public Policy Issues: A Citizen's and Administrator's Guide to the New Cultural Struggle.* New York: Harrington Park Press.

———. 1997b. "Same-Sex Marriages." In Swan 1997a, 117–20.

———. 1997c. "The Workplace Movement." In Swan 1997a, 25–33.

———. 1997d. "Workplaces, Schools, Partnerships, and Justice: An Intersection That Causes Confrontation." In Swan 1997a, 15–21.

Sweeney, John J. [1999] 2001. "The Growing Alliance between Gay and Union Activists." In Krupat and McCreery 2001, 24–30.

Swidler, Ann. 1986. "Culture in Action: Symbols and Strategies." *American Sociological Review* 51:273–86.

Tarrow, Sidney. 1989. *Struggle, Politics, and Reform: Collective Action, Social Movements, and Cycles of Protest.* Ithaca, NY: Cornell University Press.

———. 1994. *Power in Movement: Social Movements, Collective Action, and Politics.* New York: Cambridge University Press.

———. 1996. "States and Opportunities: The Political Structuring of Social Movements." In McAdam, McCarthy, and Zald 1996a, 41–61.

———. 1998. *Power in Movement: Social Movements and Contentious Politics.* 2nd ed. New York: Cambridge University Press.

———. 1999. Foreword to Giugni, McAdam, and Tilly 1999, vii–ix.

Taylor, Verta. 1989. "Sources of Continuity in Social Movements: The Women's Movement in Abeyance." *American Sociological Review* 54:761–75.

———. [1989] 1993. "Sources of Continuity in Social Movements: The Women's Movement in Abeyance." In *Collective Behavior and Social Movements,* ed.

Russell L. Curtis Jr. and Benigno E. Aguirre, 435–46. Boston: Allyn & Bacon.

———. 1995a. "Self-Labeling and Women's Mental Health: Postpartum Illness and the Reconstruction of Motherhood." *Sociological Focus* 28:23–47.

———. 1995b. "Watching for Vibes: Bringing Emotions into the Study of Feminist Organizations." In Ferree and Martin 1995, 223–33.

———. 1996. *Rock-a-By Baby: Feminism, Self-Help, and Postpartum Depression.* New York: Routledge.

———. 1999. "Gender and Social Movements: Gender Processes in Women's Self-Help Movements." *Gender and Society* 13:8–33.

———. 2000. "Mobilizing for Change in a Social Movement Society." *Contemporary Sociology* 29:219–30.

Taylor, Verta, and Nicole C. Raeburn. 1995. "Identity Politics as High-Risk Activism: Career Consequences for Lesbian, Gay, and Bisexual Sociologists." *Social Problems* 42:252–73.

Taylor, Verta, and Leila J. Rupp. 1993. "Women's Culture and Lesbian Feminist Activism: A Reconsideration of Cultural Feminism." *Signs: Journal of Women in Culture and Society* 19:32–61.

Taylor, Verta, and Marieke Van Willigen. 1996. "Women's Self-Help and the Reconstruction of Gender: The Postpartum Support and Breast Cancer Movements." *Mobilization: An International Journal* 2:123–42.

Taylor, Verta, and Nancy E. Whittier. 1992. "Collective Identity in Social Movement Communities: Lesbian Feminist Mobilization." In Morris and Mueller 1992, 104–29.

———. 1995. "Analytical Approaches to Social Movement Culture: The Culture of the Women's Movement." In Johnston and Klandermans 1995, 163–87.

———. 1997. "The New Feminist Movement." In Richardson, Taylor, and Whittier 1997, 544–61.

Teal, Donn. 1971. *The Gay Militants.* New York: St. Martin's.

Thomas, W. I., and Dorothy Swaine Thomas. 1928. *The Child in America: Behavior Problems and Programs.* New York: Knopf.

Thompson, Mark, ed. 1994. *Long Road to Freedom: The "Advocate" History of the Gay and Lesbian Movement.* New York: St. Martin's.

Thornton, Patricia H. 1995. "Accounting for Acquisition Waves: Evidence from the U.S. College Publishing Industry." In Scott and Christensen 1995b, 199–225.

Tilly, Charles. 1978. *From Mobilization to Revolution.* Reading, MA: Addison-Wesley.

———. 1993. "Contentious Repertoires in Great Britain, 1758–1834." *Social Science History* 17:253–80.

Tolbert, Pamela S., and Lynne G. Zucker. 1983. "Institutional Sources of Change in the Formal Structure of Organizations: The Diffusion of Civil Service Reform, 1880–1935." *Administrative Science Quarterly* 28:22–39.

———. 1996. "The Institutionalization of Institutional Theory." In *Handbook of Organization Studies,* ed. Stewart R. Clegg, Cynthia Hardy, and Walter R. Nord, 175–90. Thousand Oaks, CA: Sage.

Touraine, Alain. 1985. "An Introduction to the Study of Social Movements." *Social Research* 52:749–87.

Truby, Mark. 2000. "Same-Sex Partners Get Delphi Benefits: World's Largest Auto Parts Company Joins Detroit Automakers in Offering Plan." *Detroit News,* November 16. http://www.detnews.com/2000/autos/0011/16/a02-149412.htm (accessed November 29, 2002).

Turner, Ralph H. 1970. "Determinants of Social Movement Strategies." In *Human Nature and Collective Behavior: Papers in Honor of Herbert Blumer,* ed. Tamotsu Shibutani, 145–64. Englewood Cliffs, NJ: Prentice-Hall.

Unitarian Universalist Association. Office of Bisexual, Gay, Lesbian, and Transgender Concerns, with the Interweave Chapter of the Unitarian Church of Bloomington, IL. 2001. "Welcoming Congregation." July 17. http://www.uua.org/obgltc/wcp/wc1expln.html (accessed January 19, 2002).

Useem, Michael. 1979. "The Social Organization of the American Business Elite and Participation of Corporation Directors in the Governance of American Institutions." *American Sociological Review* 44:553–72.

U.S. Newswire. 2003. "NLGJA Applauds the Associated Press Decision to Offer Same-Sex Domestic Partner Benefits." June 2. http://www.lexis-nexis.com/.

Vaid, Urvashi. 1995. *Virtual Equality: The Mainstreaming of Gay and Lesbian Liberation.* New York: Anchor.

Valocchi, Steve. 1999. "Riding the Crest of a Protest Wave? Collective Action Frames in the Gay Liberation Movement, 1969–1973." *Mobilization: An International Journal* 4:59–73.

Vecchiollo, Dominic. 2001. "Variations on a Theme." *HRC Quarterly,* Spring, 21–23.

Vilanch, Bruce. 1998. "Breaking the Code." *Advocate,* October 13.

Waddington, P. A. J. 1998. "Controlling Protest in Contemporary Historical and Comparative Perspective." In della Porta and Reiter 1998, 117–40.

Walsh, Edward J. 1981. "Resource Mobilization and Citizen Protest in Communities around Three Mile Island." *Social Problems* 29:1–21.

Walsh, Edward J., and Rex H. Warland. 1983. "Social Movement Involvement in the Wake of a Nuclear Accident: Activists and Free Riders in the TMI Area." *American Sociological Review* 48:764–80.

Weedon, Chris. 1987. *Feminist Practice and Poststructuralist Theory.* Cambridge, MA: Blackwell.

Weinberg, Martin S., and Colin J. Williams. 1974. *Male Homosexuals: Their Problems and Adaptations.* New York: Penguin.

Weiser, Carl. 1996. "Legal Gay Marriage on the Nation's Horizon: Hawaii May Be First State to Take Step." *USA Today,* January 2. http://www.lexis-nexis.com/.

Wells, Susan J. 1999. "A Benefit Built for 2." *HR Magazine,* August, 68–73.

Welsh-Huggins, Andrew. 2004. "Ohio Bill Bans Gay Marriages; Law Also Bars Benefits for State Workers' Partners." *San Francisco Chronicle,* January 22.

Werum, Regina, and Bill Winders. 2001. "Who's 'In' and Who's 'Out': State Fragmentation and the Struggle over Gay Rights, 1974–1999." *Social Problems* 48:386–410.

Westby, David L. 2002. "Strategic Imperative, Ideology, and Frame." *Mobilization: An International Journal* 7:286–304.

Whaley, Douglas J. 2002. "Marriage Act Is Prelude to Harming Ohio." Forum, *Columbus Dispatch,* January 22 (received as e-mail from author, January 23).

Whittier, Nancy. 1995. *Feminist Generations: The Persistence of the Radical Women's Movement.* Philadelphia: Temple University Press.

———. 2001. "Emotional Strategies: The Collective Reconstruction and Display of Oppositional Emotions in the Movement against Child Sexual Abuse." In Goodwin, Jasper, and Polletta 2001a, 233–50.

———. 2002. "Meaning and Structure in Social Movements." In Meyer, Whittier, and Robnett 2002, 289–307.

Wilke, Michael. 2002. "Commercial Closet Report: Coors Print Campaign Reframes Longstanding Issues." http://www.hrc.org/worknet/workalert/2002/0510/article01.asp (accessed November 6, 2002).

Williams, Rhys H. 1995. "Constructing the Public Good: Social Movements and Cultural Resources." *Social Problems* 42:124–44.

———, ed. 1997. *Cultural Wars in American Politics: Critical Reviews of a Popular Myth (Social Problems and Social Issues).* New York: Aldine de Gruyter.

Williamson, Alistair D. 1993. "Is This the Right Time to Come Out?" *Harvard Business Review* 71:18–27.

Wilson, James Q., ed. 1980. *The Politics of Regulation.* New York: Basic Books.

Winfeld, Liz. 2001. "CU Regents and the New World." *Denver Post,* October 24. http://www.lexis-nexis.com/.

Winfeld, Liz, and Susan Spielman. 1995. *Straight Talk about Gays in the Workplace: Creating an Inclusive, Productive Environment for Everyone in Your Organization.* New York: Amacom.

Wockner, Rex. 1999. "American Banker: Gay Financial Network Landing Big-Name Allies." http://www.gfn.com/html/content/full_story.cfm?story_id=1764 (accessed August 14, 1999).

Woods, James D., with Jay H. Lucas. 1993. *The Corporate Closet: The Professional Lives of Gay Men in America.* New York: Free Press.

Zald, Mayer N., and Michael A. Berger. 1978. "Social Movements in Organizations: Coup d'Etat, Insurgency, and Mass Movement." *American Journal of Sociology* 83:823–61.

Zald, Mayer, and John McCarthy, eds. 1979. *The Dynamics of Social Movements: Resource Mobilization, Social Control, and Tactics.* Cambridge, MA: Winthrop.

Zucker, Lynne G. 1977. "The Role of Institutionalization in Cultural Persistence." *American Sociological Review* 42:726–43.

———. 1983. "Organizations as Institutions." In *Research in the Sociology of Organizations,* ed. S. B. Bacharach, 1–42. Greenwich, CT: JAI Press.

———, ed. 1988. *Institutional Patterns and Organizations: Culture and Environment.* Cambridge, MA: Ballinger.

Zuckerman, Amy J., and George F. Simons. 1994. *Sexual Orientation in the Workplace: Gay Men, Lesbians, Bisexuals, and Heterosexuals Working Together.* Santa Cruz, CA: International Partners Press.

Index

Gay and Lesbian Values Index
  (glvIndex), 142
Gay.com, 78
Gay Financial Network, 140, 253. *See
  also* gfn.com Web site
Gay Games, 99–100, 120, 204, 223
gay liberation fronts: emergence of, 6;
  surveys by, 7–8
gay liberation movement: corporations targeted by, 7–9; cultural
  context of, 6–7; early history of,
  6–9; protests by, 7–9; Stonewall
  Riots as start of, 5, 6, 100; tactics
  of, 6. *See also* gay rights movement; homophile movement; queer
  activism
gay press, 41–43
Gay Pride Day (San Francisco), 27
Gay Pride Month, 191
gay rights movement: charismatic
  leadership in, 203; on domino
  effect, 68–71; funding for, vs. religious Right, 57; impact on workplace organizing, 32–40, 92–99,
  206–7; national events in, 99–101;
  policy change accounts provided
  by, 250–51; workplace organizing by, 4, 92–99. *See also Corporate Equality Index*; gay liberation
  movement; homophile movement;
  Human Rights Campaign; marches
  on Washington; National Gay and
  Lesbian Task Force; queer activism;
  WorkNet workplace project, HRC;
  Workplace Project, NGLTF
GayWork.com, 220
GE. *See* General Electric
Geffen, David, 139
General Accounting Office, 55
General Electric (GE), 127

General Motors: coordinated policy
  change at, 122–23
George Kronenberger Memorial
  Award, 93, 203–4
gfn.com Web site, 140–42; on openly
  gay and lesbian executives, 205,
  253; as positive incentive, 144–45
Gilmour, Allan, 122
Girlfriends (magazine), 145
Giugni, Marco, 234
GLAAD. *See* Gay and Lesbian Alliance against Defamation
GLEAM, 97
GLUE (Gay and Lesbian United Employees) case study: 1987 march
  on Washington and, 33–34; allies
  honored by, 207; board of directors and, 167–68; CEO change
  and, 166–67; coalition partners of,
  175–76; communication technologies used by, 76–77; conservative
  boycott against, 120–21; diversity
  groups motivating, 50, 160–62,
  175–76; establishment of, 33, 50,
  161; internal struggles over tactics
  in, 38; personal narratives used
  by, 194–95; profits frame used by,
  219, 222–23; safe-space program
  of, 209; size of, 33–34, 77; unions
  and, 179–80; Web site of, 77
glvIndex. *See* Gay and Lesbian Values
  Index
Goldberg, Whoopi, 139
Golden Gate University, 48
Goodwin, Jeff, 202, 236
Gould, Deborah, 32
government employment policy: battle
  over, 256–58; equitable benefits included in, 115; Helms' antigay bill
  on, 54; homophile protests of, 6

NICOLE C. RAEBURN is assistant professor and chair of sociology at the University of San Francisco. She has published on lesbian, gay, and bisexual activism, gender, and the feminist movement. She has recently begun a new research project that will compare the adoption of gay-inclusive workplace policies in the corporate, educational, and government sectors.

Series page continued from page ii.